Italy: A Difficult Democracy
A Survey of Italian Politics

Italy

A DIFFICULT DEMOCRACY

A Survey of Italian Politics

FREDERIC SPOTTS
THEODOR WIESER

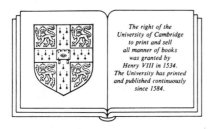

The right of the
University of Cambridge
to print and sell
all manner of books
was granted by
Henry VIII in 1534.
The University has printed
and published continuously
since 1584.

CAMBRIDGE UNIVERSITY PRESS

Cambridge

London   New York   New Rochelle

Melbourne   Sydney

Published by the Press Syndicate of the University of Cambridge
The Pitt Building,Trumpington Street, Cambridge CB2 1RP
32 East 57th Street, New York, NY 10022, USA
10 Stamford Road, Oakleigh, Melbourne 3166, Australia

© Cambridge University Press 1986

First published 1986

Printed in Canada

Library of Congress Cataloging in Publication Data
Spotts, Frederic.
Italy, a difficult democracy.
Includes index.
1. Italy – Politics and government – 1945–
I. Wieser, Theodor, 1923–   II. Title.
JN5451.S64   1986   320.945   85–17111

British Library Cataloging in Publication Data
Spotts, Frederic
Italy : a difficult democracy : a survey of Italian politics.
1. Italy – Politics and government – 1945–
I. Title   II. Wieser, Theodor
320.945   JN5451

ISBN 0 521 30451 2 hard covers
ISBN 0 521 31511 5 paperback

Contents

Contents

Preface

All Western political systems are unique, but some are more unique than others. The Italian form of government may be similar to that of most parliamentary democracies in structure and constitutional principles, but in functioning and ethos it is fundamentally different. The most obvious difference is one of which Aldo Moro frequently spoke in the last years of his life: "We know that our system is characterized by limited change of government and is therefore, in contrast to other European systems, a difficult democracy." The anomalies of government, in addition to the dark world of scandal, terrorism, and the mafia that are the staple of most media reports, make Italy a strange case in the European panorama.

Italian politics are, for all that, no impenetrable mystery. Their functioning follows remarkably clear patterns, and although these may be subtle and complex, they are deeply woven into the fabric of Italian life. In 1893 Vilfredo Pareto described the politics of the earliest years of the unified Italian state in an article, "The Parliamentary Regime in Italy," for the *Political Science Quarterly*. The Italy of Pareto seems almost as distant as the Italy of Augustus. The political system he described, however, is astonishingly similar to that of Italy today. Such is the continuity that runs through Italian political life. It is epitomized in the celebrated passage in *The Leopard* of Giuseppe Tomasi di Lampedusa: "If we want everything to remain as it is, it will be necessary for everything to change." Even though Italian politics are in a constant state of flux – and almost invariably confound prediction – their basic traits are remarkably constant.

Out of these traits – or perhaps despite them – postwar generations of Italians have for the first time in history fashioned a fully representative and firmly established democracy – if a difficult one. The main features of this political order as it has evolved since 1945 are the subject of the following pages. Because a general survey cannot cover every aspect of so broad a scene, the topics selected for attention are those considered essential for an understanding of the politics of the Italian republic and of Italy's place in

the world. The political parties are the mainspring of the country's
political life and receive careful attention at the outset, setting the
background for the body of the text, which deals with the institutions and functioning of Italian democracy. Throughout, the treatment is focused on the way the Italian political system works in
everyday practice; deeper theoretical issues must be left to other
types of work. No attempt is made to impose an ideological interpretation, a mode of analysis, or even a story line. The aim of the
account is simply to elucidate in concrete terms the dynamics of
Italian politics, showing where the Italian process of self-government succeeds, where it fails, and what problems it faces.

Readers are spared footnotes; the important works cited in the
text are listed, along with other useful published sources, at the end
of the book. Apart from such material, the study is based on conver-
sations over the years with members of parliament, government
and party officials, civil servants, trade unionists, economists,
scholars, and others involved in or well acquainted with Italian
political life. Our debt to them all is inestimable.

Ettore Scola, who has produced such perceptive film portraits of
Italian life as *We All Loved Each Other Very Much; Dirty, Mean and
Nasty; The Terrace; A Special Day; Voyage in Fiatnam;* and *Mac-
aroni,* was generous enough to take time from a busy directing
schedule to draw the cover illustration. Many of his films have
conveyed a sense of the disappointed hopes of the postwar era.
However, Scola was struck by a conclusion of this study that afflicted as Italy may be by malfunctioning political institutions and
intractable social problems, *eppur si muove* – it moves nonetheless. And so his rendering of the Italian paradox.

ITALY

showing regional
borders and capitals

1. The political context

The Italian political system is like no other Western democracy.
Over seventy parties campaign in national elections and some ten
of them sit in parliament, yet one party has dominated the country
for the entire period of its republican history. There were forty-five
governments in the first forty years after the war, yet no other
parliamentary democracy has had greater continuity in its leadership and policies. The government changes on an average every
ten months, yet essentially the same group holds all the important
political positions. Italians are contemptuous of their government,
its leaders and functioning, yet politics dominate every aspect of
the nation's life, the parties decide everything, and political patronage permeates society. A party representing a third of the electorate
is excluded from government, yet a party with 3 percent of the vote
has held the prime ministry of two administrations. There is a
greater acceptance of political diversity than in any other Western
state, yet Italy has been marred by one of the world's highest levels
of social discord and physical violence. The population is nominally 97 percent Catholic and the papacy has for centuries played a
central role in the country's life, yet today society is so secularized
that the church has almost no political influence.

Such are a few of the paradoxes that bemuse and bewilder an
observer of the Italian scene. They are symptomatic of a singularly
intricate and sophisticated political society, a society in such continuous turmoil as to appear almost ungovernable but one that
always muddles through and maintains its equipoise. The ironies
and contradictions are so pronounced as fairly to cry out for metaphor, and Italians themselves have invented many a vivid one to
convey a sense of their predicament: a ship without a rudder, its
sails torn and holds flooded, that appears to be foundering but that
rides out every storm; an insect whose physiology should keep it
earthbound but that defies all laws of aerodynamics and effortlessly
sails through the air; and even a medieval casbah where life is
colorful, cacophonic, and chaotic but where commerce and the
arts flourish. Perhaps the most apt symbol is no metaphor at all –
the leaning tower at Pisa, an object of interest precisely because it
confounds appearances and does not collapse.

1

The problems of the Italian political system have intrigued observers for years, inspiring books with such suggestive titles as *Italy – Republic without Government?, Surviving without Governing, Politics of Despair,* and *Italy Today: An Eccentric Society.* Reflecting the vicissitudes of the country's political evolution, *Italy in Transition* of 1946 was followed by the more hopeful *Italy: Change and Progress* in 1963, which was in turn succeeded by an again less committal *Italy in Transition* in 1980. It was symptomatic of the deepening gloom that *The Italian Case* of 1974 was followed by *The Italian Crisis* only four years later. By then the term and concept "crisis" were in such vogue in the domestic and international press that the notion was practically robbed of meaning. Political scientists joined in with *Italy in Crisis, Italy between Crisis and Emergency, Crisis of Parties and Governability,* and many others of a similar drift. With a good eye for the trendy issue, the Socialist party in 1978 launched a major campaign for the reform of a political system now widely considered to be in an advanced stage of decay. Eventually a parliamentary commission was established to identify the underlying problems and frame proposals that might enable national institutions to function more effectively. The ensuing debate produced universal accord that something was basically amiss but little agreement on the ultimate causes and even less on any practical solutions.

What lies behind the difficulties of this land of apparent mysteries – why it often seems about to sink but always stays afloat – is a political system whose nature and operation differ significantly from those in other Western democracies. The uniqueness is not institutional. Italy's consitutional structure is highly similar to that of other parliamentary systems. The sui generis quality of Italian politics arises instead from the impact on these institutions of the political culture of the country and the collective social behavior of the people.

The unloved state

Perhaps the most distinctive feature of Italian political life is the gulf between society and the state. A public sense of alienation from the state is deeply rooted in the country's historical experience. Centuries of foreign occupation, the hostility of the Catholic church to national unification, ineffective government after unity, and two decades of Fascism conditioned Italians to think of the state as at best ineffective and at worst an intrusive, hostile power that could do little good and much harm. After 1945 the phenomenon resumed.

Now the cohesion of the state was compromised by a profound ideological clash between two political forces, each allied to a foreign power – the Christian Democrats to the Americans and the Communists to the Soviets. The governing institutions created by the new constitution were left with weak authority and areas of competence so ambiguous as to establish no clear center of power. Even this limited authority was devalued by subsequent political practice. During the formative years of the republic, parliament refused to implement important innovations of the constitution while the dominant party – the Christian Democrats – tried to rig the electoral system so as to ensure itself a disproportionate share of parliamentary seats. As time passed the state was disgraced by a never-ending round of scandal and corruption. Political patronage seeped into every corner of society while the state industrial enterprises were eventually politicized, mismanaged, and run hopelessly into debt. Public administration, the universities, the postal and telephone systems, health care, and most other public services were turned into marvels of inefficiency.

Whatever the state touched, it seemed to debase. Its agents – parliament, the cabinet, the judiciary, and the civil service – came to be regarded with a mixture of fear and contempt, a mood perpetuating the very qualities that caused it. Popular conviction deepened that it was only outside the reach of state authority that anything functioned effectively. This attitude was described in a noted study on civic culture published in 1963 by Gabriel Almond and Sidney Verba that found Italian society "one of unrelieved political alienation and social isolation and distrust." Although this harsh conclusion may have rested on too credulous an acceptance of the average Italian's boundless self-criticism, it was essentially true. Over two decades later Giacomo Sani came to a similar conclusion, citing a 1974 poll that reaffirmed the public's low estimate of the functioning of the state apparatus. Among the respondents, 43 percent felt it was "in need of immediate major reforms," 35 percent that it required "radical change," while only 21 percent considered it "fine as is."

Nonetheless a countervailing attitude has gradually been developing. With the passage of time and against the record of many other Western countries, it has become apparent that the republican state has not been without some solid accomplishments. The most critical Italian could not deny that under its auspices the country enjoyed the greatest freedom, security, and prosperity in its history. The most disillusioned citizen could not doubt that representative democracy was deeply rooted and, for all its faults, gave Italy the least bad government it ever had. From being one of

Western Europe's most backward areas, the country had come to be one of the world's economic leaders. For all its failures, the state had proved that it alone was in a position to mount a defense against international economic crisis and a wave of terrorist violence during the 1970s.

So Italians are today deeply ambivalent. They want the state to be weak, but they would also like it to be efficient in providing services. They realize that the interventionist state required in an era of political and economic interdependence is incompatible with the laissez-faire state of their predilections. Ideal would be a "grandmother state" – there to help when asked but too feeble to interfere. Until these contradictions are resolved, the Italian state will remain unrespected and unloved. The celebrated aphorism of the country's unifiers that having created Italy, they needed to make Italians could be turned around. Italians are there; the need is to make Italy.

All-powerful parties

With the state as weak as it is, political power has flowed into other channels. By far the most important of these is the political parties. The Italy that was constructed after the war was largely their creation. They wrote the constitution and established the political system that underlay it. By the time the first parliamentary election took place in 1948 and a government was installed, they had already ruled the country for four years. Hence when the new constitutional order was launched, much of the authority that normally resides in the institutions of the state was in the hands of the party organizations. Since that time each of these institutions has either remained in the control of the parties, as in the case of parliament and the public administration, or has had to struggle for its independence, as in the case of the judicial system and the presidency. In truth, Italians have never known an essentially different mode of government. From 1922 to 1943 it was the Fascist party rather than the monarch and parliament that held power. Before that it was a small group of politicians. It is hardly surprising that the country's greatest sociologist, Vilfredo Pareto, should have developed the general theory that it is not a constitution but a political elite that counts.

Since 1945 this mode of government has been colloquially known as *partitocrazia,* or rule by party. It is one of the most characteristic features of Italian political life. To be sure, in all parliamentary democracies it is the dominant parties that determine at the outset of a legislative period who should comprise the government and what course it should follow. But once in place the government operates for the most part autonomously. In their time Konrad Adenauer, Valéry Giscard d'Estaing, and Margaret Thatcher formulated policies and took decisions without it crossing their minds to seek approval first from party headquarters. But in Italy little or no distance separates the parties from the government. The prime minister is normally little more than a figurehead who serves at the pleasure of party leaders, a fact explaining why many ambitious politicians prefer to be party secretary rather than prime minister. When there is a government crisis, it is not the cabinet members who meet to resolve the differences but the secretaries of the coalition parties. Moreover the party leaders who collaborate most closely may not even be those who are associated in government. In the latter years of the 1970s the views of the Communists and Socialists, who were out of government, were of greater importance to the ruling Christian Democrats than those of the Social Democrats, Republicans, and Liberals who were at various times in it. Effective control of the country's affairs consequently lies not with the ministers of government but with the ascendant group in the parties.

The power of Italian parties is bolstered by their tight oligarchic structures. Authority is concentrated in an executive committee of some thirty to forty persons who control a party's day-to-day activities. As chairman of this body, the secretary is the party's chief executive. The executive committee is technically answerable to a larger body – known as a central committee in some parties and as a national council in others – and ultimately to a party congress, which is formally the party's highest policymaking body. But since membership in these larger assemblies is essentially fixed by party leaders, the sessions normally have no independent authority and for the most part merely ratify decisions already worked out by the leadership. Ugo La Malfa, longtime secretary of the Republicans, exercised such draconic control over his organization that it was jestingly known as the last Stalinist party in Europe.

Partitocrazia is not simply a matter of party control of the levers of governmental power. It extends well beyond to embrace most of the entire social, economic, and cultural life of the country. One of Italy's unique features is the existence of a vast sector of public and semipublic bodies that dominate virtually every area of national life: organizations as disparate as giant industries and banks, welfare and charitable agencies, radio and television, scientific and other research institutes, La Scala and other opera houses, the Venice Biennale and other cultural festivals, sport and recreation associations, hospitals, and universities. These bodies are collectively so important they comprise what is known as the *sottogoverno,* "subgovernment" or, as it is sometimes called, "parallel government." Controlled completely or in part by the state, they are subject to government influence, which in practice means party influence.

Every country has its spoils of office, with favors dispensed to the party faithful. But the *sottogoverno* has been turned into a reservoir of partisan power, funds, and jobs without equal in any other Western democracy. The constituent organizations and the positions they control – not simply those at the policymaking level but tens of thousands down to office clerk and messenger – are parceled out among the parties by a process that has come to be called *lottizzazione,* "allotment." The party loyalists who are placed in key positions in turn command enormous amounts of patronage. They award contracts for the construction of buildings, highways, and factories; they grant bank loans, pensions, and promotions; they allocate franchises, financial subsidies, and jobs. And they do it strictly on the basis of partisanry. Since the purpose is to establish a patron–client relationship, such political favor is known as clientelism. The ultimate objective of the whole process is the accretion of power – specifically of votes at elections and of influence and funds between them. This exploitation of the *sottogoverno* by means of *lottizzazione* for the sake of clientelism through the granting of patronage is the lifeblood of the political system. Hence the general rule of Italian politics: Patronage tends to entrench in power and absolute patronage entrenches absolutely.

Even interest-group politics have been distorted by *partitocrazia.* Although some lobbying takes place in parliament and the ministries, the focus of an interest group's activities is the parties since it is they rather than the governing institutions that hold the reins of power. Moreover the method of applying influence is less the orthodox one of money, threats, and pleas than one of establishing an organic link with certain party leaders and their faction. The parties in turn designate certain deputies and senators to act as intermediaries to politically important organizations. In practice the result as often as not is that the interest group is drawn into the orbit of a party, or party faction, and serves partisan interests rather than the other way around.

The ultimate impact of *partitocrazia* is that almost everyone is sucked into this partisanry. Whether an industrialist, judge, typist, general, professor, ambassador, novelist, scientist, or factory worker, every Italian has a clear party connection or at least "belongs to the area" of a party. As a consequence the shadow of politics falls over industry, culture, academics, the law, and almost every other sector of society. Similarly with the media. In no other country do newspapers and journals represent such a wide variety of political views. But each has its party orientation and through it are filtered not just comment but news presentation. Editors are chosen for their political orientation and even then are subject to continuous partisan intervention. Alberto Cavallari, editor of the *Corriere della Sera* from 1981 to 1984, once wrote of the daily political pressures he had then been under, pressures from the prime minister on down the political scale. Cavallari drew from his experience the dramatic, but probably not overstated, conclusion that the operating principle of Italian politics is in reality "a sort of 'pluralistic Leninism' with many parties placing themselves over the state rather than [as in pure Leninism] a single party commanding the state."

It is symptomatic of the parties' jealousy of their authority that they long refused to implement the constitutional provisions that limit party power – through the establishment of a Constitutional Court to review legislation, the creation of a Superior Judicial Council to protect the legal system from political influence, the provision for popular referenda to repeal existing statues, and the establishment of regional government. The Christian Democrats above all were anxious to block any dispersion of authority beyond their control. The foundation of the court was delayed for eight years and the council for ten. The enabling legislation for referenda was passed only in 1970, and most party leaders would now like to restrict its use. It was not until 1970 that regions were finally established.

Paradoxically one of the severest constraints on party power comes from the parties themselves. Each of them, down to the smallest, is continually plagued by a compulsive formation of internal factions. The cutthroat warfare among these rival cliques is another notable peculiarity of Italian politics. The groups arise more out of never-ending power struggles among leaders than out of disagreements over party ideology and strategy. The number of factions, their adherents, and their political lines are in a nearly constant state of flux. There are generally at least three – a left, center, and right – and in the case of the Socialists and Christian Democrats many more. The differences are so open and organized that they are formally acknowledged by all the parties. The Communists alone have forbidden factions, but even in their ranks vaguely defined groups have started to form.

Party factions are political fiefdoms, each headed by its own baron and each with its own army of followers. Some even have their own publication, news service, headquarters, and source of funds. Although factions usually have a geographic center – the leader's constituency – and a specific power source – various interest groups – they exist throughout the country and often have local and regional offices. They extend their control through the party apparatus by dividing up the seats in the governing bodies in proportion to the factions' numerical strength, as determined by voting at the party congress. With this political base they then spread out into the civil service, the state commercial enterprises, and the public agencies.

Above all factions must be accommodated in the government. When a new governing coalition is formed, the twenty-six or more cabinet seats and the sixty or more subcabinet posts are distributed not only by party but by party faction. The Italian cabinet is the largest in any Western democracy precisely to permit this balancing of interests. Should a cabinet minister resign during the life of a government, he must normally be replaced by a member of the same faction without regard for professional qualifications. Moreover, because factions extend their power out of the party and into the governing institutions, disagreements among them are carried into the government itself. As a result governments have been completely paralyzed and on occasion have fallen because of factional disputes.

Factionalism blunts party power in several ways. Few leaders gain firm control of their party for very long. Party strategy and tactics are subject to sudden and drastic change as the inner balance of power shifts. The factions of one party are sometimes closer to certain factions in other parties than they are to one another and have been known to sabotage the policies of their own party leader. Since party power is therefore dispersed among competing groups, it loses focus and force.

Polarized fragmentation

Party authority is also crippled because of another important characteristic of Italian political society, its fragmentation. Some ten parties participate in national politics, and there are also two or three regional parties with representation in parliament. In addition there are dozens of tiny parties, some serious and a few manifestly whimsical, which put up candidates on the local or regional level. This proliferation is a reflection of the country's traditional social, ideological, and regional divisions. Such differences are translated into a multiparty system thanks to an election law that allocates a deputy for every 80,000 citizens (as compared with roughly 500,000 in the United States) and that is based on a proportional representation system requiring a party merely to win 300,000 votes and reach an electoral quota – that is, directly elect one deputy.

The Catholic tradition is represented by a single party, the Christian Democrats, whose vote over the years has averaged roughly 40 percent of the electorate. The Marxist heritage finds expression in the Communists and Socialists, who together account for a slightly lower average vote. The liberal, laicist middle class takes shape in the Republicans, Social Democrats, Liberals, and Radicals, whose combined vote over the years has fluctuated around 10 percent. There are also a number of parties on the left and right extremes that have the support of roughly 8 to 10 percent of the electorate. The most notable of these is the neo-Fascist Social Movement, which has been the country's fourth-largest party since it absorbed the Monarchist party in 1972. On the geographical fringes, representing ethnic minorities, are a variety of regional parties, of which the most important is the South Tyrol People's party.

Although other parties have been founded and dissolved with the passage of time, there has never been an appreciable consolidation. The Christian Democrats have been unable to absorb the parties on their left and right flanks though they have at times taken votes from them. Neither the left parties nor the lay forces have managed to amalgamate and instead have fallen prey to schismatic divisions. Therefore as long as the electoral system is retained, the party spectrum will remain fragmented to the point where for all practical purposes no single party can come close to winning an absolute majority of the popular vote.

At the same time the political spectrum is polarized. The first parliamentary election in 1948 was decisive. The Christian Democrats and Communists emerged as the two major parties and from then on together collected from two-thirds to three-quarters of the vote, in an upward swing that reached a high point in 1976. Although the trend went the other way in subsequent elections, the Christian Democrats and Communists remain the giants of the political system.

Ideological antinomy

The main difficulty of Italian politics, however, is not the fissiparation and polarization of the party system but its ideological character. It is not that Italians suffer from a philosophical mania or fascination with intellectual theories. Rather, their history left them fundamentally divided over social values and objectives. A profound and lasting cleavage ensued from the bitter clash between the liberal, secular forces that united the country and the church, which opposed unification. That created a gulf between Catholics loyal to the church and other Italians that has yet to be fully bridged. Fascism added another layer of ideology and division. After 1945 the country was dominated by two diametrically opposed forces – Catholicism and Communism – and was drawn into the East–West cold war. Once again Italian society was polarized into two warring extremes, between which there was no room for neutrality. Practical political issues were transformed into fundamental choices that both sides presented as ideological. Elections were for a time proclaimed by the church and the Christian Democrats as an alternative between Christ and Satan. The question of Italy's membership in the North Atlantic Treaty Organization was presented as a *scelta di civiltà,* a "choice of [Eastern or Western] civilization."

The resulting ideological divisions were so pronounced that they animated three subcultures – Catholic, Communist, and lay – with the adherents of each group living out much of their social and professional lives in remarkably distinct spheres. Blue collar workers are an example. Though their class interest is deep, their commitment as Catholics, Communists, or lay-party members is still stronger, as reflected in the existence of three separate trade union movements and the way they vote in elections. In the industrial and banking world as well there is a similar, if more subtle, cleavage between Catholics and the lay banking and business elite. Although these subcultures have greatly eroded over the years, ideological divisions continue to permeate Italian public life.

In everyday politics the issue comes to a head over the question of whether the ideologies of certain parties – in particular the Communists and neo-Fascists – are compatible with the constitutional order and the established domestic and foreign policy norms. The Communists have been barred from government on the national level primarily because of their historic ties to Leninist political principles and their fraternal relations with the Soviet Union. The neo-Fascists have been pariahs because some of their leaders came out of the old Fascist regime, have espoused traditional Fascist principles, and are suspected of being associated with groups seeking the violent destruction of the political system. Hence, in the terms of an analogy once used by former Prime Minister Giulio Andreotti, there are ten parties on the political field but only five – the Christian Democrats, Socialists, and three lay parties – are permitted to score a goal.

With parties representing fully 40 percent or more of the electorate thus excluded from power, governments must be formed with the remaining five parties. Such a narrow base is in itself a formidable disadvantage. The problem is compounded by the incompatible philosophies and competing constituencies of these parties. With programs, strategies, and interests pulling in contrary directions, the formation of a government is dependent on a temporary armistice in an unending war for political and electoral advantage. Every coalition is hostage to the short-term partisan interests of the governing partners, who respect almost no limits in their ceaseless jockeying for advantage. Governments are therefore of necessity weak and delicately balanced. Each member is critical to the survival of the government; one defection is fatal. This power of life and death explains the remarkable – and uniquely Italian – situation where a party with the backing of as little as 2 to 3 percent of the vote has a political weight vastly out of proportion to its electoral strength. Forming a government is difficult enough. Keeping it afloat is a day-to-day struggle.

One of the curiosities of Italian politics is that these ideological differences do not impede cooperation across the political barricade. The usual antithesis between governing responsibility and loyal opposition has never been either an ideal or a practice in Italian political life. With the establishment of a national parliament in the nineteenth century, governments were based on the technique of *trasformismo,* where amorphous parliamentary majorities were patched together from separate political fragments. This approach was symptomatic of an instinctive Italian preference for collaboration rather than conflict. The same trait has been evident throughout the country's republican history. It has been most strikingly manifested in cooperation among the Communists and Christian Democrats that began in parliament at the height of the domestic and international cold war and reached its zenith between 1976 and 1979 when the Christian Democrats formed two governments based on Communist support.

Over the years a number of scholars have drawn together the various elements of the Italian party system in a comprehensive analysis that would explain its functioning – or malfunctioning. Two contrasting interpretations have gained particular attention: Giorgio Galli's "imperfect bipartism" and Giovanni Sartori's "polarized pluralism." According to Galli, Italian politics bear some of the traits of a multiparty system; because of the hegemony of the Christian Democrats and Communists, however, it is in practice a two-party system. But this bipartism is imperfect since the former party is always in and the latter always out of power. As a result Italy suffers the worse features of both systems. Sartori's more complex analysis cannot be adequately compressed into a few words. Its essence is that Italy is characterized by a large number of parties that are widely separated by differences of ideology. Because the extremes are occupied by "anti-system" parties, the political spectrum is polarized. Political forces coalesce around polls of the left, center, and right but are driven by centrifugal forces toward the extremes. The consequence is a system dominated by ideological discord, governmental instability, irresponsible opposition, political fragmentation, and a division of the parties into factions.

Ideology and multipartism have combined to create enormous liabilities for Italian democracy. With no sign of an end to the existence of a large number of parties, a central question for the future is whether the Communists and neo-Fascists will be accepted as equal partners in national politics. "Anti-system" party and "legitimacy" are subjective notions – issues not just of a party's program and behavior but also of semantics, the electorate's perceptions, and other parties' assessment of what is expedient for themselves. When the time comes that ideology disappears as the essential divider between the parties, the Italian political system will be transformed. Differences of political philosophy will remain, and Italy will continue to be afflicted with the normal problems of multipartism. But the political game will be an utterly new one.

Plebiscitary elections

Ideology is in part responsible for another peculiarity of Italian politics: the skewing of national elections. Few other Europeans flock to the polls in as great numbers as the Italians, over 90 percent of whom have traditionally voted in national elections. Yet the outcome is essentially predetermined. The Christian Democrats will be the party of the relative majority and they will be that, as Giorgio Galli has observed, not for what they do or how they do it but for what they are, "and that is the great party of order in contrast to the great 'subversive' party, the Communists." Although much has changed in Italian politics since Galli wrote those words in the sixties, the phenomenon he described remains essentially unchanged. In 1983, as in 1948, the Christian Democrats fought the election campaign as "the party of liberty."

However, that is only part of the problem. The purpose of democratic elections – to permit an electorate to render its verdict on the previous government and to express a preference for a future one – is diffused in many multiparty systems. In Italy it is totally distorted. There is no declared candidate for prime minister, little clarity on the policy intentions of the parties, and no way of knowing what sort of coalition will be put together. These are all matters that will be decided – sometimes with surprising results – by party leaders after an election. The citizen, unable to render a judgment on any of the fundamental issues, votes for a vague party image. And that image is based primarily on a party's position on the political spectrum rather than its embodiment of specific programs, which so far as they exist are scarcely known. At most, elections have the character of a periodic plebiscite over the country's general political direction.

But often the results are ambiguous. Then party leaders read the electoral signs just as they wish. In 1963 the Christian Democrats and Socialists sought confirmation to enter into a coalition. They did not receive it but went ahead anyway. The extent to which the electorate's decision can be ignored was never more blatant than in 1981 when a new government was formed by Giovanni Spadolini, head of the Republican party – a party that had won 3 percent of the vote in the previous election. Two years later the Socialists headed the government, after winning 11 percent of the vote in that year's balloting. In short, governments are set up, govern, and fall with little or no regard for the electorate's views. The ballot is a blank check that the voter periodically endorses. Hence the paradox of an electorate that throngs to the polls but that is politically fatalistic and cynical.

A few striking exceptions apart, Italian electoral behavior has been characterized by remarkable stability, with changes normally confined to several percentage points at most. Although polarization has waxed and waned, the basic right-center-left division of the vote has scarcely altered over the years (see Appendix A). Neither the natural regeneration of the electorate, nor the decay of subcultures, nor the social and economic transformation of the country overturned traditional voting patterns. Personal prosperity and the success of capitalism did not change Mario Rossi from a

Communist to a Christian Democrat; secularization, urbanization, and feminism did not convert Maria Bianchi from a Christian Democrat into a Socialist. But why they voted as they did – and how their children voted – altered over time.

Beginning around the mid-1970s, therefore, significant changes in electoral behavior were increasingly apparent. These could be seen in the rising number of floating voters, in the establishment of new parties, in the splitting of votes on the national and the local levels, in the independent positions taken by a high proportion of voters on national referenda, and in sharp electoral reverses for the Communists and Christian Democrats. It was also apparent in the larger number of citizens who expressed their antipathy to the party system by not voting or by casting spoiled or blank ballots. After running for 30 years at a fairly steady rate of about 10 percent, the figure suddenly rose to 15 percent in 1979 and to 18 percent in 1983. In the local election in Reggio Calabria in the latter year, the number exceeded 30 percent.

Behind these changes lay a number of interrelated developments, all revealing a growing distance between the parties and the electorate. As ideological divisions softened, as subcultures shrank and weakened, and as patronage spread among the parties, voters made their decisions increasingly in accord with issues and candidates rather than traditional party loyalties. In a scholarly analysis of this phenomenon, Arturo Parisi and Gianfranco Pasquino distinguished three types of electoral behavior that were undergoing change. The "vote of opinion," reflecting a conscious choice based on a party's goals, was of growing importance. The "vote of *appartenenza*," rooted in an ideological or organizational identification, was declining. And the "vote of exchange," based on political favors, was becoming more uncertain. As a consequence the quality of the vote was changing, and this resulted in greater electoral mobility. But the impact of that mobility on electoral results would depend, in their judgment, on whether the various shifts canceled out one another and whether they affected certain parties more than others. In short, what this and other analyses have made clear is that although the long-standing bases of Italian voting behavior are altering, it is difficult to predict, given the variables, what the sum result will be. Why Italians vote the way they do is therefore likely to remain one of the mysteries of Italian politics.

Christian Democratic dominance

The most conspicuous feature of Italian politics and the one that distinguishes Italy from all other parliamentary democracies is the dominant position from 1945 to the present of a single party. The Christian Democrats have maintained their primacy in several ways. They have consistently been the largest of the parties, enjoying a solid base of electoral support that, until 1983, never fell below 38 percent. Even though surrendering the prime ministry three times between 1981 and 1983, they retained a majority of cabinet positions and ultimate control of the government. With some 40 percent of the other political forces excluded from government, the Christian Democrats have been able to transform their control of roughly one-third of the seats in parliament into nearly three-quarters of the effective political power in the state.

Christian Democratic power is not based just on electoral strength and control of the government. Over the decades the party has managed to place its loyalists in every area of the state apparatus and the *sottogoverno*, transforming them into an army of clients that not only has supported the party's electoral position but has carried its influence throughout society. So broad and effective was the Christian Democrats' control that it eventually developed into a veritable symbiosis of party, government, and state.

Because the Christian Democrats entrenched themselves in power with such success, Italy – alone among liberal democracies – has had no genuine change of rule in the whole of the postwar era. Governments come and go but essentially the same persons are in charge, merely changing cabinet seats or positions in the public industrial enterprises. Even the generational change has been amazingly gradual and limited. Most of the party's leaders began their careers under the party's initial head, Alcide De Gasperi, in the late 1940s and early 1950s and have occupied – and traded – the key positions among themselves during the intervening decades.

The most striking example is Amintore Fanfani. He became a minister for the first time in 1947 and served in one cabinet position after another in subsequent decades. Three times he was president of the Senate and twice secretary of the Christian Democratic party. Fanfani was most recently prime minister in 1982–3. He formed his first government in 1954 – when Eisenhower was American president, Churchill British prime minister, and Adenauer Federal German chancellor.

There are other cases. Emilio Colombo entered the cabinet in 1955 and since then has been minister thirty-six times; he has also been prime minister and held the treasury ministry off and on for a total of nine years. Giulio Andreotti has served in twenty-seven ministries; Paolo Emilio Taviani in twenty-two; Mariano Rumor in eighteen; Aldo Moro in sixteen; and so on. Fanfani, Andreotti,

Rumor, and Moro were each prime minister five times. According to a study by Mauro Calise and Renato Mannheimer, some 152 politicians held two-thirds of the 1,331 ministerial and subcabinet positions distributed between 1946 and 1976. Indeed 31 persons alone occupied 480 such positions during that period. Thus the aphorism that the Christian Democrats are their own alternative government.

Even in coalition the Christian Democrats have always maintained control of the government and the state apparatus. At a minimum they have held on to a majority of the ministries. Those that wield influence or a lot of patronage – State Participation, Agriculture, Public Education, Post and Telecommunications, Interior, Foreign Affairs, Defense, and Economics – have never or only rarely been ceded to other parties. Coalition partners have traditionally parlayed their small portion of electoral support into cabinet positions, in that way gaining a voice in government and access to some patronage. But their influence over policy has generally been slight. Only on those relatively rare occasions when they united on a specific issue – such as divorce and abortion – have they been able to prevail against the Christian Democrats. Otherwise their influence is largely negative: the ability to bring down a government.

With the passage of time the foundation of Christian Democratic hegemony has been chipped away. Internal problems, electoral losses, involvement in scandal, and increasing pressure from the Socialists and lay parties have loosened the party's grip on power at every level. It remains the dominant party. But one of the key questions of Italian politics is whether its decline is reversible or whether it is on the way to being displaced as the country's controlling political force.

Instability in stability

Remarkably enough, the Christian Democrats have maintained their hegemony over the years without ever having won an absolute majority in any election. Control of the government has therefore depended on gaining the parliamentary backing of other parties. Forging arrangements to perpetuate itself in power is the party's paramount aim. How it has accomplished this is the central theme of Italy's postwar political history. It is possible to distinguish five general phases.

The initial stage, from 1944 to 1953, marked the Christian Democrats' rise to ascendancy. The earliest party governments after the fall of Fascism were all broad coalitions of Christian Democrats, Communists, Socialists, and lay forces. By the end of 1945 the Christian Democrats, with Communist support, took over the prime ministry and successfully asserted a position of political leadership. The first postwar election – in 1946 for a Constitutional Assembly – affirmed their primacy. By 1947 they felt strong enough to eject the Communists and Socialists and set up a centrist–conservative coalition. Riding a wave of anti-Communism created by the cold war, the Christian Democrats scored a stunning victory in the first parliamentary election in 1948 when they won, though not quite an electoral majority, a majority of seats in parliament. Their position of hegemony was established.

A new stage began with the 1953 election, when the Christian Democrats lost their parliamentary majority and became dependent on other parties to form a government. At times they ruled alone with the parliamentary backing of political allies – a so-called *monocolore* government – and at other times in coalition. A durable governing formula proved elusive, however, and the Christian Democrats edged further and further to the right in their search for partners. Twice in the late fifties they ruled for short periods with the parliamentary backing of the Monarchists and neo-Fascists. But in 1960 they went too far when they allowed Fernando Tambroni to form a government that not only rested on neo-Fascist support but that appeared to veer dangerously to the right in its political orientation. Popular opposition exploded in rioting in which ten persons died. Tambroni fell in ignominy after only four months. With that, the door was closed to coalitions of the right.

A third phase opened with the Christian Democrats' turning to the Socialists to find a solid basis for governing. The center-left option entailed years of ideological and political anguish on both sides and had to await the accord of the Vatican and the Americans. The first coalition was inaugurated in 1963. It was ill-starred from the outset. The country's economic miracle was winding down, and the welfare state the Socialists wanted to establish was blocked by the Christian Democrats for budgetary reasons. After rocking along for a decade, the center-left collapsed in an atmosphere of bitter acrimony when the Socialists withdrew from the coalition in 1974 and two years later brought down the government by refusing even to support it in parliament. Now another door was closed.

Meanwhile a radically new situation was evolving. Step by claudicant step the Communists were moving away from Leninism and the Soviet Union. In 1973 they proclaimed a new tactic, which aimed at sharing power with the Christian Democrats rather than replacing them in government. This development culminated in a dramatic success by the Communists in the national election of 1976, giving them and the Christian Democrats together more than three-quarters of the seats in parliament.

With this turn of events a fourth stage began in which the Christian Democrats had no choice but to accept some degree of Communist cooperation in governing. Although the tactic involved risks for both sides, an agreement was reached on a *monocolore* government with indirect Communist support. Two years later the collaboration was extended to the point where a new government was formed with explicit Communist parliamentary backing.

But even more quickly than it had been conjured into being, the accord came apart. The Communists found that cooperation with the Christian Democrats was increasingly unpopular with their members and was not leading to its desired goal, full entry into the government. Early in 1979 they therefore withdrew their support, precipitating another early national election. The campaign was conducted as a plebiscite on full Communist entry into the government. The result was an emphatic negative. Not only did the Communists suffer the first election defeat in their history, they lost a full 4 percent of their electorate, a substantial figure by Italian standards. The door that had been slammed shut on the right in 1960 and on the center-left in 1976 was now closed on the Communists.

A fifth stage opened at the outset of the 1980s when, once again, the center-left formula was the only viable basis of governing. The Socialists, now controlled by a new group of young leaders who could scarcely wait to get their hands on power, agreed to take their party back into government, and a coalition was formed in 1980. Scarcely had the country settled back for the usual monotonous rise and fall of governments when the mood of déjà vu was destroyed by two startling developments.

In 1981 the police, in investigating a banking scandal, discovered the existence of a secret Masonic lodge, known as P2, whose members included hundreds of prominent persons, including party and government officials. The exposure of what seemed to be an invisible power at the heart of the state blew up into the biggest political scandal of the postwar period. The Christian Democrats had to surrender the prime ministry, which was turned over to a Republican. No sooner had they claimed back the position the following year than they suffered more than a 5 percent loss at the polls in the 1983 parliamentary election. Once again they had to step aside, this time allowing a government to be formed by the Socialists, despite that party's mediocre performance in the voting. Although these developments left the Italian political scene in a state of unprecedented ambiguity, the Christian Democrats remained as they had been since 1945, the ultimate controlling force.

The overall record of the intervening forty years shows that for all the changes of regime, the governing system itself has been stable, stable to the point of near immobility. For all the ministerial shifts, there has been no essential change of ruling elite. The De Gasperi era apart, the essence of Italian self-government over these decades has been little more than one of brokering new coalitions. What in other countries is merely the starting point of the governing process – getting a regime in place so that the implementation of policy can begin – is in Italy almost its totality. As time has passed, finding a stable governing formula has become progressively more difficult. Coalitions of the center, right, and left have been tried in turn, with similar results in the end: governments so weak that they have spent more time presiding than governing.

Nonetheless the ship, rudderless and flooded, sails on in defiance of every prediction that it cannot possibly stay afloat. The crew is largely unchanged, the course remarkably steady, and every storm – political, economic, and social; domestic and international – is always ridden out with astonishing ease. None of the encumbering freight – multipartism, weak government, a mistrusted state, and party primacy – can be jettisoned. But might there be a change at the helm? With the Christian Democrats having lost their hegemony, question arises whether they may lose their centrality. With the Communists having undergone a transformation, they may gain full acceptability. Although the strength of the Socialists and lay parties waxes and wanes, they have been making an unprecedented effort to provide an alternative to the two major parties.

Elements of potential change are visible and could fundamentally alter the way Italian politics have been played since 1945. But Italian history is littered with turning points that never turned. Everything could remain essentially as it is. If change does occur, it is in the parties that the seeds of it are to be found.

2. The Christian Democrats: The indispensable center?

The Italian Christian Democrats have enjoyed a longer period of unbroken political dominance than any other democratic party in the world. For four decades after the war they consistently won more votes than any competitor; were the dominant force in every government; provided every prime minister but three; occupied all or a majority of the cabinet seats; and controlled most of the key positions in the civil service, the state industries and banks, and the thousands of public bodies in every area of society. The author of a history of the party up to 1975 could aptly entitle his book *L'Occupazione del potere* (The occupation of power). As a political success story, it has been without parallel.

At the outset of the 1980s the occupation was clearly coming to an end. Although still the most powerful force in the field, the party was in retreat on almost every front. Its electoral strength, long in decline on the local level, had suddenly plummeted in the parliamentary election of 1983. It had already lost the presidency in 1978 and the prime ministry in 1981 and the two following years. Important positions in the state-controlled business sector and public agencies were being wrested out of its hands by other parties. Over the years the Christian Democrats have been renowned for their powers of recovery. But the crisis of the eighties bore signs of being systemic. For the first time the question arose whether the party would be able to pull itself together and if not recapture what it held in the past, at least hang on to the commanding high ground. Or would it be pushed out of even its most entrenched positions? Having been the controlling force in Italy throughout the postwar period, the answer to these questions would inevitably have a profound impact on the future of the country.

What had launched the Christian Democrats on their remarkable conquest of power was a combination of factors: outstanding leadership, the help of the Catholic church, broad interclass support, popular fear of Communism, the weakness of competing parties, a successful foreign policy, a unique relationship with the United States, and an ability to catch and harness the political mood of the time. These added up to a winning formula, one that no other party could match. Even many who would not vote for the Christian Democrats wanted them to be the fulcrum of the country's government. Such were the elements of the party's success. Now they are the essence of its problems.

"Medio tutissimus ibis"

The Christian Democatic party was organized in 1943 by veterans of the pre-Fascist Catholic Popular party, Catholic trade unionists, and young leaders of Catholic professional organizations. From the start the undisputed leader was the former secretary of the Popular party, Alcide De Gasperi, who even before Mussolini's fall had drafted a general program for a party that was to be Christian, interclass, centrist, and socially progressive. It took years to define and refine the various programmatic ideas that circulated among Catholic political figures in those years. Only with the first party congress in 1946 was any coherence achieved, and even then it was the coherence of ambiguity. The state was not to be confessional but neither was it to be secular. Church and state were to be separate but the 1929 concordat giving the church sweeping privileges in civil affairs was to be maintained. Private property was inviolable but land reform was to be carried out and economic privilege was to be eradicated through progressive taxation. Traditional Catholic suspicion of the state was muted but governing institutions were to be weak, powers were to be devolved to regions, and parliamentary representation was in part to be corporatist.

In time the various pieces were cobbled together into programs with features appealing to every social category from socialistic workers to reactionary landowners, Catholic and non-Catholic alike – all united in a "democratic front" against the "popular front" of the Communists and Socialists. In an often-quoted statement to the party's 1946 congress, De Gasperi described the Christian Democrats as "a party of the center that leans to the left." More precise would have been: a moderate conservative party that can show a suitable face to any electoral constituency.

In taking institutional shape the Christian Democrats' most urgent need, especially with two rapidly reviving Marxist parties on the scene, was to erect a national organization. With no foundation to build on, the party turned to its natural ally, the church. There it could not have found a more ubiquitous, influential, and highly motivated friend. Frightened by a seeming threat of revolution from the left, Pope Pius XII and the Italian hierarchy, parish priests, and the Catholic laity joined in a massive effort to build a party structure and recruit members. Assistance of every sort – from money to meeting places – was unstintingly provided. In the Catholic laymen's associations the party found not only a ready leadership but a veritable army of local activists. With such help, the party had by the end of 1945 recruited over a half-million members and established over 7,000 local offices, nine daily newspapers, and eighty weeklies. With that amount of support De Gasperi was strong enough to lay successful claim to the prime ministry, as he did in December of that year.

In the critical election of a Constitutional Assembly in 1946 and the first parliamentary election in 1948 the Vatican, the clergy, and Catholic laymen's associations conducted a political crusade on the Christian Democrats' behalf. Although the party had other strong forces behind it – such as the business community and the American government – and exploited a widespread fear of Communism in the wake of the Prague coup, the church and its associations were by far the party's most important institutional support. The electoral successes on both occasions amazed the Christian Democrats no less than their opponents. Whereas the old Popular party had never gained more than 20 percent in any election, the Christian Democrats won 35 percent in 1946 and 48 percent in 1948 – margins without precedent for any party in Italian democratic history.

But if the party's multifaceted character and its links to the church were major elements of Christian Democratic success, they also caused grave problems for De Gasperi and his successors. In turning to the church for support to launch the party organizationally and electorally, the party mortgaged its independence. The price demanded by the pope – essentially the right to direct Italian politics from the Vatican and use the party as his political instrument – was so exorbitant that it eventually shocked most Catholics and even some high church officials. De Gasperi made enormous concessions but like Konrad Adenauer, another Catholic statesman with a similar problem, he was a secular Catholic and knew that to be the tool of the church would damage not only the party but also Italian democracy.

His apprehensions came to a head over "Operation Sturzo." In 1952 the Vatican was greatly alarmed that the left parties might win the Rome city election in May of that year and come to power in the pope's own diocese. The best way of turning back the threat, in Pius's view, was to put together an election list independent of the Christian Democratic ticket. The list was to comprise right-wing candidates, including neo-Fascists, headed by the former leader of the Popular party, Don Luigi Sturzo, himself a priest. Unwilling to cooperate with the neo-Fascists and fearing that this maneuver was the first step toward a church-sponsored rightist party, De Gasperi demurred and the proposal collapsed. Pius was so incensed that he declined a short time later to receive the party leader on the occasion of his thirtieth wedding anniversary and his daughter's investiture as a nun. De Gasperi, who the previous year had received greetings on his seventieth birthday from Stalin but not the pope, remarked that while he accepted the humiliation as a Christian, he resented it as prime minister of Italy. Despite the contretemps, ecclesiastical interference went on and the basic issue – whether the party or the church should decide what belonged to Caesar and what to God – was one that De Gasperi and his successors had to fight over and over again.

De Gasperi's other big problem was that in having created a broadly based party that included social utopians, trade unionists, middle-class entrepreneurs and professionals, artisans, shopkeepers, civil servants, housewives, farmers, and landowners, he had to forge these groups into a coalition able to agree on common goals. The deep fear of Communism in those cold war years was an important catalyst in transforming this heterogeneous mass into a solid political force. But De Gasperi's personal role was critical. A man of foresight, patience, and skill, he articulated the median position around which others could unite while leading the party on a course equidistant from the socialist dreams of the party's left and the reactionary clericalism of its right.

By linking two incompatible elements – political Catholicism and liberal democracy – De Gasperi integrated the mass of Catholics for the first time into democratic parliamentarism. He did this by welding together a type of party new to Italy, a coalition of almost every social group, Catholic or not, from left to right – the postwar Western European phenomenon, the "catch-all party." That was only part of his achievement. He also succeeded in laying the foundation of a viable, long-term governing system by insisting that his party should forge alliances with other democratic forces. The Catholic social doctrines of the old Popular party were therefore replaced by economic policies developed by such liberals as Luigi Einaudi and Ugo La Malfa while the lay parties themselves were increasingly included in Christian Democratic governments. In this way he created a centrist coalition formula that has been the basis of almost every subsequent government. On being awarded an honorary degree at Oxford in 1953, De Gasperi was praised by the university orator for having commended to Italians the precept of Daedalus: *"Medio tutissimus ibis"* – "You will be safest if you go the middle way." This principle was De Gasperi's legacy. It guided a country with little living tradition of liberal parliamentarism but much social and ideological division along the road to successful democracy.

As with the acceptance of church support, however, there was a price to be paid. The party's various constituencies tended at times to checkmate one another to the point where agreement on policies was almost impossible to achieve. The original promises of social reforms had bit by bit to be abandoned. In no time the party became a centrist formation in all but essentials – and there it was conservative. The different elements of the party gradually formed groups that were difficult even for De Gasperi to control. Eventually he also paid a heavy personal price. In the 1953 parliamentary election the Christian Democrats, though remaining the largest party, lost 8 percent of its electors. As if to demonstrate that pragmatism – the pure selfish interest in success – rather than any sort of idealism was paramount, the party abandoned De Gasperi. His government fell and, after having been prime minister eight times, he resigned for good.

The party as a power machine

If the party's moderate-conservative character was fixed by De Gasperi, its trait as a deeply rooted mass party was largely the contribution of his successor, Amintore Fanfani. The situation confronting Fanfani was epitomized in a saying current in those days that to get into parliament a Christian Democratic candidate needed twenty priests or 2 million lire. It was a situation Fanfani intended to change, and whatever he did, he did with gusto. His objective was to create a strong party organization and to extricate the party from its dependence on the church and private industry so that it could operate with complete autonomy.

Within five years he revamped the party structure, nearly doubled the number of local party offices, almost quadrupled the number of active party workers, and virtually doubled party membership. At the summit he fashioned a modern party machine with a single objective, the conquest of power. Catholic support continued to be necessary and he could not stop ecclesiastical interference, but he reduced the party's subservience to the church. His boldest stroke was establishing an independent power base in the state-controlled industries and banks. These he began systematically transforming from firms operated by professional managers who followed purely economic principles into firms managed by persons increasingly selected for their party credentials and their willingness to direct operations in ways useful to the party. The Christian Democrats thereby gained access to funds and an enormous store of patronage, which were turned into support at election time. In 1956 he established a Ministry of State Participation to facilitate party control over the public-sector economy, which was now rapidly expanding in the context of Italy's economic miracle. This was the moment when the Christian Democrats' occupation of power – the triangular state–government–party link – was set in place.

The annexation of the state economic sector unleashed a veritable war among the various party groups for a share of the jobs and funds. With the creation of the first institutionalized faction, Fanfani's own, in 1952, others rapidly took shape, and at the 1954 party congress as many as eight were identifiable. These groups not only compromised party unity but also virtually invited the Vatican, the state corporations, and other interest groups to link themselves to certain factions and use them as channels of influence within the party. From this time forward the history of the party was essentially the history of factions, their metamorphoses and their power struggles. Given the differences among factions, it was increasingly difficult for the party to agree on policies. Governments were one stopgap after another; already from the mid-fifties muddling through was the political norm. Not only were social reforms put off year after year but the country's first long-term economic program, developed by Budget Minister Ezio Vanoni in 1955, was so chewed apart by the factions that it came to nothing. By now Christian Democracy stood for the status quo, indeed immobilism. Its claim of being a centrist party was true only in the sense that there were even more conservative parties – the Liberals and neo-Fascists – to its right.

So if Fanfani left the party stronger in terms of organization and financing, he left it weaker as a result of its internal divisions. And, like De Gasperi before him, he paid a heavy personal price. In 1959 right-wing factions rebelled, and Fanfani resigned both as party secretary and prime minister. There now emerged a new faction, the Dorotei – so-called because the group was founded in the Santa Dorotea monastery in Rome – which became so powerful that it controlled the party for the next ten years and dominated it for a further ten after that. It was a political machine with no ideology and no objective other than power for itself and the party. Too big for any individual to dominate, its leaders came and went. From 1959 until 1969 it almost unilaterally chose and dispensed with party secretaries and set the party's course. After opposing a coalition with the Socialists, it led the party into one. It selected and rejected prime ministers, raised and destroyed governments. It chose Antonio Segni as the party's candidate for the presidency in 1962 and, after his incapacitation two years later, secured the election of the Social Democrats' Saragat over the Christian Democratic candidate, Fanfani. Prime ministers who announced government policies without having secured the prior concurrence of the Dorotei found that their policies were eventually scuttled by the party. With the formation of a center-left government in 1963, the faction was determined to dilute the reforms that were agreed on as the basis of the coalition. To show who was in control, they brought down the first such regime after only six months in office.

By the end of the sixties other factions began to challenge the Dorotei. The disputes spilled over from the party into national politics, making it difficult for governments to be formed or to govern once in office. As time went on the party became so fragmented and so crippled by factional maneuverings that it could not agree on much of any political line. So bad was the situation that faction chiefs finally agreed in 1973 to bring back Fanfani as party secretary and to increase his powers in the hope that he could unify and revitalize the party. What Christian Democratic leaders could not bring themselves to acknowledge was that the party had been so self-absorbed for so long that it had fallen completely out of touch with the mood of society.

How far out of touch was soon evident. Fanfani's first decision was to throw the party's full weight behind the Catholic-sponsored 1974 referendum to repeal a divorce law that had been passed four years earlier. In a colossal tactical misjudgment, he presented the issue as a choice between militant Catholicism and secular Communism. This antique Manichaeism backfired, and the referendum was decisively defeated, a setback at least as much for the Christian Democrats as for the church. In the regional and communal elections of the following year the party fell to the lowest level in its history while the Communists advanced to within 3 percent of the Christian Democrats. Fanfani was finished.

The end of hegemony

With the party's dominance threatened for the first time since 1945, Christian Democratic leaders realized that drastic action was needed to improve the party's image. Benigno Zaccagnini, one of the party's old and honorable stalwarts, was brought in as party secretary. "Honest Zac," as he was known because he had never

2. **The Christian Democrats** 27

been tainted by scandal, was presented as a symbol of a party to be cleansed and reoriented on its original idealistic purposes. The 1976 party congress was billed as marking the "refoundation" of the party. And in fact the Christian Democrats pulled themselves together in time for the 1976 election and once again played their well-worn trump card – they were the only plausible barrier against the Communist threat. Indro Montanelli, the lively, conservative editor of the influential *Giornale Nuovo,* advised voters: "Hold your nose but vote for the Christian Democrats." A sufficient number of electors did both and, though the Communists advanced, they could not overtake the Christian Democrats, who maintained their long-held position as the largest party. The rejuvenation, however, came to nothing. The parliamentary party had its most sweeping change in decades, with many new and young representatives entering the Chamber and Senate. But the old bosses remained in command and the newcomers were allowed no real influence. If the electorate kept the party in power, it was only in apprehension of the alternative.

Nonetheless with the outcome of the 1976 election, Communist support was necessary to form a government. The Christian Democrats faced one of the most difficult and delicate tasks in their history. Despite the anti-Communist tone of the election campaign, Christian Democratic leaders had already come to the view that the Communist party had undergone a radical change, that it was no longer a Leninist organization, and that it did not take orders from Moscow. They did not want to legitimize it in the eyes of the wider public, thereby opening the way to an eventual challenge for the leadership of the country, or give it seats in the cabinet, and in that way compromise their power. But they calculated that Communist cooperation would provide a strong basis for Christian Democratic rule and at the same time saddle the Communists with some responsibility for the austerity measures necessary to deal with the country's severe economic problems at the time. To secure that cooperation they were willing to turn over a few positions in parliament and the *sottogoverno* and to consult the party on government policies. A sizable group of Christian Democratic backbenchers, including many of the new entries, opposed this tactic but were easily whipped into line.

Aldo Moro, who had successfully brought together the Christian Democrats and Socialists in the early sixties, now came forward to guide the process. At this point the most influential person in the party, Moro was the sole figure who enjoyed the trust both of his own party leadership and that of the Communists. If the strategy was his, the delicate task of making the practical arrangements fell to Giulio Andreotti, a conservative Christian Democrat of great cunning and subtlety. Against the interventions of the American government, which the party leadership deeply resented, Andreotti succeeded in forming two governments with the accord of the Communist party.

It was a bravura performance. The Christian Democrats used the Communist party simultaneously as a bogeyman to frighten voters and as a partner to guarantee the country's governability. Obviously this arrangement was not satisfactory to the Communists for long, and in 1979 they broke it off. Although the national election that year was interpreted as a popular decision against Communist entry into the government, it was not until their 1980 congress that the Christian Democrats resolved to abandon the Moro line. The decision marked a critical point. The Christian Democrats were now left with no alternative but to return to the center-left formula – and in having no alternative were at the mercy of the Socialists if any durable government was to be formed. For the first time in history the Christian Democrats could not dictate the terms of the coalition contract. The conditions on which the Socialists insisted – an unprecedented role in both the government and the *sottogoverno* – compromised Christian Democratic control as never before.

The Christian Democrats' defeat in the local and regional elections of 1975, which cost them the governments in most large cities and a number of regions, combined with the new offensive of the Socialists had already weakened the party's position when two events occurred that shook the very foundation of its long hegemony. The first was the P2 scandal. Although almost all parties were touched, the affair ultimately was seen as a symptom of the corruption of the system over which the Christian Democrats had presided for thirty-five years. They could not therefore object when the president offered the position of prime minister to a non–Christian Democrat for the first time since 1945. When that blow was followed by the election debacle of 1983, the party had once again to allow the government to be formed by another party. By now the party was in the worst crisis of its history, having lost its iron grip not only on the government and *sottogoverno* but even on its own traditional electorate.

Who runs the party

One of the important contributory causes of the Christian Democratic decline is leadership. Only for brief periods has the party been headed by someone who was strong, effective, and respected. De Gasperi possessed all three traits in great measure. At a time when he bore responsibility as a prime minister and foreign minister for conducting Italy through the critical formative period of its postwar history, he was also molding, managing, and leading his party. The only other person to gain full command of the party and to leave a strong imprint on it was Fanfani. In building up a party machine and extending the party's power into the state economic sector, he made himself in Giorgio Galli's view the most powerful man in Italy since Mussolini. He also made himself probably the most widely disliked. A man of great personal and professional talents, Fanfani displayed enormous energy and a political staying power without equal anywhere. Yet as Giuseppe Saragat once said, "Wherever he lays his hands, he creates confusion."

No one could have been more unlike this ebullient Tuscan than his Puglian successor, Aldo Moro. An archetypical figure of the deep South, Moro was a politician's politician. A man of oriental patience, he possessed the qualities that made him the ideal person to lead his party into coalition with the Socialists in the sixties and into cooperation with the Communists in the seventies. Moro was legendary for the obscurity of his ideas, his pleonastic discourses, and his neologistic phrases – such as "converging parallels," to describe the center-left. With tragic irony and not by chance, he was kidnapped by left-wing terrorists on the day of his greatest achievement, the establishment of a government supported by the Communists.

Otherwise the party has been in the hands of the factions. Amoeba-like organisms, the factions themselves have been in a constant state of change – growing, dividing, dissolving, and re-grouping while changing names, members, and policies. This phenomenon was largely set in motion in the mid-fifties with the country's economic boom and in particular the rapid expansion of the state industries, which enticed party groups to develop their own centers of economic power. There have generally been at least seven major factions, at times as many as a dozen. With their own organization and funds, faction leaders have their own supporters, territorial bases, and links to organized interests. Collectively they have been described as an oligarchy, a crown council, a league of tribal chieftains. Since factions are in a constant struggle for power, party leadership rests on temporary alliances among them. The formal party leader, the party secretary, is himself a creature of the factions and serves at their pleasure.

Although factions are essentially power machines, they originally reflected differences of ideology and social interests. The first faction was organized by Fanfani in 1952 as a means of controlling the party. Others soon took shape with names – such as "new forces," "new chronicles," "spring," and "bridge builders" – as arbitrary and meaningless as the political philosophies behind them. Some have carried eponyms of their leader – hence, Andreottiani, Fanfaniani, Morotei. Although they occupy specific positions along the party spectrum, their political identities are subject to sudden and drastic change. Andreotti and his faction began on the far right in the 1950s and by the 1970s were on the far left. With Fanfani it was the reverse. Carlo Donat-Cattin, a trade unionist and head of the one faction that has never strayed from its position on the left, repeatedly supported conservative positions after 1976.

Until the mid-1970s one faction or group of factions was clearly ascendant, if only briefly, and gave the party some political coherence. Subsequently, however, they crumbled into such amorphous groups that political command has been utterly fragmented. At the party congresses of 1982 and 1984 the Dorotei split up and a variety of small factions evolved under the old party hierarchs. A number of these formed temporary coalitions strong enough to elect Ciriaco De Mita party secretary on both occasions but too divided to agree on anything more.

Factionalism is a grave liability to the party. It forces each party official to align himself with a specific group and support the group on every issue. It institutionalizes and intensifies party divisions and leads to power struggles for their own sake. Factionalism has also concentrated and perpetuated control in the hands of the same circle of men who have run the party for most of its history. This is the "second generation" that took over upon the defenestration of De Gasperi in 1953. Fanfani, Moro, Andreotti, and Donat-Cattin are key members. Other notables are Emilio Colombo, who has a strong base in Basilicata and links to banking and is consistently on the party right; Flaminio Piccoli, who has his base in Trent and is a stalwart of the party center; Silvio Gava, whose political and economic base is in Naples; Antonino Gullotti, who is a political power in eastern Sicily and has an economic base in the construction industry; Rumor, whose power is anchored in Catholic circles in the Veneto; and Taviani, who enjoys strong support in Catholic circles and the Genoa shipbuilding industry.

Although age is no particular liability in Italian political life, the old barons and their long years in power give the party leadership the image of an aging and self-perpetuating oligarchy. Some of them – such as Rumor and Taviani – have already lost their influence; by the end of the 1980s most of the others will have retired from active political life. In the meantime, however, they have made it all but impossible even for the aging "third generation" to rise to positions of leadership, and only a few – notably Arnaldo Forlani, Ciriaco De Mita, and Vincenzo Scotti – have managed to be coopted into the magic circle. The resulting blockage of fresh talent has had a debilitating effect on the party by further weakening its leadership capacity.

The evils of factionalism are carried over into the government in a variety of ways. Most directly, it is the factions that select the party members who serve in the government. The division of the ministerial and subcabinet positions is so critical and delicate that it has followed a fixed procedure, set out in what is known as the "Cencelli manual." The formula, administered for many years by a Christian Democratic subcabinet official named Massimo Cencelli, establishes the criteria for a division of positions proportionate to the faction's strength in the party; this apportionment is followed scrupulously and must be adhered to for the duration of any particular government. A minister who leaves the cabinet during the life of a government has to be replaced by a person of the same faction. Since factional credentials rather than professional qualifications are all-important, ministers are at times notoriously unqualified. Although factions attach great importance to placing their men in ministerial positions, as often as not the leaders themselves do not aspire to serve in the cabinet; they all sit in parliament, but only Fanfani, Moro, Rumor, and Andreotti have made a career in government. The others are normally content to direct their surrogates from the outside while they concentrate on their party role.

It is not surprising that the quality of government is degraded by factionalism. Disputes can be so severe as to paralyze the regime or even cause it to fall – as happened on at least six occasions. With the party so wrapped up in internal power struggles, it has little energy left for governing. A Christian Democratic minister constantly looks over his shoulder at what is going on in the party since he must be ever alert to protect and advance his party position. Nor is there any incentive for a minister to perform well. The case of Vincenzo Scotti is not atypical; after achieving remarkable successes as labor minister in two governments, he was demoted in subsequent cabinet reshuffles – once to minister-without-portfolio – and without responsibilities – and on the second occasion to culture minister. In truth, running the country does not appear to be of much interest to the heirs of De Gasperi.

Christian Democratic factionalism is roundly condemned, especially by those outside the party. To some extent, however, it is a
natural and inevitable consequence of the great diversity of interests and constituencies that find their home in the ample realm of
Christian Democracy. Moreover, separate and defined factions
ensure that the wide variety of views in the party are represented,
can be voiced, and have an influence. Any coterie of like-minded
associates is free to form a group that can work within the party for
their objectives. To this extent factionalism promotes and guarantees democracy in the party. Such diffusion of power has no doubt
helped to prevent schisms and has contributed to the striking coherence and unity that the party can demonstrate at critical moments. Almost alone among the parties, the Christian Democrats
have been spared secessions by disgruntled minorities. But these
considerations are small compensation for the heavy costs to the
party, the government, and the country.

How the party runs

It is in the party apparatus where factions take shape and determine
party policy. Theoretically, the party's general direction and the
parameters within which its executive officials must operate are
fixed by the party's biennial congress. For example, it was the 1962
congress that gave the green light for a center-left coalition and the
1980 one that ruled out a future coalition with the Communists.
Party leaders would have found it virtually impossible to bring the
Communists into the government, as was much discussed in the
late 1970s, without having first taken the issue to the congress for a
debate and vote.

However, as often as not the congress is little more than a political festival where the 1,200 delegates meet, argue, and let off
steam. Although it is a democratic forum, the real contenders are
factions rather than individuals. During the deliberations, factional alliances shift and factions themselves sometimes break
apart when the critical voting takes place. In the end it is the faction
leaders who meet separately – in a back room befitting the
occasion – and take the vital decisions, which their followers have
no choice but to accept. The congress therefore amounts to a
periodic settling of accounts among the factions, determining what
alliances prevail and indirectly the policy direction the party will
follow.

Between sessions of the congress, policy issues and important
matters are taken up by the national council. This body has 160

members – half of them parliamentarians – elected by the congress. There are 30 additional ex officio members, among whom are faction leaders and regional party secretaries. Management of day-to-day affairs lies with an executive committee of 45 members, most of whom have specific operational functions in the party. Its members are elected by the national council and they generally meet every month or so. The party's chief executive, the secretary, was once chosen by the national council but since 1976 has been directly elected by the congress. There is also a party president, but the position is normally honorific.

In each of these bodies the seats are distributed to the factions in proportion to their strength in the party – as reflected in the support the faction receives in the final vote on the key issues before the congress. Election to the subordinate bodies is conducted on the basis of separate factional lists. Hence factional differences and competition are extended throughout the entire party apparatus. This arrangement ensures that each faction is represented and plays a role at every level of the party.

Such a rigid and dogmatic division of party offices perpetuates the party's internal disunity and the ceaseless maneuvering for advantage. As factional divisions have become more volatile and confusing, the party command has been ever more seriously lamed. Since Fanfani's fall in 1959 and with the partial and brief exception of Moro, party secretaries have been at best first among equals. When De Mita sought to use the 1984 congress to trim back the powers of the factions, he failed completely. The lesson of the party's history is clear: The factions will not tolerate strong, central leadership.

Who supports the party

Membership in the party has little if any meaning. Theoretically a party card is taken out or renewed every year. In fact membership cards are widely falsified. Dead people, fictitious persons, and names picked at random from telephone directories are registered along with genuine applicants. Since party cards are parceled out according to factional strength, potential new members are often discouraged from joining the party since they could endanger factional balances. This manipulation of membership has been acknowledged over the years with varying degress of candor by party officials. In 1976 two Christian Democratic senators openly charged that roughly half the party cards were bogus. Although one academic study has questioned whether the irregularities are so massive, other observers have confirmed that there is a wide-spread misuse of party cards. In any case membership has little or no relevance to party activity. Even those living persons who know they are members rarely attend party meetings or assist in electoral campaigns.

Under the circumstances it is difficult to attach much significance to membership statistics. Nonetheless they can be briefly summarized. From 500,000 members in 1945, the party grew to over 1 million by 1953 and reached a high point of 1.8 million in 1973, fluctuating since then between the two latter figures. Although in the early years the majority of members was in the North, since 1963 roughly 58 percent have been in the South, 13 percent in the Center, and 29 percent in the North. The party has always had a relatively high proportion of female members – between 34 and 38 percent in the 1960s and 1970s, which is roughly 10 percent higher than in the Communist party.

What counts is the substantial and, during most of the life of the republic, consistent electoral support that the party has amassed. The Christian Democrats' success has rested on three pillars – Catholicism, clientelism, and anti-Communism. On these supports the party has erected a unique coalition of social groups. The most solid and stable bloc of votes has always come from women and rural residents, largely a result of the fact that church attendance is higher among women and in most of the countryside. But the breadth of the party's appeal can be glimpsed in data provided in Paolo Sylos Labini's classic study, *Saggio sulle classi sociali* (Essay on social classes). According to this 1968 estimate, Christian Democrats received the votes of 29 percent of the upper middle class; 35 percent of middle-class employees; 48 percent of farmers, artisans, and shopkeepers; 36 percent of wage earners in agriculture and industry; and 40 percent of special categories, such as the military and religious. A 1975 survey by Giovanni Sartori and Alberto Marradi viewed Christian Democratic supporters from another angle, finding 39 percent males, 63 percent blue collar workers, 48 percent rural residents, and 66 percent regular church attenders. None of the other parties can boast an electorate of such a wide social background. How was this coalition forged?

Support by practicing Catholics has always been considered the single most important component of the party's strength. Although Christian Democracy may not be a Catholic party, it has been essentially a party of Catholics. The church has supported it, the faithful have voted for it, and party leaders have come out of a strict Catholic orthodoxy. In fact one of the marked features of postwar

Italy was the inextricable, mutually supporting relationship that existed between the church, the organizations for Catholic laymen, and the party.

Normally a career in the party began in Catholic Action or one of the similar associations. The Catholic University Students' Federation, FUCI, and the University Graduates Movement were a veritable breeding ground for party leaders. Out of these two groups came one president of the republic (Giovanni Leone), five prime ministers (Andreotti, Moro, Leone, Colombo, and Mario Scelba), four party secretaries, and two dozen ministers. Giovanni Battista Montini, later Pope Paul VI, was the group's religious counselor from 1925 to 1933 and ever after maintained friendly personal relations with FUCI leaders. Among the working class, leadership and electoral support were cultivated by the Christian Workers' Associations, ACLI, and later by the Catholic trade union, CISL. Until the end of the 1960s the institutional links between them and the party were extremely close – key trade union leaders were party officials – and they supported the party's economic and social policy even when these were not to their members' advantage. Thanks to the Confederation of Small Farmers, Coldiretti, Catholic farmers were a main pillar of Christian Democratic electoral strength; in return the association for many years dictated who was appointed agriculture minister and what policies the ministry followed.

The relationship between these groups and the party began unraveling in the 1960s. The change of mood after the Second Vatican Council and the social upheavals at the end of the decade set Catholic Action and the other professional associations into a sharp decline. Membership fell off drastically and links with the party were broken. ACLI had already loosened its ties as early as 1959 and severed them completely in 1970. CISL, always more distant from the party, took up an independent line from 1969 on. With the exodus of farmers to the cities, the Confederation of Small Farmers lost members and influence. With the wave of secularization that spread across Italy in the 1970s, the old relationship between the party and the church itself was fundamentally changed.

The pivotal event was the divorce referendum of 1974. As a result of the decisive defeat of the referendum, the party started moving away from an institution it suddenly realized was no longer able to deliver massive electoral support and was to some extent a political liability because of its reactionary position on major social issues. The Christian Democrats never doubted, then or later, that

Catholic support was crucial and that good relations with the church had to be maintained. But from then on when major political issues arose – such as a referendum over abortion and problems in church–state relations – the party held itself ostentatiously aloof.

Nonetheless significant links remain between the party and the Catholic world. Even today a glance at the biographic register of members of parliament makes clear that a large number of Christian Democratic deputies and senators began their careers in Catholic organizations. Almost half those in top party positions in parliament have or once held a position in one or several of these bodies; more than one-fifth of all Christian Democratic parliamentarians are or were active in them. The Confederation of Small Farmers continues to guarantee some Christian Democratic influence in the countryside – a reason for the party's strong showing for many years in the Northeast – and exerts a strong conservative and anti-Communist influence in the party.

But these organizational ties have less and less electoral significance. In the mid-1970s a number of lively new groups developed – most significantly Communion and Liberation – which aimed to revivify political Catholicism and to reform the Christian Democratic party and make it more responsive to ecclesiastical viewpoints. These groups had a brief impact in some middle-class circles in the North and elected a few of their leaders to parliament in 1976. It is symptomatic of the contemporary mood, however, that their efforts to resuscitate a Catholic political consciousness have had slight success. By the late 1970s, in short, not only had relations between the party and the church become distant but the Catholic subculture had greatly diminished in size, vigor, and political commitment. With this, the very cornerstone of the party's electoral position was undermined.

Or was it? There is no reason to doubt the conventional wisdom that the huge Christian Democratic vote in the elections of 1948 and 1953 resulted in large part from the ideological mobilization of the faithful by the church and that the impact of this continued for a time. But after the end of the 1960s, with the secularization of the country and the wide popular support for divorce and abortion in the referenda on those issues, it was difficult to resist the conclusion that Catholics were voting for the Christian Democrats as a matter of choice rather than faith, as a political decision rather than a reflex action as a member of the Catholic subculture.

Another vital source of Christian Democratic support – financial and electoral – comes from the vast network of patronage that the Christian Democrats have established through their control of the state industrial and banking enterprises, local and national public agencies, and the government bureaucracy. They use the jobs and funds at the disposition of these bodies as a reservoir of partisan favoritism. The activities of ministries, state enterprises, and public agencies are subject to party control, and it is doubtful that any important decision is made without party approval. In this way public-works projects, pensions, jobs, and favors are handed out in a way that will cultivate votes and extend party influence. Agencies and ministries with control over large amounts of patronage have been turned into Christian Democratic preserves, seldom if ever surrendered even in coalition governments. It is largely as a result of this blatant plundering of the state that the Christian Democrats have earned their reputation for brazen corruption. At the same time the situation explains in part why the Christian Democrats have remained the dominant party despite that very reputation. In a political system where electors cannot punish or reward a party for its performance, patronage is a key to power.

The Christian Democratic near-monopoly of patronage was eventually broken. The party lost much of its influence on the regional and local level in the course of the seventies when it was ousted from government in cities and many of the newly established regions. By the early eighties it was forced to share an increasing number of top positions in the state industries and banks and other areas of the *sottogoverno*. The management of pensions and other welfare programs came more and more under the control of regions and trade unions. As a result the clientelistic foundation of Christian Democratic power has come under challenge.

There is still one further consideration to explain the Christian Democrats' electoral performance. For all the support it has received from the church, all the votes it has bought through its clientelistic network, and all the interest groups it has corralled, the party has in and of itself stood for something that appealed year after year to the largest single bloc of Italian voters – the widespread perception that it is the organization that brought Italy the greatest prosperity in its history, its longest period of succcessful self-government, and its most successful external links. To this the Christian Democrats have added an ideological element, presenting themselves as the one great barrier to Communism and the best guarantor of liberty and democracy. Vital to the success of this electoral tactic lay in convincing as much of the public as possible that the Communists were not to be trusted to maintain the country's free economic and political system. Maintaining the illegitimacy of the Communist party had a further extremely important effect. By keeping its main opponent out of the political game, the Christian Democrats have been able to dominate the field. To this extent the "Communist menace" was critical to Christian Democratic hegemony.

The change in the bases of Christian Democratic support is clearly reflected in election results over the years. During the period 1948 to 1958 – at the height of Catholic solidarity, of the perceived Communist threat, and of East–West tensions – the Christian Democrats won an average of 44 percent of the vote in the three elections of that period. In the five elections of the next two decades they held a steady 38 percent. During this period the electors who may have defected because of the changed domestic and international situation were compensated with support cultivated through the party's growing clientelistic network, especially in the South. From the mid-seventies on, however, the party steadily lost hold on its traditional electorate, as could be seen in the results of local and regional elections after 1975 and the outcome of the various referenda. The Christian Democratic decline was particularly marked not only in large cities but even in the Northeast, the so-called white area where the Catholic rural subculture had been especially solid. These trends culminated in the party's decline to an all-time low of 33 percent in 1983.

The party's main failure – resulting from an electoral system that encourages multipartism – is that, unlike its sister party in Germany, it has never succeeded in absorbing the small parties on its right and left fringes. So far the losses have been limited and mostly on the right. But the party's greatest fear is a hemorrhage on the left, which explains the party's ambivalent attitude toward the Socialists and its need to deprive the Communists of full acceptability.

Can the center hold?

The Christian Democrats have been sneered at by intellectuals, neglected by scholars, and despised on all sides for their wanton exploitation of state resources, their poor administration of government, and their reputation for corruption. The party has a lot to answer for. Having created a near-identity of the administrative state and the party, it infected the entire political, economic, and social system with some of its own illnesses. After the mid-fifties it neither led, nor planned, nor managed. It simply maintained itself in power.

For most of the postwar period a plurality of Italians was willing to overlook the party's vices because its virtues seemed more important. It was leader of the process that conducted Italy out of two decades of Fascist dictatorship into democratic self-government. For all its evangelistic campaign oratory, it always practiced pragmatic, essentially nonideological politics and forced the other parties to compete on that basis. It brought conservative industrialists and landowners, the middle class, and ultimately even the church – among whom there was only a shaky respect for democracy at the end of the war – into the mainstream of liberal representative democracy. By incorporating the lay parties, later the Socialists, and still later the Communists into the governing process, it demonstrated a flexibility that contributed to the tolerant and adaptable character of Italian political life. As a result, the fulcrum of Italian politics was firmly fixed in the center of a broad ideological spectrum. Its cautious foreign-policy goals were well suited to the temper of the Italian people and earned the confidence of the country's Atlantic and European partners. It presided over an economic miracle and, despite a terrifying wave of left- and right-wing violence, maintained the country's freedom and rule of law at a critical moment.

By the mid-1980s, however, there was not much left of the main elements that originally underlay the Christian Democrats' long years of success. The party was virtually bereft of leadership or even a controlling group. Its factionalism had decomposed into a factiousness so uncontrolled as to leave the party in a state of disorientation and confusion. The old party barons, having prevented the emergence of a new generation of leaders, now comprised a gerontocracy without successors. The diverse elements of the economic community were finding more effective support from other parties or defending their interests on their own. Even the party's distinction of being the great bulwark against domestic and foreign communism was losing relevance. And far from embodying the spirit of the times, the Christian Democrats presented the image of an exhausted, uncertain, and divided party unable to understand much less meet the needs of the country. The party's electoral decline after 1974 was therefore only one sign of a gradual but steady erosion of power in every sphere.

Still, the party retained its primacy since there continued to be no substitute for a coalition grouped around "the party of the relative majority" even if the position of prime minister had now to be shared. As much as ever, the Christian Democrats' position in the political system ultimately rested on the lack of a popularly acceptable alternative. But whether they could remain the indispensable center of the governing system depended on developments in the other two major parties – whether the Communists would cross the bounds of acceptability and the Socialists show promise of developing into a solid force capable of initiating a genuine alternation of government.

3. The Communists' struggle for legitimacy and acceptance

It is not easy to take the measure of the Italian Communist party. It has been in such continuous transition that what is true of it at any particular moment is not necessarily true at another. Moreover it is a party that has lived between two worlds – the ideological world of Marx, Lenin, and Stalin and the practical political world of Western parliamentarism and pluralism. And it is a party that has always been internally divided between those to whom democracy and those to whom socialism is more important. Consequently its historic course has been marked by continuity, change, contradiction, and ambiguity in almost equal measure. Even today, after an evolution of decades, the party presents two faces: One was born of the Bolshevik revolution, insists that it is intrinsically different from other parties, rejects social democracy, and advocates a transformation of the economic and social system. The other was shaped by Italy's free political and economic system which the party has supported as loyally as any institution and more than some. Which face is real? Or are both real? Or is one a mask for the other?

No other questions about postwar Italy have so engaged politicians, journalists, scholars, diplomatists, and the business community – not to mention the simple Italian voter. The issue is anything but hypothetical. The party has long been the country's second political force, could become the largest, and may someday participate in the national government and even lead it. In practical terms the debate that has raged over the party has concerned essentially two matters: whether its ideology is consistent with the democratic norms of the constitutional system and whether its programs lie within the acceptable bounds of the country's domestic and foreign policies. Identity and objectives: These have been the twin issues of importance about contemporary Italian Communism.

The party's identity is rooted in its origin – the decision in 1921 to secede from the Socialists. The dispute was essentially over three points. Believing that Italy was in an objective revolutionary situation, the Communists insisted that the existing political order had to be overthrown by force and replaced by a dictatorship of the proletariat. Further they emphasized the supreme role of the party

41

as spearhead of the revolution and the need for strict control of the party from the top. Finally they insisted on the party's complete submission to the Soviet Union through the Communist International. The history of the party since then has been one of a gradual but steady move away from these precepts.

A strategy of cooperation

When the Fascist government fell in 1943, Communist leaders recognized that the party's original character and purposes were totally inappropriate to the times. They were under no illusion that the party had any chance of seizing power in a country that was occupied by the British and Americans, heavily influenced by a powerful Catholic church, and weary of political nostrums and dictatorship. Moreover, the Soviets considered Italy a part of the Anglo-American sphere of influence and, to ensure that there would be no attempt by Italian Communists to seize power by force, instructed the party after the war to disarm its several hundred thousand partisans. Although the party's ultimate objective of a communist society remained unaltered, the route to the destination would be different from what the party's founders had had in mind.

The new strategy was outlined by the party's leader, Palmiro Togliatti, on his return to Italy in March 1944 in a meeting at Salerno. To the dismay of the more eager and dogmatic comrades, Togliatti made clear that the old small revolutionary party was to be replaced by a mass party. This "new party" would seek to establish a "presence" in all areas of society and to collaborate with other democratic forces – in particular Socialists and Catholics – through a policy of alliances. The transformation of society would be achieved not through subversion but by working within democratic institutions and rules. Because it represented a radical change in the party's original 1921 position, Togliatti's policy was known as the *svolta di Salerno,* the "turning point of Salerno."

From then to the present the party's paramount and unchanging goal has been to gain acceptance as a legitimate partner in the political system and to participate in government. For a time the party had considerable success. Thanks to its leadership of the anti-Fascist resistance and its rapidly growing strength, the party was included in every coalition government from 1944 to 1947. It cooperated in bringing De Gasperi to power in 1945, played an important role in drafting the republican constitution, and concurred in the government's signature of the 1947 peace treaty. It formed a popular front alliance with the Socialists. As an earnest of its desire to collaborate with other social forces it was willing to accept the monarchy as well as Mussolini's concordat with the Holy See. It went along with an inadequate purge of Fascists in the public administration. And it put forward moderate social and economic policies.

The collaboration came to an end in the spring of 1947. On the one hand De Gasperi finally found it opportune, as coincidentally did his counterparts in France and Belgium, to expel the Communists from government. On the other the Kremlin ordered Communist parties in the West to cease collaboration with bourgeois parties and to launch a campaign of massive opposition to the Marshall Plan.

Despite this headlong confrontation and the deep ideological split of the country, the Communists never wavered from their strategy as enunciated at Salerno. The question was whether the turning point marked a genuine commitment to democratic constitutionalism or was merely a ruse. Ironically many of the Communist rank and file were initially as convinced as the average anti-Communist that Togliatti's strategy was, in the words of the party's official historian Paolo Spriano, in reality "a Trojan horse in the bourgeois citadel." Party officials today frankly admit that Togliatti was engaged in a double game. But this *doppiezza*, many of them maintain, was directed not to the Italian public but to party militants. It was a tactic to keep rank and file in line by allowing them to think that a revolution was just around the corner even though Togliatti was convinced that the road to power lay through the ballot box. Although *doppiezza* took still other forms, its uniform trait was a disjunction between doctrine and practice, between what was said at one time and said at another, between what was said and what was done; as such it was in Donald Blackmer's phrase "an inherent structural characteristic of the party, . . . a kind of institutionalized schizophrenia."

No idiosyncrasy has been more difficult for the party to overcome than this split personality. The first effort toward achieving an integration was taken in 1956. In that year the Cominform was dissolved and at the Soviet twentieth party congress Nikita Khrushchev not only inaugurated a process of de-Stalinization but also acknowledged the possibility of different roads to socialism. With these developments Togliatti gained leeway to commit his party more unambiguously to the established democratic system. Speaking to the Soviet party congress in Moscow and later to his own party congress, he declared that every communist party had to be free to follow its own course, that socialism could be achieved through parliamentary institutions, and that the goal was a socialist democracy along the lines neither of capitalism nor of Soviet Communism. When the Italian party congress approved this "Italian way to socialism," it committed the party to democratic parliamentarism and national autonomy inside the communist camp. Even though it was far from clear at the time – and was questioned by skeptics through the 1970s – the party's ratification of Togliatti's policy was a political watershed.

The succeeding years were not easy. The demythologizing of Stalin, the Soviet invasion of Hungary in the same year, Italy's economic miracle, and the shift of the Socialists from an alliance with the Communists to one with the Christian Democrats were hard blows, forcing the party into the very isolation that it wanted at all costs to avoid. For over a decade and a half the party found itself largely excluded from the country's political and social developments. It was left behind by the sudden surge of student and labor militancy that swept through Italy at the end of the 1960s. Politically and ideologically it was outflanked on the left by militant Marxist and Maoist groups. On the labor front it engaged itself on behalf of better wages and conditions for workers but raised no challenge to the capitalist system itself. In the social sphere it watched from the sidelines as the Socialists and lay parties led the way to overdue reforms, such as divorce legislation. Consequently the Communist party emerged from the sixties still mistrusted by those on its right while detested by the ultraleft as nothing better than a crypto-social democratic party that had ratted on the revolution. So as it struggled to demonstrate its democratic credentials, it lost its radical ones.

The 1970s saw a dramatic reversal in the party's fortunes. With the long-delayed devolution of power to the regions, the Communists soon found themselves in control of several regional governments and went on to capture one government after another on the communal and provincial levels as well. The 1974 divorce referendum, which the Christian Democrats tried to turn against the Communists, gave the party another significant success. By now the long series of center-left governments was coming to an end, making the formation of government on the national level more difficult than ever.

In the meantime the party was gradually feeling its way toward a new assessment of the overall political situation. Given the decline of the Socialists, the seemingly unshakable entrenchment in power of the Christian Democrats, and the example of the overthrow of the leftist government of Salvador Allende in Chile by a right-wing military group, party leaders concluded that there was no plausible

prospect of the parties of the left replacing the Christian Democrats in power. Ousting the Christian Democrats and seeking to
govern with a bare majority would provoke a crisis in both Italy and
NATO. Instead the only practical course lay in governing in alliance with its traditional enemy, the Christian Democrats. The
model of the "grand coalition" in Germany, where the Social
Democrats first joined the Christian Democrats and then booted
them out of the government, had not gone unnoted south of the
Alps. This new tactic, formally unveiled by party secretary Enrico
Berlinguer in the fall of 1973, was labeled a "historic compromise," representing as it did a collaboration between ideological
opposites. Although it created a stir at the time and deep conster-
nation in the party ranks, the approach was actually in the best
tradition of *trasformismo*. Moreover it was an idea whose time had
come, coinciding with a great spurt in the party's electorate in the
1975 communal and regional elections and the national election in
the following year.

As a result, the Christian Democrats began to reintegrate the
Communists into the governing system for the first time since
1947. The Andreotti government formed in 1976 was based on
indirect Communist support in parliament, and the Communists
were given the presidency of the Chamber of Deputies and the
chairmanship of seven parliamentary committees. More
significantly – and behind the scenes – Prime Minister Andreotti and the Christian Democratic leadership coordinated major
policy issues with Communist leaders. Although the socialists
and lay parties resented this preferential relationship between
the two, they acquiesced in the broadened collaboration in
the belief that the country could not otherwise be effectively
governed.

Reflecting this mood of political rapprochement, a common
program for legislation in the domestic sphere was agreed on in
1977, and a short time later the Chamber and the Senate adopted
foreign policy resolutions designed to ring the Communists further
into political orthodoxy. To describe this de facto coalition, the
term "constitutional arch" came into widespread usage, lending a
preferred status to those parties that had participated in drafting the
constitution – thereby including the Communists while excluding the neo-Fascists and parties of the extreme left. In 1978 the
process went further when another Christian Democratic government was established with formal Communist parliamentary support. Communist collaboration during this period – at the height
of leftist terrorism, of economic crisis, and of a general atmosphere

of tension and uncertainty – went far to remove lingering doubts about the party's commitment to the political order.

Now on the threshold of power, with its participation in the government seemingly only a matter of time, the party found the ground cut out from under it. Aldo Moro, its trusted interlocutor in the Christian Democratic party, was kidnapped and assassinated in the spring of 1978. In the following months it was increasingly evident that the Christian Democrats had no intention of giving the Communists seats in the cabinet. At the same time the Communist rank and file as well as powerful groups of trade unionists were becoming acutely discontented, feeling that the workers were paying the price for the government's austerity program while receiving nothing in return. By withdrawing from the government and forcing an election in June 1979, party leaders wanted a showdown on the issue of their entry into the government. They lost the gamble and a full 4 percent of their vote. Most Italians still did not want them in the government.

Late in 1980 party leaders convened in Salerno, a city much damaged by an earthquake a short time before. The location was particularly apt. The party's strategy, like part of the city, was in a shambles. The "historic compromise" was damaged beyond repair and, at Berlinguer's encouragement, the party reverted to the older tactic, now labeled "democratic alternative," which aimed at an alliance of the Communists with the Socialists and left Catholics. But since this "second 'turning point of Salerno,'" as it was sardonically known, evoked the interest of neither of the other two components, the party once again found itself in the isolation it dreaded. Uncertain and immobile, the party was able neither to mount a constructive opposition nor to propose concrete alternatives.

After forty years, the course down which Togliatti had launched his party had not reached its destination. The Communists were neither in the cabinet nor considered a fully acceptable alternative party of government. The journey, however, was not a failure. Even if the party found itself in a cul de sac, its loyalty to the constitutional system was by now all but universally acknowledged and its legitimacy beyond question.

From unity to diversity

The commitment to the "Italian way to socialism" and the corollary principle of representative democracy ineluctably led to a change in attitude toward the Soviet Union as a model society and leader of the world socialist movement. Italian Communism's ideological association with a totalitarian system and the reflection of its links to Moscow in pro-Soviet and anti-Western positions on foreign and security issues were an enormous liability, giving the impression of a party loyal not to the interests and values of Italy but to those of the Russian state – in fact a party that belonged to "the other side." No obstacle to the party's legitimacy was greater, no form of *doppiezza* more damaging.

At the time of the party's founding and after the war as well, Communist leaders calculated that the party's only chance to survive, expand, and eventually come to power was with the support of the Soviet Union. If De Gasperi needed the Vatican and Washington, Togliatti needed Moscow. For many years after the fall of Fascism relations between the party and the Soviets were close and untroubled. In fact many Italians were drawn to the party because of the enormous prestige of Stalin and the role of the Soviet Union in the Second World War. The Soviets gave Togliatti broad latitude to follow a strategy both agreed on. And in any case there were few issues during the cold war years on which they did not see eye to eye. In fact, as far as can be judged, Togliatti had to put up with less interference from Stalin than De Gasperi from Pius XII.

It was Khrushchev's denunciation of Stalin at the Soviet party congress in 1956 that, all unintentionally, opened the way to a fundamental revision of relations. For the average Italian Communist, the revelations destroyed a world. In the turmoil and disillusionment that spread through the party, Togliatti faced the delicate task of maintaining the party's equilibrium while preserving his own credibility as an erstwhile collaborator of Stalin. In a noted article in *Nuovi argumenti,* he shifted some of the blame for Stalin's grim record to the Soviet system itself and, hinting that the old relationship between the Italian party and the Soviet Union could never be the same, coined the term "polycentrism" to describe the sort of international system that was evolving.

The crack in the old unity was only slight, and the party defended the Soviet suppression of the Hungarian revolution a short time later. But ultimately what had been called into question was not only the myth of Stalin but the myth of the Soviet Union. For a time, as it gazed in two directions at once, the party disguised its uncertainties and divisions under a characteristically ambiguous slogan: "Unity in diversity." A fundamental psychological change, however, had occurred. From then on, the separation widened steadily if slowly; by the end of 1961 the Italian party's autonomy in the Communist camp was a fixed principle.

Three years later while at Yalta, Togliatti reformulated his idea of polycentrism and, with an eye to the Soviet–Chinese schism, warned against convening a world conference of Communist parties under Soviet aegis to read the Chinese out of the movement. He outlined these views in a memorandum for use in a meeting to have been held a short time later with Khrushchev. Though he died before the session, the memorandum acquired the status of a political testament. Not only did it criticize Soviet leadership, it emphasized the position that the PCI had been pressing – and would promote ever more outspokenly in future years – that the old Soviet-imposed unity was finished and that the deeper unity of international socialism could be preserved only if the various parties were permitted to develop independently and without external interference.

The first open breach with the Soviet Union – and a critical turning point in relations – occurred in 1968 when the Italian party harshly condemned the Soviet invasion of Czechoslovakia. The following year Berlinguer stood before the World Conference of Communist and Workers' Parties in Moscow and declared that there was no single model of a socialist society. By the mid-1970s the breach was becoming an open gulf. The PCI had established relations with the British Labor party and other West European socialists and developed particularly close links to the German Social Democrats. It was shifting from opposition to acceptance of NATO as it had done a decade earlier in the case of the European Community. To avoid isolation and to strenghten polycentrism, the party took the lead in establishing what came to be known as Eurocommunism, a collaborative effort among the Communist parties of Western Europe to coordinate their positions on practical and theoretical issues. The ultimate purpose was to establish a system that would replace capitalism with a socialist system based on parliamentary democracy and individual freedom. Many non-Communists hoped that this development would fully emancipate Western communism from the thrall of the Soviet model and Leninist ideals while transforming these parties into something essentially along the lines of Western social democracy.

But Eurocommunism never came to much. There was a joint declaration of the Italian, French, and Spanish parties in March 1977, a meeting in Brussels in June of the same year of all West European Communist parties, and later on a number of bilateral meetings and joint communiques. Of real collaboration there was little. And the differences, ideological and practical, could not be bridged. Since the French party never really left Moscow's orbit, foreign-policy issues and attitudes toward the Soviet Union repeatedly divided them.

Although Eurocommunism was abhorrent to the Soviets – who condemned it as revisionist deviation and a ploy of the imperialists – Moscow went to remarkable lengths to avoid an open break. The Soviets had long been willing to allow the Western parties, particularly the influential PCI, a substantial degree of independence as long as Soviet foreign-policy positions and ultimate Soviet control of the international communist movement were not challenged. Soviet party media drenched Eurocommunism, the "historic compromise," and other contemporaneous heresies in scorn, but they did not attack the party itself and in effect appealed to the rank and file over the heads of their leaders.

However, the Italian Communist leaders were caught in a momentum most of them could not and did not wish to control, and this was driving them further away from the Soviets. They would not be provocative – after all, some of the rank and file still looked benevolently on the Soviet Union – and for a time they pursued an uneasy truce with the Soviet party. But they considered their party completely independent and committed to a pluralist, liberal parliamentary system.

Berlinguer made this point openly at a ceremony in Moscow in 1977 celebrating the sixtieth anniversary of the October Revolution. While this declaration did not constitute the "definitive break" that some Italians – such as Ugo La Malfa – considered it to be at the time, it gave further emphasis to the changing relationship. The Communist party's inclusion in the joint foreign-policy resolutions of the Chamber and Senate a short time later marked another important step. In 1979 the party congress condemned the Soviet-backed invasion of Cambodia by the Vietnamese. Later in the year the party was critical of the Soviet deployment of SS-20 missiles and, though not supporting, did not catagorically oppose the American plan for the installation of new weapons systems in Western Europe in response.

It was in 1980 that a fundamental split developed. In early January the party condemned the Soviet invasion of Afghanistan. A few weeks later meetings were held with the "autonomist communists" of Eastern Europe – Yugoslavia and Romania. To encourage the idea of a nonaligned Western bloc, Berlinguer met not long afterward with Willy Brandt and François Mitterrand. By April Berlinguer was in Peking where, after years of delay in deference to the Soviets, he announced the reestablishment of relations with the Chinese party. In the same month the PCI boycotted the Moscow-sponsored disarmament conference of Communist parties that was held in Paris.

The following year opened with Berlinguer's refusal to attend the Soviet party congress and ended with the PCI's condemning martial law in Poland, which the Italians accused the Russians of instigating. It was the Polish events that caused the critical break. For the Italian party condemned not just the event but the Soviet system and what lay behind it. Berlinguer went on television to declare that the October Revolution – which he described as "the greatest event of our time" – had become a spent force. The party itself issued a long denunciation of the Soviets for having imposed their political system on Eastern Europe and having repeatedly repressed reform efforts in those countries. It concluded that "completely new forms must be found to spread democracy and socialism" and that these would have to come from the West European left. In other words, the Soviet model was no longer a model.

To this *Pravda* responded with an attack on the PCI leadership that was more scathing than anything since Moscow's diatribes against Yugoslavia and China decades earlier. Virtually relegating the Italian party to the enemy camp, the paper accused the Italian party of "direct aid to imperialism," of "slandering" the Soviet Union, of following a domestic course of "opportunism and revisionism," of "calumnious assertions" about the Soviet military threat to Europe, and of an attitude toward Soviet foreign policy that was "truly sacrilegious." It concluded: "Something monstrous has happened." *Kommunist*, a Soviet party monthly, chimed in with what it no doubt considered the ultimate malediction, accusing the Italian party leaders of "repeating almost word for word the fabrications of Reagan, Weinberger, Haig, Brzezinski and other imperialist politicians."

The counterreply of the Italian party was equally outspoken and could scarcely have been harsher had it been written by Reagan and his fellow imperialists. After reiterating the condemnation of Soviet interference in Eastern Europe and its armed intervention in Czechoslovakia and Afghanistan, it ridiculed the notion that the problems in Communist countries came from the machinations of Western imperialists. In their behavior toward other parties, the reply commented ominously, the Soviets had learned nothing from their break with Yugoslavia and China.

By 1982, in short, relations between the Italian party and Moscow were in shreds. The tremendous oedipal struggle with the Communist fatherland concluded with both sides insisting that there was no formal rupture. Presumably the Russians wanted to avoid the embarrassment of an open break and maintain the basis for an eventual restoration of relations. In Italy the term *strappo,* or "tear," was used to characterize the relationship, thereby lessening the pain of the situation for the hardline minority. But in practice the relationship was left with little if any more substance than diplomatic links between two hostile states. Functionaries of the two parties continue occasionally to meet. But the number and level of the sessions have steadily declined while ties with West European social democratic parties have tightened. Since the late seventies the party has sought, whenever possible, to align itself with positions taken by the German and Swedish Social Democrats and has appeared to be encouraging the formation of a "Eurosocialist" left of which it would be an integral part. By now few, if any, Italians doubted that the party was fully independent.

Party power – democracy versus centralism

Each of the central elements of the Communist system is part of an interlocking whole, and as one element changed others were called into question. One of these was the highly controverted Leninist principle of "democratic centralism" – the principle of strict internal discipline and monolithic unity. The party's first leader, Amedeo Bordiga, who had been ruthless in cracking down on the slightest deviation, was himself expelled from the party in 1924 for not toeing the Stalinist line. Expulsions regularly followed in subsequent decades, and though they have been rare in the postwar period, in 1968 a group of party members who criticized the party for a lack of democracy and its links to the Soviet Union – and who started up a newspaper, *Manifesto,* to say so – were thrown out en masse. Although Communists have disagreed as passionately as members of any party, they alone insist on maintaining a facade of impregnable solidarity. A policy may be debated by the leadership up to the moment of decision, but then it must be accepted and followed. The question therefore arises whether a party that will not tolerate open diversity and dissent in its own ranks can be genuinely committed to democracy and pluralism in the country at large.

Despite the changes in the party statute over the years, democratic centralism remains in the preamble as the underlying principle of the party's organization. In addition Article 8 forbids "factional activities" in the interest of party cohesion, and Article 52 declares that party discipline is the prerequisite of party unity. What do these precepts mean in terms of party operations?

Formally it is the triennial party congress that is the party's supreme organ and that sets policy. In practice the congress has no real independent authority. Its sessions are prefixed and allow little possibility for spontaneous initiatives. Delegate selection is controlled and works against minorities. At the sessions only one overall policy motion is tabled. Since it has already been worked over and amended at lower levels in the months before the meeting, it is presented as an authoritative statement of party views and is put to a vote on a take-it-or-leave-it basis. Uninhibited debate and open disagreement are further stifled by the Communist ethic of supporting the leadership. Such discord as occurs is easily disposed of. After the party's denunciation of the Soviets following the declaration of martial law in Poland, one party official, Armando Cossutta, ostentatiously disassociated himself from the party's position. In the preparations for the 1983 party congress, few of his supporters were selected as representatives to the session, and his position received the endorsement of a mere 5 percent at the congress. In fact the rank-and-file support for Cossutta's viewpoint greatly exceeded that figure and may have been as high as 25 percent.

Between the sessions of the congress, the 170-member central committee is responsible for determining party policy. Although its meetings are not without some give and take, it also rubber stamps the policies already laid down by the leadership. In reality power lies in the hands of the 33-member executive committee and in particular the 7-member secretariat, headed by the party secretary. This centralization of authority is no greater than in other parties. What distinguishes the Communists is their strong sense of discipline, ensuring the secretary a degree of security that is unique among party heads.

Of the postwar leaders, the one who had by far the most influence on the party and the country was Palmiro Togliatti. A founder of the party, Togliatti spent most of the Fascist period in Moscow. Surviving all the purges, he returned to relaunch the party, which he then led until his death in 1964. Like Lenin, Togliatti was a consummate pragmatist, turning every opportunity to advantage. Like Stalin, he was ruthless in running the party and cracking down on dissidence. But he also had the finesse, patience, and subtlety that could have come only from his roots in the culture and religion of his own country. His successor, Luigi Longo, a veteran of the Spanish civil war and the Italian resistance, had been the party's organizational genius after 1944. Under his leadership the revisionist course continued. Since he was ailing during much of his tenure, effective authority in the party passed increasingly to Enrico Berlinguer, who became secretary in 1972 when not quite fifty years old.

With Berlinguer the party skipped over its second-generation leaders – such noted party figures as Pietro Ingrao and Giorgio Amendola – and chose someone who in a sense epitomized the new Communist party in its growing political ecumenism. Berlinguer came from an aristocratic Sardinian family; his father was a Socialist deputy until 1968, and his wife was a practicing Catholic. Recessive and austere, the opposite of a fiery demagogue, he led the party from its vital center and took it through a period of profound transformation up to the edge of government power. With the failure of the "historic compromise," however, his leadership was fatally wounded. Although he remained in command – thanks to a strong party machine – the party stagnated. After having taken the party to its greatest electoral success in 1976 and its severest defeat in 1979, he achieved his ultimate victory only posthumously when his party outpolled the Christian Democrats in the election to the European parliament four days after his death in June 1984.

In selecting Alessandro Natta as his successor, the party passed over such leaders as Giorgio Napolitano who might have restored its momentum, for an aging and unexciting party bureaucrat who would ensure no change, forward or back. At his initial press conference, Natta reiterated the party's endorsement of Italy's membership in NATO and its full independence of Moscow, adding: "I may make trips abroad, perhaps to socialist countries, but they will not be pilgrimages and I do not feel part of any sort of church." That safe was not sure, however, soon became clear. Just in the first year of his leadership the party slipped ever deeper into confusion and disunity, suffered serious political and electoral defeats, and fell ever further behind the rapidly changing mood of Italian society.

A longtime problem of party management is one that has afflicted all communist parties: the distance that separates a starkly bureaucratized leadership group from the rank and file. This problem has persisted in the PCI throughout the postwar period, with the leaders frequently in advance of members and cadres. Each critical development – the establishment of the "new party," the adoption of the "Italian way to socialism," the differences with the Soviet Union, the "historic compromise," and the criticism of the Polish government in 1981 – was resented and resisted by "conservatives" in the party ranks. It is generally estimated that these hardliners have comprised 20 to 25 percent of the party members. Given the party's obsession with unity, this recalcitrant minority has persistently impeded the leadership's flexibility and the party's capacity to evolve. As a result the party advances haltingly and for periods has been wholly inert.

With its rigid discipline and the most extensive and effective organizational network of all the parties, the PCI stands as a unique phenomenon on a landscape of factionalized, squabbling parties. Indeed its almost un-Italian cohesion, earnestness, and efficiency have made it seem a fearsome organization to its competitors and the Italian public. But if the centralism is obvious, is the party also democratic?

Perhaps the harshest criticism of the party's preoccupation with unity comes from inside the organization itself. Younger functionaries in particular complain that there is too much secrecy on the part of leadership and that it is impossible to express dissent in any effective way or to buck the machine that party leaders have built up. Others who have examined the party on the inside have come to a similar conclusion. Lucio Colletti, a Marxist philosopher and former party member, maintained in a study published in 1975 that the party was as much as ever essentially a Stalinist organization. He characterized party members not as a vanguard but as a rearguard whose function was merely to carry out directives from above. A few years later a young Communist sociologist, Salvatore Sechi, maintained that despite changes in the party statute, in practice any divergence from the view of the leadership was not only pointless but resulted in ostracism. He argued that as long as the party's apparatus operated on the basis of cooption and collegial responsibility, the open manifestation of dissent – whether in discussions or voting in party councils – remained empty rhetoric even if permitted by party regulations.

Despite these strictures there can be no doubt that the rigid democratic centralism of the past has loosened under the cumulative impact of changes in the party and Italian society. The party is coming increasingly into the hands of a new generation of functionaries who are more managers than the "professional revolutionaries" referred to in the old party statutes. With the turnover in party membership, new social groups who take free debate for granted are being incorporated into the ranks. And as more party functionaries are appointed or elected to communal and regional governments, they have adopted the free give and take of the system. Party leaders have come to tolerate wide differences of view among members at all levels. Something suspiciously like amorphous factions have begun to form, and leaders are willing to speak more openly of their disagreements with prevailing party policy. The new mood in the party was reflected in the changes in the statute approved at the 1983 congress. These deemphasized the operational relevance of democratic centralism and obligated the party's executives to explain to the rank and file why and how they have reached their policy decisions. Disputed issues were to be referred to the central committee for resolution and not swept under the carpet.

It would be difficult to argue that the Christian Democratic mode of decision making through backroom deals by a few party oligarchs or that the autocratic management of their parties by Ugo La Malfa and Bettino Craxi has been more democratic than the Communist manner of reaching decisions. In the end what differentiates the Communists is the almost monastic atmosphere that prevails. There is among party officials at times a strong intellectual arrogance and a difficulty in crediting views that do not accord with the truth as seen by the party. The hierarchs expect obedience, and while tolerating dissidence, they tend to regard it as disloyalty. By the same token the faithful may disagree with their leaders but still tend to feel a religious – and therefore essentially uncritical – devotion to the party. That said, most Communists genuinely do not want their party to suffer the factionalism and incessant bickering that characterize the other parties. To that extent the prevailing ethic is accepted for quite practical reasons. Disagreements are regarded as family matters, to be kept inside the family. It is this self-imposed ideal that leads to the effort to minimize and conceal differences in an effort to create an external appearance of monolithic unity.

From belief to agnosticism

In what sense is a party that has forsaken insurrection, rejected the Soviet Union as a model, and established its ideological and organizational independence while embracing parliamentary democracy and political pluralism still Leninist, in what sense communist? Clearly it is a party that has abandoned Leninist – or other revolutionary – tactics for coming to power. But the question remains whether it is a party that is wedded to Leninist – or other revolutionary – concepts of the state and society. Although few of even its harshest critics any longer believe the party's commitment to democratic principles is merely a mask that would be torn off once it gained power, there is widespread uncertainty about the policies the PCI would pursue in government even though it would of necessity be part of a coalition and dependent on the cooperation of other parties. The PCI's substantive goals are consequently a vital issue, even if trying to understand them verges more on psychoanalysis than political analysis.

It is in fact the question of final aims that most nakedly exposes Communism's Janus face. The party has persistently suffered from an inner conflict between – expressed crudely – a part that has looked toward a radical reordering of society along Leninist lines and a part that has looked toward an accommodation of the Leninist vision with the social and economic realities of postwar Italy. As the PCI moved down the "Italian way to socialism" and away from the Soviet ideal, the Leninist articles of belief were piece by piece called into question. However, it was one thing for party leaders to abandon Leninist tactics – as patently impractical – but another to give up Leninist goals. After all Leninism in this sense was not just the party's philosophical underpinning but the basis of its identity and purpose; to renounce that would be to sacrifice much of itself. Once again Togliatti finessed the dilemma and maintained the party's unity while altering its position by developing a national communist philosophy based on the writings of Antonio Gramsci.

Gramsci, one of the founders of the party and its secretary from 1924 to 1926, had been imprisoned by the Fascists in the latter year and from 1929 until his death in 1937 spent his time jotting down his thoughts, not only on politics but also on philosophy, history, and literature. The result was a series of fragmentary writings which, when published after the war as *Prison Notebooks,* made Gramsci both one of the leading figures of modern Italian intellectual history and one of the most important interpreters of Marxism. Because of the conditions in which they were written, the works are so disjointed and at times obscure they have given rise to a veritable academic industry of interpretation of what their author actually said and meant. For some he emerges as almost a Stalinist totalitarian, for others a larvated social democrat. It was this very ambivalence that a party that thrived on ambiguity needed to paper over its paradoxes and preserve its unity and sense of continuity. By choosing among Gramsci's thoughts, the party was able to produce and propagate a political doctrine that was relatively congenial and relevant to contemporary Italy and the postwar development of Western capitalism.

Even though the party's Leninist patrimony had in the meantime been reduced almost to rhetorical imagery, formally interring the body of the party's ideological ancestor was a matter of deep anguish. By the 1970s the issue could no longer be repressed. Not only had the party internalized much of the country's liberal democratic ethos, Italian society had been changed through its own inner dynamic and the decent standard of living Communists thought could be achieved only through social revolution was being squeezed out of the capitalist system by peaceful negotiation. The contrasting suppression of democracy in Czechoslovakia and of dissidence in the Soviet Union along with the poor economic performance in Eastern Europe brought about the open acknowledgment by 1969 that the Soviet system – which fairly or not was identified with Leninism – was no model for Italy. Even the blindest faith could not obscure the practical benefits of the Western system and the ills of that in the East.

A revisionist process that was already well under way received further impulse in 1978 when Socialist leader Bettino Craxi provocatively challenged the Communists to make plain once and for all which side of the fence they were on: that of Western democratic socialism or that of Marxist-Leninist socialism. Again Leninism was highlighted as an ultimate test of the party's commitment to the country's political values. Out of this ferment came at last a frank handling of the Leninist issue within the party in a series of discussions, articles, and conferences. The openness of the debate, however belated, was in itself an indication of the party's changing mood. Gradually a consensus emerged that candidly recognized Leninism's lack of relevance to industrially advanced Western democracies, even if some of Lenin's analysis of capitalism was still considered valid. The commemoration of the October Revolution, the holiest date in the Communist calendar, was downgraded, and in 1981 Berlinguer pronounced his anathema – that the event no longer had any practical relevance, for all its historic value.

These changes were given official sanction through a series of revisions in the party statute approved by the 1979 congress. Deleted was a section in Article 5 obligating members to possess a knowledge of Marxism-Leninism and to apply it to concrete issues. Article 7, regarding the duties of membership, was revised to state merely that every adherent must deepen his knowledge of the history of the party and the revolutionary workers' movement. All that remains of the party's doctrinal past is a reference in the preamble to the thinking of Marx and Engels which, it is stated, was given "an impetus of historic importance" by Lenin. To the writings of Gramsci and Togliatti were now added for the first time the works of the nineteenth-century Socialist Antonio Labriola, and none of them were presented as dogma but as "sources of orientation." The Leninist body had disappeared, leaving nothing more than a socialist grin.

If the PCI is not Leninist, the question arises what it is and what it seeks. Here the party's twin souls rise up. On the one hand party leaders insist that their aim is not a reformed and regulated capitalist society but a new, authentically socialist community. The party's intention, expressed in typical terms by Pietro Ingrao, is "to change not merely a government and a parliamentary majority but the relations of production, the foundation and norms of the state and ultimately the very working of human society." On the other hand the party has in everyday practice increasingly replaced dogmatism with pragmatism, utopian goals with real-world policies. It has shifted its whole intellectual focus from Marx, Lenin, and international communism to the Western world of liberal democracy, European integration, and Atlantic cooperation. Where and when in power it has governed with all due regard for pluralist and capitalist economic and social structures. Over time it has absorbed so many of the elements of the existing system in which it lived, it has itself been changed.

The contradictions and ambiguities are evident in the party's record. In the social area the PCI has tended to be a cautious, even a passive, and indeed at times a conservative force. It has lagged behind the Socialists and lay parties on most of the important issues, such as divorce, feminism, nuclear power, sexual questions, the environment, abortion, youth and student problems, and civil liberties. These were sensitive and often politically divisive matters, unhelpful to the party in its struggle for acceptance; after sidestepping them for as long as possible, the PCI usually joined the reformist parties but only at the moment of showdown. All in all its opportunistic handling of social problems left the impression of a party with little sincere commitment to anything but its own advancement – perhaps reassuring evidence of its domestication.

In the economic sphere the party was generally well behind the curve of developments but espoused policies, however mistaken at times, that were moderate in substance and usually similar to those of social democratic parties elsewhere in Western Europe. In the early postwar period it called for various fundamental reforms – such as nationalization of big monopolies, a redistribution of farmland, and a broad program of economic planning. However, private-property rights and free-enterprise capitalism were not called into question as the operating principles of the country's economic system. Where in government it promoted policies designed to mitigate the lot of the poor, the workers, and the peasants but even in defending employment and wage levels and agricultural reform, it was less than doctrinaire. Blinded by Marxist determinism, it totally failed to anticipate and was at a loss to explain the economic boom that began in the mid-1950s, and it erred equally wildly in predicting that Italy's participation in the Common Market would spell ruin for the country's economy and working class. Nonetheless much of its critique of Italy's uneven economic development was cogent, and the party correctly foresaw that the gulf between some areas and some sectors would result in substantial disequilibria and a perpetuation of the gulf between North and South.

As poverty disappeared in the wake of national prosperity and as Eastern European economies stagnated, some in the party, led by Giorgio Amendola, advocated a mixed economy that would avoid the inefficiency of capitalism and the overcentralization of communism. In the course of the 1960s the Communists emerged as some of the most hardheaded proponents of industrial efficiency and the operation of the profit motive in state industries. European economic integration was accepted, the goal of nationalization was dropped, and by the mid-1970s the party was among the firmest advocates of fiscal and monetary austerity, a reduction of the budget deficit, and wage restraint – positions that attracted respect – and some votes – in middle-class and entrepreneurial circles. That the support for austerity and wage restraint was chiefly a function of the party's drive to enter the government seemed evident when the party later reversed itself upon going into the opposition. That shift undid much of the party's reputation for probity in the economics field.

These convolutions were the sign of a party in painful transition. That the party had abandoned Leninist socialism without subscribing to Western social democracy, which it regarded as a sellout to the capitalist system, was formalized in 1978 when it attempted to stake out a middle position. The new economic and social approach that it then unveiled was labeled *la terza via,* "the third way." As its appellation suggests, the concept purports to be an alternative to both capitalism and communism. Party leaders candidly admit they cannot define "the third way" with any precision. Although many of the broad objectives of the approach parallel those of European social democrats, they are often elaborated in Leninist-sounding verbiage about "the conquest of state power," "the destruction of capitalism," and "working class hegemony" that sends a chill up the spines of a good many Italians. So in the end Communists try to square the circle: being a party like the others and yet being different; being loyal to the established order and yet wanting to change it; seeking acceptance and yet maintaining a separateness. Although Italian Communism no longer equals Leninism, what it does mean remains in some respects obscure. The well-known line from Eugenio Montale's poem is all too apt: "This alone can we tell you today/ That is what we are *not*/ That is what we want *not.*" To some extent, however, this very uncertainty explains the party's attraction and its repulsion, its growth and its decline.

Members and electorate

At its birth in 1921 the Communist party was scarcely more than a small band of revolutionaries, its number reduced during the Fascist period not only by police repression but also by defections. In August 1943, just after Mussolini's fall, the party was down to 3,000 members. From then on its growth was phenomenal. At the time of its first postwar congress in December 1945, the number had already risen to 1.7 million and by 1947 reached 2.225 million, the all-time high. The initial explosion of membership by and large resulted from the party's tremendous prestige as leader of the resistance to the Fascists and the German army, its outstanding organizational ability, its successful infiltration of the trade union and cooperative movements, and simply the party's aggressive political strategy. From the mid-1950s membership began to decline, in the wake of the revelations about Stalin and the invasion of Hungary, and fell to a low of 1.5 million in 1968 following the Soviet invasion of Czechoslovakia. After reviving, it steadily declined after 1976 to its 1984 figure of 1.619 million. As such it remains the largest party in Western Europe and the largest communist party outside the communist world.

Although the turnover in membership has been quite high, the party has succeeded in solidifying its social and geographical bases. The party is very much a workers' organization, with workers representing about 40 percent of its national membership – with a high of 53 percent in Lombardy and a low of 27 percent in Sicily. Its most notable weakness has been its failure to break the Christian Democrats' hold on farmers and agricultural workers. In fact their proportion of the party membership has steadily declined to the point that farm laborers and small landholders by 1984 represented only 5 percent of the membership. By contrast the party has had a notable growth among civil servants and intellectuals and in the tertiary sector generally. Between 1971 and 1979 the number of white collar workers and skilled laborers rose from 3 to 7 percent; in

Lazio and its capital, Rome, from 7 to 15 percent. Artisans comprise 5 percent, as in the Christian Democratic party. Pensioners represent 21 percent and housewives 8 percent. Women as a whole are 23 percent of the membership. The Christian Democrats have 10 percent more women and twice as many housewives; on the other hand three times more pensioners are Communists than Christian Democrats.

Geographically about half the party's members are concentrated in the industrial cities of the North with their large working-class populations and in the "red belt" – Emilia-Romagna, Tuscany, and Umbria – where the Communists have exploited the historic socialist and republican legacy to build up strong support in all social and economic strata. Even in the South, where there is neither a working-class nor a Socialist and laicist tradition, the Communists have succeeded in recruiting a solid membership. In the early 1970s the party made its greatest headway in Naples, Salerno, and the area of Isernia. They have also worked hard, though with less success, to break into the Christian Democratic strongholds in the Veneto and Trentino and in the homeland of the South Tyrol People's party in the German-speaking area adjacent to the Austrian frontier. By the mid-1970s the Communists had succeeded in establishing themselves – both in terms of members and electoral following – as a genuinely national party, albeit still weak in much of the South.

The foundation of the party's membership has rested on the substantial Communist subculture. Institutionally, this takes shape in various mass organizations that the party has established or has come to control – the National Farmers' League, the Union of Women, the National Association of Partisans, the National Peasants' Alliance, along with a number of recreational, cultural, athletic, and similar organizations. In recruiting members for the party, in swaying opinion or in getting votes, these organizations have probably not had the importance sometimes attributed to them. However, two other organizations that the Communists succeeded in taking over after the war, the General Confederation of Labor, CGIL, and the National League of Cooperatives, have been of the utmost importance. The CGIL was crucial to the Communists in first gaining and then keeping the support of a high proportion of workers. The cooperatives, with influence in the construction, agricultural, and consumer-goods industries, have provided an important source of funds for the party, in particular through its control of much of Italy's trade with Eastern Europe and the Soviet Union.

Of all the parties the Communists have the most extensive communications apparatus. Their daily, *l'Unità*, has by far the largest circulation of any party journal, reaching over a million copies on Sundays. They also publish a variety of journals, such as *Rinascita, Critica Marxista, Politica ed Economia,* and *Studi Storici,* which have wide intellectual prestige. But they cannot compete on the popular level with the Christian Democrats, and to a lesser extent the Socialists, who have the state radio and television network at their disposal and one or another of the major national dailies behind them. The party also maintains educational centers as well as professional institutes for economic affairs (CeSPE) and international affairs (CeSPI), as well as the Gramsci Institute, a center for research and conferences. The party operates its own publishing house, Editori Riuniti, and has broad influence in the book trade.

The party's growing attraction was evident in voting results over the postwar period. In the 1946 election to the Constituent Assembly, the Communists were the third party, with 19 percent of the vote. In the 1953 parliamentary election they received 23 percent, nearly twice as much as the Socialists, whom they replaced as the second party. They continued to gain, slowly but steadily, until 1976 when they achieved a stunning breakthrough, reaching over 34 percent and with that the brink of power on the national level. In thirty years the Communists had almost doubled their vote, having gained the support of one of every three of the 36 million Italian voters. Not until 1979 did they suffer a setback, losing a full 4 percent in the election of that year. Although the lion's share of their electoral gains over the years was at the expense of the Socialists, the Communists' critical failure was their inability completely to absorb that party.

The Communists' electoral success has been even more marked on the local and regional levels. Although Communist support has always been concentrated in urban centers, it has also taken deep root in some areas of rural radicalism in the North and South. No section of the country has been more staunchly Communist, for instance, than the Tuscan countryside. The great heartland of Italian Communism is Emilia-Romagna and its capital, Bologna, which the party has governed without break since the end of the war. By ensuring that the buses ran on time, by providing a broad range of social services, and by gaining a reputation for efficient and honest government, the Communists created if not a socialist paradise, a clearly well-run city that was for decades a model throughout the country.

With the first regional elections in 1970, the PCI predictably captured the three traditional "red" regions. In the next round in 1975, they added Liguria, Lazio, and Piedmont. Still more remarkable was its advance in the cities. By 1975 Rome, Naples, Florence, Genoa, Turin, Milan, Bologna, and Venice – indeed all the large cities except Palermo – had Communist-Socialist governments and in most cases Communist mayors. The overall Communist vote in the regional and local elections of that year rose to 33 percent, while the Christian Democrats fell to 35 percent, producing the greatest "red scare" in Washington and among the Italian rich since 1948. A noteworthy element of this success was the solid Communist advance in the South, the culmination of a trend that Joseph LaPalombara characterized as "the single most important transformation in Italian electoral geography since the birth of the Republic." By 1978 over half the provinces had Communist-Socialist administrations and, in all, over 50 percent of the country's population lived in municipalities governed by Communist mayors or electoral councils controlled by the Communists.

These results reflected the fact that where it governed, the party built up a reputation for being on the whole responsive, honest, and efficient. As exasperation with the corruption and incompetence of the other parties grew, voters at the communal, provincial, and regional levels turned to "the party with clean hands" and, though Communist administrations did not produce the miracles that had been hoped, they were at least marginally better than their predecessors and in most cases were reelected. By the mid-seventies many Italians who would never vote for the Communists in a national election willingly did so in other contests – reflecting a confidence in the Communists' ability to administer but a lingering doubt about their policies on the national level.

However, even on the national level an important psychological change occurred around the mid-seventies. The corruption scandals involving the Christian Democrats and other parties, the breakdown of the center-left formula, and the changes in the Communist party made the PCI's participation in government seem less horrifying and potentially beneficial. In some bourgeois circles the party became downright chic. The party's support for the Christian Democrats in combating left-wing terrorism and in dealing with the economic crisis strengthened the confidence of the political establishment and society at large that the party's ideological change and its loyalty to the constitutional system were genuine. By now the assessment of the party was changing far more rapidly in Italy than outside, particularly in some Western governments, which fell ever further behind in recognizing the extent of the party's transformation.

The new attitude was evident even in industrial circles. Business leaders had a growing sense that though the party was no friend of capitalist interests, it had changed drastically and was in any case far too powerful a force to be ignored. Above all, as a result of the world economic crisis after 1973, which hit Italy with particular severity, they were convinced that cooperation with the party and CGIL was necessary if Italy's economic and financial problems were to be solved. A number of leading entrepreneurs, such as Gianni Agnelli, head of Fiat and the country's most influential industrialist, and Guido Carli, president of the Confederation of Industry, publicly argued that the Communists had to be allowed some voice in shaping the country's economic policies.

One institutional obstacle, however, has never been sur- mounted. At the end of the war the party recognized that its most powerful ideological opponent would be the Catholic church and that the two of them would be engaged in a veritable war for the allegiance of the Catholic electorate. The party considered it par- ticularly crucial to remove Catholic workers and farmers from the dilemma of having to choose between their religious faith and class interests. Over the years communist leaders have tried two ap- proaches: on the one hand to gain the political neutrality of the church and on the other to go around the church and reach the Catholic faithful through appeals to their economic and social concerns. The "new party" that Togliatti launched in 1944 had explicitly envisaged collaboration not only with the Socialists but with Catholics as well. On his entry to Rome in 1944 Togliatti declared: "We, the Communist party, have declared – and I repeat this declaration today in Rome, the capital of the Catholic world – that we respect the traditional faith of the majority of the Italian people. . . ." This sentiment was embodied in the 1945 party statute, where it has since remained, stating that party membership is independent of "religious faith and philosophical convictions." How such a position was to be reconciled with the party's Marxist- Leninist ideology that was to be studied by every member was not explained.

Obviously the best that could be hoped for was a modus vivendi. To achieve it the party was willing to make great concessions. At its first postwar congress in 1945 Togliatti insisted that the new con- stitution would have to contain full guarantees for freedom of religion and freedom for the church. He added that the 1929 church–state accords between Italy and the Vatican were final and irrevocable. As good as his word, the Communists voted along with the Christian Democrats in the Constitutional Assembly to incor- porate these agreements into the constitution. These efforts to placate the church failed utterly. Pope Pius XII regarded Commu- nism as by far the greatest danger to Western civilization of the century and saw the PCI not just as a political opponent but also as politically incarnate evil. In 1949 the Vatican declared that anyone who joined the party or even voted for it was excommunicate. After the death of Pius XII in 1958 the hostility softened somewhat in tone though not at all in substance.

Nevertheless the party persevered, placing great hopes in the tolerant approach of John XXIII in the late period of his papacy. In 1963 Togliatti appealed for mutual understanding and respect while acknowledging that there could be no compromise of principles on either side. Within that limit, he maintained, Catholics and Communists should be able to march together toward the common goal of a more just society. In his Yalta memorandum of the following year, he admonished his party to "put aside the old atheist propaganda that leads to nothing." Anticlericalism was outmoded, and religion should not be regarded as an instrument of the conservative classes, he maintained. Longo carried on this policy, telling the party congress in 1966: "As we are against a confessional state, so we are against state atheism."

Despite their steady growth, the Communists made few inroads into the Catholic electorate. In a play for legitimation, the party invited eleven well-known Catholics to run on Communist election lists in the 1976 election. While this greatly alarmed the church, only six of the candidates were elected and the action failed in its real objective.

The following year Berlinguer tried another approach. In an open letter to one of the most progressive members of the hierarchy, Bishop Luigi Bettazzi, Berlinguer reiterated that Catholic belief was compatible with Communist party membership as spelled out in the party statute. The claim was immediately rejected by the Catholic Episcopal Conference, and the correspondence never went further. In 1979, undoubtedly as a result of this standoff, the preamble of the party statute was rewritten to confirm the party's respect for a religious concept of life and to declare that the party recognized the Christian conscience could act as a stimulus in the struggle for the socialist transformation of society.

Since that time the two sides have largely ignored one another, the Communists making no further gestures and the church avoiding open attacks but unrelenting in its refusal to legitimize the party for the faithful.

Protestants of the Communist church?

The Communist party itself is often likened to a church and its functionaries to a priesthood. The party is an all-embracing institution with a millennial ideology and its equivalent of a liturgy and holy days, saints and martyrs, converts and apostates. Like a church it cannot easily admit errors and changes only with difficulty. In a way the evolution of the party has some similarities to the Reformation, with its condemnation of the central organization for betraying original purposes, with its organizational separation, its changes in practices and beliefs, its insistence on following its own national way, and even its return to original texts. The party still acknowledges the underlying faith – socialism – but it has reinterpreted the content of that belief and has destroyed the old organizational unity.

In the years since 1944 the party has distanced itself from each of the grounds for its secession from the Socialists. Yet the party has not really come to terms with its past. Two of its historic leaders – Giorgio Amendola and Umberto Terracini – raised the question late in their lives whether the schism with the Socialists had not after all been an error. Similarly, despite the condemnation of the Soviets over Czechoslovakia, Afghanistan, and Poland, the party has never reassessed its support for suppression of the Hungarian revolution. Relics of Leninism litter the party landscape. Contradictions and ambiguities abound.

In the end the party's image therefore leaves the observer puzzled. Here is a party that has endorsed a political system that it has always vowed to transform and transform into something it cannot precisely describe but that includes features that are presumably outside the bounds of Italian political and economic orthodoxy. In truth the objective of the proposed fundamental economic and social changes does not appear to differ from that of left socialists elsewhere in Western Europe. But because of its past it must earn public trust; unlike other parties, it has a record to live down. Like an ex-prisoner who insists he has gone straight, it is still watched for any sign of backsliding. "What would the party actually do if it were in power?" is a question that remains in the backs of the minds of a large number of Italian voters.

At the same time there can be no doubt that the other parties are frightened of the Communists for reasons of pure power politics. With its discipline and efficiency, the PCI might easily dominate the scene once allowed in government. Certainly the other parties do not want to compromise their monopoly over the clientelistic prerogatives of government power. Patronage is a zero-sum game, where more for one means less for the others. So partisan objections to the Communists are at times camouflaged by bogus ideological arguments – a reverse *doppiezza*.

The question arises why the Communist party does not itself finally sweep away the ambiguities and, like the German Social Democrats, hold an equivalent of the Bad Godesberg party congress, declaring once and for all and without any qualification that it accepts the practices and policies of the existing political and economic order. Apart from the fact that Italians – who have never had either a revolution or a reformation – do not by nature like clean sweeps, the party cannot yet go so far.

The Communist party has proceeded to the ideological brink. Any further substantial change will involve a surrender of its origin and its identity. To abandon its distinction from Western social democratic parties would be tantamount to admitting that the secession of 1921 was a mistake and that the entire course of the party's development, the struggles that the party undertook and suffered for in the subsequent decades, had been futile and that the Socialists were right all along. Nor is the party's commitment to its working-class ideology something it is willing to trade for electoral advantage. Communists feel profoundly that they deserve a place in government because of their decades of support for the constitutional system and because they represent a third of the electorate. They resent the notion that they should have to repent of anything for that place.

It is the lesson of postwar European politics, however, that the party that occupies the middle ground is the party that has access to power. In Italy this fact implies a full endorsement not just of parliamentary democracy and political pluralism but also of capitalism, the European Community, NATO, and alliance with the United States. Until the Communists – like the German Social Democrats before them – take steps to remove the remaining ambiguities, doubt will remain about their acceptability as a governing alternative. The party must not just be but must be seen to be a loyal supporter of both the rules and the objectives of the political system. Otherwise the party's quest for acceptance and its struggle to maintain its identity will continue to pull in opposite directions. And the party will go on, in a phrase of Matthew Arnold, "wandering between two worlds, one dead/ The other powerless to be born."

4. The ambiguous role of the Socialists

Of all the Italian parties, none has changed more dramatically in the course of the postwar period than the Socialists. It is indeed no exaggeration to speak of a genuine mutation. From being a vacillating, faction-ridden, Marxist-Leninist party subordinate to the Communists at the outset of the postwar period, the party had transformed itself by the early 1980s into a unified, self-confident, moderate-left party in the mainstream of European social democracy. By then it was not only in the hands of the youngest group of political leaders in the country, its organization had been completely revamped and its ideological program thoroughly revised. This veritable transfiguration culminated with Bettino Craxi's inauguration in 1983 as the first Socialist prime minister in Italian history.

The resurrection and glory of the party was celebrated at the forty-third Socialist congress in Verona in May 1984. Shortly before the event Luciano Pellicani, editor of the party monthly, *Mondoperaio,* commented that the occasion marked the first time in history when the party would hold a congress with a unified leadership, a clear program of reforms, and a plainly liberal-socialist platform. This novel development, combined with Craxi's qualities as a great "political impresario," according to Pellicani, were what had made the Socialist party the axis around which the country's politics turned.

This flattering self-portrait was symptomatic of the Socialist party of the early 1980s: aggressive, pragmatic, highly self-conscious, and to a great extent a one-man show. Although some of the bravado was a facade concealing an inner uncertainty, no other party in the postwar period had fallen so low and pulled itself together so well. It was small wonder that after 1979 the Socialists replaced the Communists as the main topic of the country's political discussion. But the full extent of Craxi's achievement can be properly gauged only by comparing the party of the early 1980s with the party as it was at any previous time.

"Barnum's circus"

One of the most puzzling questions of postwar Italian politics is why socialism failed to be the strong political force that it has been elsewhere in Western Europe. In the early years of the unified Italian state, the Socialists were in every sense the country's first party. They were the first to be founded, the first mass party, and quickly became the first in political strength. Not only were they the best-organized party, but they also controlled the trade union movement with 2 million members and had a powerful appeal to intellectuals and students. Only in Germany was democratic socialism stronger at the end of the First World War. In succeeding decades, however, while socialist parties flourished and eventually came to power in every other European democracy, Italian Socialism went into steady decline, to the point that by the 1970s it was the smallest socialist party in Western Europe. Its 34 percent of the vote in 1919 fell to 25 percent in 1921, to 21 percent in 1946, and to roughly 10 percent in 1972 and in the three following elections. In 1977 Craxi could say with little exaggeration in an interview with *Le Monde*, "The Socialist party is struggling for its very existence."

The main problem of Italian Socialism was that it always had difficulty deciding what it was and what it wanted. Rooted in a late-nineteenth-century mixture of syndicalism, anarchism, and Marxism – with a heritage going back to the French revolution, the ferment of 1848, and the Paris commune of 1871 – it never succeeded in integrating these various strands to achieve political focus, a clear identity, and intellectual consistency. As founded in 1892 under the leadership of Filippo Turati, the Socialist party repudiated the existing "bourgeois" system but advocated altering it by democratic reform rather than destroying it by violence. This position was too mild for some and too extreme for others. In 1908 Turati expelled the revolutionary syndicalists. In 1922 Turati himself was pushed aside and the moderates were thrown out. His successor, Giacinto Serrati, tried to amalgamate the party with the Communists. He was expelled after a year. The party's neutralist stance at the time of the First World War had already caused another sort of rift when Benito Mussolini and other Socialists who favored Italian support of the Allied Powers were expelled, some of them following Mussolini into the Fascist party.

From the time of its birth, therefore, Italian Socialism was divided between those advocating radical action and those wanting moderate reform – between the "maximalists" and the "minimalists," in Socialist parlance. Every European Socialist party has had

to reconcile its Marxist origins with its dedication to political freedom and to choose between evolution and revolution. Although
each has done so in its own time and manner, the Italian Socialists
have had singular difficulty in resolving the dilemma. At the turn
of the century they would neither accept nor reject the established
governing institutions. So while they participated in elections and
sat in parliament, they would not join the government or even
collaborate with other political forces. In 1912 they proclaimed
themselves a revolutionary party. The characterization was rhetorical and fooled no one, except possibly the Socialists themselves.
As the years passed they demanded increasingly radical changes
and did nothing to achieve them. Lenin saw through this sham
militancy, writing to them in 1920: "You seem to yourselves to be
'terribly revolutionary,' oh dear abstentionists and antiparliamen-
tarians, but in reality *you are frightened* by the relatively small
problems of the struggle against bourgeois influences inside the
workers' movement. . . ." With equal disdain, Gramsci once likened the party to "Barnum's circus," remarking that it "never takes
anything seriously" and has "always fled from assuming full responsibility" for its actions – charges that were repeated in a constant refrain on all sides in the following half-century.

The Russian revolution was a catalytic event, forcing the party to
decide whether it wanted revolution or reform, proletarian dictatorship or liberal democracy. The issue came to a head at the 1921
party congress at Livorno, where a strong majority accepted Leninism and the principles of the Third International but insisted on
an independent – Italian – way to socialism and on following democratic principles in running the party. As a result the extreme left
seceded and founded the Communist party.

Having shed its syndicalists, Communists, and moderates, the
remnant party was by 1922 in the hands of the victorious "maximalists" who were mesmerized by the notion that destiny would
create a socialist state and they needed only to wait. So they waited.
When destiny took events in the opposite direction, they consoled
themselves with the belief, shared by the Communists, that Fascism was a mere prelude to the destruction of capitalism and the
establishment of a Marxist state. Once the Fascists were firmly in
power the Socialists, unlike the Communists, gave up the struggle.
They calculated that they had been proved wrong and that democracy had no future in Italy. Some of them fled and the party was
eventually reconstituted in Paris under Pietro Nenni. There it soon
fell under Communist domination.

Nothing better exemplifies the Socialist party's good intentions and inner softness than its relationship to the Communists. In 1935 it allied itself with them in a "unity of action pact." This accord was renewed in 1943 when both parties recognized the Soviet Union as the common leader and advocated their own ultimate fusion. After the collapse of Fascism the Socialists went even further, proclaiming their party formally to be Marxist-Leninist and campaigning in the first crucial postwar parliamentary election with a joint electoral list with the Communists. In 1949 the party broke off its contacts with the trade unions in Western countries. Party ranks were infiltrated with Communists and for a time Socialist leaders took major decisions only with Communist agreement. By the early 1950s the party was little more than a Communist front, no longer recognized by the Socialist International as a socialist party.

What had led the Socialists in Italy, in contrast to those elsewhere in Europe, to subordinate themselves to the Communists was a deep conviction that wherever Socialists and Communists had been divided, the working class had been defeated and their enemies had come to power. Another element was the perception that at the critical moments of the 1930s the Soviet Union had defended democracy – in Spain – while Britain and France had knuckled under to Fascism – at Munich. In 1945 they therefore regarded the Soviet Union, not the British and Americans, as the prime vanquisher of German Fascism. The postwar world in their view was divided into a predatory capitalist camp, headed by the United States, and a peaceful socialist camp, led by the Soviet Union. Behind these political calculations was also a sense of psychological inferiority arising from the fact that it had been the Communists not the Socialists who had led the effective resistance to Italian Fascism.

The consequences were disastrous. By making itself little more than an appendage of the Communists, the party squandered its Socialist heritage, obfuscated its liberal character, and destroyed its individuality. Its position between Stalinism and reform socialism required intellectual distinctions that neither the workers nor the liberal middle class could comprehend – so they chose the "real thing," the Communists on the left or the Christian Democrats on the right. Moreover, a party so passive and lacking in self-confidence could not begin to compete with the iron discipline and ideological certitude of the Communists. Between the fall of Fascism and the end of the war, the Communists had already undermined the twin pillars of Socialist strength, the trade unions and the agricultural cooperatives. By 1946 half the Socialist rank and file in the North had switched to the Communists; by 1948 the control of the trade union movement had also passed to them. After being the country's second-largest party in the initial postwar election in 1946, the Socialists fell below the Communists in 1948 and continued to decline, as the Communists grew, for the next thirty years.

The party's alignment with the Communists also provoked ruinous schism. In 1947 a group of moderates refused any longer to tolerate the party's pro-Soviet and anti-American stance and, with the encouragement and financing of the United States, withdrew to form the Social Democratic party under the leadership of Giuseppe Saragat. This group represented a full third of the party, including almost the entire youth movement, and was subsequently joined by other groups that walked out as the Socialists' leftward drift continued. Between 1947 and 1950 the Socialist party lost 400,000 members, half its total.

Pietro Nenni, the party's leader after 1930, began to awaken from his trance by the mid-fifties. But it was not until after the Hungarian uprising and Khrushchev's denunciation of Stalin in 1956 that the party, albeit divided, began to reassert its autonomy. This shift culminated in the decision in 1963 to join the Christian Democrats in a center-left coalition. Now the Socialist left rebelled. In 1964 a third of the central commitee and an equal percentage of the party's parliamentary representatives quit the party and formed the Socialist party of Proletarian Unity, a secession that cost the Socialists an important segment of their working-class support. This blow was temporarily offset two years later when Nenni and Saragat reunited their parties. But the merger was more organizational than ideological and political. When the unified party won fewer votes in the 1968 election than the two parties had won separately in the previous one, the union collapsed.

Even at this point the Socialist party's ambiguous and vacillating attitude toward the Communists had not fully run its course. As the center-left unraveled and the Socialists witnessed their steady electoral decline – attributed in part to the Communists' ability to win over the moderate-left protest vote – the party again shifted course. In 1974 it withdrew from the government and – in a precisely mistimed stroke, since the Communists were now committed to the "historic compromise" – espoused a policy of "left alternative" – a Communist-Socialist coalition to replace the Christian Democrats in government. This new strategy was so distant from political reality as to create still deeper confusion. Not until four years later, with Craxi then in command, did the Socialists finally initiate a clean break with the Communists.

Strong factions, weak leaders

The party's failure to project a clear profile or to follow a convincing political line has been greatly compounded by internal division. An uncontrolled factionalism has ravaged the party since its earliest days. To some extent the Socialists epitomize the libertarian, individualistic, voluble, and self-critical side of the Italian character. They revel in disputation and fractiousness. "What a beautiful thing socialism would be," Turati himself lamented late in his life, "if there were no socialists." In the course of European history there have been few parties of a major philosophical tradition that tore themselves so thoroughly apart as the Italian Socialists. Although their factionalism may have been no more intense than among the Christian Democrats, it was more damaging. It generally had greater ideological content and therefore cut deeper. And it was not always subordinated to party unity and therefore led to disastrous secessions. At times Socialist factions were virtual parties in themselves, closer to another party than to other Socialist factions. Some were simply political machines to which an ideological facade had been attached. With the passage of time ideological differences became thinner and thinner to the point that by the mid-1970s factions were essentially bases of personal power.

The battlefield of the factions was the party apparatus – an executive committee of around 30 members, a central committee with some 225 members, and a triennial national congress attended by 1,000 or more delegates. The main contest was usually held on the provincial level, where delegates to the congress were chosen. This selection process was critical because it was the congress that elected the central committee, which in turn coopted the executive committee, which elected the secretary. At every level party management suffered from indiscipline and inefficiency and an attitude more akin to one of running a political club than a political party. Instead of possessing an effective instrument to carry out his policies, a party secretary generally found himself presiding over a squabbling band of less than loyal subordinates. Until the early 1980s, no one ever rose to the top who could put an end to this factionalism or even control it. Since leaders could do nothing without the acquiescence of faction chiefs, the secretary's position was insecure and the policies he pursued were the minimum acceptable to the various factions. The party selected and ejected secretaries in rapid order.

The only one who endured was Pietro Nenni, the dominant figure of Italian Socialism in this century. Born the year before the party was founded, Nenni died the year after Craxi had gained full control. His errors of judgment were excelled only by his honesty in recognizing his mistakes and his willingness to change course. Nenni kept the party alive under Fascism, led it into subservience to the Communists in the 1940s, and, within a few years of accepting the Stalin peace prize in 1951, emancipated it from Communist domination. At the height of his influence in the 1950s he was guided by three successive objectives: to reunite his party with the Social Democrats, to reestablish the party's independence of the Communists, and to take the party into the government where it could work for social reform.

Each of these steps was possible only after a tremendous struggle within the party organization, where Nenni and his allies were a minority. Despite his great prestige, he was decisively beaten on the reunification issue in 1957, which delayed the merger until 1966 by which time a successful fusion was too late to achieve. The decisive battle over the party's political orientation – its autonomy from the Communists and its acceptance of NATO – was fought out at the 1959 congress, where Nenni won a clear majority. But no sooner had the congress concluded than a leftist subgroup developed inside Nenni's own faction, once again crippling the secretary's leadership. Not until 1963 had he solidified his position to the point where he could conduct the party into a center-left coalition.

Craxi's rise to leadership provides another example of strife between the party leader and the apparatus, operating as a front for the factions. Following the party's poor performance in the 1976 election – an election precipitated by the party's inept secretary at the time, Francesco De Martino – there was a revolt by a new generation of party officials known as the "forty-year olds," who deposed De Martino and elected Nenni's forty-two-year-old protégé, Craxi, to succeed him. At the time of his election Craxi probably had control of no more than 30 percent of the party apparatus. When the cabal that put him in office fell apart a year later, Craxi was a virtual prisoner of the executive committee and could not lead the party in any direction. There were even a number of party officials at this time who did not make a move without first checking with the Communist headquarters. To save the situation Craxi struck a bargain with the leader of the leftist faction,

Claudio Signorile, to divide power between themselves. In March 1978 they convened an extraordinary session of the party congress, swept up support in the provincial conventions, and at the congress won the greatest measure of support – 63 percent – in the party's history. But, true to Socialist form, Signorile soon challenged Craxi's leadership and, after a year of sparring, the secretary demolished his rival by splitting the left and forming an alliance with a splinter group headed by an ambitious young Venetian, Gianni De Michelis. Craxi now had a free hand, and he set about creating what amounted to a new organization.

The Craxi reformation

The party that Craxi conquered was not simply beset with internal problems; it was one that seemed to prove Bismarck's aphorism that every political system needs a whipping boy. Since its foundation it has somehow been the party everyone – historians, political scientists, journalists, and politicians of all colors – has loved to hate. It has been condemned for its weaknesses – for failing to block the Fascists in the 1920s, for being outsmarted by the Communists in the 1940s, for being outwitted by the Christian Democrats in the 1960s, and for bringing the country near to ungovernability in the 1970s. It has been criticized in effect for its strength – for constituting a modest "third force," autonomous of both the Christian Democrats and the Communists, that prevented the development of an essentially two-party system. But above all it has been reproached for its ambiguity – for failing to make a lasting and unqualified commitment to a specific course of action and consequently for being a party no one could rely on. It so often said one thing, meant a second, and did a third that it was victim of the jibe, "It does not know what it wants but wants it right away."

Nonetheless the Socialists themselves seem almost joyously to have provoked exasperation. Their frequent shifts of course – toward the Communists, away from them, toward the Christian Democrats, back to the Communists, and then a return to the Christian Democrats after years of proclaiming that this was out of the question – left the impression of a party that was irresolute and stood for nothing solid. For decades the Socialists emphasized their claim of being the party that could guarantee the country's governability. But by their actions, they were a major force for instability – pulling down governments, forcing elections, and making it hard for anyone to rule. The resulting image of opportunism, unreliability, and unpredictability gave rise to the most damning and frequent charge of all: "They simply cannot be taken seriously."

This reputation, despite everything, was by no means balanced and just. In domestic affairs no other party had more consistently supported progressive causes. In the initial postwar period the Socialists had opposed the monarchy, the concordat, and the decision to stop the anti-Fascist purge, while the Communists had supported all three. The party was the prime mover of social and governmental reforms and the main defender, until the Radicals came along, of civil liberties and minority rights. In foreign and security affairs the party's switch from opposition to support of European integration, NATO, and the Italian defense effort reinforced the country's international links. And, during the first series of center-left governments, it was they who initiated divorce legislation, insisted on the establishment of regions, and drove through parliament a statute of workers' rights.

It was a measure of the Socialists' ineffectiveness that their achievements were greatly overshadowed in the public mind by their failings. The condition for their entering the center-left in 1963, for instance, was Christian Democratic acceptance of a program of economic and social innovation intended to make Italy a welfare state based on broad economic planning. This objective clashed directly with a Christian Democratic commitment to economic austerity in the face of mounting inflation. Blocked by the Christian Democrats, much of the reform program never materialized, and the Socialists were seen as being more interested in the spoils of office than in the power of government to reform society. The Socialists felt they had been duped by the Christian Democrats, who had accepted their parliamentary support but sabotaged their goals. The Socialists found themselves increasingly vulnerable to the charge that they were propping up a series of governments hostile to the interests of their electorate. They looked on in anguish as workers and other elements of their constituency shifted to the Communists. Eventually the strain between the party's left-leaning working-class tradition and its alliance with a rightward-moving Christian Democratic party became intolerable. After having dreamed of being the intermediary between the two major parties, the Socialists found themselves being destroyed by them. So the center-left, far from being the historic turning point that would lead Italy into an alternating two-party system, ended in bitterness and recrimination.

By the mid-1970s the party's fortunes, reputation, and self-respect were at an all-time low. The party had been weakened by alliance with the Communists; it had been damaged by alliance with the Christian Democrats. It lost votes when it was in the opposition; it lost them when it was in government. It hurt itself by letting the Social Democrats go; it damaged itself by letting them back. With each failure the party's credibility – and electoral support – dropped. And with that decline the hope vanished that the Socialists could offer the country a convincing alternative.

Like any good general who takes command of a battered army, Craxi recognized that restoring morale and reorganizing command were the requisite first steps to make the party an effective fighting force. To universal amazement he succeeded in the course of a few years in revamping the structure, gaining complete control over the party apparatus, and infusing the party with an unprecedented sense of unity and purpose.

Craxi first strenghtened the position of party secretary. By changing the party statute in 1981 to provide for his election by the congress instead of the central committee, he augmented the leader's authority by preventing his ouster between sessions of the congress. It was a sign of the changed mood that even those who did not always like the way Craxi was leading the party recognized the value of strong central leadership and supported him because they were thereby supporting the party – an utterly novel attitude among Italian Socialists. The spirit of unity went so far that the 1984 congress did not bother formally to count votes but elected Craxi by acclamation.

Craxi's next step was taken at the 1984 party congress when the central committee, with its Leninist connotation, was replaced by an entirely new type of body, a 473-member national assembly comprising a cross section of Italian public life – to include roughly 200 representatives of local party organizations and over 100 deputies, senators, and Italian representatives to the European parliament as well as 100 prominent figures from the world of culture, science, economics, entertainment, and sports who are party members or sympathetic to Socialist causes. While the purpose of this broadly based organization is to demonstrate the party's openness to modern society and contemporary ideas, its size and membership derogate from any serious role it might play and therefore further impede the formation of an internal party opposition. Similarly, the enlargement of the executive committee, from its 30-odd members to more than 50, reduces that body's central place in the party, disperses its authority, and reduces its ability to challenge the position and policies of the secretary.

While extending his control over the party organization, Craxi had in the meantime taken steps to neutralize the old factionalism. In 1978 factions were – not for the first time in party history – formally dissolved. Although they continued to operate for several more years, the power of the "first-generation" leaders – Riccardo Lombardi, De Martino, and Giuseppe Mancini – was already in eclipse and by the end of the decade had passed into history. In another move to disarm or forestall opposition, Craxi brought into the central party organization some of the persons who had been fervent opponents. The political science professor Giuliano Amato, for example, became his principal adviser on government affairs during his years as prime minister. Although factionalism and internal wrangling are at an all-time historic low, a left faction under Claudio Signorile continues to exist. At the 1981 congress it won 30 percent and at the congress three years later 20 percent of the delegates. Another grouping, around Gianni De Michelis and Rino Formica, maintains its own identity ready to challenge Craxi.

If ever there was a party that needed a strong dose of democratic centralism, the Socialists were that party and from Craxi they got it. But after arrogating to the secretary an unprecedented degree of control and enforcing a greater sense of internal discipline than ever before, Craxi failed to use his authority to forge an effective political machine. A notoriously bad manager himself, he refused to delegate responsibility for organizational matters and on becoming prime minister had no time for such things himself. Poor management was one of the party's historic problems and an important reason why the Socialists had so easily been outmaneuvered by the Communists after 1945. Even the triumphant Verona congress took note of the party's continuing weakness in this regard – stagnation in local and provincial organizations and inadequate internal communication.

To some extent a generational change in the late seventies heightened the problem. In the past it had been the cadres on the left of the party and Socialist trade unionists who had devoted themselves to party organization and activities. The newcomers – often political amateurs of middle-class or academic background – tended to regard their party positions merely as springboards to positions in public administration or elective office. As a result the Socialists have come to be known as "the party of local officials," with the officials themselves more interested in their own careers than in the advancement of the party's goals. The party's lack of a professional and dedicated organizational cadre is a serious liability and goes far to explain both the party's operational problems at all levels and its inability to raise itself out of electoral stagnation.

If centralization was one critical aspect of the party's change, establishing a clearer identity was another. Beginning in 1978 Craxi launched a full-scale offensive to alter the party's image, develop a coherent ideology, rally the forces, and set the party on the psychological offensive. A program adopted at the congress of that year initiated the process. The document addressed itself to the major topical issues of the moment – unemployment, labor mobility, the cost of welfare services, and the operations of government – with the intent of creating the impression of a party able to deal flexibly and pragmatically with the country's difficulties. The main point, however, was to signal a shift from the "left alternative" to the "Socialist alternative," thereby announcing the party's move away from the Communists and its intention of following an independent course. Privately, party leaders were already preparing for a new sort of center-left coalition.

Next, Craxi declared ideological war on the Communists. This was a daring act since the ideal of a united left went very deep among Socialists. Even during the years of the center-left, hostility toward Communists had been eschewed. Now, inaugurating a media blitz intended to show how different the two parties were and which was truly democratic, Craxi published a highly polemical article in *L'Espresso* contrasting the socialism of the democratic, reformist sort, associated with the liberal tradition of Proudhon, with the authoritarian socialism that culminated in Leninism. Norberto Bobbio, Massimo Salvadori, and other respected Socialist intellectuals joined the fray, with the result that the Communists, who had been making vast strides toward political acceptability, suddenly found themselves on the intellectual defensive. As Gianfranco Pasquino remarked, "The Socialist goal seemed to be not to prod the Communists to change but to embarrass them, to expose their backwardness and unreliability in order to reap electoral and political benefits as the democratic, reliable, modern party of the left." The attacks were therefore designed to cause a clean break between the two parties of the left and make plain the reasons for it. To remove even symbolic doubt about where the party stood, the hammer and sickle, which had been the party's emblem since its foundation – and which the Communists had usurped – was replaced by a red carnation, a Socialist symbol of the turn of the century with less revolutionary intimations. Newspaper caricaturists had a field day picturing Marx having his beard trimmed, a bust of Marx in the trash can, and a portrait of Marx relegated to the attic. Of course that was just what Craxi wanted.

Other issues were successively picked up and exploited. Addressing the concerns of the late seventies about the country's growing "ungovernability," the party adopted the cause of institutional reform and recommended ways of altering the constitutional system to increase the government's efficiency and stability. Efforts were also made to invigorate the party's ties with the other European socialist parties, which enjoyed wide prestige in Italy. However, because François Mitterrand, Willy Brandt, and Helmut Schmidt did not have much regard for Craxi and his party, a close and warm relationship never developed. The Socialists were somewhat more successful in highlighting their European credentials through their commitment to the European Community and their Atlanticist loyalty by supporting American arms policies.

The revisionist process reached its doctrinal acme with the program that the 1981 party congress adopted, which stressed the themes that lay behind all the various maneuvers: "pragmatism, gradualism, and reform." The themes may have been banal and the steps leading to them may have been largely media hype. But at the end of the course no one could doubt that the Socialist party had left Marx, Lenin, and the Communist party far behind and was now unambiguously within the fold of Western European social democracy.

The third aim of the Socialist revival was the establishment of the party as a force able to break the bipolar nature of Italian politics and specifically to crack the Christian Democrats' domination of the government, thereby unblocking the democratic world's most stagnant political system. At the outset of his endeavor in 1978 no one would have given Craxi much chance of success. Not only did his party lack credibility and respect, he personally attracted antipathy. Even though he had spent his entire career in politics, he was by choice a political outsider and ostentatiously maintained his residence in Milan rather than Rome. He kept his own counsel, took decisions alone and in secret, maintained an office without windows in a building separate from party headquarters, and held himself as much as possible aloof from the everyday political world. Because of his tenacity, his inner insecurity, and his alleged dictatorial behavior, he was occasionally called a Hitler and often portrayed as a Mussolini in newspaper cartoons.

At an early stage in his campaign for power Craxi committed two blunders. In the desire to make his party the center of public attention and to demonstrate its full autonomy, Craxi took a stand independent of the other parties when Aldo Moro was kidnapped, advocating talks with the Red Brigade kidnappers. To most Italians such a position looked more like frivolous opportunism than compassion. The other error lay in his failure to perceive the libertarian mood among leftist youth and intellectuals in the late seventies. The support that the Socialists might have won in these circles went instead to the Radicals. So despite the party's rejuvenation and its vast campaign expenditure, Craxi failed his first big electoral test, the 1979 parliamentary election. Instead of advancing to the vaunted 15 to 20 percent, the Socialists vote went up from 9.6 to 9.8 percent.

Nothing daunted and saved by the Communists' debacle in the election, Craxi proceeded to the final stage of his march to power, one that would take the Socialists back into the government and give him the prime ministry. The way was opened by a series of fortuitous events: the Communist election setback, a shift in the power balance among the Christian Democrats in favor of the pro-Socialists, and a decision by the 1980 Christian Democratic congress ruling out any further collaboration with the Communists. As a result the Christian Democrats had no choice but to do a deal with Craxi and to do it largely on his terms.

For the Socialists the new center-left government formed in 1980 was not a revival of the old center-left. For one thing it was constructed on the basis of greater equality. The Socialists had their pick of important cabinet positions and a much larger share of positions in the *sottogoverno*. More important still, it was regarded as a critical step toward demonstrating the Socialists' ability to govern, to govern well, and then to be rewarded at the polls for their dynamism and imagination.

This approach was the reverse of the usual democratic mode of coming to power. Instead of electoral advance being followed by government office, power was to come first and produce electoral growth. In banking on a substantial improvement in their position, the Socialists had been much beguiled by the example of Mitterrand's dramatic improvement of the French Socialists' fortunes and also had hoped that some of that success would have an impact on Italian voters. Although they may not have believed their own predictions – of doubling their vote overnight – they based their whole strategy on making a sufficient electoral breakthrough to initiate a process leading to a fundamental political realignment. Where were the votes to come from? Craxi's aim was sometimes understood to be a "reequilibration" of the left, with the Socialists achieving a closer balance with the Communists. Such an objective was certainly an aspiration of all Socialists. But Pasquino was precisely on the mark in observing: "Briefly, there is no simple way to remedy a situation of imbalance within the Italian left that is the product of thirty years of struggles, transformations, and mistakes." Since the Socialists knew this, their objective was to construct in the center of the political spectrum a "Socialist and lay area" of nearly equal strength to the Christian Democrats and Communists. Although some additional votes might be picked up on the left, the crucial battle would be with the Christian Democrats over the uncommitted middle-class electorate.

The outcome of the 1983 election, when the Socialists advanced by a mere 1.6 percent – precisely when the Christian Democrats declined by over 5 percent – was consequently a bitter disappointment. Craxi's own position was saved only by the shocking setback to the Christian Democrats. Now, paradoxically, in a position to play his final card, Craxi insisted on becoming prime minister. The Christian Democrats were in such disarray they had no choice but to agree.

At last Craxi had his chance. The determination and aggressiveness he had displayed in transforming his party, he now demonstrated in running the government. To display a capacity to cope with domestic economic problems, he faced down the Communists by cutting back the escalator clause in wage contracts while supporting the Republicans in pushing through parliament a bill reducing tax evasion. To chalk up a historic success, he signed a revised concordat with the Holy See. To give the impression of being an international leader, he visited major world capitals. He proved his soundness on Western security by easing through parliament formal approval for a new American missile system in Italy and at the same time took steps to ensure that relations with the Soviets and Eastern Europe did not deteriorate. All the while he managed to keep his five-party coalition going far beyond the normal lifetime of an Italian government and thereby provided an exceptional period of political stability.

In the end none of these achievements translated into votes for his party. In the 1984 election for the European parliament, both the Christian Democrats and the Communists advanced while the Socialists, who usually did well in European elections, made no gain. In the regional, provincial, and communal elections the following year, the Socialists registered only a meager improvement. Although the Christian Democrats allowed Craxi to remain prime minister after both elections – precisely because his premiership was worth no votes for his party – these outcomes dashed Socialist hopes that Craxi would initiate a new political era.

Italy's "Socialist problem"

Even in a period when the two major parties were on the defensive, when the number of "floating voters" was rising, and political subcultures were weakening, the Socialists had been unable to achieve an appreciable electoral advance, much less a dramatic breakthrough. Prestidigitation could win the prime ministry but it could not win votes. Craxi had presented the Italian voters an alternative and they had not accepted it. What had gone wrong?

For all its newfound unity and leadership, the party in essence had not overcome its structural weaknesses. In material terms the Socialist party was far from a negligible force and, though markedly weaker than its two rivals, was solidly established as the country's third party. Membership, which stood at 830,000 in 1946, averaged about a half-million after the early 1960s. Despite the party's working-class origin, members came from all segments of society. Around 35 percent were workers, 21 percent white-collar employees, technocrats, and managers, 13 percent farmers, and 7 percent artisans. The party enjoyed the backing of a large number of intellectual and cultural figures and most of the leading economists. It dominated one trade union, the UIL, and occupied a secondary position in another, the CGIL. Although concentrated in the North and in urban and industrial areas, its support came from every area.

Greatly magnifying its material strength was the party's pivotal position between the two main parties. With the Christian Democrats unwilling to govern at any level with the Communists and the Communists unacceptable in the national government, the Socialists were often indispensable if governments were to be formed anywhere. By 1985, for instance, they had inserted themselves into the governments of thirteen regions, seventy-nine provinces, and sixty-nine large cities. Able to throw their support in either direction when governments were formed, they had great leverage to extract benefits from their coalition partners and dexterously used this blackmail potential – in the phrase of its critics – to extract a share of positions and patronage markedly disproportionate to their electoral strength. This practice became such a dominant trait the party was gradually transmogrified into a political animal that compensated for its small body by developing a huge head with an insatiable appetite for the spoils of office, devouring an ever-larger portion of the *sottogoverno*.

Instead of forming a disciplined army determined to win the war for Socialism, most Socialist functionaries operated essentially like a band of freebooters who preferred to stay behind the lines of political battle and find an easy job with the possibility of personal profit. "They would sooner steal than govern," one of Craxi's loyal lieutenants said with typical Socialist candor and self-criticism. As a result the Socialists, for all their skill in appropriating political spoils, failed to turn the jobs and patronage to electoral advantage. Even in its historic stronghold of Milan – whose popular mayor in the early 1980s was the Socialist Carlo Tognoli – the party did not enjoy great prestige and in the 1983 national election was even outpolled by the Republicans. Nowhere did the Socialists exert themselves sufficiently to determine the course of local government and were therefore never able to transform certain cities or regions into shop windows of good Socialist administration. Moreover, there were those among the party leaders who had already positioned themselves to bring down their chief at the first sign of vulnerability, even at the cost of recommencing the party's perpetual power struggle. All this had two broad consequences. On the one hand the party lacked an effective, loyal organization from the grass roots to the top and remained in danger of slipping back into its old ways. On the other it suffered from a bad image; appearing corrupt, selfish, inefficient, and part of the mistrusted system – all descriptions used by Socialists themselves – was the sum of the party's defects.

For such reasons the party had been unable to broaden its constituency. Existing in an ideological no-man's-land between the Christian Democrats and Communists, the Socialists lacked a defined subculture or distinctive philosophy on which to build. As a party official lamented: "The Communists stand for the working class and social change; the Christian Democrats for the mother of the family and the pope; we are just a party." Indeed it was part of the Socialist ethos to be nondoctrinaire, even antidoctrinaire. Apart from the older-generation working class who were Socialist by tradition, the party's appeal therefore did not go much beyond professional and middle-class elements who were attracted by the party's liberal, secularist stance, who shared some of the social goals of the Communists and some of the economic and foreign-policy positions of the Christian Democrats but who found the ideologies of those two parties repugnant. Having been cut loose from its working-class moorings, it failed to get hold of a firm alternative support.

After nearly a decade as Socialist leader, Craxi had succeeded in transforming the Socialist party but not in transforming party politics. Too weak to replace the Christian Democrats, the Socialists remained too strong to be left out of any government; too strong to be a compliant satellite of the Christian Democrats, they remained too weak to be an equal partner. They insisted on playing at the high stakes table of politics even though they lacked the electoral chips. So there remained at the heart of the political system a continuing instability and an inherent ambiguity. In this sense the problem of the Socialists was the problem of Italy. Until it was resolved, Italian democracy would continue to be blocked by a Christian Democratic party with power but no interest in governing, a Communist party wanting to govern but with no power, and a Socialist party unable to provide an alternative.

5. The small parties: The lay forces and the extremes

The most striking change in Italian politics before and after Fascism has been the complete reversal of the dominant group. Prior to Mussolini's rise to power the liberal bourgeoisie was ascendant while the Catholics and Marxists had no part in governing. Since 1945 power has been in the hands of Catholics while the rest of the political spectrum has been dominated by the Communists and Socialists. This radical transformation was probably inevitable. The liberal, secular forces of the *risorgimento* that united Italy and governed for the next sixty years were always more a political spirit than a solid political entity. Since the country was a late industrial developer with an essentially peasant society, the middle class was small and never put down deep roots. Already in decline after the First World War, bourgeois liberalism was dealt a fatal blow with the triumph of Fascism. Though it revived after the war, time had clearly passed it by.

Any chance that an essentially nonideological formation based on old middle-class, secularist values might secure a firm foothold had depended on the Action party, formed soon after the fall of Mussolini by members of the liberal anti-Fascist resistance. This party epitomized what H. Stuart Hughes has described as "the vague and widespread longing for an Italy that would be 'purer' than the Italy of tradition." Although the party was not without its astute politicians, most *Azionisti* were high-minded intellectuals with no clear strategy for achieving their lefty ideals. Moreover, social and moral revolution was not what the Allied armies, the Christian Democrats, or the Communists had in mind after the war. By the end of 1945 the Action party collapsed and its leader, Italy's first postwar prime minister, Ferruccio Parri, was ousted by an alliance of Christian Democrats and Communists – forces far stronger, numerically and ideologically. This turn of events has generally been considered a critical one in Italy's postwar development, marking the moment when politics took on the character of doctrinal warfare between two millennial forces.

Since that time the parties of the liberal middle class tradition – the Republicans, Liberals, and Social Democrats – have eked out meager existences, averaging together in the course of the postwar elections a mere 10 percent of the vote. What modest role falls to them is based on the prestige of the traditions they embody and the simple fact that their parliamentary support is essential if a government without the Communists or neo-Fascists is to be formed. But while they have been victims of political polarization, they could also be the beneficiaries of a decline of the two dominant parties. One of the recurrent questions of Italian politics is whether the lay parties might expand and in alliance with the Socialists forge a coalition strong enough to offer an alternative to the Christian Democrats.

Little parties, big ideas

The three lay parties share a number of important traits that distinguish them from the other parties. They are all rooted in the Italian political tradition of the late nineteenth century – the Republicans looking back to Mazzini, the Liberals to Cavour, and the Social Democrats to Leonida Bissolati. Their approach to politics is pragmatic rather than ideological. Individual rights are more important to them than broad social goals. And they are, if no longer anticlerical, strongly secularist. It is because of their liberal principles and laicist approach that the three are known as lay parties.

The three stand in contrast to the other parties in additional ways. A higher proportion of their leaders and membership have been educated abroad or have personal and business links with other countries, usually America, Britain, and France. The parties are therefore more internationalist in outlook and better informed on world affairs. They are obsessive about Italy's maintaining its position as a leading industrial state and on emphasizing its Western European over its Mediterranean character. These are the parties that are automatic and unqualified proponents of European integration and Atlantic cooperation. Moreover, it is from this milieu that a fair portion of the management elite of Italy's private industry and banking world comes.

The lay parties also have one coincidental similarity. All three were dominated for much of their postwar history by a single leader – Ugo La Malfa of the Republicans, Giuseppe Saragat of the Social Democrats, and Giovanni Malagodi of the Liberals. Each built up his party and led it to its greatest success. Each also became so closely identified with his party, however, that his departure resulted in a leadership crisis that took years to resolve.

Despite their similarities, the lay parties differ substantially in their domestic policies. These differences arise primarily because their preeminent interest is economic and here their philosophy and electoral constituency diverge significantly.

For the Republicans the issue of greatest national moment is the maintenance of Italy as a technologically advanced industrial state tightly linked to northern Europe and the United States. They are therefore preoccupied with the country's economic condition and would subordinate every element of daily politics to achieving a sound economy. To forestall a politically motivated stop–go economic policy, the Republicans favor some form of long-term economic program, even though they deeply distrust government interference in the private sector. To achieve an effective incomes policy, they argue for some type of social contract with the unions and the association of the Communist party with the government's economic policies. To modernize society, they have supported legislation for land reform, divorce, abortion, and similar measures. To encourage Italians to resist their traditional self-absorption and the psychological pull of the Mediterranean, they champion any cause that will integrate Italy further into the European Community and the Atlantic Alliance.

Above all they support whatever parliamentary arrangement will produce a government strong enough to take the hard economic decisions necessary to deal with the country's structural economic problems and specifically, since the early 1970s, inflation, tax evasion, and the ever-expanding budget deficit. The Republicans were an early and enthusiastic proponent of Socialist entry into the government. With the breakdown of the center-left, they became – and remain – deeply disillusioned with the Socialists. After the Communist advance in the 1976 election, the Republicans argued that no government without Communist cooperation, if not participation, could deal with Italy's deepening economic difficulties. By 1979 they were disenchanted with the Communists in turn and since then have favored broad coalitions without them. But whatever the format of government, the Republicans have always sought for themselves one of the ministries dealing with economic affairs.

Thanks to the caliber of its leadership and the acknowledged sagacity of its economic policies, the Republicans are the most prestigious of the lay parties. Some of the country's leading entrepreneurs – Gianni Agnelli, Carlo De Benedetti, and Bruno Visentini – support the party, and Visentini succeeded La Malfa as party president in 1979. Not surprisingly, when President Alessandro Pertini in 1979 turned to a non–Christian Democrat to form a government for the first time in the postwar era, the choice fell on a

Republican, Ugo La Malfa. Although that effort failed, when the
Christian Democrats did finally agree in 1981 to give up the prime
ministry, it was to another Republican, Giovanni Spadolini. As
Italy's "economic conscience" the Republicans enjoy the support
of many technocrats, industrialists, managers, and middle-class
professionals.

Yet the respect the party enjoys has never translated into votes
and – despite historic roots in Romagna, the Marches, and Sicily –
the Republicans have astonishingly little electoral appeal. Over the
years their vote has averaged a mere 2.5 percent. The party's record
in prescribing sound economic policies and its image as a modern,
Europeanist, and Atlanticist party have nonetheless earned it a
political weight and status vastly out of proportion to its size. Anxious to exploit this prestige, the Christian Democrats have always
invited the Republicans to join its coalitions, and the Republicans
have in fact been a member of more governments than any other
party except the Christian Democrats themselves. Although the
Republicans have rarely been able to force the government to
follow the economic policies they have advocated, they take satis-
faction in having prevented worse ones.

Although they began edging toward the center at the end of the
1970s, the traditionally most conservative of the lay parties has
been the Liberals. Upon the fall of Fascism they enjoyed wide
esteem, in part because they counted among their members some
of the major figures of pre-Fascist Italy, including the country's
revered intellectual leader, Benedetto Croce, who was party president until 1947. From the start the Liberals were split, between the
old rich – southern landowners and northern entrepreneurs – and
new secularist, social reformers. In many respects they remain a
party of the late nineteenth century and therefore suffer from an
image of being both liberal and reactionary, principled and irrelevant. By instinct they are a champion of civil liberties, a critic of
church prerogatives, and a proponent of such social reforms as
divorce and abortion. But above all they are the country's foremost
advocate of a free-market economy and the zealous enemy of government regulation of the private business sector. In practice this
has made the Liberals the defenders of the rich, big business, and
large landowners, at times criticized by their own left wing for
being little more than a spokesman for the Confederation of Industry.

Increasingly the party sacrificed its liberal politics to its conservative economics. The decisive shift to the right occurred in 1954
when Malagodi was elected secretary. After that the Liberals became the most inflexible opponent of social reform and state inter-

vention. They resisted the formation of a center-left government, and in the widespread apprehension about Socialist entry into the government, the Liberals scored their greatest success in the 1963 election when they won 7 percent of the vote – 10 percent in the northern industrial cities. However, once it became clear that the center-left would not lead to the Bolshevization of Italy, support for the Liberals melted away to the point where in 1976 they barely remained in parliament, having won a mere 1 percent of the vote. Malagodi was finished, eventually replaced by the bland but more progressive and pragmatic Valerio Zanone. Under the new leadership the Liberals moved slightly leftward and in 1979 joined the government for the first time in some years. They revived their interest in civil liberties and rejuvenated the party ranks with bright young professionals. Above all Zanone led his party out of self-isolation and improved relations with the other lay parties and the Socialists in the hope of creating a strong centrist bloc between the Communists and Christian Democrats.

At the same time the Liberals were looking for a new constituency, if not a new identity. While remaining an essentially upper-middle-class party, they appealed with some success for the support of small businessmen, shopkeepers, and other self-employed persons who found appeal in the Liberal policy of maximum free enterprise and minimum government regulation. Nonetheless their modicum of electoral support remains confined to the traditional strongholds of Turin and the industrial North, and even there every decimal point has to be fought for at election time.

The largest and most ambiguous of the lay parties is the Social Democrats. An anti-Communist party of Marxist heritage, a socialist party with almost no working-class support, a conservative party born in protest, the Social Democrats have a blurred profile. The party was founded in 1947 when Giuseppe Saragat, an eminent anti-Fascist Socialist, broke with his party over its pro-Communist, pro-Soviet, and anti-American stance. During the cold war years Saragat's group, with American financial suppport, was the rallying point for further Socialist defectors but never developed into the mass party of which Saragat dreamed. Indeed, however respectable their reasons for seceding, the Social Democrats have never been able fully to shake the reputation of being a "bought" party and a "betrayer of the working class." Moreover the party suffers from an extreme case of the intellectual splits. On the one hand it retains all the traditional Marxist paraphernalia – its members addressing one another as "comrade," its policymaking body being called the "central committee," and so on. On the other hand its very existence is based on its sharp disassociation from the other parties of Marxist origin, and its policies are often to the right of the Christian Democrats. At times it treats the Communists as a mortal foe and the Christian Democrats an an eternal friend; at other times it acts as though both are enemies. But it happily joins with either in local and regional governments, even while proclaiming that the Communists are entirely unacceptable in the national government.

Although the Social Democrats are unwaveringly loyal to their European and Atlanticist principles, they are a party of little intellectual substance. Their constituency further emphasizes their amorphism. The Social Democratic voter is most often an independent artisan, a self-employed shopkeeper, a pensioner, or a low-ranking civil servant. Being of the lower middle class, he is not attracted to the Liberals; being critical of the church, he will not vote for the Christian Democrats; and being conservative, he cannot support the Socialists much less the Communists. Fashioning this electoral melange into a solid political bloc is the party's never-ending labor, and it is in large part accomplished by using public office to dispense favors for votes. The Social Democrats consequently have the reputation of being preeminently a party of patronage. Their main electoral target since the late seventies has been pensioners.

When in coalition, the party has been particularly undisciplined, never hesitating to oppose the government's policies when it thinks it can thereby earn a vote. Even the party's anti-Communism is subordinate to this clientelistic approach and is stepped up or backpeddled according to the mood of the moment. Pietro Longo, a dynamic one-time protégé of Nenni, took over the party in 1979 and has given it a good deal of zest without, however, gaining any particular success at the polls.

There is a widespread view that the Social Democrats should disappear because they have little plausible reason to exist. And in fact the party has steadily declined since 1948, when it won 7 percent of the vote, to the point where it has averaged just about half that figure in elections since the mid-seventies. The party has twice suffered from damaging scandals. In 1975 its secretary, Mario Tanassi, was indicted – and later sentenced to prison – for receiving payoffs from the Lockheed Aircraft Corporation while he was defense minister. In 1984 after it was established that he had been a member of the P2 Masonic lodge, Pietro Longo was forced to resign as budget minister. Nonetheless the frequent reports of the party's death have always proved to be exaggerated.

The influence of the three lay parties can be easily misassessed. In cold political terms they provide the Christian Democrats with a broader political base and the necessary parliamentary support to govern. In return they receive a few cabinet positions, generally of minor importance, and a little bit of patronage. Lay leaders privately acknowledge that their parties have not appreciably affected the course that Christian Democratic governments have followed. They make essentially two claims. On the one hand they have been able – in conjunction with the Socialists and Communists – to bring about such important social reforms as divorce and abortion. On the other hand they have given the Christian Democrats the impetus, support, and occasional prodding needed to keep Italy firmly linked to the European Community and NATO.

When the issue of Italian membership in the European Monetary System came to a head in late 1978, for instance, Prime Minister Andreotti tried to postpone Italy's entry as a concession to the Communists who were opposed to adherence at that time. The Republicans immediately threatened to withdraw from the government, which would have caused its collapse. Andreotti was forced to back down and Italy became a founding member of the EMS. Six years later they used a similar threat to force the Craxi government to enact tax-reform legislation. Such pressure is not always possible and not always effective. Unlike third parties in some other countries, the lay forces have no alternative party with which to form a government. They must either serve with the Christian Democrats or stay out of government. Therefore precisely because they are necessary to guarantee Italy's governability, their bargaining power is limited.

As a political force the lay parties are crippled by two disabilities. They are weakened by their own differing objectives and constituencies. And there is little place for them on the party spectrum. After 1945 they were crushed between the opposing weights of the Catholics and Marxists. To the vast majority of Italians, the lay parties seemed marginal to the great struggle taking place between Communists and Christian Democrats at home and betweeen East and West internationally. In the years that followed, the electoral strength of the middle-class parties has grown and declined – within narrow limits – as a function of the fortunes of the major parties. When disenchantment with the Christian Democrats and Communists heightened after 1979, the lay parties made steady advances in each national and local election. Even so their appeal has been limited to a small segment of society, attracted for reasons of tradition or economic interest.

Nevertheless by keeping the liberal spirit alive through the early years of the republic, the lay parties were able to contribute to the deep social and psychological changes that swept through Italy after the sixties. Eventually politics lost their ideological fervor, society was secularized, and the prevailing social mood became pragmatic and tolerant. Giulio Andreotti has recounted that Togliatti, once listening to a Republican leader's speech, whispered in Andreotti's ear: "Little parties; little ideas." In the end the laugh was on Togliatti. It has been the lay parties' values that have prevailed. Perhaps the greatest irony of postwar politics is that contemporary Italy is far more in the image and likeness of the internationalist, nonideological, modernizing, northern European, Atlanticist, and secularist ideals of the lay parties than in that of either of the two major parties. The Christian Democrats and Communists, as Giorgio Galli and Alfonso Prandi pointed out already in the sixties, "are the product of Italy yesterday rather than of Italy today. Italy's history, interpreted in terms of subcultures, is the basis of their success. The principal reason for their persistent influence is their continuous and massive organization in a society that does not encourage spontaneous, articulate pluralism."

But if the lay parties have won some of the most important political arguments, they have never won many votes. In the late seventies and early eighties there was a slight resurgence in their electoral support, particularly in the large cities of the North. As the Christian Democrats' reputation for corruption caught up with them, the Republicans and Liberals presented themselves as a force that would lead to "moral and institutional renewal." Some saw in this development the vague hope of a fundamental restructuring of Italian politics. This long-dreamed-of third force would introduce an alternation of power, genuine political competition, and other normal features of Western democracy.

A dream, however, it certainly is. The idea that Italians are waiting for a Socialist and lay-party coalition to lead them through the Red Sea of *partitocrazia,* clientelism, ineffective government, and corruption into a purified democratic promised land is an illusion. Italian politics are full of surprises, but sea changes in voting patterns are not one of them. There is no chance that these parties will become mass parties. And a government of the "Socialist and lay area," as it is known, would be inherently weak, a loose coalition of parties whose lay ideals unite them less than their practical policies divide them. The consequence would be a political scene characterized by less rather than greater stability.

The Radical cousins

Out of the lay-party tradition has come what is one of Europe's most exotic parties – the colorful, unorthodox, tumultuous, silly-serious Radicals. Founded in 1955 as a secessionist offshoot of the Liberal party following its shift to the right under Malagodi, the Radicals share with the lay parties a political outlook that is liberal, secularist, and Europeanist. Like the lay parties, they have an impact beyond their electoral strength. Also like the lay parties, they have been dominated by one man, in their case Marco Pannella. Beyond that, however, they are a unique – and in the view of the other parties a uniquely troublesome – phenomenon in Italian politics.

Originally the Radicals were a coterie of essentially upper-middle-class intellectuals who aspired to bring together the Socialists and lay parties in a centrist bloc that would take the government away from the "clericalist Christian Democrats" while keeping it out of the hands of the "totalitarian Communists." Reorganized in the early 1970s by Pannella, today's Radical party is a younger, rougher group of libertarians who are determined to replace *partitocrazia* with participatory democracy and to force reforms on a political system it regards as unwilling to respond to social change. Far too small to launch a frontal assault on an entrenched system, the Radicals have simultaneously tried to shake up the system while working through it to bring about social and political reform.

Radical aims and tactics have changed in emphasis over the years but there are a number of constants. No party ever practiced more firmly the political dictum that the cure for the ills of democracy is more democracy. Their most consistent cause has been the advancement of civil liberties and minority rights. Virtually the only opponents of the harsh law-and-order measures passed by parliament in the 1970s, they are also the strongest promoters of rights for conscientious objectors, homosexuals, feminists, and various social minorities. They played a vital role in mobilizing public opinion behind divorce and abortion legislation and in defeating the referenda to repeal those laws.

With the governing institutions in the control of the established parties, the Radicals have appealed directly to the public through mass demonstrations, sit-ins, hunger strikes, an astute use of the media, and national referenda. The referendum in particular has been regarded as a way of imbuing Italians with a sense of popular democracy. Parliamentary activity was long regarded as secondary, and only in 1976 did the Radicals enter a national election, to wide surprise winning four seats. During the late seventies the Radicals capitalized on a widespread libertarian mood among youth and made themselves a poll of attraction for nonviolent protesters and social outsiders, especially of the far left. They also appealed to floating voters, social outsiders, and a sprinkling of intellectuals and artists, such as the Sicilian writer Leonardo Sciascia. Trebling their vote – largely at Communist expense – they were the biggest winner in the 1979 election. In subsequent elections the Radicals scarcely bothered to campaign but held on to much of their support.

In parliament the Radicals proved to be both a friend and an enemy of that body. They did their best to make it a forum for genuine debate of national issues rather than a front for decisions taken in committees and party headquarters. But they also made unprecedented use of the filibuster to block legislation they opposed, leaving it difficult at times for the chamber to function.

The Radicals have disproved the common wisdom that they could not long survive, though it is not clear they have the coherence and self-discipline to maintain themselves in the longer run. Nonetheless they have already made a contribution to Italian democracy. In a country with almost no public interest groups for social causes, the party has given tens of thousands of Italians a sense of participation in the political process and offered unorthodox youth the possibility of legitimate political activity – at a time when the alternative for some might have been terrorism.

Of an entirely different order of radicalism are the left and right extremes. Italy has probably the world's richest array of political fringe groups and extremist parties, a fact that reflects the country's continuing ideological individualism and fragmentation. Some of these parties and groups are legitimate and devoted to the democratic order; others are of questionable constitutionality; still others inhabit a murky area between legal extraparliamentarism and outright subversion. Together these extremist forces collect an average of about 10 percent of the vote in any national election. Because of their ultrist positions, however, they cannot join a government on the national level. Indeed no government today could accept their support if it were necessary to survive a confidence vote or pass legislation. Hence these parties pose a twofold problem for the political system. They represent a significant bloc of the electorate that is excluded from participating in government. And some of them have fostered and perhaps participated in terrorist violence.

The far right

The extreme right finds its expression in the Italian Social Movement, MSI. This anemic reincarnation of Fascism owes its name, ideals, and leaders to the Italian Social Republic that Mussolini established in 1943 behind the German lines in the town of Salò on Lake Garda. The party has always been as much an expression of a political mood – a nostalgia for an idealized past, a protest against the present – as a concrete political movement. The Missini themselves have always been a remarkably variegated lot: republicans and monarchists, Catholics and anticlericals, conservative capitalists and radical anticapitalists, revolutionaries and corporatists, rich and poor.

Since a strategy for restoring a vanished era is not easy to map out, the party's programs have always been vague. The basic stance is that of right-wing parties everywhere: esteem for the church, the family, old social values, stringent law-and-order measures, the police, the military, and the intelligence services combined with hostility toward the unions, social minorities, civil liberties, and unconventionality in any form. All ideologies to the left of its own as well as social permissiveness, divorce, abortion, rock music, the international communist menace, and – for whatever reason – vivisection are condemned. The MSI advocates a highly centralized state with no devolution of powers to regions and a presidential rather than a parliamentary form of government. In foreign affairs it is loudly nationalistic but was for a long time internally divided between "third force" and pro-NATO groups. When parliament voted on Italian entry into NATO in 1949, the party abstained. In later years it gave ever more unambiguous support to the Atlantic Alliance and the European Community. It supported Italian adhesion to the European Monetary System in 1979 and the installation of American cruise missiles in Sicily in 1983. It has always cultivated support in the armed forces, police, and intelligence services. Several prominent military officers have sat as MSI deputies in parliament.

The important question about the neo-Fascists is whether they are loyal to the constitutional order. Formally speaking, the MSI advocates an "alternative to the system" – in the slogan of its 1973 congress. It insists that it has a strong "sense of the state" but identifies this with the nation rather than the existing institutions, which it disdains. Though never explicitly accepting the constitution, it repudiates force to alter the established form of government.

Because of its origins and ideology, the Social Movement has always been considered politically unsavory. It harked back to a regime – Mussolini's Salò republic – that fought alongside the Germans after 1943. Organized some months after the 1946 constituent assembly was elected, the party did not participate in drafting the constitution and was therefore not one of the founders of the republic. Its legitimacy has consequently always been in question in a way that was never the case with the Communists. For this reason the party's overriding strategy has been to gain acceptance by the other parties and insert itself into the political process in order to force the center of political gravity as far as possible to the right.

The party has been profoundly divided on how to go about this – a division reflecting a deep split between its wing in the North, which provides most of the leadership, and that in the South, where most of the votes come from. The northern group is radical, republican, and the more genuinely fascist; its objective is to destroy the influence of the left and create a right-wing regime. In practice it has always worked within the parliamentary system, believing that expediency dictates cooperating with – and conditioning – the Christian Democrats. A radical element, however, has favored a militant course that would give the political system a forceful shove toward a resurrected fascist state. With the ultras in this group, that push is to be an actual physical one. These have been the street agitators and leaders of various paramilitary and other extremist groups – notably Guiseppe Rauti's New Order – that have operated somewhere between legality and clandestinity, between harmless fantasy and terrorist violence.

The southern wing is an assembly of reactionaries, outsiders, social malcontents, ex-monarchists, and lower-middle-class white collar workers, in large part linked by the age-old southern feeling of neglect and mistreatment by a "northern" government. It wants social order, discipline, and the preservation of "old social values."

For two decades, from 1950 to 1969, the MSI followed a moderate course. It created an organization similar to that of the other parties, developed a form of right-wing subculture – with a party newspaper, *Il Secolo d'Italia;* its own professional and student organizations; and even a trade union, CISNAL – and generally sought to create an impression of democratic respectability. For the radical wing of the party this course was so much weak-willed temporizing and in 1956 some extremists, led by Rauti, pulled out.

With De Gasperi and their parliamentary majority gone after 1953, the Christian Democrats accepted discreet neo-Fascist support and in return brought the party into a number of local governments. Already in 1947 the Christian Democrats used MSI votes to keep the Communists out of the Rome city government. Then through the fifties they accepted the party's backing in the national parliament to prop up several governments. Even after the Tambroni government, which was based on open MSI parliamentary support, collapsed in violence and killing, they accepted, indeed sought, neo-Fascist votes to secure the election of their presidential candidates, Segni in 1962 and Leone in 1971.

Clearly the Christian Democrats tried to play a double game with the MSI. Until the way was open to a center-left government in 1963, they had little choice but to accept its support, embarrassing though this was. But they have always been frightened of losing votes to it. Their concern was such that in 1951 the government tabled a bill to outlaw the Social Movement on the ground that it was Fascist and therefore fell under the constitutional ban on a reestablished Fascist party. Although parliament passed the statute – known as the "Scelba law" for the name of the interior minister who drafted it – successive governments never enforced it, despite occasional appeals of the left parties and former resistance groups. For the Christian Democrats the threat of dissolution made it possible to use the MSI while keeping it under some control.

Once the taboo against the center-left was broken, the Christian Democrats no longer needed the Social Movement's parliamentary support. The MSI was relegated to the sideline and its objective ever since has been to get back in the political game. In 1969 the party's radical wing took over, with Giorgio Almirante, a secondary official in the Salò Republic and the party's initial secretary, at the head. Almirante pursued a dual tactic: overt democratic respectability and covert encouragement of what came to be known as "a strategy of tension." To unite and revivify the far right he brought about a merger with the declining Monarchist party. In parliament the MSI generally supported the foreign policy of successive governments while posing as the true democratic opposition on domestic issues. The party also cleverly exploited the conservative backlash that followed the student and worker unrest of the late sixties, winning notable electoral successes on the local level in 1971 and nationally a year later.

At the same time, Almirante reintegrated hotheads like Rauti – whose views he generally espoused – and allowed them to take to the streets. The party engaged in public agitation and exploited social unrest, most notably the riots that broke out in the South in 1970. It is not clear whether the party was also involved in the acts of right-wing terrorism that occurred throughout the seventies. Party leaders categorically disclaimed any association with terrorists and denounced the killings of those years as playing into the hands of the Communists. But the party was widely perceived as at least sympathetic to the extreme right's efforts to destabilize the country. Moreover, some of the party's prominent parliamentarians were men suspected of plotting against the state.

The MSI vote has fluctuated around 5 percent, with a high of nearly 9 percent in 1972. Support is centered in Rome, Naples, and Sicily and comprises surviving old Fascists, lower-middle-class shopkeepers and artisans, and a sprinkling of bureaucrats, police, and military. They vote for the MSI for various reasons – as a protest to whatever is especially unpopular at the moment; in nostalgia for a simpler, more orderly, and hierarchic society; out of disgust with party and parliamentary "games"; because of southern resentment of the North; and simply in support for traditional right-wing causes. That much of this electorate wants to bring about anything like a revived Fascist regime is extremely doubtful.

Suspicion of the MSI has gradually receded. The party's ever more insistent denunciations of violence have gained credibility, and its rejection of "the system" has come to be regarded as rhetorical routine. Not long after becoming prime minister in 1983, Craxi met with neo-Fascist leaders, and his office later issued a statement regretting the "ghettoization" of the party. The following year, high-level representatives of the Christian Democratic, Liberal, and Social Democratic parties for the first time attended the MSI party congress. In 1985 the party was given one position on the board of directors of the state radio and television network (RAI). With these symbolic steps the party was emerging from its long isolation.

The far left

For about ten years, beginning around 1968, a self-styled revolutionary left was a prominent feature of the Italian political scene. In its original form it was a product of the wave of ideological radicalism that swept intellectual, academic, and professional circles in Western Europe and the United States in the late sixties. The ferment hit Italy with particularly strong and lasting force, taking shape in a wide variety of miniparties, groups, and movements that had one theme in common: the Communist party had abandoned its original principles and become a component of the established order, a bulwark of the status quo. Drawing on heroes as varied as

Marx, Lenin, Mao, Theodor Adorno, Herbert Marcuse, and "Che" Guevara, they established a "new left" to the left of the Communists from which they would launch their assault on the social system.

One of these groups was Manifesto, a circle of Communist intellectuals who were expelled from their parent party after criticizing it for having turned its back on the class struggle. Another was Continuous Struggle, a movement of students and other youth who, radicalized by the turmoil of 1968 and 1969, felt repelled by the consumer society and wanted to replace it with a new egalitarian order. It was always more free thinking than serious acting, but for a time was a not insignificant force among some young people. In addition there were a number of groups that wanted to encourage greater class consciousness and political activity among workers. These included the Political Movement of Workers, a tiny left Catholic group, and Workers' Vanguard, a small "revolutionary" Marxist-Leninist group. At the same time there grew up a variety of other Marxist-Leninist parties as well as anarchist, Trotskyist, and Maoist groups. The most serious and radical of all was Workers' Power, particularly strong in the Fiat works in Turin, which called for the destruction not only of capitalism but – harking back to an old radical Italian idea – of work itself. It endeavored to be the spearhead of a workers' movement and regarded terrorism in some circumstances to be legitimate.

These extreme groups were the "sects" of the Italian political system. Like their religious counterparts, they were characterized by deep individual commitment, ideological fanaticism, exclusiveness, alienation from the prevailing culture, and hostility toward established institutions. And, as with sects, expulsions and secessions were continual. Consequently the groups had a tendency to divide and subdivide. Their identity, leadership, and names were in a state of nearly constant change. In doctrine and practice they shaded by imperceptible degree from orthodox Marxism to extraparliamentarism, from advocates of peaceful change to practicioners of revolutionary violence. But, again as in the case of dissident religious movements, most of them eventually conformed. After initially rejecting the established political institutions, they joined the system – participating in elections, sitting in parliament, and, along with the other parties, accepting the funds that are allocated by the state to the parties. After proposing revolution, they agitated for reform. After each going its own way, they began seeking unity.

The most notable step in this direction occurred in 1974 with the formation of the Party of Proletarian Unity (PdUP). This brought together the Manifesto group, the Proletarian Movement of Workers, and those remnants of the old Socialist party of Proletarian Unity. Although PdUP failed to integrate large parts of the far left, it became the most significant party in this area of the political spectrum. The greatest success in bringing the far left together occurred at the 1976 election when all of them, except Workers' Power, formed an electoral federation that was poised, so they thought, to win 1 million votes and, with resurgent Communist and Socialist parties, throw out the Christian Democrats and bring the entire left to power. In the event this slate won only a half-million votes and sent a mere six deputies into the chamber. The defeat was one from which the far left never recovered.

Two subsequent developments finished it off. One was the "movement of '77," a highly amorphous group of students and young people who reenacted briefly but violently the student and youth revolt of the previous decade. They represented a spontaneous, unorganized revolt against society by unemployed, alienated, and angry youth. They were nonpolitical, not to say antipolitical, and so far as their underlying sentiment can be defined, it was one of searching for personal fulfillment. The basis of its ideology and its vocabulary was "liberation"; its mouthpiece was the daily newspaper *Lotta Continua;* its novel was *Porci con le ali* (Pigs with wings). At an early stage a violent, armed element developed. During March and April 1977 open street battles exploded in Rome and Bologna. The agitation of that year took place outside, indeed against the parties of the left, in particular the Communists. It marked a significant break with the orthodox left by young people, many of whom went over to the Radicals. The other development was the increase in left terrorism. That had the effect of exposing the emptiness of the extreme left's claim of being revolutionary and, in causing a revulsion to violence, forced these groups to the right.

The far left has failed to achieve almost any goal it set for itself. After all the slogans were shouted and all the demonstrations organized, not only was there no revolution but society remained untransformed, alienated groups were no more integrated or more liberated, workers' political consciousness was unraised, and the universities were in a shambles. Their doctrinal objective was to improve the conditions of the workers. But these groups had so few contacts with the workers they did not even know that the working class of their theories had largely vanished years earlier. The far left was engaged in an intellectual not a class struggle and its weapons were words and slogans. Once terrorism began, it renounced the legitimacy of violence and thereby surrendered its revolutionary militancy.

The ultraleft is consequently a moribund political force. Continuous Struggle was dissolved in 1977 and its eponymous newspaper, *Lotta Continua,* was closed down some years later. PdUP was for a time a satellite of the Communist party and in 1984 amalgamated with it. Proletarian Democracy created in 1978 in the illusory hope of unifying the extreme left, is the sole party from this area with representation in parliament. It is a movement of young militants, some devoted to working-class causes, others to ecology and pacifism. Workers' Power was long ago transformed into Workers' Autonomy, the only remaining revolutionary movement but itself decapitated when Antonio Negri and its leaders were arrested in 1979. All the others are little more than political clubs or organizations whose political aim appears to be little more than covering walls with posters and graffiti.

The extreme left has not been without its value, even if that value is more social than political. These organizations gave shape to radical sentiments, offering alienated youth a way to express their aspirations and to participate in the country's political life. Altogether they raised a challenge to prevailing values and institutions and provided young people an alternative to terrorism. Their demise marked the death of the ideal of social revolution in Italy.

6. Parliament, prime minister, and president

Although an Italian government remained juridically intact both with the ouster of Mussolini in 1943 and throughout the American and British occupation, it was not until 1946 that political leaders could come to grips with the task of giving shape to the postwar state. In June of that year Italian electors, who now for the first time included women, were summoned to vote on two important issues. One was a referendum on whether to maintain the monarchy. In this, 54 percent of the voters favored a republic. Despite a strong majority for the monarchy in the South and the existence of a Monarchist party there for many years, royalist sentiment evaporated almost immediately. The other issue was the election of an assembly to draft a new constitution. The voting produced a modest majority for parties of the center and right. But no single group dominated the drafting sessions and even in the face of the deepening cleavage at the time between the Communists and Christian Democrats, the final document represented a broad consensus and was approved by virtually all delegates except the Monarchists. It went into effect on the first day of January 1948.

The constitution created governing institutions essentially along the lines of orthodox parliamentary democracy. In their eagerness to erect barriers against the possible rise of another dictatorship, however, the drafters circumscribed these institutions with a variety of checks. In novel departures from Italian constitutional tradition, they provided for a devolution of a measure of central authority to nineteen proposed regions, for referenda to repeal laws, and for a Constitutional Court to review the constitutionality of legislation and government actions. Further to strengthen the concept of a government of laws rather than men, the constitution was made difficult to amend, the judicial system was given complete independence, and a full list of civil liberties was guaranteed.

One of the constitution's unusual features is its elaborate catalog of social and economic rights. These provisions were a concession by conservatives to the left for the social revolution that did not take place after the fall of Fascism. Some of the prerogatives are practical and enforceable – as the right to form unions and hold strikes. Others are utopian and hortatory – as the right of every individual not simply to a job but to "recompense proportionate to the quantity and quality of his work and in any case adequate to the needs of a free and dignified existence for himself and his family." This sort of idealism is reinforced by the very first article of the constitution, which declares with solemn meaninglessness that "Italy is a democratic republic founded on labor." In agreeing to such clauses, the left gambled on winning control of parliament and then turning the vague principles into laws; the right on winning and keeping them rhetorical. The immediate effect, in any case, as the eminent constitutionalist Piero Calamandrei maintained at the time, was to devalue the entire document in the eyes of the Italian people.

A more serious defect is the incompatibility between the liberal rights guaranteed in the constitution and the repressive clauses of the civil and criminal codes of the Fascists, which were left in force. This problem was compounded by the assembly's decision to incorporate into the constitution the 1929 concordat without any amendments that would make it consistent with the letter and spirit of the new constitution. The resulting legal tangles placed a burden on the courts that has never been fully removed.

All in all the Italian people were given a constitution that was based on good intentions and fine ideals but that left the country with weak governing institutions, unclear and dispersed political authority, and a patchwork of incompatible laws. With proper nurturing the new state might have strengthened itself. However, the Italian republic was dominated at its birth by two groups – Catholics and Communists – which lacked a sense of the state in the normal Western tradition. Their point of reference was well caught in the pronouncement, "It is above all the party that counts!" Thus spake, not Togliatti, but Aldo Moro at the 1962 Christian Democratic congress. The effect of this approach on the functioning of the Italian republic during its first ten years has been traced with great lucidity by Giorgio Galli and Alfonso Prandi in *Patterns of Political Participation in Italy*. The authors point out that although the Christian Democrats and Communists gave lip service to the central role of parliament, for instance, they in fact saw its purpose merely "as that of sanctioning a political will of the people that is formed outside of parliament." And, as they further observe, "the task of evoking, articulating, and enforcing that will" is clearly reserved to the party rather than to parliament.

The two leading parties therefore envisaged governing institutions not as bodies with an inherent autonomy and integrity but as instruments to be manipulated or ignored by the parties as their interests dictated. The Communists at first calculated that this could best be achieved by a strongly centralized system with no devolution of power to regions; the Christian Democrats took the opposite position. Once the latter won an absolute parliamentary majority, the two parties reversed their stands. At that point the Christian Democrats had no scruples in exploiting state institutions for their own purposes. They took advantage of their parliamentary majority to pass legislation – called the "swindle law" by its opponents – which was designed to give them a disproportionate share of parliamentary seats in future elections. The constitutional innovations that would reduce the parties' powers – the provisions for regions, referenda, an independent judiciary, and judicial review – they refused to implement as long as possible. On losing control of parliament in 1953, they shifted the focus of power away from the governing institutions and into the *sottogoverno*. Therefore from the outset of the republic and throughout its formative years, the principle of party supremacy was established as the controlling dynamic of the Italian political system. Italy consequently emerged as the Western world's leading example of *partitocrazia* – a fact evident from then to now in the day-to-day functioning of the institutions of government.

The parliamentary sideshow

By the terms of the constitution, parliament is the strongest organ of the state. It has authority to pass laws, ratify treaties, and amend the constitution. It elects the president and has ultimate control over the government through votes of confidence and the right to impeach the president and cabinet ministers. It elects one-third of the members of the Constitutional Court and the Superior Judicial Council. It sets its own rules and may meet as briefly or as long as it wants, providing it convenes twice a year.

But anyone who sits as an observer in the gallery of the Chamber of Deputies or the Senate quickly becomes aware that something is amiss. Even on those relatively rare occasions when parliament meets in plenary session – to debate a new government's program, important legislation, or some major public controversy – the houses do not then come to life as forums for genuine deliberation or as arenas where issues of national importance are settled. Instead the prime minister and the party spokesmen deliberately avoid blunt talk and do their best to evade an open clash. Extemporaneous exchanges, the essence of good parliamentary debate, are rare.

To put forward some novel or unexpected proposal is treated as a betrayal of unwritten parliamentary rules. Palazzo Montecitorio, the site of the Chamber, and Palazzo Madama, the home of the Senate, are useful places to make contacts and conduct informal business. But it is unmistakably apparent that decisions are being taken elsewhere and that parliament's primacy is a fiction.

This fact is most glaring in the fall of governments. Formally speaking, the prime minister and his cabinet are dependent on the confidence of the two houses; they need their approval to take office and must resign when they lose their support. In practice, however, few governments ever fall as a consequence of a parliamentary vote of no confidence. Rather they collapse when one party withdraws its support from the government. At that point a no-confidence vote on the floor of parliament is regarded as not only superfluous but an undesirable overdramatization of differences, making the formation of a new government – most likely with the same parties – more difficult. So the prime minister, without awaiting or seeking a formal no-confidence vote, goes directly to the Quirinale to turn in his resignation to the president of the republic.

The reason a party withdraws its support from a government has nothing to do with the stated aims of the government or parliament's failure to carry out the agreed program. Rather it reflects a party's decision that its partisan interests are no longer served by allowing the government to continue. Or it can result from a shift in the power balance within the Christian Democratic party; the governments of De Gasperi in 1953, Moro in 1964 and 1966, Rumor in 1970, Andreotti in 1973, and Cossiga in 1980 all came to an end for this reason. Once a government falls it normally takes about six weeks to organize a new one, though in 1979 the process stretched out over five months. During the entire period, parliamentary activity comes to an effective halt.

Parliament has developed little sense of institutional autonomy. Most deputies and senators think of themselves as party functionaries first and parliamentarians second. Party headquarters reinforces this attitude by treating a seat in parliament as something to be offered as a reward for loyal service or to be taken away if the party decides to place the incumbent in some other position. Deputies are therefore liable to be moved from the Chamber to the Senate or out of Rome to a position in local government. The wishes of the parliamentarian or his constituents count for nothing. This practice is particularly marked in the case of Communist backbenchers, who are rotated precisely to prevent their developing a separate parliamentary identity. Although Communist leaders sit in parliament, which they regard as a useful platform for debates of national issues, it is their party position that is all-important; symptomatically Pietro Ingrao, the first Communist to be president of the Chamber of Deputies, decided after one legislative period to return to the party apparatus. It is in this sense that Giuseppe Di Palma speaks of the Communist party's "limited parliamentarism."

At every turn party bureaucracies keep parliamentarians, individually and collectively, reined in. Decisions that would be thought to belong to members of parliament – such as the selection of the leaders of the party groups in the Chamber and Senate and the designation of members and chairmen of parliamentary committees – are taken by party chiefs. Any display of autonomy is rare and is always suppressed. The Communist party's expulsion of the Manifesto group is a famous case. Another is the effective neutralization by Christian Democratic leaders of the so-called Group of One Hundred, a centumvirate of young, conservative Christian Democratic deputies formed in 1978 to resist their party's cooperation with the Communists. It was also symptomatic that a law passed in 1974 providing public financing for the parties – ostensibly to put an end to the growing scandal of political bribes and payoffs by business firms – was administered in such a way that the funds were channeled not directly to candidates for parliament – since that would have allowed them a measure of independence of the party machine – but to party headquarters, which dispensed the monies according to their own designs.

Parliamentary organization

Yet in investing popular sovereignty in parliament, the drafters of the constitution clearly wanted a legislative body of real authority and gave careful thought to its structure. Originally the Christian Democrats favored an upper house organized along corporatist lines while the Communists pressed for a single chamber in keeping with their desire for a strongly centralized government. Discredited by the Fascists, the Christian Democrats' model was not widely acceptable, while a unicameral parliament risked too stark a break with tradition. So an unhappy compromise was reached on a bicameral parliament with a Chamber of Deputies and a Senate with identical powers. The Chamber has 630 members, the Senate 315; both deputies and senators are elected for five years.

The establishment of legislative bodies with coequal authority and identical functions was criticized from the start, and there has been recurrent talk of either transforming the Senate or abolishing it. In the 1970s, when regional government was being instituted, some consideration was given to turning the Senate into a body representing the regions. Nothing came of the idea. The work of the two houses therefore overlaps and since there are no joint coordinating committees, the resultant duplication complicates and slows the legislative process. A law passed in one house and amended, however slightly, in the other must be reenacted ab initio.

What differences exist between the two bodies are minor. The voting age for the Chamber is eighteen, for the Senate twenty-five. Deputies must be at least twenty-five years old and senators forty. Electoral constituencies for the two houses are divided differently and since direct election to the Senate requires a 60 percent majority of the vote, almost all senators are elected through a special proportional representation system. In daily politics the Chamber is decidedly the more active and important body. It is there where the party secretaries and almost all party leaders sit and normally where the authoritative position of the parties is enunciated. It is also there where the younger and more ambitious politicians go.

The Senate, reincarnating somewhat the tone of the prerepublican body whose members were appointed by the monarch, is more honorific and includes among its members prestigious senators-for-life – all former presidents of the republic and five eminent persons, such as leaders in cultural, intellectual, or some area of public life, who may be chosen by each head of state. The atmosphere in the Senate is appropriately somnolent. Yet its president ranks just after the president of the republic in precedence and becomes acting chief of state in the case of the latter's incapacitation, death, or resignation. Only four prime ministers have come out of that body: Adone Zoli, Giovanni Leone, Giovanni Spadolini, and Amintore Fanfani.

Italian parliamentary procedure follows two unusual practices. One is the requirement that the final vote on all legislation before the whole house must be secret. Although this rule theoretically offers a way for backbenchers to vote their conscience on controversial legislation, it is in practice used as a way of surreptitiously subverting a government of which their party is a member. One of the main weaknesses of every government is its inability to count on the support of its own parliamentary majority. Defectors repeatedly take governments to the brink and on several occasions – the

Cossiga government of 1980 is a late example – have pushed them over.

The other and more important anomaly is the authority of committees to legislate on behalf of the whole house. As a consequence the fulcrum of parliamentary life has been shifted from the floor of parliament to the committees, where most legislation is enacted. This procedure makes the passage of bills easier but, in removing deliberations and decisions from public gaze, weakens parliament's already thin ties to the electorate.

The Chamber has fourteen permanent committees, the Senate twelve. Committees are organized to parallel government ministries or groups of ministries. In handling legislation the committees act in an advisory, or a drafting, or a legislative capacity. It is the president of the house who divides the work among the committees and decides in which manner the committee is to act. It is the president's further prerogative to decide whether a matter should be handled in committee or by the whole house, though issues relating to the constitution, voting rights, international agreements, and the budget must be dealt with in plenary session. The president also fixes the parliamentary agenda in consultation with the committee chairmen.

Parliament's performance

Even though the Chamber and Senate are outside the center of real political power, most Italian experts find that on balance parliament has performed as well as circumstances have allowed. They point to legislation on such difficult social issues as labor relations, divorce, abortion, the family, university reform, a national health service, and rent control. Moreover, parliament offers a site where the country's manifold regional, social, and other interests can be articulated and discussed. It is the focal point of the debate of important national issues. And it provides the principal means by which political outsiders – the Communists, neo-Fascists, and fringe parties – play a role in the state and participate in the operations of the political system.

The failures have not primarily been failures of parliament as an institution. With no effective autonomy, the Chamber and Senate can do no more than the governing parties permit. And the parties, divided internally and among themselves, are rarely able to compose their own differences to the point where they can deal with any but the most pressing issues. Existing statutes that cry out for revision remain unamended. The Fascist penal code has never been fully replaced and leaves on the books a number of extraordinarily obsolete and repressive provisions. The rules for the customs police have not been substantially amended since the 1890s. Activities that urgently need regulation are untouched. Countless examples could be cited where an acute need for reforms, guidelines, or new legislation has been ignored. By and large parliament has been able to act on tough issues only when there is massive social pressure and a correspondingly broad parliamentary majority. In cases such as divorce and abortion the ad hoc coalition included the Communists and excluded the governing Christian Democrats.

In terms of quantity, however, the Chamber and Senate have produced a flood of legislation that generally well surpasses the output of other Western European parliaments and the American congress. Between 1953 and 1957, for instance, the Chamber and Senate approved over 2,000 statutes; in approximately the same period the German parliament passed roughly 500. Behind this remarkable record lie a number of important features of Italian parliamentarism. One is that matters handled by administrative action in other countries are turned into formal statutes. Another lies in the power of committees; having authority to legislate, two dozen persons sitting around a conference table are able to resolve differences and exchange favors more easily than hundreds of persons meeting in plenary session. A third consideration is that members of parliament have an unrestricted right to introduce legislation. It is a privilege that parliamentarians of all major parties make full use of, and in each legislative period thousands of private member bills are put forward. Heavily involved in patronage, legislation of this sort is more discreetly handled in committee than in full session. As a result, if legislation is neither significant nor controversial, it is almost sure of enactment. But the product tends to be narrow in scope, clientelistic in nature, and fragmented in its treatment of national problems. From 1948 to 1976 no less than three and in some legislative periods four times more legislation was passed in committee than on the floor of parliament. Since then the proportions have almost evened out – as many special-interest matters have passed to the regions – but a slight majority of legislation still comes from committees.

That quality has been sacrificed for quantity is evident when the content of the legislation is examined. The great majority of these statutes concerns matters of such slight importance that they are known as *leggine*, "little laws." In a study of parliament, Giuseppe Di Palma took a careful look at these *leggine* and found that a high proportion of them was devoted to bettering the condition of government employees. Fully 37 percent of the legislative proposals between 1963 and 1972, for example, concerned financial and career benefits for the civil service or dealt with civil-service regulations and related legal matters. Other *leggine* were similarly clientelistic in nature and trivial in substance. Since the early 1970s, the number of *leggine* has declined – in part because regional governments now deal with some of these matters, in part because the issues are encompassed in major statutes and in part because of stricter parliamentary control over money matters. For most of its existence, however, parliament has distinguished itself by producing masses of trivial statutes. Indeed, a marked feature of Italy's institutional crisis, Sidney Tarrow has pointed out, is "a Parliament that is inundated with thousands of private member bills but becomes paralyzed when faced with major programmatic legislation. . . ."

As a way of asserting a measure of autonomy, parliament has become increasingly recalcitrant, with the result that the tempo and outcome of the legislative process have been more and more beyond executive control. Since the mid-1970s the secret vote, the filibuster, and mass absenteeism have slowed or stopped parliamentary activity for long periods and have wrought havoc with the government's legislative program. Relations between parliament and the executive have consequently developed into a serious problem. A constitutional lawyer, Andrea Manzella, commented ruefully of his experience as Prime Minister Spadolini's *chef de cabinet:* "No modern parliament raises so many negative conditions for a government; no government is weaker in parliament than the Italian." He meant, more concretely, that the executive has no way of knowing how much time will be consumed in getting a legislative proposal through parliament and lacks the authority or sanctions to cajole or force parliament to act.

The sum result is a parliament whose operations are obstructed by the parties and that in turn obstructs the executive authorities. As a consequence prime ministers have more and more relied on decrees to govern. According to the constitution, decrees may be issued only in an emergency and must be enacted into law within sixty days. For more than two decades resort to this right was never made. Then in 1970 it was discovered that issuing a decree was a way of forcing parliament's hand, putting it under pressure to act before the sixty-day limit expired. Sixty-nine decrees were issued in the following two years. In subsequent legislative periods their number rose – to 124 between 1972 and 1976, 167 between 1976 and 1979, and 274 between 1979 and 1983. As early as 1978 President Pertini, though new in office, was sufficiently alarmed by this escalation to dispatch a letter to Prime Minister Andreotti in effect protesting the drastic overuse of a constitutional instrument intended for use only in exceptional circumstances.

The reliance on decrees shows that the triangular relationship – parties – parliament – government – is on the whole deteriorating. By the 1980s even the palliative of decrees was losing effectiveness. Of the executive's 124 decrees during the sixth legislative period, 100 were eventually enacted into law; of the 167 during the seventh, only 136; and of the 274 during the eighth, merely 189. Parliamentary critics are concerned not only by the number of decrees, their incongruity with the constitution, and their derogation from parliament's prerogative but also by the quality of the legislation that results when parliament has a political pistol held at its head.

Turning from legislation to parliament's other function – oversight of executive actions – the record is not impressive, despite efforts to improve it. The right of members to question the government or a specific minister in plenary session or in committee is employed often enough but without real effect. Although parliament's budget authority provides ultimate control over the administrative apparatus, no attempt is made to use this power. However, there has been a conscious effort to extend parliament's influence in other ways. Oversight of the state radio and television was established in 1975. When the intelligence services were restructured in 1977, parliament was given certain controls over their operations and the prime minister was required to submit a biannual report on their activities, with a special committee having the right to demand supplementary information. The budget committee was given responsibility in 1979 to assess the suitability of nominees to top positions in the state business enterprises. As far as can be judged, in none of these cases has parliamentary oversight been aggressively pursued or effective in its results.

Parliamentary commissions to study important national problems have existed almost as long as parliament. The mafia commissions are famous, and in the 1970s and 1980s there were major inquiries into such questions as the kidnapping of Aldo Moro, the activities of the international banker, Michele Sindona, and the P2 Masonic lodge. In most cases the hearings go on for years but in the end produce more bickering among the political parties than light on the mysteries. In 1971 a new type of parliamentary investigation was instituted. Modeled to some extent on the hearings of the

American congress, they are closed sessions in which nonparliamentary experts testify on topical issues. They have proved useful in providing specialized information for use in preparing legislation.

Return to *trasformismo*

Behind parliament's malfunctioning lies a deeper problem. The principle of responsible government and loyal opposition – an underlying ideal of parliamentary democracy – has never really existed in Italy. It did not exist before, during, or in the early years after Fascism. Once the Christian Democrats won their parliamentary majority in 1948 and went on to fasten a grip on the country's political and economic life, the other parties reasoned that the only chance of playing a role and of gaining access to the patronage of the *sottogoverno* was to abandon the opposition and join the government. Since the outset of the republic, therefore, the way to power has not been through the dialectic of opposition-winning-governing but of cooptation-cooperation-coalition.

What opposition has existed – the Communists and neo-Fascists – has not been considered loyal and for its part has not wanted to oppose. The Communists may have bitterly attacked the government's foreign, security, and European integration policies, but they were profoundly anguished on being expelled from the government in 1947 and wanted nothing more than to be readmitted. With this out of the question, they calculated that their only possibility of influencing the country's political life was to play a role in parliament and in the regions. They thereupon propounded the concept of "parliamentary centrality." This did not mean that they regarded the Chamber and Senate in Westminsterian terms but rather as stepping-stones to legitimacy and power. Collaboration was the keynote. And so there quickly developed a type of parliamentary government that one expert on the constitution, Valerio Onida, has called "an alliance of imperfect consociation" – or what might less elegantly be described as collaborative back scratching. Eventually three-quarters of the government's legislative program was being approved with Communist votes. Even between 1948 and 1953, when the Christian Democrats and Communists were engaged in outright ideological warfare, proposals tabled in committee by the Christian Democrats and their allies received Communist approval in 70 percent of the cases, a figure that later exceeded 90 percent. By the same token the government parties helped to pass a fair number of Communist private member bills. In this manner both government and opposition submerged their ideological differences to assist one another in cultivating their respective constituencies.

Over time, even the substantive differences between the left and the Christian Democrats steadily diminished. By 1963 the Socialists had moved from illegitimacy to government without ever going through the intervening stage of loyal opposition. The apotheosis of this mode of parliamentarism was reached with the special relationship that developed between the Christian Democrats and Communists from 1976 and 1979. Although no formal coalition was possible, the Communists were given an important institutional role in parliament while the Christian Democrats treated them almost as a coalition partner – altering policies, working out legislative compromises, and coordinating programs. As a consequence the separation of government and opposition – apart from the right and left fringes – broke down completely in those years. "What we see in Italy today," Sidney Tarrow wrote at the time, "is a progressive decline of opposition – not the decline of *the* opposition, for the PCI is stronger than ever organizationally – but a decline in the level of dialogue, both between government and opposition and between the summit and the base, that is the hallmark of classical parliamentary democracy."

The announced aim of this cooperation was the establishment of a government strong enough to adopt the unpopular economic measures necessary to cope with the country's economic crisis. But in examining the two Andreotti governments of that period Franco Cazzola, concluded that, despite some improvement in the control of the legislative process, they had nothing more to show in the end than had their predecessors. Gianfranco Pasquino was even more critical, finding that instead of contributing to a dynamic capacity of the government to reach decisions, the sharing of power had the reverse effect. Andreotti himself in later years claimed only that during those two terms inflation had been checked, the balance of payments had improved, and the public debt had been slightly reduced. He did not mention that the Bank of Italy had been responsible for the financial improvements, that the major economic program of those years, the Pandolfi plan, had never gotten off the ground, and that abortion legislation and several other laws had been enacted only under the threat of a national referendum.

Viewed in the perspective of the first four postwar decades, the line between a government that governs and an opposition that opposes has been ever more blurred. To this extent contemporary Italian parliamentarism has reverted to a form of the old practice of *trasformismo,* with opposition parties being enticed into the governing system and governments being constructed out of various combinations of them. For the Christian Democrats this mode of governing has been a perfect recipe for holding on to power. By maintaining themselves as sole mediator between the parties, they have made themselves the pivot of the governing system. To keep the arrangement going they have had to share more positions, patronage, and power. But whatever the shifts and changes in the electoral strength, they remain at the center of any coalition that is formed.

This republican form of *trasformismo* has had the advantage of generating governments well calibrated to the political mood of the moment and the balance of power within and among the parties. But because the majority cannot or will not govern without the acquiescence of the minority, Italy moves only when there is massive consensus – sometimes quantified as around 80 percent of the parliamentary forces. With an inhibited government and a toothless opposition, the Italian political system lacks that vital propulsion, that indispensable dialectic that lifts a country's government from the minimum level of action necessary for the country's survival to a plane where it can lead, innovate, and deal with social and economic problems. This is the situation Italian politicians have in mind when they contend that Italy has never actually been governed in the whole of the postwar period.

Weak executive

In almost all European democracies the power of the prime minister and the cabinet has steadily grown as the executive has absorbed more and more of parliament's authority, leading to a system sometimes labeled prime ministerial dictatorship. Not so in Italy. Here parliament's debility is matched by the government's weakness. The reasons for this are both political and institutional.

In practical terms the executive must spend as much time in partisan power struggles as in directing the country's affairs. Since the foundation of every government rests on the shifting sands of coalition politics, prime ministers must above all devote themselves to holding together the political base of the government. The average life span of the forty-odd governments since 1948 has been about ten months. The longest was Moro's third government, which lasted 833 days; the shortest was Andreotti's first, which fell after 9. Until a new government is formed – a process generally lasting around six weeks – the old government remains in caretaker status and can do no more than tend to the most urgent matters.

The difficulty of forming a solid governing bloc is due to the fact that five of the ten parties represented in parliament – and most notably the Communists and neo-Fascists – are excluded from governing. With the other five occupying the same center ground, they are therefore in competition for essentially the same electorate. As a result the coalition partners are in a state of continuous warfare among one another for electoral advantage. With communal, provincial, regional, national, European, or presidential elections usually around the corner, tensions steadily grow.

Hence a government is based on nothing more than a delicate truce. The truce itself is in constant peril since each party exploits the day-to-day issues for its own advantage. Occasionally partisan interests coincide, and then the government can govern and the legislature can legislate. But more often than not the junior partners of a government see greater electoral advantage in causing the prime minister and his government to fail than in helping him to succeed.

There is a fairly precise rhythm in the rise and fall of the average Italian government. As soon as installed, it finds itself embroiled in disputes that extend from economic and social policies to passionate quarrels over patronage positions in the *sottogoverno*. These disputes lead in turn to personal and professional squabbles among cabinet ministers that acquire political substance in themselves. By the third or fourth month the government finds that its proposals are being defeated in parliament as discord among coalition partners breaks into open feuding. Time is gained by a decree law covering some especially troublesome issue. Or a vote of confidence is put down that brings the bickering to a temporary halt. By the seventh or eighth month the range of disagreements and resentments has reached the explosion point. At that stage one or more of the coalition partners initiates a crisis by attacking the government in the press, by sniping in parliament, or by obstruction in the cabinet. Then any symbolic issue is seized on to precipitate a collapse of the truce – and the fall of the government. Such is the normal life cycle of a government.

The problem is compounded by the extraordinary weakness of the prime minister himself. In other parliamentary democracies the head of the government is normally the person who is the acknowledged head of the party and its leader at election time – someone who possesses substantial personal political power. In Italy he is rarely the strongest man in his party and can never claim to have the weight of the electorate behind him. With rare exceptions those who reach the top of the greasy pole do so not because they have climbed there themselves but because they have been put there by the parties. Hence the prime minister is a creature of party leaders. He is free neither to hire nor fire his cabinet ministers. On becoming prime minister in 1981, Spadolini loudly proclaimed that he personally intended to select his ministers and would choose them on the basis of their qualifications. Leaders of the other parties wasted no time in deflating that dream.

A prime minister's weakness is also institutional. In defining his powers, the constitution is remarkably vague. They key passage, Article 95, says merely, "The prime minister directs the general policy of the government and bears responsibility for it. He maintains the unity of political and administrative policy by promoting and coordinating the activities of the ministers." The constitution left it to parliament to spell out how the prime minister's office should be organized and to determine the number, responsibilities, and structure of the ministries. The requisite legislation has never been enacted. As a result the prime minister has ill-defined authority and no staff to control the government or coordinate its various parts.

The cabinet itself is a chorus of prima donnas. Since ministers owe their positions to their party or faction, they are not linked to the prime minister by any sense of self-interest, much less loyalty. Most ministers consider themselves essentially autonomous and are often inclined to regard the prime minister's "promoting and coordinating" their activities as unacceptable interference. When his government fell in 1982 as a result of a dispute between two ministers, Prime Minister Spadolini notified parliament that he was resigning in order to "defend the validity of the principle of collegiality and coresponsibility among ministers." But his gesture was futile. In practice a prime minister is first among equals, if that.

The cabinet is large, unwieldy, and not in all respects rationally organized.The size is dictated by the need to satisfy party and factional demands; if all the competing interests cannot be accommodated by appointments to the standard ministries, ministers-without-portfolio are added, even if the portfolio is all but empty. The typical government comprises at least twenty ministers and six or seven ministers-without-portfolio. Each minister is "balanced" by several under secretaries who as a rule are from another faction or party than the minister. A government thus numbers close to a hundred appointees, meticulously selected according to party and faction. Any interim change must leave this balance intact. When

Foreign Minister Franco Maria Malfatti resigned for health reasons in 1980, he was replaced by Attilio Ruffini, a man completely out of his depth in international affairs but, like his predecessor, a member of the Fanfani faction. Once in a while a nonpolitical expert is brought into the cabinet, but he rarely lasts long. One such "technician," Rinaldo Ossola, was one of Italy's best foreign-trade ministers in the postwar period. He was dropped from the cabinet after only two years to make way for a septuagenarian Christian Democrat.

There are still other problems. When the three ministries in the economics area – Economics, Treasury, and Budget – are occupied by persons of different parties, great policy turmoil can result. Moreover no attempt is made to follow the example of the Third and Fourth French republics, which also suffered from acute cabinet instability, by exempting such ministries as foreign affairs and economics from partisan politics for the sake of good administration and national prestige. Nor is it normally possible for ministers, even though they may serve in the cabinet for many years, to develop expertise in any one field. Yesterday's defense minister is today's minister of tourism; today's labor minister is tomorrow's minister for culture. The constant ministerial shifts not only weaken the country domestically but in an era of complex bilateral and multilateral relations they are extremely damaging to Italy's international effectiveness and standing.

To compensate for the prime minister's weakness and the cumbersome operation of the cabinet, interministerial committees have been set up. There are eight of them, of which the most important is the Committee for Economic Planning (CIPE). So far the committees have not been a success as coordinating and directing bodies, a failure attributed by Giuliano Amato to the resistance of the individual ministries' administrative apparatus, which sabotages efforts to hammer out unified policies. There is a growing recognition that if the government is to meet its responsibilities as the executive of an advanced industrial state, it will have to find new institutional arrangements, especially in the economic, financial, and social areas.

For many years there has been recurrent talk of reforms that might bring about a more effective parliament, a stronger executive, and above all more stable government. Incessant cabinet crises and the early dissolution of the last four parliaments because of a complete breakdown in relations among coalition partners has deepened concern that the existing system is dragging Italy into ungovernability. In 1983 parliament established a commission to prepare a set of specific proposals. Suggestions ran the gamut from fundamental alterations of the constitutional system to technical revisions of parliamentary procedures. After more than a year's study, the commission reached a consensus supporting a retention of the existing constitutional system but advocated better parliamentary procedures, improved relations between parliament and the government, a strengthening of the prime minister, and a restriction both on decree laws and the use of referenda. Since any of the expedients to strengthen the roles of parliament and the prime minister would be at the expense of the parties, however, the outlook for significant reforms is dim. Before the physicians can cure the system, they will have to heal themselves.

Referenda: Monkey wrench or democratic tool?

Political life has been complicated since the early 1970s by national referenda initiated not by the government to test public opinion on some major issue – as has occurred in some other European countries – but rather organized at the grass roots level and in effect imposed on the government by the public. This mode of direct democracy is provided for in Article 75 of the constitution, which requires a referendum whenever requested by 500,000 qualified voters or five regional councils. Although referenda cannot initiate legislation but only repeal it and may not abrogate international treaties, budget laws, or pardons, their scope is otherwise unrestricted. The validity of a referendum must be verified by the Constitutional Court; when voted upon the referendum carries if a majority of the electorate votes and a majority of those voting approves.

By opening the way for the public to circumvent parliament or force it into action, the referendum is deeply mistrusted by the political parties. Though the drafters of the constitution were divided on the issue – albeit not along party lines – the attitude of the parties can best be gauged by the refusal of parliament to enact the necessary legislation implementing the constitutional provision until 1970. The law was put on the books at that time at the initiative of the Christian Democrats, who saw the device as a way of repealing a law passed that year that for the first time in Italian history permitted civil divorce.

Catholics were therefore the first group to take advantage of the referendum provision. When the vote was held in 1974, it resulted in a decisive reaffirmation of the law – 20 million votes against 13 million – and went far to demonstrate the validity of the principles behind the referendum. The vote made possible the direct and unmistakable expression of the public's view, unfiltered through either the parties or parliament. And once the electorate had spoken the issue was removed for good as a matter of public controversy.

In the years after that it was almost always the Radical party that promoted referenda, using them as a way of going around parliament, of encouraging greater public involvement in politics, and of forcing reforms of what it regarded as outmoded and repressive laws. By 1978 the Radicals had collected the necessary signatures for nine referenda. The Constitutional Court declared early that year that four of these, including one that would have abrogated the concordat, were not valid. Later in the spring, and only in the nick of time, parliament enacted legislation on three other referendum issues, thus automatically canceling the referenda on those matters. In the end therefore only two came to a vote. One of these was on public financing of political parties, which lost by 56 to 44 percent, and the other concerned a 1976 law-and-order measure that had expanded police powers, which failed by 77 to 33 percent.

The Radicals claimed a moral victory, pointing out that referenda opposed by parties representing 95 percent of the electorate had won the support of fully a third or more of the voters. This outcome demonstrated in their view that there was an appreciable number of Italians whose views were being ignored by the traditional parties. So, nothing daunted, they sponsored another ten referenda, some of which were supported by the Socialists. Once again the Constitutional Court quashed four of these. Parliament enacted legislation – limiting the jurisdiction of military courts – on a fifth. Of the remaining five, the overriding issue was abortion.

Pressure for legislation on this question had become irresistible in the mid-seventies. By then roughly 800,000 illegal abortions, according to estimates of the World Health Organization, were being performed every year in Italy. This was the highest rate of illegal abortion – with the highest number of accidental deaths – in Europe. Countless other Italians went abroad for the operation. While legislation was blocked in parliament by the Christian Democrats and neo-Fascists, the Radicals had collected signatures for a referendum that would remove all restrictions on abortion. To maintain some legal control, parliament in 1978 hastily enacted a law – one of Western Europe's most liberal – permitting abortion on demand at state expense for women eighteen years old and over. But that was far from the end of the matter.

For the Catholic church and many Catholic laity, the law was immoral; for feminist groups and the Radicals, the age limit and other provisions of the statute were too restrictive. Both sides therefore sponsored several new referenda; the Catholics to abolish the law and the Radicals to make it freer. It was the Catholics' referendum that was the most hotly contested and, despite the outspoken campaigning of the pope, only 30 percent of the voters supported it when it went to a vote in May 1981. The outcome marked, as had the divorce referendum, an important moment in the country's social development, making clear how far secularization had advanced. In the same voting, the Radical's other referenda – on security laws, life imprisonment, and handgun control – were decisively beaten.

In 1984 the Communists, after years of lambasting the Radicals for their frequent recourse to the practice, sponsored a referendum to cancel a key provision of the Craxi government's economic policy, a reduction in the escalator clause in wage contracts. On going to a vote the following year, the referendum failed to carry by 46 to 54 percent.

Even though no statute has yet been repealed, the referenda have had a clarifying and pacifying effect. Most of the standard arguments in favor of them – encouraging political interest, allowing direct expression of the public's views, and bringing decisions closer to the people – have been amply fulfilled. Participation has not been markedly lower than in parliamentary elections, running from 89 percent on the monarchy and divorce issues to 80 percent in the various referenda of 1981. Moreover, no nation wastes less time on lost causes. Once referenda were held, the results were accepted and the issues vanished as matters of public contention.

Nonetheless the referendum frightens the political establishment. It is an instrument beyond the control of the parties and forces them to take stands on issues that are often highly divisive. The proposed 1978 referendum on abortion, for instance, threatened to bring the Christian Democrats and Communists into a head-on clash, interfering with the deepening collaboration between them at the time. Whether the parties, in their anxiety to avoid referenda, have brought pressure on the Constitutional Court is not clear. However, the reasons the court has given for rejecting some referenda – reasons sometimes given only many months later – have not always been convincing.

Ever since the Radicals began sponsoring referenda, the other parties have been talking about abolishing or limiting their use. They maintain that the Radicals have employed the device in ways, for issues, and to an extent not intended by the drafters of the constitution. And they argue that it is so easy to set a referendum in motion that a small number of persons can start the process over issues that are of interest only to a tiny minority. Certainly there is a risk that improper use of the referendum could sour the public's interest and defeat the very purpose of engaging the public in topical social issues. But so far referenda have done far more good than harm.

The peripheral role of the president

With the abolition of the monarchy – by a majority of only 2 million out of a total of 23 million votes in the 1946 referendum – a president replaced a king as head of the Italian state. Enrico De Nicola, an eminent Neapolitan lawyer and politican, acted as interim president until the republican constitution came into force. Then Luigi Einaudi, a Liberal and a member of the Constitutional Assembly, was elected and moved into the Quirinale, the former papal summer palace and after 1870 the residence of the monarch. In spite of his simple, almost puritanical nature, Einaudi allowed some of the pomp of the monarchy – its cuirassiers and palace attendants – to remain. But the question always asked is whether the president himself is anything more than a decorative symbol, a *fainéant,* as the octogenarian statesman Vittorio Orlando asserted provocatively to his codrafters of the constitution.

Throughout the decades since the constitution took effect, the presidency has become the one fixed point in an ever-changing scene. Against a background of falling governments and malfunctioning parliaments, it represents an element of continuity. Although the office has not always been kept above politics, as the constitution no doubt intended, it has on the whole functioned with fewer problems – and less partisanship – than the other state institutions.

De Nicola and Einaudi brought to the presidency an incontestable intellectual authority and a clear moral stature. The former, an old-fashioned liberal of the pre-Fascist era, was the unanimous choice of the parties to be provisional president. Sagacious, scrupulous, punctilious, and notoriously prickly, De Nicola capably discharged his functions under delicate circumstances. Failing to be elected to a regular term in 1948, he went back to Naples in a huff but later returned to Rome as president of the Senate and initial president of the Constitutional Court. Einaudi, an economist of international repute, governor of the Bank of Italy after 1944, and the architect of the country's postwar economic recovery, was cautious in interpreting presidential powers but firmly rejected Christian Democratic attempts to deprive the office of any authority. On stepping down in 1955, he left a legacy of rectitude and responsible constitutionalism.

His successor, Giovanni Gronchi, claimed a far broader role and tried to guide the country's domestic and international course. A Christian Democratic trade unionist, Gronchi wanted to steer politics to the left though he paradoxically encouraged the formation of governments ever more to the right. His forays into foreign affairs – dispatching a letter to President Eisenhower criticizing American Middle Eastern policy and making a controversial visit to the Soviet Union – were widely regarded as both inept and incompatible with his constitutional role.

Antonio Segni, a rich Sardinian landowner, followed Gronchi in 1962 and presented the opposite paradox of favoring a right-wing course when Italian politics were turning to the left. Although originally on the left of the Christian Democratic party and a promoter of land reform, he had become steadily more conservative and strongly opposed the entry of the Socialists into the government in 1963. In fact his nomination for the presidency was intended to reassure the country's conservatives that the center-left would be kept in control. Segni resigned for health reasons after only two years in office and was succeeded in 1964 by Giuseppe Saragat. Elected with the support of the Communists and against the bitter opposition of some Christian Democrats, Saragat saw himself as a moderator as Italy went through the vagaries of center-left government, the student and labor unrest after 1968, and the subsequent shift to the right. Saragat was succeeded in 1971 by Giovanni Leone, a brilliant penal law professor but a lackluster Christian Democratic politician, who was elected on Christmas Eve when the weary delegates wanted to end the stalemate in balloting. Though he carried out his presidential responsibilities better than many expected, he was forced to resign six months before the end of his term following allegations of financial wrongdoing.

Few presidential elections had a more surprising and fortunate outcome than the one in 1978 that put the vigorous octogenarian Socialist, Alessandro Pertini, into the Quirinale. No doubt because he had spent all his young manhood – from 1927 to 1943 – in Fascist prisons, he was profoundly committed to social justice and individual liberty. Although president of the Chamber from 1968 to 1976, Pertini had always been rather an outsider and in 1978 was not even his own party's preferred candidate. Elected because of the disarray in the Christian Democratic ranks, Pertini was exactly what Italy needed at the time, a person of total integrity. Warm, unpretentious, a man of the people in the highest sense, and almost compulsively conscientious, he quickly became the most esteemed in the succession of presidents, and his honorable performance had the effect of strengthening popular respect for governing institutions.

Determined to have back the presidency in 1985, the Christian Democrats united around Francesco Cossiga and – gaining the accord of the Socialists, who wanted to keep the prime ministry in return, and the Communists, who were anxious to come in from the political cold – easily and decisively secured his election. The man they chose, a protégé of Aldo Moro, had served the party loyally as under secretary of defense, interior minister at the time of Moro's kidnapping, and prime minister for about a year. He was president of the Senate when promoted to the Quirinale. The way to his election was smoothed by his own traits. Relaxed, amiable, jovial, and not wildly ambitious – rare qualities in an Italian politician – Cossiga was a weak but respected politician who, typical of the sort the world around, was liked by many and disliked by few. With his election, the Quirinale was once again secure in the hands of the Christian Democratic party headquarters.

Such are the aleatory results of the electoral process. Election of the president, who serves for seven years, is by an "electoral college" comprising all members of the Chamber and Senate along with delegates from the twenty regions. It is inevitably a highly partisan contest, and the outcome of the balloting is entirely unpredictable. Segni was the only initial frontrunner to emerge a winner. Behind-the-scenes deals have become increasingly difficult to arrange, with a corresponding increase in the number of ballots. Einaudi and Gronchi were elected in four, Segni in nine ballots. But Saragat needed twenty-one and Leone twenty-three. Pertini, the darkest of dark horses, was elected in sixteen ballots, while Cossiga broke precedent by being elected in one.

The president's powers are both ceremonial and substantive, incontestable and controversial. By far his most important prerogative is that of selecting the prime minister. Although his latitude is limited – and throughout most of the life of the republic limited to Christian Democrats – he has some scope for choice, and his selection helps to set the tone and direction of the government. Pertini broadened the scope by deliberately breaking precedent and giving non–Christian Democrats a chance to form a government. This initiative, which would have been inconceivable had a

Christian Democrat been in the Quirinale, was the greatest direct influence any president has had in shaping Italian politics.

The president also has a measure of control over political developments through his authority to dissolve one or both houses of parliament – or to refuse to do so with the intent of forcing the parties to form a viable government. Before deciding on dissolution he must consult with the presidents of the Chamber and Senate, though whether he is bound to follow their advice is unclear. He may not dissolve parliament during the last six months of his own term of office, a period known as the "white semester."

The remaining presidential powers have only indirect political influence. The president appoints one-third of the members of the Constitutional Court, may send messages to parliament, and has authority to summon parliament to special sessions. Laws and regulations are valid only if signed by him, and he may refuse to authorize the government to present bills to parliament. Legislation may be sent back to parliament but whether he may veto it is a matter of controversy. He ratifies treaties and has the power of amnesty. Finally he is commander-in-chief of the armed forces, chairman of the Supreme Defense Council, and chairman of the Superior Judicial Council – ceremonial positions, though potentially of great importance at a moment of national emergency.

Apart from the ultimate threat of impeachment and trial by parliament, the greatest limit on presidential powers is the highly ambiguous constitutional requirement that his official acts must be approved by an appropriate minister. In some cases, such as the nomination of the prime minister and the dissolution of parliament, approval would not make much sense. The president's acts as commander-in-chief, however, could presumably be exercised only with cabinet approval. Between these two extremes lies a legal no-man's-land.

Because of these uncertainties in the constitution, the president confronts two difficult and delicate issues: how far he is independent of political authority and how far he may go in trying to influence policy. Gronchi felt little restraint in either respect and even the far more cautious Einaudi was forthright in repulsing incursions into what he considered his prerogatives. Since those early years a convention has evolved, based on limited presidential authority. Subsequent presidents have claimed no more than those powers that Walter Bagehot in the late nineteenth century attributed to the British monarch: "the right to be consulted, the right to encourage, the right to warn." A president who attempted to do more would provoke a grave political and constitutional crisis.

The idea has from time to time been broached of strengthening the president by having him popularly elected. To augment his personal authority in this way, however, would risk intensifying the dispersion of power that is already the cause of much confusion, inefficiency, and ambiguity. A variant of this proposal would replace the present system with a presidential one. Only the neo-Fascists advocate this. Clearly, an underlying problem of the Italian constitutional system is similar to that of the Fourth French Republic – a parliament that is formally powerful while in practice victim of many warring parties that perpetuate the country's basic social divisions and produce chronic governmental instability. But the situation that provoked the collapse of the latter regime and the adoption of a presidential system were the existence of a profound national crisis and the presence of a commanding national leader – conditions that are not on the horizon in Italy.

7. Public administration and *sottogoverno*

In October of 1976 a tinsmith named Vito Pennetta rented an airplane and flew over Rome's Piazza Venezia, sending 1.5 million lire in bank notes fluttering down on passersby. His spectacular gesture was a desperate attempt to embarrass the government into providing information about the cause of an accident in which his son Roberto had been killed a year and a half previously in the crash of a sailplane just outside the Italian capital. Despite all his frantic efforts up to that time, Pennetta had been unable to obtain a copy of either the results of the court investigation or the technical evaluation of the incident. The official justification was always that no one was available in the Air Ministry to type up the technical data of the experts' report.

Over a year and a half is a long time for a distraught father to wait for a simple report. But the Italian civil service reckons in long time spans. When someone retires, he may wait many months or even years before he receives his state pension. In tax offices throughout the country sacks of unopened returns are piled in corridors where they gather dust. The Treasury Ministry still has a war damages bureau with some 150 officials. While France and Germany settled all their war damage claims years ago, in Italy hundreds of thousands of such cases remain to be dealt with. Permission for a normal construction project generally requires three years. In the case of subsidized construction, so many public agencies must approve the proposal that the time stretches far beyond that, while the credits for the project are eaten up by inflation. Massimo Severo Giannini, minister for Public Administration in 1979–80, found that decisions by government agencies take an average of at least three times longer than those in private business.

If slowness is one obvious problem, formalism is another. Even the simplest request of a government agency – to procure a document or just to have it stamped – can mean a peregrination through a seemingly endless labyrinth of referrals. Here is bureaucracy that has become an end in itself. Here are officials who practice what Gaetano Salvemini referred to as "bureaucratic absolutism." And here is where are perpetrated such incidents as the one involving the mayor of a Sicilian town damaged in an earthquake whose application for funds to construct emergency housing was returned from Rome unopened because the dossier had not been bound with the official ribbon bearing the colors of the Italian flag.

Of course any organization, public or private, can appear incompetent if judged by the inevitable anecdote. And in almost every country the civil service is an object of mistrust if not derision. The question is whether the anecdotes are the tip of an iceberg of ineptitude or exceptions to the general performance. In Italy, where parliament falls short of its constitutional role and the prime minister and cabinet are weak and embroiled in continuous political crisis, the capacity of the civil service to keep the government running is of more than normal importance. As elsewhere in Europe, public agencies also shoulder the growing burden of managing social welfare programs and directing the country's economy. Moreover, state corporations in Italy control 80 percent of the country's banking, more than a quarter of its industrial employment, and half its fixed investment. Clearly Italy's public administration bears an exceptionally important role in the country's economic and social life.

Civil service organization and personnel

The core of government administration – the ministries and their civil service staff – is organized along the standard lines for all parliamentary democracies. The ministers and their under secretaries are appointed by the party of government. In the case of coalitions these positions are distributed among the governing parties, though the Christian Democrats almost invariably hold on to at least one subcabinet position whoever is minister. The ministries themselves are divided into directorates, which are subdivided into divisions that are broken down into sections. These offices are all occupied by career civil servants.

Government administration in Italy is heir to a number of structural weaknesses that go back to the early days of the unified state. Modeled on the French system, the civil service is rigidly centralized and hierarchical. There is so little delegation of authority that some ministers must sign as many as 200 documents a day. Coordination within and among ministries is effected only at the top. Reforms have never succeeded in breaking down these horizontal and vertical barriers. Fastidious and complex, bureaucratic procedures breathe the authentic spirit of the last century. According to a

government survey released in 1982, half the time and resources of
a ministry are devoted to self-administration.

Because of the vast number of regulations – tens of thousands of
them, codified in thirty-three hefty volumes – the prevailing atmosphere is slow-moving and legalistic, with the emphasis on following rules rather than achieving results. The expenditure of funds,
for example, is so cumbersome that ministries are usually unable to
spend all their allocation. Since the late seventies an average of 20
percent of each ministry's budget went unspent. These funds then
accumulated in the Treasury, not only impairing systematic budget planning but also compromising parliament's control over
spending. Another bureaucratic casualty are monies earmarked for
Italy by the European Community's regional development fund. A
portion of these is regularly forfeited because Italian government
agencies cannot manage to propose projects within the allotted
time.

In Italy as in all countries, government offices are always accused
of being overstaffed, and in Italy as in most countries, the number
of government employees has steadily risen. Personnel of the
"central administration" (principally, the ministerial civil service,
school and university teachers, the career military, and postal employees) numbered 768,000 in 1950, 970,000 a decade later, 1.3
million in 1970, and 1.5 million in 1980. As of 1983 the ministerial
civil service alone totaled 400,000, with roughly one-quarter in
Rome and the remainder in field offices around the country. Sabino Cassese, an authority on public administration, maintains that
such a figure is not excessive to bureaucratic needs and is no
greater than in other major European states. Government personnel also include career members of the armed forces and police
(320,000); all school and university teachers (865,000); doctors,
nurses, and administrative staff of the national health service
(680,000); employees of the post and telephone service and railways (465,000); employees of other public agencies (400,000);
employees in the public sector enterprises (690,000); and local,
provincial, and regional administration staff (652,000).

Italian public administration therefore accounts for a total of
roughly 4.5 million persons. Large as it is, this figure compares
favorably with that in other Western European countries. For every
100,000 inhabitants, Italy has 5.3 public employees, as compared
to 5.9 in Germany, 6.2 in France, and 8.2 in Britain. The problem
lies less in size than in the distribution of positions and resources.
Relatively unimportant sectors have large staffs while vital areas
are sometimes too spare. The number of personnel devoted to law

and order, for instance, remained essentially unchanged despite the enormous increase in terrorism and criminality after the early 1970s. By contrast, the Treasury has twenty-four bureaus for pensions; according to Giannini, "12 of these do absolutely nothing." There is also a problem of disparities within the ministerial civil service itself, with far too small an administrative staff (16%) and far too many clerical and custodial personnel (73%).

It is said that any institution can function well, whatever its organizational structure, if it is staffed with good personnel. In the Italian case the quality of the civil service, far from minimizing the structural weakness of government administration, magnifies it. One fault lies with personnel policy, which is misfocused and maladministered. Recruitment is the responsibility of each ministry and is by public examination. However, examination procedures can take years, and the tests temselves are based more on law and theory than on managerial aptitude and the social sciences. Far worse, formal entry procedures can be bypassed by those with the right political connections.

Here is what insiders generally regard as the main weakness of Italian public administration – its use as an enormous patronage machine. The state apparatus is treated by the parties not just as an instrument of administrative control over the country but also as a means of dispensing partisan favor. By placing their nominees throughout the bureaucracy, they are able to consolidate their power while extending their clientelistic network. In this way the civil service and its operations have been shamelessly politicized. For most of the postwar period it was the Christian Democrats who bore most responsibility for this situation. With the partial regionalization of public administration in 1977, however, the other parties have played the same game in those regions where they are in control.

As a result potential candidates of real merit are inclined to look elsewhere for a career, the wrong type of person is recruited, and professional equity is undermined by unfair and clientelistic entry procedures. Despite the generally high quality of the diplomatic service and a sprinkling of outstandingly competent officials in the higher echelons of the entire ministerial system, Italy therefore lacks the solid, well-trained administrative elite of the sort found in most other Western countries. Attempts have been made over the years to remedy this situation. A professional training institute, the School of Public Administration, was established in Caserta in 1962, but it proved to be notoriously inadequate. Reorganized and moved to the North after 1977, the school still made no headway against the entrenched forces of party patronage.

The civil service is divided into four classes: executive, administrative, clerical, and custodial. Promotion within each civil service class is by seniority and merit, though in fact the former prevails. There is little mobility among ministries and almost no movement into and out of government service. One of the attractions of government employment is nearly absolute job security; in practice no one can be dismissed short of egregious wrongdoing. Further to protect themselves, civil servants are organized in a variety of unions and have the right to strike. They are eligible for retirement after only fourteen-and-a-half years of service, with university study counting toward retirement. This provision has resulted in the extraordinary phenomenon of "baby pensioners" – persons who have retired while merely in their late twenties or early thirties. In practice therefore Italian public administration has created for itself the worst of all possible worlds. With only seniority counting for promotion and no possibility of being fired, the government employee regards his position as a sinecure to be occupied rather than a job with responsibilities to fulfill.

The conditions of government service accentuate these problems. Promotion is slow. Pay is poor and administered so inequitably as to have created what one expert has called "a salaries jungle." The prevailing ministerial atmosphere, like the structure, is hierarchical and discourages any initiative, exertion, or dedication. One special assistant to a minister, recruited temporarily from the outside, found that as a result of her hard work, she was in no time known derisively by her ministerial colleagues as *la prussiana,* "the Prussian." Personnel regulations are so numerous and overlapping that they spread confusion rather than establish order. Worse, they can be manipulated to produce promotions and wage increases for those with the right political friends. To say that morale is poor is drastically to understate the indifference and cynicism that enshroud public administration in Italy.

These problems also afflict the higher executive ranks. In a study in the early 1970s of the British, German, and Italian civil services, Robert Putnam found that the Italians were older and had served longer than officials of the other nationalities as a result of slow promotion procedures. Three decades into the postwar era, public administration was consequently still in the hands of persons who had begun their careers under Fascism. The study found the typical member of the administrative inner circle to be "legalistic, illiberal, elitist, hostile to the usages and practice of pluralist politics, fundamentally undemocratic" and the atmosphere in the ministries to be one of "deep and bitter alienation" from the country's political institutions. Since that study was conducted, most of those persons reached the mandatory retirement age of sixty-five and retired. They were replaced, however, by a generation whose formative years were of a much different but still highly politicized background.

There are two other important characteristics of the civil service that some critics believe weaken the administrative system. One is the high proportion – roughly 40 percent – of lawyers in the higher civil service. In Cassese's view, legal training produces functionaries who think more in terms of applying norms than of solving administrative problems. From this arises the public perception of a civil service that is legalistic, remote, and overbearing. The other trait is the dominance of southerners, who have a reputation – at least among northerners – of regarding a job as a natural right and their salaries as an obligation of the state irrespective of their qualifications or performance. In the North the higher level of industrialization and business activity has traditionally offered university graduates well-paying careers in industry and banking; in the South such outlets have been relatively rare and the social cachet of government service along with the security of a position with practically automatic promotion have great allure. Already by the mid-1960s, 75 percent of the higher grades were from the South; in some ministries, such as Interior and Treasury, the percentage was even higher. Only the Foreign Ministry has resisted the encroachment; there the southerner has remained virtually an oppressed minority.

Civil service performance

The problems of government administration start at the very top – with the ministers themselves. On the one hand they must put up with constant interference from their party, which regards them as nothing more than its instruments. On the other they are in office for a period normally counted in months. They consequently have little or no feeling of responsibility to their ministry and its staff while the latter has little sense of loyalty to its newest transient chief. Lack of direction and continuity are heavy liabilities to the civil service in discharging its functions. The burden of ministerial responsibility falls on the top level of permanent officials, who must make do with little or no overall policy direction. Under the circumstances the quality of administration varies greatly. Some ministries – such as Foreign Affairs, Justice, Interior, and Treasury – generally discharge their responsibilities efficiently and creditably. By contrast Labor, Merchant Marine, and Foreign Trade have poor reputations, whereas the huge Public Education Ministry is renowned for its red tape and slowness. Throughout the bureaucratic hierarchy, however, there are higher officials with an astonishing capacity for work and no regard for hours spent in the office. Consequently work tends to float to the top in every ministry, where it is dealt with by a few extremely hardworking officials.

Most others are timeservers. Low pay, no risk of being fired, and no incentive to strive for promotion are fatal to efficient performance. For one thing they lead to "moonlighting." When ministries close for the day at two in the afternoon, thousands of civil servants at all levels return home for a postprandial siesta and then go off to a second job in private business – as a bookkeeper, bartender, or business consultant. The ministerial position with its modest salary provides the basis for financial security; the second one offers the means for a comfortable life, a university education for the children, a bigger car, or a vacation apartment at the sea. According to a 1978 poll by the Rome employment office, 74 percent of the higher civil service, 40 percent of the middle-level officials, and 76 percent of staff and custodial personnel hold a second job. As a result office performance suffers, work piles up, and absenteeism hovers at around 10 percent.

In the spring of 1982 government investigators without warning had a spot check on absentees. One of the cases they discovered was that of a postal worker who showed up at the office only once a month – to collect his pay. The rest of the time he worked in his wife's electrical appliance shop. He divided his government wage among five other postal employees, who covered for him. The random investigation – and the arrest of the postal worker – caused a wave of panic in Rome ministries. Morning buses were suddenly jammed, and some civil servants reported seeing one another in the office for the first time in years.

Despite such cavalier personal behavior, the prevailing professional atmosphere in a typical ministry is one of a juristic perfection that has little regard for practical administration. The citizen who needs some decision or action from a government agency must start at the *tabaccheria,* the state-licensed tobacco shop where he buys a *carta bollata,* a blank form with a government stamp that is the prerequisite for initiating any bureaucratic action. Once submitted, this certificate begins its course through innumerable offices, wanders through an endless rank of anonymous desks, disappears under a mountain of files, is found again and carried further by clerks until finally a decision is reached and possibly translated into results. A request for authority to construct a building, for example, must pass through sixty-four offices for approval.

The citizen, under the circumstances, is the powerless partner. Small wonder that he sees the state and its administrative apparatus as a foreign power and regards the civil service not as a service – and certainly not civil – but as an institution whose demands he tries to avoid while exploiting every opening. Who would not cheat in paying taxes when, after years of genuine improvement in tax collection, the average factory or shop owner still pays less tax than the average factory worker or shop assistant; when in 1983 only 14,000 persons declared an income of over $40,000; when the nearly 1 million shopkeepers declared an average annual income of less than $3,600; when doctors, dentists, artisans, and the self-employed pay little, if any, tax? The tax-collecting bureaucracy is so badly organized that one of its top officials told the press in 1984 that five or six years of bureaucratic reform would be necessary before tax collecting could be systematized and enforced – even if the political will to do so existed, which he doubted. And who would not despair over the national health service? As reorganized in 1979, it was well-planned in theory but from the start became embroiled in political patronage at every level, damaging its reputation and effectiveness. After the reform, just as much as before, if the average patient was to receive proper meals and nursing care, his family had virtually to move into the hospital with him to provide it.

At times the inefficient operation of the system has other consequences. Since taking the route of the normal chain of command is so frustrating and time-consuming and is in any event not promising, the person who needs a government decision looks for a shortcut or a surer way. He turns to the *raccomandazione,* the personal "recommendation," in the hope of surmounting the obstacles of a malfunctioning apparatus. In a country where intercession has always been an important part of religion, whether pagan or Christian, this expedient is a central trait of the national psychology. Recommendations are submitted in the tens, or probably hundreds, of thousands every year by anyone who might have influence – a business leader, a priest, a trade union official, or above all a politician. Everyone must have his *santo in paradiso,* his well-placed contact.

Use of the recommendation is such an unabashed feature of ministerial operations that the government printing office issues a standard form for them, complete with blanks to fill in concerning who is being recommended by whom and for what. Ministries in turn maintain large staffs to handle the flood of requests. The routine destroys the bureaucratic ideal of impartiality but it at least produces results. And it is a further instance of how Italians work around the system to get what they want.

Faced with bureaucratic inertia, the temptation also exists to apply a bit of "grease." Would it not be more effective to slip a few bank notes into the documents and save hours or days of waiting? An attorney unobtrusively hands over some money to ensure that the court clerk's office will write out the verdict by the weekend instead of at the end of the month. And most commonplace of all are cases where a bit of money has eased the path of a request for a building permit. In this fashion bribery becomes another means of keeping the administrative apparatus in motion – for the one a welcome source of additional income and for the other a handy method of having business taken care of promptly. The country's poor administration is a veritable invitation to the *bustarella,* the envelope filled with money. As one civil servant bluntly put it: "It is impossible to get anything done without a *bustarella."*

Alas, the *bustarella* has escalated into an epidemic of bribes and rake-offs of large sums, particularly in connection with government contracts. The most notorious case was the payoffs made by the Lockheed Aircraft Corporation to Italian officials in the 1970s. Since then indictments, arrests, and trials for similar, if less spectacular, types of malfeasance have been reported in the press almost daily.

The problems of public administration have been recognized throughout the history of the republic. Proposals to correct the weaknesses and create an independent civil service with uniform regulations have never been lacking. A Ministry for Administrative Reform, under one name or another, has existed off and on since 1950 without ever accomplishing much, if anything. A Superior Council for Administration, founded around the same time to coordinate ministerial practices, does little more than administer itself. One of the most impressive reform plans was submitted to parliament in 1979 by Massimo Severo Giannini, then minister of Public Administration and a leading administrative expert.

Giannini's report was particularly incisive in summing up the breadth and depth of the problem. Whereas the function of the state had historically been one of maintaining order, the document observed, it had become one of managing services and of dividing and transferring funds. Many advanced industrial countries had made this shift, but Italy had not. The report saw the core of the problem in the mutually reinforcing disdain of the civil servant and the citizen. Because of its performance, the state is viewed not as a reliable friend but an "equivocal, irrational, and distant creature," which is guided by a civil service of "incompetent and lazy officials," of "specialists in formalism." Public authority, Giannini concluded, represents for the average citizen a "singular legal malefactor," doing in its own sphere what it forbids in the private sector.

In the years since it was submitted, Giannini's report and the suggested changes have been much praised but almost entirely ignored. Only one concrete proposal has ever emerged: a suggestion by Prime Minister Spadolini in 1982 to reorganize the prime minister's office in a way that Giannini described in a press interview at the time as "a farrago of nonsense." Asked why no action had been taken on his recommendations, Giannini responded crisply, "There is no political will to solve the problem."

As so often, the problem comes back to the parties. Since they cannot resist using public administration as an instrument of partisan control and clientelism, no genuine reform of the system is possible. The establishment of a respected and competent administrative bureaucracy, difficult in every country, remains one of the great uncompleted tasks of the Italian state. Until it is achieved, the Mediterranean and baroque Italy will continue to be a great burden on the Western and innovative Italy.

Autonomous agencies and public corporations

Public administration in Italy also comprises other important bodies, some of them unique. Most simple are the autonomous administrations responsible for the country's relatively modest nationalized sector – primarily the railroads, post and telecommunications, electricity (ENEL), road construction, and the state monopolies of such items as tobacco and salt. Although each of these has its own board and director general, the ministry to which it is responsible holds considerable authority over policy direction. Apart from the postal system, most of the nationalized industries are managed satisfactorily, although railroad service has been greatly disrupted in recent years by labor problems.

The unique component of Italian public administration is the public corporations. These comprise an amazing archipelago of some 45,000 entities, which with Italianate ambiguity are *of* the government but not *in* it. These bodies are hypothetically independent in their operations and those that are commercial have private stockholders. But since they receive state funds and are managed by persons appointed by the government, they are subject to political control. They include most of Italy's large industrial firms, the major banks and credit institutions, social security and welfare agencies, state radio and television, hospitals, universities, research centers, opera houses, theaters, museums, and organizations for sport, culture, and recreation. Together these public corporations reach every corner of society and touch each individual in it.

This conglomeration of public entities is the heart of the *sottogoverno* and comprises a power, diffuse as it may be, that is roughly coequal to that of the government itself. How these public agencies have been turned into a parallel system of political power is a key to understanding Italian politics.

The heart of this domain is the state industrial corporations (see Figure 1). It comprises four giant state holding companies that control over 1,000 subsidiaries. The largest is IRI, the Institute for Industrial Reconstruction; it was set up in 1933 to take over banks and industries facing bankruptcy in the wake of the international depression. After the war IRI steadily expanded into broader sectors of the economy, producing a system of nationalization *all'italiana*. IRI normally holds a majority but until around 1980 rarely a monopoly of a company's stock; financing is largely secured on the open market rather than through government grants. Although its goals have increasingly been set by the state, IRI was originally free both to define its objectives and to decide how to achieve them. That was the origin of what became famous in postwar Europe as "the IRI formula" – a combination of state and private enterprise based equally on free competition and national planning, with management in the hands of professional businessmen and economists rather than government officials. This innovative approach proved an effective means of developing key sectors of the economy that private companies alone could not finance, such as steel, shipbuilding, chemicals, and other heavy industries. As a result IRI became a major stimulus to the postwar economic miracle and its "formula" a widely admired model.

Today IRI is Europe's largest corporation – indeed the biggest firm outside America, oil companies apart – and its largest business employer. The IRI realm is vast. Through 600 subsidiary holding companies it owns a controlling interest in most of the

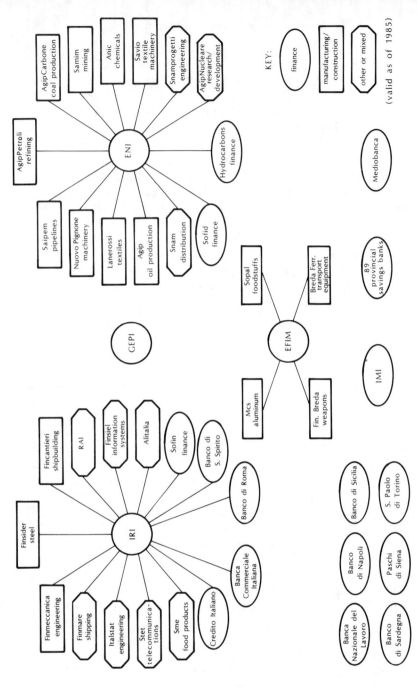

Figure 1. Public-sector banks and holding companies, with principal subsidiaries.

country's iron and steel production; most shipbuilding and shipping; a high proportion of the telecommunications and electronics industry; much of the engineering industry, including Alfa Romeo and aircraft construction; the state radio and television (RAI); most *autostrade;* Alitalia; miscellaneous industries and services in the food and hotel business; a variety of national and local construction and city-planning projects; television advertising; some airports and local transportation lines; and the Italian half of the Mont Blanc tunnel. IRI also owns most of the shares of three large banks – Banca Commerciale Italiana, Credito Italiano, and Banco di Roma – and entirely owns the Banco di Santo Spirito.

Yet IRI is only one state holding company. Three other state corporations were established after the war along the lines of the IRI model. By far the most important of these is ENI, the National Corporation for Hydrocarbons, which controls the petroleum company, Agip, as well as most of the country's nuclear energy and chemical industry along with a number of textile and engineering firms. ENI is Italy's largest company in terms of sales and, according to *Fortune,* the world's ninth largest firm, the fourth largest outside the U.S. It is one of the biggest oil and chemical concerns in the world and controls nearly 300 subsidiaries. Agip alone is the world's fourteenth largest petroleum firm. The other two holding companies, EFIM and GEPI, were founded primarily to nurse sick companies back to health and to create a number of new basic industries. Altogether the four holding companies account for one-third of Italy's total sales and half its fixed investment.

A no less important part of the public sector is the banking system. All the major commercial banks, savings banks, and special credit institutions are public corporations under autonomous management. On the commercial side there are – in addition to the three large IRI banks – six chartered public banks – Banca Nazionale del Lavoro, Banco di Napoli, Monte dei Paschi di Siena, Istituto Bancario San Paolo di Torino, Banco di Sicilia, and Banco di Sardegna. In addition there are eighty-nine savings banks, organized regionally. These are a power in their own right – the one in Milan is the largest savings bank in the world. Finally there are special credit institutions – such as the Istituto Mobiliare Italiano (IMI) – that make long-term loans for industrial and public-works projects and extend credit for agriculture and construction. Altogether the thirty-one commercial banks along with the savings banks and special credit facilities account for roughly 80 percent of Italy's banking facilities and therefore hold nearly complete control over the country's investment funds.

Social security and welfare agencies are another important group of public corporations. These bodies, rather than the government, manage all the various social services – pensions, unemployment compensation, health benefits, and family allowances. Since almost every economic and social group has its own program, there are thousands of such bodies. Their funds – contributions by members, employers and the state – are enormous. The largest of these service organizations, and the one into which all the others are being merged, is the National Institute for Social Security (INPS), which in 1983 had a budget that was the equivalent of 21 percent of the country's gross national product (GNP).

In addition there is another type of welfare agency that elsewhere would be private but in Italy is public and receives state funds – organizations for the blind, orphans, war victims, the impoverished, and almost every other conceivable group of unfortunates. The total number of all such bodies is amazing; in 1945 there were already 30,000 of them; by the mid-1970s the number was estimated to be 42,000. A high proportion of them are simply self-legitimizing organizations that exist solely to exist, consuming all or most of their funds and energy in self-administration.

Repeated efforts by parliament and various ministries to reduce the number of these agencies have invariably been frustrated by the entrenched interests they represent. In 1956 an office was established under the Treasury to eliminate obsolete and useless bodies. In the following fourteen years, it managed to shut down or amalgamate a grand total of seventy-three organizations – including several responsible for the colonization of Abyssinia and an agency set up in 1938 to administer property confiscated from Jews. A law passed in 1975 identified 7,500 organizations to be abolished. So far only several hundred of them have been dissolved.

Sottogoverno + party control = political power

Even the raw data do not fully convey the weight and influence of Italy's public corporations. The state industries and banks occupy the heights of economic power. The other public entities have in some cases substantial financial resources and in others great social influence. All of them together create a web of thousands of administrative and staff positions that in turn possess enormous collateral authority. Some Western states have large public sectors but none has such a breadth of economic power with such a depth of national influence.

Having been established as autonomous organizations with independently recruited personnel rather than government civil servants, the state commercial enterprises were intended to be immune from political influences. But since it is the government that appoints the top managers, a loophole has always existed through which politics could enter. The Fascists generally respected the autonomy of the public corporations. And so, for a time, did the Christian Democrats. Generally speaking, executives and managers were selected for their professional abilities. Operational independence was honored. Investment decisions were normally based on economic considerations alone. But in the wake of the loss of their parliamentary majority in 1953, the Christian Democrats looked for ways of entrenching themselves in power and freeing themselves from financial dependence on private industry. Under Fanfani's guidance they conceived the idea of constructing a power base outside the government. In the public enterprises and other agencies they saw a potential empire that could provide great political and financial riches.

The colonization started in the mid-1950s, at first primarily in the noncommercial areas. After that the industrial firms and banks were subjected to steadily mounting political pressure. One by one the key positions throughout the public sector were filled with party loyalists. By the late 1960s IRI, ENI, and their subsidiaries as well as the commercial and savings banks, Italcasse (the central financing corporation of the savings banks), the social security and welfare agencies, as well as the multitude of other public entities were all in the party's direct or indirect control. Some spheres became the preserve of a specific faction. Monte dei Paschi di Siena, for example, was for many years in the hands of the Fanfani faction. Similarly the state radio and television was built up be a Fanfani protégé, Ettore Bernabei, into a citadel of factional and party patronage and influence. Four large chemical groups were set up with lavish state funding, each of them the affiliate of a specific Christian Democratic faction. Only a few sectors managed to withstand the blitz. These included the Banca Commerciale Italiana, a traditional stronghold of lay influence, Credito Italiano, and a number of IRI and ENI subsidiaries.

As time passed, executives were chosen less and less for their professional abilities and more and more for their party allegiances and connections. Sometimes an executive's only qualification was political. For instance, as of 1980 half the presidents of the savings banks were without any economic or other relevant training. The head of the Turin savings bank was someone whose academic background was in the fine arts; her predecessor was a schoolteacher. The Bank of Italy has always fought against such blatant patronage but with little success. Normally all that stands in the way of such an appointment is a disagreement among party factions. Then the position is left vacant, sometimes for long periods. More than sixty savings banks were without a president in 1980; one bank had been so for more than a dozen years. And so it has been throughout the public sector, even with the top positions in IRI and ENI. One state holding company, EGAM, was saddled with so many incompetent managers over the years that it finally had to be dissolved in 1977. Wherever the political meddling spread, the quality of management usually declined.

But even in those cases where the executive has been someone of proven managerial talent, the fact that he held his position because of his party affiliations could not but compromise his independence. He owed a debt. And such debts never went uncollected. Those who refused to pay up had to go. Establishing this web of clientelistic relationships was an important means by which the Christian Democrats extended their power throughout the country. Once they had asserted a right to decide who would occupy the top positions and then inserted their nominees in them, they were poised to control the operations. In no time industries and banks found themselves under ever-increasing political direction, to the point where there was little room left for economic considerations. A broad range of investment decisions – whether or where to construct a factory, whether to close an unproductive plant, whether to build a highway and what route it should follow – were taken so as to reinforce the political influence and electoral strength of the Christian Democratic party or a particular faction or a particular leader.

The national network of highways and *autostrade* was so notorious for being constructed in areas that would help Christian Democratic leaders in their home districts that various branches are specifically associated with them by name – the Arezzo section of the Rome–Florence *autostrada* with Fanfani; a stretch near Avellino with De Mita; a highway south of Rome with Andreotti; the *autostrada* from Rome to L'Aquila with Lorenzo Natali; and the partially constructed "PiRuBi" *autostrada* in the North with Piccoli, Rumor, and Antonio Bisaglia. Highway construction is but one of the various public-works projects and public-works projects are but one of the various ways the government and the *sottogoverno* are used to dispense jobs, contracts, and funds – all of which translate into votes.

The manipulation has been equally crass in other areas. The

state radio and television network (RAI), once the preserve of the
Fanfani faction, has long been one of the most hotly contested of
all objects of the *sottogoverno*. In a series of articles in 1984, the
Corriere della Sera found not only that RAI's personnel policy from
top to bottom was dictated by party affiliation rather than professional qualifications but also that the entire programming operation was determined by the parties. "The presence of the parties is
suffocating and their pressures are on all of us," one official was
quoted as saying. The issue exploded in controversy in 1984 when
the sixteen-member board of directors came up for appointment.
That the ten members selected by parliament would be political
was taken for granted. But when the parties arrogated to themselves the remaining six – two for the Christian Democrats and
one each for the Socialists, Social Democrats, Communists, and
Republicans – and then designated the appointees by name, they
set in motion an avalanche of public criticism. Romano Prodi, the
head of IRI, of which RAI was a subsidiary, flatly refused to confirm the appointments.

Nor have the private media been able to withstand party pressures. Most newspapers and magazines are financially weak and
need periodic loans to continue to publish. Loans are arranged
with a political understanding, and the paper's editorial position is
adjusted accordingly. A particularly notable case was that of the
Corriere della Sera, which was bought by the Rizzoli family in
1974. Running into financial difficulties, the Rizzolis found that
bank loans were not available because of the paper's critical attitude toward the Christian Democrats. In 1977 funds were secured,
in an operation finagled by the head of the P2 Masonic lodge, after
which the newspaper dropped its left-leaning editor and took a
friendlier attitude toward the Christian Democrats. And so it is in
other spheres for anyone who wants a line of credit. Whether the
loan applicant is a large industrial firm, a shopkeeper, a builder, a
small manufacturer, or simply a family man who needs a mortgage
for a house, each must have political backing and in the normal
case that must come from the Christian Democrats.

Even the welfare agencies have been managed by administrators
who followed elastic procedures, based on partisan favoritism, in
collecting dues and dispensing benefits. Pensions are a particularly
notorious case, especially in the South where they are a vital source
of income for the unemployed, underemployed, and self-employed. Two and even three pensions are not uncommon, with the
result that the total national figures work out to one Italian in ten
being a statistical invalid. In the banking world the Christian Dem-

ocrats, in the words of a 1980 study by the respected economic weekly *Il Mondo,* have transformed the whole system "into a supermarket of credit at their own disposition." Agricultural credits, to cite an example in one area, are vital to all farmers. But unless the farmer belongs to the Christian Democratic–controlled Confederation of Small Farmers, he finds it difficult to obtain a loan. If a member, he is not only assisted in applying for the loan but also may be given a favorable interest rate. The resulting political credit is an important element in the solid hold the Christian Democrats maintain in agricultural areas.

Influencing the operations of the public entities was not the Christian Democrats' only objective in taking control of the public sector. Equally important was jobbery pure and simple. Every country has its spoils system where at least some top government posts – in the United States 3,000 federal positions – go to party supporters. But in Italy the political-selection process was extended from the top to the bottom of the government and then spread into the public agencies, where it influenced virtually every appointment, including secretaries, messengers, and clerks. In this way the *sottogoverno,* with its thousands of public entities and hundreds of thousands of jobs, was transformed by the Christian Democrats into the biggest pool of patronage in any democratic state. This is how the party card became almost as important in Italy as in Communist countries.

Political patronage in Italy works like the economic multiplier – one favor creates many times that number of supporters and voters. Ambitious young managers in IRI and ENI – like their counterparts in the ministerial civil service – quickly learn that the way to the top of their profession lies in cultivating the support of a faction leader who acts as their sponsor. In a country where clientelism is the lifeblood of society, the authority to offer a job, arrange a promotion, make a loan, let a contract, build a factory, give a franchise, or provide a tip on land speculation is the royal road to political influence and electoral support. A double pension to a poor person in the South is usually sufficient to keep the person in the Christian Democratic ranks even if his community lacks paved streets, proper sewage facilities, or other minimal urban services. And a political appointment, economic decision, or personal favor is only the beginning. It is followed by the payback, in the form of other jobs for the party faithful and politically helpful decisions. In the words of a Socialist politician: "The results of clientelism can be seen in election results. Who governs, stays in power." Hence

Italy's remarkable electoral stability has to some extent been traced to the patronage of the *sottogoverno*.

To keep the process going, cash is needed. Consequently, the state enterprises must also agree, as Cesare Merzagora, a prominent financier, declared publicly in 1979, to falsify the company books and conduct transactions through "black accounts" that never appear in official bookkeeping records. A prominent Socialist economist and cabinet minister in the 1980s, Francesco Forte, resigned as vice-president of ENI in 1975 when he was refused an honest balance sheet for the company and would not endorse a bogus one because he knew it concealed funds used for political payoffs and sums that ENI illegally kept abroad. In 1977 *Il Mondo* estimated that various Christian Democratic factions had received roughly $100 million from public corporations in the preceding dozen years. Undoubtedly other parties also benefited from this largess. Such graft has been the ruin of several leading managers. In 1975 Camillo Crociani, head of an IRI subsidiary, fled to Mexico because of his involvement in the Lockheed bribery scandal. Five years later the president of ENI, Giorgio Mazzanti, though personally innocent, was forced to resign because ENI was involved in a kickback scheme for a number of Italian politicians in connection with a huge oil deal with Saudi Arabia. In 1984 it was discovered that IRI's books had been falsified during the previous decade and that almost $200 million had been channeled into a slush fund for a wide variety of purposes, largely though not solely benefiting the Christian Democrats.

Even more than the industrial corporations, since the mid-seventies the banking system has been rocked by scandals involving payoffs for political favors and illegal party financing. The most notorious of these concerned Italcasse. For several years during the 1970s that body made unsecured loans of hundreds of millions of dollars on the basis of personal and political favors. The chairman at the time, Giuseppe Arcaini, is said not only to have embezzled large sums but also to have maintained a political slush fund with money that never appeared in the official books. Arcaini died before the scandal was uncovered in 1980. But when it became known that one of the main beneficiaries of the loans had given some funds to Franco Evangelisti, a Christian Democratic minister, the latter had to resign from the cabinet. As the scandal spread, forty-nine savings bank presidents were arrested for suspected involvement in the affair.

The political plundering of the state sector has damaged the performance of the very industrial enterprises that were a major element in the Italian economic miracle. As a result, the "IRI formula" as a model for Europe was discredited and the once proud tower of Italian enterprise was defaced by corruption, bad management, and near bankruptcy. Shortly after stepping down as minister for state enterprises in 1980, Antonio Bisaglia publicly acknowledged that "the state enterprises went into a crisis when they had to submit to decisions which the management could not reject because politics were supreme." Never were truer words spoken; no one knew the truth of them better than Bisaglia; and few persons bore greater responsibility than he. Those areas that were well-run and technologically advanced – firms in engineering, construction, natural gas technology, and gas pipeline construction – were generally those that had escaped political tampering.

The most telling judgment is that of the balance sheets. After twenty-five years of profits, the state corporations sank into a period of almost consistent and mounting deficits. Since 1970 their only profitable year was 1973. By 1983 IRI had a debt of $24.6 billion (American billion), an annual loss of $2.1 billion, and an annual gross revenue of $25 billion. In January 1984 Prodi told the press: "The entire IRI group is in danger of financial collapse." In 1983 ENI had a debt of nearly $12 billion and EFIM of over $2 billion. The combined public-sector debt in that year approached $40 billion, and its annual loss amounted to $3.5 billion.

To be sure, this dismal record is not the consequence of political exploitation alone but also reflects the widespread recession after the 1973 oil crisis as well as organizational deficiencies within the holding companies. Moreover, some political direction has always been implicit in the objectives of the public sector. The central aim of the public enterprises is to combine free-enterprise principles with national social goals. The Ligurian shipyards, for instance, were kept going long after they were clearly unprofitable. Moreover, the state enterprises were required to put an increasing proportion of their investment into the Mezzogiorno – in projects that were designed more for political than economic purposes, resulting at times in enormous losses. After the mid-1970s they and the banks were under intense pressure from the major parties and the trade unions to keep unprofitable industries in operation to avoid increasing unemployment. So instead of restructuring to adjust to the changing world economy, the state enterprises had to maintain their labor staff, which destroyed their profitability and drove them ever further into the red. Exempt from these political pressures, private firms in similar lines of activity came through the economic difficulties of that period and began turning profits.

At the same time it should not be overlooked that the state enterprises have not been only the politicians' victims. Having greater stability and continuity of leadership than the government, their influence is considerable, and they sometimes use the parties. It was in fact Enrico Mattei, the founder of ENI, who taught the Christian Democrats in the early fifties how to link economic and political power, how funds could be used to buy politicians, factions, newspapers, and influence. It was he who formed one of the first and strongest of Christian Democratic factions, the Base. With his enormous influence in the party – and therefore the government – he had a completely free hand to conduct ENI's overseas operations – Italy's foreign policy, some thought – without interference from the Foreign Ministry. Another such mogul was Eugenio Cefis, quondam head of ENI and Montedison, a huge chemical and fibers firm. Like Mattei, Cefis was no mere chief executive officer of his firm but a wheeler-dealer in both politics and economics to such an extent that he has been described as the most influential man in Italy during the early 1970s.

The initial challenge to the Christian Democratic monopoly of the public entities came with the formation of the center-left government of 1963. Up to then the Christian Democrats had appeased their small coalition partners with a few crumbs, positions with little political or financial benefit. Now the Socialists demanded their "fair share" of *sottogoverno* jobs. In numbers they extracted quite a few but these were almost always subordinate ones, making them "the party of the vice presidencies," in Giuseppe Tamburrano's phrase. A partial exception was the state radio and television, which was of such importance to the Socialists that a division of the positions was a requisite part of every coalition accord. Even so the Christian Democrats have invariably held on to the most important post, that of director general.

It was not until the end of the 1970s that the Christian Democrats' hold on the *sottogoverno* was loosened. By then the problems of the state enterprises were so grave and the jealousy of the other parties so intense that they could no longer resist. Far from objecting to the politicization of the public agencies, the competitors wanted only to share in the spoils. For the Socialists, key positions in the *sottogoverno* – with the resulting access to funds and patronage – were more important than positions in the cabinet. With the fading of the "historic compromise" in 1979, the Christian Democrats were dependent on Socialist cooperation, and Craxi drove a hard bargain.

The struggle began with a veritable war over ENI, which in five years had six different heads until it was definitively ceded to the Socialists in 1982. On entering the government in 1980 the Socialists forced the Christian Democrats to hand over the Ministry of State Participation for the first time since it had been established in 1956. They also took the top positions in the Banca Nazionale del Lavoro, the country's largest bank, positions in some savings banks, and roughly a quarter of the board positions in the state enterprises. That these were then run as annexes of the party was well illustrated in 1983 when Nerio Nesi, the man the Socialists put at the head of the Banca Nazionale del Lavoro, broke ranks with all the other banks and, at the direction of his party, lowered the bank's interest rate. In the cultural area the Venice Biennale has long been in Socialist hands, and they have used it on occasion for the party's own politico-cultural purposes. The Social Democrats' share of the booty has included the top positions in EFIM and the Istituto Bancario San Paolo di Torino. By the mid-1980s the Liberals had gained a vice-presidency in both IRI and ENI as well as a seat on the board of ENEL, ENEA, and a number of banks. The Republicans held comparable positions, though more of them as a result of their longer participation in government.

As of the early 1980s the Christian Democrats had given up roughly half the positions in the state industrial enterprises but still held tenaciously on to three-quarters of the banks. In theaters, opera houses, and so on, Christian Democrats were estimated to hold 40 percent, the Socialists 26 percent, and the Communists 22 percent of the positions. In health and social welfare, the positions were split according to a formula that gave the Socialists and Communists about 20 percent each and the Christian Democrats 37 percent.

In distributing the parts of the public sector like so many trophies of the political battle, the parties also claim the right to designate the person to fill the position and a veto right over candidates of other parties. Moreover, the persons designated must obey the political terms of the contract. When they do not they have to step down. Egidio Egidi resigned twice, in 1977 as head of Agip and in 1980 as head of ENI. In 1982 Rinaldo Ossola, a former director general of the Bank of Italy and ex-minister of foreign trade, was compelled to resign as chairman of the Banco di Napoli, a Christian Democratic stronghold, because in trying to clean it up he had stepped on the toes of too many politicians. The next year Umberto

Colombo, the head of ENI was forced out because he would not accept as his director general Leonardo Di Donna, a man whom Craxi insisted on having in the position for personal and partisan reasons.

By now, however, even the most hard-bitten practitioner of *partitocrazia* realized that the public-sector economy had been pushed so near financial ruin as a result of politics that proper management and sound reorganization were urgent. The goose had to be rescued if there were to be any golden eggs at all to be pilfered. It was at this point that Romano Prodi, a young Christian Democrat, was placed at the head of IRI and Franco Reviglio, a Socialist, in charge of ENI. These two experienced and competent technocrats gradually restructured their organizations, divested some of the weak subsidiaries, and began to place the two holding companies on a sounder operational and financial footing. Even so, they were hounded by the parties. For instance, Prodi's effort to sell off the food-production subsidiary, SME, provoked a bitter struggle between the Socialists and Christian Democrats. The political tampering has therefore continued, now at least below the threshold of economic ruin.

The scandals and corruption are so much taken for granted that they never become a serious political or electoral issue. From time to time the Republicans wag a self-righteous finger at the other parties only to have fingers wagged back at them. Nor do the Communists exploit the *sottogoverno* any less than the other parties. On the regional, provincial, and communal levels where they are in control, they direct the process with equal partisanship though perhaps with less corruption.

The dispersion of the power of the *sottogoverno* has been one of the most effective ways of destroying the concentration of Christian Democratic power and of finding some degree of alternative to the lack of an alternation in the government. It perpetuates, however, a system of gross maladministration with grave economic and social effects.

8. The administration of justice

One of the outstanding paradoxes in Italian public life is the contrast between the heavy web of laws that hangs over everyday life and the contempt that the person in the street generally exhibits toward all legal regulations. Cynics maintain that violating the law is one of the requisites in the art of survival in Italy and that the country indeed functions only because laws of greater or lesser importance are ignored. In any case the dichotomy between the *paese legale* and the *paese reale,* between the "legal Italy" and the "real Italy," is a fundamental one. The country's legal tradition extends far back into the past and is still cultivated in the universities. But the everyday world of legal reality is all too often one of malfunctioning courts, a politicized judiciary, arbitrary judges, and inadequately protected civil liberties. Hence the taunt that Italy is the cradle of law but the grave of justice.

The administration of justice faces growing problems throughout the Western world but probably nowhere more than in Italy. The dramatic rise of political terrorism, mafia operations, domestic and international drug trafficking, massive illegal arms sales, kidnapping, and ordinary criminality places crushing burdens on the judicial system while exposing its weaknesses more clearly than ever. As a consequence the problems of the legal system vie with the economic situation as the predominant concern of the public and government alike.

The place of the judiciary

If the constitution leaves ambiguities in the role and powers of the country's executive authorities, it is clear and emphatic in its intent to have a completely separate judicial branch that, in the words of Article 104, is "an autonomous order independent of every other power." To give this provision practical effect, the constitution provides that judges shall be appointed for life and that their recruitment, training, promotion, assignment, and transfer as well as disciplinary authority over them shall be not in the hands of the government but of other judges. It therefore set up an independent

150

body of judges, lawyers, and legal experts – the Superior Judicial Council – to discharge these responsibilities.

The constitution goes further and, in one of its major innovations, introduces into Italian political life a supreme constitutional authority. This it does by establishing a Constitutional Court with responsibility to review the constitutionality of all legislation, to adjudicate disputes among government agencies as well as between the regions and the central government, to determine the validity of referenda, and, with parliamentary approval, to impeach principal executive officials.

Implementing these provisions was a long, arduous struggle and one that in certain respects continues. The concept of an independent judiciary with the right of judicial review presented an obvious challange to parliamentary power and party supremacy. The Christian Democrats, once they had won their parliamentary majority in 1948, had no interest in a powerful and competing authority in the state. Successive governments simply refused to enact the legislation necessary to put the constitutional provisions into effect. Only when the Christian Democrats lost their majority in 1953 was the way finally open.

The Constitutional Court was established in 1956. It has fifteen members; they serve for nine years and are not eligible for immediate reappointment. Five of them are chosen by the president, five by parliament, and five by the judges of the highest civil, criminal, and administrative courts. The Superior Judicial Council was set up in 1958. It now has thirty-two members, twenty are judges selected by the judiciary itself and ten are legal experts chosen by parliament. The first president of the Court of Cassation and the attorney general belong ex officio. Members serve for four years and may not succeed themselves. The body is nominally chaired by the president of the republic, though its functioning executive is its vice-president.

Once these bodies were founded, Christian Democratic governments at the time attempted to deprive them of the independence that the constitution intended. The Superior Judicial Council it tried to hobble by subordinating it to the Justice Ministry, thereby destroying its very autonomy. The law to this effect was later declared unconstitutional. The Constitutional Court it sought to control by claiming that the president's five appointees should be selected by the government – in practice the Christian Democrats. It also tried to tame the court by refusing to enforce some of its early decisions, eventually provoking the resignation of the court's president, Enrico De Nicola. Parliament contributed to the court's difficulty by refusing to clear away old laws, many of the Fascist era, that conflicted with the letter and spirit of the republican constitution. Resistance to the court also came as well from the senior judges, who were strongly opposed to judicial review, not only of their decisions but also of parliamentary legislation. Since cases can be tried only if sent up by lower courts, the Constitutional Court's functioning was for a time impeded by recalcitrance within the judicial system itself. Not surprisingly the court was extremely diffident in its decisions during its early years.

Since then it has won acceptance as the supreme interpreter of the constitution and, despite certain lapses, has gradually earned a position of solid prestige. It not only has established itself as the ultimate arbiter of acts of parliament but has opened the way to significant social reforms. It also has played a role, which it did not seek, of in effect reforming statutes that parliament was unwilling to deal with. By annulling, for example, certain repressive laws of the Fascist period, the court partially solved a thorny legal and political problem. It drastically altered legal relations between church and state by gutting key provisions of the 1929 concordat, which the Vatican and the Italian government could not agree to amend. And it rid Italian law of such bizarre statutes as that which provided for up to fifteen years' imprisonment for *plagio*, or "spiritual manipulation," which was actually enforced until the court abrogated it in 1981.

There is no rule of precedent in Italian law, and decisions have been shaped, as with courts everywhere, partly by the political outlook of the judges and partly by the mood in society and parliament. While displaying no uniform ideological bias – on some issues being uniformly conservative and on others consistently liberal – it has on the whole become more daring in challenging old statutes and more progressive in its decisions on social questions.

Although the court has been uncompromising in its defense of property rights, it upheld the nationalization of the electricity industry in 1963 and has ruled against industrial lockouts. Its decisions have been generally favorable to the trade unions, workers' rights, and not only the right to strike but also to hold political strikes. The court's record of defending civil liberties is good, marred only by its defense of "crimes of opinion" and certain public-security regulations of Fascist vintage. Its rulings in favor of parity of the sexes and between marriage partners initiated a marked advance in women's rights and in time compelled parliament to reform family legislation. After years of caution regarding church–state issues, the court adopted a strongly secularist position. In disputes between regions and the central government, it has usually sided with the latter. It has been permissive in allowing European Community regulations to be applied in Italy. Among its dubious decisions are certain of those that disallowed eight proposed referenda to be put to a vote.

Only once has the court sat as an impeachment panel, when its membership is augmented by sixteen persons chosen by parliament. The occasion was to try two former defense ministers, Mario Tanassi and Luigi Gui, on charges of having accepted bribes from the Lockheed Aircraft Corporation.

The weakness of the court, as of the judicial system as a whole, is its entanglement in politics. Most appointments to the court are partisan. The five nominees of parliament are selected in accord with an unwritten agreement among the parties that two will go to the Christian Democrats and one each to the Communists, Socialists, and lay parties. In making his five appointments, the president of the republic is not deaf to partisan suggestions. No president has so far selected a Communist. The five appointed by the judiciary are the least political. But all in all a majority of the court's members owe their positions in one way or another to party considerations. These political links are reinforced by a party's repertoire of potential rewards. A member of the court with aspirations of a later career in public life – as a deputy, senator, or head of a prestigious state organization – must be receptive to party views. And the parties are not bashful about sending signals – an article in the party newspaper, for instance – on how to vote. Not all court members heed such views all the time. And most cases are of no political interest. But some decisions are undoubtedly conditioned by partisan pressures.

The independence of the judiciary itself – the judges and public prosecutors – is even more blatantly compromised, though in this case less because of the parties than the judges themselves. At the end of the war the senior judges, thanks to their authority over promotion and assignment, exerted absolute control over the judicial system. As veterans of the Fascist state, they were deeply conservative. Although they injected this tone into the operations and decisions of the judiciary, they kept the courts out of overt politics. But once their authority over promotion was broken, as a result of reforms in the late 1960s, they lost their hold on the other judges, many of whom reacted to their new freedom by taking up political causes. In no time factions developed within the judiciary and spread to the Superior Judicial Council itself. With that, the principle of an independent and politically neutral judiciary was destroyed.

The creaking machinery of justice

The biggest problem in the operation of the Italian judicial system is the extraordinarily slow operation of the courts. Some cases are notorious. A disagreement over fishing rights in the island waters of Cabras in Sardinia went to trial in 1858 and was settled only in 1981. A dispute over the legacy of Don Carmelo Parisis, duke of Leucadi and Casalecchio, began in Messina in 1914 and was not concluded until 1980. It was resolved then because, the properties in ruin and the bank notes no longer of value, his heirs concluded there was no further point in pursuing the case. Although such examples are patently exceptional, it is anything but unusual for a trial to drag on for a dozen years or more. One of the most important cases of the postwar period concerned the bombing in 1969 of a bank on Piazza Fontana in Milan in which sixteen persons were killed and ninety injured. The trial began in 1972 in Rome and was transferred first to Milan and then to Catanzaro, where it did not resume until 1974, only to be postponed until 1977. The case was decided in 1979; the decision was appealed and a second trial was concluded in 1982. A higher court annulled that decision, however, and another retrial got under way only in 1985. Although this case is also not typical, the overall record of the Italian legal system is so bad that the European Court of Human Rights in 1982 sharply criticized Italian courts for excessive slowness and in one case levied a fine against the government.

The time for the average case to make its way through the three main tiers of courts is from seven to ten years. First a case goes either before a single judge, if it is a relatively minor matter, or to a tribunal of three judges. If appealed, it goes to an appellate court, which sits as a panel of five judges. Finally it can be referred to the Court of Cassation in Rome, which constitutes, except in constitutional matters, the final appeal court. Before a single judge, cases usually take between 470 and 550 days; in a tribunal, from 800 to 900 days; before a court of appeal, 770 days; in the Court of Cassation, almost a full three years. Therefore the normal case – assuming it is appealed, as almost always occurs – runs for fully seven years and can go for three additional years if it is taken to the highest court. The inevitable result is a huge backlog of cases at every jurisdictional level. In each year since 1980 there have been roughly 1.5 million criminal cases and over 1 million civil cases pending on court dockets.

The slow and inefficient operation of the courts can be traced to a wide variety of causes. From the preparation of a case to its decision, the natural pace of judicial action is leisurely. The courts themselves are often woefully lacking in adequate and qualified administrative staff. They are usually situated in antiquated and cramped buildings and lack the funds and personnel to maintain even modern filing systems and data banks. It is not unknown for a judge to have to write out his decisions himself for lack of secretarial assistance. To visit an Italian courthouse is to go back to an earlier century.

Judges themselves are part of the problem. Many take only forty or fifty cases a year. As a group they are badly allocated, both within the court system and among the judicial districts. There are too few judges in the lower courts but more than are necessary in the multimember panels at the appellate level. The geographic distribution of judges was set in 1941 and today is drastically at variance with the radical population shifts since then. Moreover, many judges – roughly 40 percent – are from the South; many of them, after brief service elsewhere, press to be assigned back home. The resulting dislocations are substantial. In 1983, of the 7,352 judgeships, 952 were vacant and some 300 were identified for transfer from areas where they are not needed to those where a grave shortage existed. But in the face of obdurate local resistance, the government and parliament year after year flinch from moving judgeships. As a consequence in large cities, such as Turin and Milan, but also in Sardinia and peripheral areas of northern Italy, courts are so shorthanded that even the hardest-working judges have trouble keeping abreast of the cases reaching the court dockets.

Italian appeals procedures are a further part of the problem. In contrast to those judicial systems where findings of fact are rarely at issue and only points of law may be appealed, Italian appellate courts treat each case as though it had never been tried. Years can therefore be consumed in studying the old record, taking new testimony, and reevaluating previously established facts. As a consequence trials are protracted and results can be surprisingly different, even flatly contradictory. In the Piazza Fontana bombing trial, the accused were first found guilty. On appeal they were judged innocent, not because of any legal error in the previous trial but because of a different assessment of the facts. That decision was in turn overruled on grounds both of the legal proceedings and of the treatment of facts. In another case, a priest accused in 1973 of the murder of his female housekeeper was found innocent both in the original trial in Bolzano and on appeal in Trent. Ordered by the Court of Cassation to be retried on points of law, an appellate court in Venice found him guilty and sentenced him to fourteen years' imprisonment. The Court of Cassation again ordered a retrial on points of law and an appellate court in Brescia found him innocent on grounds of fact. However, the decision was once more found wanting and a fourth trial was held, concluding in 1982 with the defendant's being found innocent for lack of evidence.

Another difficulty for the courts is the disorder in the legal codes. Both civil and criminal codes were drawn up during the Fascist period. After the war the principles of the republican constitution were superimposed on the old statutes, creating confusion and contradictions. The Constitutional Court annulled some provisions, and parliament amended others. But parliament has never rewritten the codes from scratch and therefore has left the courts to deal with a crazy quilt of judicial and legislative accretions. The overall situation has been vividly described by Luigi Barzini: "A tropical tangle of statutes, norms, regulations, customs, some hundreds of years old, some voted last week by Parliament and signed this morning by the President, could paralyze every activity in the land, stop trains, planes, cars and ships, shut every shop, industrial plant, hospital, school and office, if they were suddenly applied. The late Luigi Einaudi, Italy's formost economist and ex-President of the Republic, calculated that, if every tax on the statute books was fully collected, the State would absorb 110 percent of the national income."

Although courts in almost all Western countries have faced a steadily increasing workload, the problems have been particularly severe in Italy. In addition to ordinary crime and less ordinary violence by terrorists and the mafia, Italy was by the early 1980s one of the world's leading centers of international drug trafficking and illegal arms sales. Kidnappings reached the highest level in the world. On top of that the courts have been deluged by a wave of corruption cases that has swept over the republic from its earliest years. A number of the scandals made the headlines of the international press – the Montesi affair, which involved drugs, orgies, and politics; the Lockheed case, which concerned graft and eventually put former Defense Minister Tanassi behind bars; the affair of Michele Sindona, in which the Vatican lost millions in investments and a major American bank collapsed; the case of Roberto Calvi, involving the biggest bank failure in history; and, most sensational of all, the secret Masonic lodge, P2, that was engaged in illegal and unconstitutional activities. But they were merely the most notorious in an unending pageant of squalid plots, blackmail, graft, payoffs, intrigues, fraud, misappropriations of funds, thievery, and cover-ups that has touched almost every part of society.

From Giorgio Galli's survey of some of these scandals in *L'Italia sotteranea* (The underground Italy) it becomes clear that political figures, criminals, and officials of the intelligence service – and even on occasion Vatican functionaries – are so hopelessly enmeshed in the cases that investigations and trials sink into mystification, conspiracy theories, and wild speculation. In the end facts are rarely established and few persons are ever punished. The practical upshot is that these cases are a tremendous burden on prosecutors and judges, who sometimes find that the only way to resolve a case is to delay it or let it slide along until it peters out.

At the formal opening of the new judicial year, the attorney general has regularly reiterated that the crisis in the judicial system has worsened, with court dockets fuller, judges fewer, and trials slower than ever. And on taking office, every new government in years has put forward a plan to rectify these problems. Little has ever been done. Already in the 1970s the magistrates' exasperation had reached the explosion point. Their grievances were also personal. Before 1945 magistrates had enjoyed the highest prestige and wages of all professions; in the course of the postwar period their relative status and income declined. Being responsible for the investigations and trials of terrorists, mafia members, and big-time criminals, they were at times in daily risk of their lives. Even though some were in fact murdered, the government for years made little or no provision for their physical protection.

Eventually judges went on strike. Their first major action was a wage strike in March 1975. When President Leone criticized the stoppage as inconsistent with the magistrates' constitutional duties, the judges responded that they enjoyed the same right to strike as all Italian civil servants. Since then there have been repeated strikes, wildcat actions, and work slowdowns not only for better wages and better physical safeguards but also for improvements in the court system. In time judges secured better conditions for themselves. But they have never been able to goad the government and parliament into dealing with the structural problems of the judicial system, or even to improve the existing situation with some money. In the 1984 budget an exiguous .76 percent of expenditures went for the administration of justice, a sum that included wages and the operating costs of prisons.

Politicized justice

Despite its difficulties, the Italian *magistratura* remains a select profession, a career service with entry through a stiff annual public examination. Magistrates are the elite of the civil service and again stand at the top of the government wage scale. In contrast to the United States, Britain, and many other countries, the Italian judiciary comprises not only judges but also investigating magistrates and prosecuting attorneys. In other words the functions of a grand jury, district attorney, and trial judge are all exercised within the same organization. Entrants, usually fresh from a university law school, serve an initial period of internship with either a judge or a prosecutor. From then on they normally remain in one or the other branch of the judiciary. Appointed for life, magistrates are responsible only to the Superior Judicial Council and therefore have a great latitude of personal discretion. They are promoted by seniority throughout their career; transfer, by a Superior Judicial Council, requires their agreement. The purpose of establishing a separate and autonomous judiciary with its members subject only to other magistrates was to create a system that would be both independent of government and immune from politics. The postwar history of the Italian judiciary is essentially a struggle over this ideal.

Today the principal defect of the Italian judiciary is precisely its immersion in politics and ideology. The problem began in the Fascist era when the Piedmontese model of a politically neutral judiciary was increasingly compromised. By 1945 Italy was in the hands of a judiciary that was deeply conservative in its approach to the law and the role of the courts. The senior judges, being at the top of a tightly organized judicial system, tacitly imposed their own points of view on the new judges as they rose through the ranks. But when they lost control of promotions, they lost their hold on the subordinate judges. A sense of intellectual liberation swept through the judiciary. Younger judges in particular began to challenge both their superiors' authority and their theory of law.

This disagreement coincided with the wave of student and worker unrest in 1968–69, which radicalized a large number of judges, especially the younger ones in the North, driving many of them to the extreme left. By the end of the 1960s the judiciary was split from top to bottom over issues as basic as the nature of law and the role of judges. The consequence was a political polarization that fractured the unity of the judiciary and has impeded the administration of justice. Probably a majority of judges adhere to the conventional view that the operation of the courts is essentially mechanical rather than discretionary. Even so, the judiciary as a whole is deeply divided over how laws are to be interpreted, how old statutes and the new constitution are to be reconciled, and the extent to which legislation should be molded to meet the changing needs of society.

Conservative and right-wing judges have explicitly endorsed the most restrictive view of the judicial role. But in practice they impose their own conservative ideology on the law and its application. In the past some of them have regularly banned books, plays, films, and magazines and have taken action against those whose mode of social behavior – the wearing of bikinis at the beach, for instance – they found distasteful. One magistrate in particular, Donato Bartolomei, made himself notorious – or much admired by some – for having banned most of the films and novels for which Italy was famous in the postwar period. These prohibitions rarely lasted long and, given the strong Italian instinct for tolerance, were generally treated as a joke.

For the leftist judges, organized in a group called the "democratic magistrates," the use of ideology goes even further and is explicit. These judges openly, indeed proudly, acknowledge their ideological commitment, occasionally even expressing it on cases that are *sub judice*. For them, the courts are an instrument in the class struggle. In their view, as summed up by a noted jurist, Federico Mancini, "All laws should be interpreted with this yardstick: partisanship is a virtue and neutrality a misconception or a fraud; so is independence; a judiciary cloaking itself with these sham values is a servant of power and ought to be told as much; judges must defend the oppressed and the downtrodden, cooperate with the labor movement, act as a countervailing force *vis-à-vis* the political and industrial government."

It was in this spirit that many younger judges, conducting political crusades from the bench, earned the title *pretori d'assalto*, "fighting judges." In their hands the social provisions of the constitution, up to then considered platitudes about economic equality and social justice, were treated as an enforceable legal code. In labor disputes these judges almost invariably decided in favor of workers and unions. "For an employer," Mancini remarked, "to emerge from their hands as a winner was harder than for a camel to go through the eye of a needle." At the same time they were also responsible for much judicial legislation by establishing new standards of environmental protection against industrial pollution and real estate speculation, outlawing food adulteration, and the like. In seeking to be the country's social conscience, these judges hoped to revolutionize the role of the Italian judiciary. In the course of the 1970s some "democratic magistrates" became increasingly radical, occasionally denouncing other judges as "trucklers to the bourgeoisie" and appearing at public meetings at the side of extremist leaders. Ultimately a few even became involved with the Red Brigades.

Given the pronounced politicization of every other area of Italian public life and the ideological cleavages in the country, the political infection of the judiciary was probably unavoidable and once it occurred was destined to be more virulent than anywhere else in Western Europe. Since the mid-1970s, it has gradually subsided. The old right-wing judges have now retired. The "democratic magistrates," splintered by repeated secessions, have been stepping back from political causes. And the Communist party, seeking to enter the government after 1976, told the Communists on the bench to leave social reform to the party in parliament.

But political differences remain and have damaged the various judicial organizations. The National Association of Magistrates, the judges' professional organization to which all judges traditionally belonged, was already in the hands of the younger judges by 1969. The senior judges walked out a short time later and formed their own strongly conservative body, the Union of Italian Magistrates, which they dissolved in 1979. The political factions in the association itself hardened over time into groups as distinct and hostile as those among the political parties. Of those identifiable in the early 1980s, roughly 37 percent belonged to the conservative "independent magistrates," 45 percent to the center-left "unity for the constitution," and the remainder to the "democratic magistrates."

Inevitably these divisions have been carried into the Superior Judicial Council, subverting its political autonomy and neutrality. Even at the best of times the council's independence was far from immaculate. The ten members appointed by parliament have in fact always been selected by the parties, with four falling to the Christian Democrats, three to the Communists, two to the Socialists, and one to the lay parties. After the judges themselves became politically factionalized, the remaining twenty appointments – chosen by the judiciary – were also subject to ideological selection, each faction voting for its own adherents. In practice this works out to the Christian Democrats and Communists having a decisive voice in selecting members of the council. And that is only the beginning. Judges argue long and hard to ensure that the panels of the courts are formed in accord with factional divisions. Assignments to the courts themselves – unlike promotions, which are automatic, based on seniority – are also subject to political considerations. The result is a political spoils process that infects the judiciary as it does other public institutions. Even the council's disciplinary function has been compromised; by appealing to their faction for support, offenders are almost always absolved.

The judicial system is also prey to a different type of problem: external pressures, political and other, that are occasionally brought to bear both on individual magistrates and on the *pubblico ministero,* "district attorney's office." Whether these influences come from the government, a political party, or some group or individual, the intent is to cajole or intimidate magistrates into redirecting their activities or dropping a case. The atmosphere in which some magistrates work can at times be tense and dangerous, and many an individual prosecutor has shown tremendous moral and physical courage in the face of threats and blandishments. Others have given in. Three cases in Western Sicily illustrate the situation. Giangiacomo Montalto, deputy district attorney in Trapani, was murdered in 1983 because he would not be deterred from his probe of mafia activities. His successor on the other hand cooperated with the mafia, was exposed, and landed in prison. *His* successor in turn again went after the mafia and was promptly the object of an assassination attempt.

The situation is somewhat similar for one or another *pubblico ministero.* Some are hard hitting and courageous. The Rome office, however, has had a reputation for being "sensitive" to the interests of political parties and the concerns of persons with good political connections. Cases that properly lay in the jurisdiction of the magistrates in Milan or other cities have at times been transferred to Rome for that reason. The result has on occasion been skewed investigations and even downright judicial iniquity.

One example must suffice. It concerns the Bank of Italy, probably the country's most prestigious institution and the only one to maintain its freedom from the control of the political parties; Paolo Baffi, its governor, a man of unblemished integrity and architect of the country's remarkable financial recovery in the mid-1970s; and Mario Sarcinelli, deputy director of the bank and the official in charge of investigating suspect members of the banking system.

In March 1979, at the order of Antonio Alibrandi, a right-wing Rome magistrate, the police marched into the Bank of Italy, arrested Sarcinelli, and imprisoned him for nearly two weeks. He was then released and the court acknowledged that there were no legal grounds to hold him. In the meantime Baffi, who traveled often to international bankers' meetings, had been subjected to the humiliation of being deprived of his passport. Sarcinelli, due to become director general of the bank several months later, could not be promoted because technically he was still under investigation. Baffi retired soon afterward in disgust. It was widely suspected at the time and later became more evident that Alibrandi's action was intended to bring to a halt the bank's investigation of the Banco Ambrosiano, whose illegal operations caused its collapse in 1982. The case demonstrated the turpitude a politically motivated judge can wreak, in this case not only against two men doing their duty but also against one of the few Italian institutions with any integrity left. It was an Ibsenesque affair, with the villains portraying the heroes as enemies of the people.

Embattled civil liberties

Although cases like Sarcinelli's are not everyday occurrences, they are not entirely exceptional. In the late 1970s alone several dozen impresarios of theater and opera, a number of professors of medicine, forty-nine savings bank presidents and ex-presidents – to say nothing of countless less prominent citizens – have been rounded up and summarily put behind bars, often on charges that were prima facie flimsy. Sometimes the arrests were at dawn, involved aged men, and took in masses of suspects at one time. Gradually a pattern has developed. Dramatic arrests are followed by even more dramatic newspaper headlines. The shadow of corruption once again seems to cover the land. Judges and prosecutors do not remain anonymous and in the background; they become celebrities and give interviews. Then rumors begin to circulate that the arrests were motivated for some unrelated reason, possibly political. After one or two days, weeks, or months the suspects are released. Sometimes the charges are declared to be unfounded, as in Sarcinelli's case. Or, years later perhaps, a trial commences that often comes to nothing.

During the late seventies and early eighties there was still another type of sweeping arrest and imprisonment: of persons accused of terrorist acts or of participation in groups practicing armed violence. Some suspects were imprisoned with no stated evidence against them and had to wait years before being charged, much less tried. Some youths were sentenced to as much as thirty years in prison merely for belonging to "criminal associations" without having committed any crime. The trials of terrorists have always been conducted with scrupulous fairness. But prior abuses of judicial and police authority, though not systematic, have undoubtedly resulted in some cases of gross injustice.

On April 7, 1979, to cite a notable example, the police arrested twenty Marxist intellectuals, including Antonio Negri, a Padua University professor. Negri was accused of involvement in the kidnapping and murder of Aldo Moro. These allegations were later dropped, but Negri was in prison for a year and a half before formal legal charges were brought against him for armed insurrection and other felonies. When his trial finally began in 1983, he had been behind bars for four years. The Negri case is not the only or even the most flagrant example of such abuses. The Amnesty International annual reports for 1981 and several years following cite a number of similar cases where the original charges could not be sustained, were dropped, and were immediately replaced with new charges, creating strong suspicion that the detention was for political reasons. To highlight the situation, the Radical party took the sensational – and, to many, scandalous – step of placing Negri on their candidate list in the 1983 parliamentary election. Negri was elected and, automatically gaining legal immunity as a parliamentarian, was released from prison. While parliament debated whether to lift his immunity so his trial could proceed, Negri fled the country. A year later he was sentenced in absentia to thirty years imprisonment for terrorist activities.

These infractions of civil liberties fly in the face of the provisions of a genuinely liberal constitution. That establishes, in Articles 13 through 28, a comprehensive bill of rights along classic lines. It includes the normal freedoms – such as speech, press, assembly, and religion – and the normal protections – such as freedom from unwarranted arrest, detention, search, and seizure. By and large the Constitutional Court has a good record of defending these rights in cases that reach them. The problems arise from three statutes that stand in uneasy relation to the spirit and letter of the liberal constitution.

One is the criminal code of 1931, which, though in part nullified by Constitutional Court decisions, contains still valid provisions limiting basic freedoms. It is under one such clause or another that books and other publications are still sometimes banned, though the injunction is brief and usually ignored by vendors. Under a provision punishing *vilipendio,* "contempt," persons may be sentenced to years of imprisonment for disrespect toward state institutions, the national flag, the armed forces, the Italian nation, religion, and prominent public figures, including the pope. This law was occasionally enforced with shocking results in the early years of the republic and is still not a dead letter. In 1980 the editor of a satirical weekly, *Male,* was sentenced to two-and-a-half years imprisonment for having staged an impromptu skit poking gentle fun at John Paul II, who was by remarkable coincidence speaking at the same moment to the Rome press corps on freedom of expression. In 1983 an American writer was sentenced to a prison term of one-and-a-half years for a book considered insulting to the memory of Pius XII. A year later a court ordered the confiscation of a poster with a reproduction of *The Last Supper* advertising a brand of grapefruit juice. The enforcement of the repressive provisions of this code are increasingly rare. But having them on the books adds to the very uncertainty that is the result of one of the most pervasive problems in the Italian administration of justice, its capriciousness.

A more immediate risk to civil liberties results from two acts passed in response to the wave of political terrorism of the 1970s. Both concern that neuralgic point in every legal system, arrest and detention. The first was the 1976 "Reale law," named for the then Republican minister of justice, Oronzo Reale, which was intended to improve public security following a number of grave acts of right-wing terrorism. In particular the statute loosened up arrest provisions to include very elastic and ambiguous criteria, thereby broadening judicial discretion at the expense of suspects' rights. By reducing the categories of persons who could be released while awaiting trial, the Reale law increased the risk of long and unjustified detentions. And by relaxing restrictions on the use of weapons by the police, it raised the danger of a trigger-happy police force. It is reckoned that nearly 150 persons were shot to death by police in the following decade.

The other set of statutes, the antiterrorist legislation of 1979–80, empowered the police to detain any suspect for forty-eight hours without notifying a magistrate and to hold him for a week or more once a magistrate has been informed. The police were also authorized to interrogate suspects without a judicial official or defense counsel being present. Most extreme of all, suspects could be held in preventive detention for three years and three months before trial, for another three years and three months if the case were appealed, and for yet a further period of the same length if the case went to the highest court – meaning that someone could be in jail for a total of nearly ten years before a final disposition of his case. Since Italy, like most other European countries, has no law establishing habeas corpus and an extremely limited bail system, suspects can therefore find themselves in preventive detention for more than three years before even entering a courtroom.

Ironically it was not the tough detention provisions of the 1979–80 statutes that eventually broke the left-wing terrorist movement but the offer of a lenient sentence to anyone who cooperated with the police. By the end of 1983 some 400 ex-terrorists benefited from the law, in many instances receiving sentences that appalled the country for their leniency. Once again, despite good intentions, justice was offended.

Although many of the provisions of the 1979–80 laws have expired, judges and prosecutors retain sweeping authority to hold suspects in prolonged detention on evidence that is at times tenuous and even unstated. Their powers intensify a long-standing problem that goes far beyond the relatively few terrorist suspects and includes a far larger number of persons accused of ordinary crimes. As the conditions for obligatory arrest were broadened and those for provisional release were drastically narrowed, the inevitable consequence was further incursions into elementary civil liberties, augmenting the number of persons in preventive detention and causing an ever more drastic overcrowding of prisons. By the mid-seventies the number of individuals in jail awaiting trial was roughly 20,000; by the early eighties the number was up to 30,000.

In 1982 an effort was initiated to ameliorate the situation by requiring courts to respond within three days to a suspect's formal appeal for release. At first the procedure helped little, however, since many suspects did not know of the arrangement or were too mistrustful to avail themselves of it. By mid-1984 over 10,000 cases had been reviewed with the result that 1,781 arrests were quashed.

In the meantime the public scandal had mounted. Once again the Radicals used the issue in an election – this time the 1984 balloting for the European parliament – by selecting as a candidate another victim of the system, Enzo Tortora. Tortora, a popular television figure, had been accused of involvement in drug trafficking and held in prison without trial for nearly a year. His case, which catalyzed the public contempt for the country's judicial procedures, resulted in his winning a half-million preference votes in his constituency.

But no one and no cause was served by a parliamentary and judicial system where a man accused of a serious crime was not brought to trial in a reasonable time and who gained release from improper detention through an electoral gimmick. Neither the Tortora nor the Negri case was the first time a political party had adopted someone as a parliamentary candidate so that, once elected, he would be immune from prosecution. The procedure neither added prestige to the state nor advanced the cause of justice.

In the summer of 1984 preventive detention, now discreetly renamed "precautionary detention," was revised to reduce the time spent in prison prior to trial. But the change dealt with symptoms rather than causes since its implementation presupposed efficiently operating courts and an adequate number of judges and prosecutors. The danger consequently arose that suspects would be released before trials could be held – still punishing the innocent, by imprisoning them for long periods without trial, and allowing the guilty to go free because they could not be tried before the statute of limitations had expired. The new law was popularly disparaged as a "creeping amnesty." Although parliament patted itseld on the back for a "reform," magistrates wrung their hands at the thought of the number of criminals who would never be punished.

Criminal justice and the penal system

Another set of difficulties, far from unique to Italy, arises from the malfunctioning of criminal justice. A large part of the problem is that the punitive process itself is not swift, effective, and certain enough to forestall crime. According to a 1976 report of the Superior Judicial Council, the percentage of unsolved crimes between 1970 and 1974 rose from 55 to 78 percent. Moreover only 3 to 4 percent of those apprehended were arrested and charged; even of this small number, many were never tried because the statute of limitations had expired before they could be brought into court. Such a drastic failure of law and order clearly goes far to undermine the very notion of criminal deterrence.

The slowness of the courts also adds to the drastic overcrowding of prisons. As of 1984 there were about 46,000 persons in jails built for a maximum of 27,000 prisoners, with the number increasing at a rate of nearly 700 a month. One way authorities have dealt with the problem is to declare periodic amnesties. In 1978 over 7,000 and in 1981 around 14,000 persons were released from pretrial detention or from sentences for minor crimes. The Superior Judicial Council's 1976 report stated that normally only 20 percent of those sentenced serve out their full terms; 55 percent are released provisionally; and the others are amnestied. But neither the severity of long detention nor the leniency of summary release contributes to a sense of having a fair and effective criminal-justice system.

Prison conditions add to the problem. Most prisons are reconstructed medieval fortresses or monasteries where the cells, food, and treatment have traditionally reflected an archaic and repressive philosophy. Frequent prison revolts have been one of the consequences. In 1975 parliament passed legislation to introduce more humane treatment and initiate a program of prisoner rehabilitation – by such means as abolishing striped prison garb, modernizing prisons, separating suspects from convicts, and providing immediate vocational training for short-term prisoners. The reforms ran into trouble from the start. The government budget squeeze in the following years reduced the funds available for the necessary additional personnel and for building construction. Where funds were not an issue, good intentions were spoiled by excess, by an exaggerated leniency after harsh restraints. Some reforms were botched by authorities, some abused by prisoners.

The efforts on behalf of prison reform were also set back because they got under way as terrorism was reaching flood tide. The national mood changed. Some reforms that had been approved by the Chamber of Deputies were voted down by the Senate as a result of the increase in terrorism and criminality. Inside the prisons terrorists and criminals exploited the easier conditions to weaken the prison system. Prisons became an important breeding ground for terrorism, and for a time ranked just after universities and large industrial plants as places where terrorists were recruited.

Public safety and the police

The problems of public order have varied drastically over the years. In the early postwar period when the Communists organized mass demonstrations against the Marshall Plan and NATO, the Interior Ministry under Mario Scelba, a conservative Christian Democrat, reacted with great brutality. As a result of police actions, in the two years alone after July 1948, 62 persons were killed, 3,000 injured, and 92,000 arrested, most of them Communists.

As the demonstrations and police counteractions tapered off in the fifties, urban crime began sweeping through a society that had up to then been remarkably safe and orderly. As millions moved from the countryside to the cities and from South to North, social mores were shaken loose and well-administered cities, such as Turin and Milan, were overwhelmed with poor, homeless – and often exploited – emigrants. Such films as *Rocco and His Brothers* and *Voyage in Fiatnam* portrayed the resulting social problems and criminality. Although robbery, homicide, and other crimes have been steadily on the rise since then, their incidence remains moderate by other European countries' standards.

Where Italy does hold the world record is in kidnappings. From 1960 with the first case to the end of 1983, 586 persons had been reported to have been kidnapped, and it is thought that there were many additional cases of which the police were not notified. The persons were young and old, rich and poor, and in the 1980s even included children and babies. The practice began in Sardinia and was limited to there until 1968. In 1972 when the mafia became involved, kidnapping graduated from being a cottage industry to a big-time business with thousands of persons involved in kidnapping rings. Most of these rings were centered in Sardinia, Calabria, and Sicily, but some were operated in the North by Sicilian emigrants. Ransoms are always paid, kidnappers are all but never found, and 3 percent of the victims do not survive. The impotence of the police in the face of a kidnapping threat of this magnitude is a cause of the public's lack of confidence in the police.

Law enforcement and related activities are for the most part carried out by police who are organized on a national basis and who receive orders from Rome. The most important force, and the one enjoying some popular respect, is the carabinieri. They are a major buttress to law and order, especially in the countryside where they are a significant element in the social fabric of small towns. They have a strength of 85,000 men and though organizationally a part of the army, they are subordinate to the Interior Ministry. With few exceptions, carabinieri chiefs have prided themselves on remaining aloof from politics. Another force is the 82,000-man national police, who are commanded by the Interior Ministry either directly or through the local prefect. Primary responsibility for guarding the borders and for enforcing customs and fiscal regulations are the 40,000 uniformed finance guards who are under the control of the Finance Ministry. Only the municipal street police, *vigili urbani,* are under the control of local authorities.

Another element of the security situation is the intelligence services. Since 1977 these have been divided into a domestic branch, SISDE, in the control of the Interior Ministry, and an external branch, SISMI, under the Defense Ministry, with a section of the prime minister's office, CESIS, responsible for overall coordination. In addition, the three branches of the armed forces, the carabinieri, the finance guards, and the police have their own intelligence services, each operating independently.

The intelligence agencies have been increasingly criticized over the years both for incompetence and for illegal and even subversive activities. The latter problem stems from the fact that when they were established after the war, the agencies were highly political and generally well to the right. Not only did many of their officials come out of the Fascist regime but their primary mission was to operate against the Communists and Socialists. Having from the start a political function, they dabbled in domestic politics – activities that extended from snooping on the private lives of individual Italians to involvement in right-wing terrorism and other unconstitutional affairs. Successful operations against terrorists and criminals were few. As more and more became known of their failures and illicit actions, the services were thoroughly discredited.

The Christian Democrats, who have maintained unbroken control of the Interior Ministry since January 1946, never exercised effective control over the intelligence services and at times used them for partisan purposes. Gradually the practice of "political espionage" was taken up by the other parties, eventually leading to a situation where nearly everyone "had something" on nearly everyone else. The situation intensified not only the political corruption of the services but also the dichotomy between the real Italy and the legal Italy.

All in all the problems in administering justice and in maintaining law and order constitute for the average Italian the weakest point in the whole political system. On the one hand he is inadequately protected from crime and on the other liable to grave abuses from the legal authority itself. No legal system can be reorganized and put right overnight. But the inability of government and parliament to undertake a full-scale program that would create more order in the legal system, correct the problems of the courts, and give greater assurance that the innocent will be safeguarded and the guilty punished must be accounted an inexcusable failure of political will, a major reason for the mistrust of the state by its citizenry, and one of the important causes of the corrosion of public morality.

9. Dangers to the state: Plots, terrorism, and the mafia

Unlike other Western democracies Italy suffers from not just one or two but almost all the ills to which the contemporary state is susceptible – a fragmented party system, weak and unstable governments, inefficient public administration, a politicized judiciary, and political patronage that reaches everywhere. Added to that it not only lacks the ballast of a long democratic tradition but has at times been shaken by a number of exceptional problems – ultraconservative conspiracies, illegal and subversive activities on the part of intelligence services, terrorism from the right and left, and the expanding power of the world's strongest criminal organization. To a great extent, these ills can ultimately be traced to a weak state whose institutions are regarded not as sovereign, respected bodies but as feeble entities to be ignored, manipulated, or even destroyed. Hence whenever one or another of these threats to the state erupts anew, concern arises over the ability of the democratic system to deal with it or even to survive.

Obviously it is difficult to penetrate this occult world. Few hard facts ever come to light and although exposés are not lacking, they are long on speculation and short on verifiable information. But enough has been revealed to offer a glimpse into this underground realm and a basis for assessing its danger to the state.

Conspiracies and "conspiracies"

Paradoxically one of the main subversive threats has come from within the system itself. Having undergone no genuine political or psychological purge after the fall of Fascism, civil society retained a fascistic residue. Within the Interior Ministry, the intelligence services, and the police there were for many years officials who regarded any political group to the left of center – including some Christian Democrats – as an intolerable menace and who dreamed of an authoritarian, ultraconservative political order. Their concerns came to a head with the formation of a center-left government in 1963, which to them represented a dangerous shift to the left. One such person was Giovanni De Lorenzo, commanding

170

general of the carabinieri and former head of the intelligence service. In the summer of 1964 De Lorenzo drew up a plan for the carabinieri to arrest a large number of political figures and imprison them on Sardinia, occupy prefectures throughout the country, take over the national radio and television network, and seize the headquarters and newspaper offices of the left parties.

The operation was never mounted. Even though the plan was presumably known to some government and political leaders, De Lorenzo remained head of the carabinieri and was promoted – or perhaps kicked upstairs – to be army chief of staff two years later. Eventually reports leaked out, possibly through his enemies in the military, that while head of the intelligence service, De Lorenzo engaged in domestic political espionage: compiling files on public figures and indulging in blackmail and bribery. Early in 1967 a parliamentary commission was established to investigate these activities, and a short time later he was dismissed. Soon after that two journalists exposed the 1964 plan, asserting that De Lorenzo had in fact intended to overthrow the government. The majority report of the parliamentary commission concluded that although the general was guilty of improper conduct, he had not plotted an actual putsch, a conclusion that some regarded as a whitewash. In 1970 a judicial investigation found that he had acted contrary to the laws and the constitution. By then De Lorenzo enjoyed parliamentary immunity, having been elected to the Chamber of Deputies, first as a Monarchist and later as a neo-Fascist.

The purpose of De Lorenzo's machinations and the persons involved in them remain a mystery. Nowadays few believe that De Lorenzo seriously intended to launch a coup d'état. One view is that the plan was a preemptive threat, intended to warn the center-left government not to veer from established domestic and foreign policies. It has long been rumored that President Segni, a known enemy of the center-left, was at least aware of the plan or – as De Lorenzo himself later maintained – actually inspired it. Other theories implicate the Christian Democratic leadership at the time. In his *catalogue raisonné* of postwar scandals, Giorgio Galli views the De Lorenzo affair as part of a longer-term scheme by the Christian Democrats, assisted by De Lorenzo, to weaken the Socialist party and turn it into a passive coalition satellite.

Whatever the truth, the important fact is that De Lorenzo infected republican Italy with two lasting viruses. It was he who started the practice of compiling files with derogatory information on public figures. The dossier with photocopies and tape recordings soon became a common weapon of major politicians in the country's unending partisan warfare. And it was he who initiated the black art of power brokering through backstairs conspiracy. The desire for power outside the institutions of the state eventually led to the formation of a vast political underground.

Coup plotting itself was not yet over. One far-right group actually launched an overt attempt to overthrow the government. On the night of December 7–8, 1970, Prince Valerio Borghese, a legendary Fascist submarine commander and Nazi collaborator, assembled on the outskirts of Rome a group of his National Front followers along with 200 members of the National Forestry Service. His intention was to oust the government, which he regarded as too pusillanimous in the face of student and worker agitation, and replace it with a military regime. The plot collapsed in ineptitude, confusion, and sheer farce as the key commanders disagreed among themselves and issued contradictory orders. By sunrise the conspirators had all vanished.

The plot itself was too preposterous to have had the slightest chance of success. What was alarming, however, was that the intelligence services – presumably with the collusion of some Interior Ministry officials – managed so successfully to hush up the affair and prevent an investigation that rumors of it reached the press only after four months and solid information after four years. After repeated government denials, Defense Minister Andreotti acknowledged that some of Borghese's armed men had in fact succeeded in entering the Interior Ministry on the fateful night. He stated that he had also come upon information that right-wing terrorist groups possessed plans to poison water supplies with radioactive material to be stolen from a reactor in northern Italy. Magistrates who subsequently investigated the affair discovered that the head of the intelligence services, General Vito Miceli, was linked to Borghese's group. Miceli was arrested on suspicion of subversion but the charges that he knew about and concealed the plot were never proved. Like De Lorenzo, Miceli later became an MSI deputy in parliament. Borghese, who fled when the first rumors of his action reached the press, died in Spain in 1974.

In the meantime, late in 1973, the police stumbled on yet another right-wing underground group that had cooked up yet another conspiracy. The group was known as Compass Rose; its members included two generals and a number of senior military officers, some veterans of the Salò regime. It was financed in part by one of the country's richest industrialists and was evidently masterminded by Borghese. Its plan to overthrow the government and set up a neo-fascist regime involved the assassination of 1,617 persons identified on a "death list" that included almost every political figure of note from Berlinguer to Almirante. The conspiracy was broken up before any action was initiated.

If these schemers could be dismissed as a lunatic fringe, an organization was in gestation during this time that was not on the margin but right in the center of Italian political life and whose participants were anything but harebrained fanatics. Although rumors had been rampant for years in Rome political circles that "real power" in Italy was held by a small group of Masons, the public was astounded to learn in March 1981 of a secret Masonic lodge called Propaganda 2 to which hundreds of prominent persons belonged. The lodge was exposed when police raided the office of its grand master, Licio Gelli, and discovered membership lists and other documents of a sensational nature. The membership lists contained the names of 962 persons from every walk of life: 4 cabinet ministers, 3 under secretaries, 38 parliamentarians, 195 military officers, political figures from every party except the Communists and Radicals, industrialists, bankers, diplomats, civil servants, judges, the leading official of the Superior Judicial Council, the chief of the general staff, the heads of the two intelligence services, the head of the financial police, journalists, television stars, and police officials – a cross section of Italian public life. Gelli, a self-made millionaire who had spent much of his life in Latin America, immediately fled and was eventually arrested in Switzerland, where he bribed his way out of prison and disappeared.

The P2 affair was the worst scandal of the postwar period. Some of the highest officials were sooner or later forced to resign. The Christian Democratic party was so disgraced that the government, headed by Arnaldo Forlani, fell. For the first time in the history of the republic, the Christian Democrats had to hand over the prime ministry to someone from another party. The lodge, which had existed since the late nineteenth century and became involved in politics only when Gelli entered it in 1971, was promptly dissolved by virtue of the constitutional ban on secret societies and as a threat to the security of the state. In the meantime the press reported that Gelli had ultraconservative political views, thereby arousing suspicion that the lodge was the front for another right-wing conspiracy.

After conducting a two-and-a-half-year investigation, a parliamentary commission issued a report, couched in ambiguous language and toned down before its release to remove names and references to the political parties, which suggested that P2 was ultimately subversive in its design to use the officials and institutions of the state for illegitimate purposes. The commission insisted that the membership list was genuine if not complete, that many of the military officers on the list had been involved in some episodes of a subversive nature, that there was some evidence of P2's involvement with right-wing terrorist groups, and that Gelli was recruiting military officials for an eventual move against the state. The report noted that links existed between P2 and the Borghese group and that the lodge had helped to conceal the 1970 plot. The report also raised many intriguing points – the fact, for instance, that at the time of Moro's kidnapping the entire leadership of the intelligence services were members of P2 – which raised more suspicions than it resolved.

Giovanni Spadolini called P2 a "creeping coup." And in a sense it did represent an attempt to establish a parallel structure of power. Its right-wing slant would explain why so many military and intelligence officials were involved in it. Lodge members included General Giuseppe Santovito, chief of military intelligence, General Pietro Musumeci, his deputy, and Francesco Pazienza, his close aide. The parliamentary commission's report implicated the three in the establishment of a secret group inside SISMI, known as "Super S," which engaged in various illegal activities such as arms smuggling, contacts with the mafia, and actions against the Communist party. Santovito and Musumeci were eventually indicted for their activities, and Pazienza was arrested in New York for suspected involvement in the Banco Ambrosiano collapse. Into the 1980s, therefore, at least one of the intelligence services was engaged in illegal activities and blatant tampering in domestic politics. Equally disturbing, its operations presumably remained beyond the control of a series of prime ministers and defense ministers.

What all this adds up to – and what it meant for the democratic system – remains unclear. In the end, the entire scheme collapsed like a house of cards with the merest puff of publicity, its members insisting that they were not members. Such is hardly the stuff of which true subversion is made. In essence the basis of the lodge's activities, especially after 1976 when Gelli became its grand master, was essentially political and financial influence peddling. Gelli, at the center, apparently saw himself as Italy's supreme *eminence grise* – pushing buttons, pulling strings, brokering power. In return for information from his vast web of contacts, Gelli provided assistance and introductions. Most lodge members were opportunists on the lookout for the main chance, the shortcut to money and power.

P2 was the apotheosis of the technique of the *raccomandazione* –
personal advance through knowing the right people. As such, P2
was woven out of the threads of several traits that run through
Italian life: the conviction that institutions exist to be exploited; a
weakness for the devious and covert; a belief in the existence of
hidden centers of influence; and the continual search for a sponsor
and protector. Combined with this was the basic ingredient of all
the conspiracies and terrorism of postwar Italy: the confidence that
a small coterie of zealots could achieve its goals and impose its will
on an entire nation.

The right's "strategy of tension"

Such plots have been only one aspect of right-wing designs against
the constitutional order. There is a still uglier and more lethal
side – outright terrorism. Faith in the liberating and purifying
effects of violence has a long history in Italy and in this century was
an important element in the Fascist rise to power. In its postwar
form political terrorism was born in the South Tyrol in the 1950s
when the German-speaking minority blew up railroad and electrical power lines in its battle for autonomy. Terrorism became a
nationwide problem in the 1960s when it was taken up by the far
right. There eventually sprung up over 100 right-wing organizations espousing violence. The groups differed widely. Some were
nothing more than bands of adolescents who hung out in bars and
spent weekends in paramilitary training camps in the mountains
east of Rome. Others were old-fashioned gangs of fascist thugs who
occasionally beat up or shot leftists on the streets. The inner core
were professional terrorists who bombed buildings and murdered.
No doubt some of the groups had contact with one another and
with similar formations elsewhere in Europe and Latin America.
They have also been said to receive funds from the Libyans. But
there has never been evidence of central direction at home or
control from abroad.

Right-wing terrorists are a motley group. Most who have fallen
into police hands have been found to be social misfits, often with
strong personality disorders – "borderline nuts," in the blunt language of an Italian expert. They are guided not so much by a
philosophy or social analysis as by foggy notions rooted in an
authoritarian and nihilistic outlook. Some of the younger ones are
motivated simply by an adulation of force. "Against a world of mice
will arise a nation of wolves" was the mindless slogan of one group.
So far as there is a creed it is one of warmed-over fascist notions of

racism, elitism, contempt for democracy, and anticommunism onto which have been grafted such contemporary causes as support for capital punishment and opposition to abortion and "loose" social morals. To this end they have sought to demonstrate a radical-right "presence" as a counterforce to the left and an instrument of support for the right. The most fanatical are dedicated to a "strategy of tension," which is designed to create panic sufficient to bring down the democratic system and replace it with an authoritarian military regime or outright fascist state. Hence they aim at achieving strict social order by means of social disorder.

Terrorism of the right began in the mid-1960s with small-scale bombings along railroad lines. No one was killed, and the press ignored the incidents. But in December 1969 right extremists committed an act of violence unprecedented in postwar Italy when they blew up a bank in Piazza Fontana in Milan, killing sixteen persons and wounding ninety. A few hours later bombings occurred in three locations in Rome as well as in Palermo, Messina, and Reggio Calabria. The year after, a train was derailed in Gioia Tauro, killing six persons. The next major incidents took place in 1974 when a bomb was thrown at an antifascist demonstration in Brescia, taking eight lives, and later the same year when the express train *Italicus* was bombed, resulting in twelve deaths.

For the next five years there was little right-wing violence – in all ten assassinations and occasional inconsequential bombings – and what took place was completely overshadowed by a sudden and dramatic increase in terrorism by the left. Behind the scenes, however, right-wing terrorists were regrouping and at least some of the old organizations – such as National Vanguard, Mussolini Action Squads, and New Order, which were all banned in 1973 – were being supplanted by such new ones as Black Order, Third Position, and Armed Revolutionary Nuclei or NAR. Although Black Order was charged with the 1974 bombings, NAR quickly became the leading terrorist organization on the right. Between 1978 and 1980, it bombed some ninety buildings. In Rome it hit the foreign ministry, the main city prison, the offices of the Superior Judicial Council, and the renaissance city hall on the Capitoline Hill. The group also assassinated six persons, among them the Rome magistrate who was investigating the organization. In August 1980 a bomb exploded in the Bologna railroad station killing 85 persons and injuring nearly 200, the bloodiest act of terrorism in Europe in the postwar period. Since the bombing occurred one day after a court indicted four persons for the *Italicus* bombing and within a few days of the sixth anniversary of that event, it has been assumed that a right-wing organization, probably NAR, was responsible.

The distinguishing feature of rightest terrorism is the sheer illogic and randomness of its operations. Alberto Ronchey has characterized this violence as "blind, indiscriminate and impersonal." With few exceptions the targets have had neither rational nor symbolic relation to rightist causes. Rather the objects have been historic buildings and the victims innocent bystanders. It is the act of destruction and killing that is important. Nor has right-wing violence had any evident link to the political situation. In the early sixties and seventies it appeared to respond to the growing strength of the left – the entry of the Socialists into the government, the increasing power of the Communists, and the student and worker unrest of 1968 and 1969. Thus fascist violence began during the years of the center-left, was most active in the wake of the "hot autumn," and tapered off after the Socialists left the government in 1974. However, it did not revive between 1975 and 1979 when the Communists were at the height of their influence. And the Bologna bombing occurred when the Communists were in the opposition for the first time in six years.

The most mysterious and important question is how far these groups have enjoyed the connivance of the Interior Ministry, intelligence services, and police. Among the Italian public there was a suspicion, originally confined to the left but increasingly widespread during the 1970s, that the links were so definite that fascist violence could be considered, in the slogan of the left, "terrorism of the state." In particular it was believed that key officials of the Interior Ministry and the intelligence services at times not only protected right-wing terrorists but also were involved in their activities. Over the years the feeling deepened that, in the words of the *Corriere della Sera* in May 1980, "top political and police authorities inspired, planned, designed and covered up for" the Piazza Fontana bombing.

In fact the police had insisted from the start that the Piazza Fontana bombing was a leftist operation, and they immediately arrested several known anarchists. One of them was killed a few days later in a fall from a window in police headquarters. Another, Pietro Valpreda, was held in prison for almost three full years before being released. Investigating magistrates eventually discovered that the police had concealed evidence pointing to the far right as responsible and many years later found that the evidence against the two men had been fabricated by intelligence agents. In

1972 two neo-Fascists, Franco Freda and Giovanni Ventura, were arrested and tried. In the course of the trial, an agent of the intelligence services, Guido Giannettini, was exposed as one of the main conspirators. In 1979 the trial concluded with sentences of life imprisonment for Freda, Ventura, and Giannettini and the acquittal of Valpreda. A subsequent decision to overturn the sentences for lack of evidence was annulled, and the new trial began in 1985.

It was also evident throughout the 1970s that the police did not devote anything like the effort and resources against terrorists of the right that they did in combating those of the left. In fact they used the Piazza Fontana bombing for a time as an excuse to investigate and arrest trade unionists and members of left-wing parties and organizations – at the very time that neo-Fascist gangs were roaming the streets in some areas committing acts of violence and terrorism without any police counteraction. When the Communists complained, they were chided by some Christian Democrats for playing up right-wing activities for partisan advantage.

As public patience wore thin, the government shuffled around a number of high officials and promised a reform of the intelligence services. But it was not until 1977 that the intelligence apparatus was reorganized. Even then suspicions remained. Not long after the Bologna bombing the Socialist transport minister, Rino Formica, called for an investigation of possible remaining links between police officials and right-wing terrorists. That there was good reason to doubt the probity of intelligence officials was all too evident with the P2 revelations.

Prodded by the public horror over the Bologna bombing, authorities took firmer action against the ultraright. In the several years that followed, Third Position was destroyed and some 500 suspects were rounded up, 164 of whom were put on trial in 1985. Nonetheless these far-right activities remain enshrouded in an obscurity that can only be likened to products of neorealist Italian cinema, where the boundary between fact and fantasy, dream and reality is so shadowy and indistinct as to produce a sense of near hallucination. In most cases the perpetrators of the plots and terrorism have not been found, have been exonerated, or their trials have dragged on to absurd lengths. "A story of blood and absolution," one newspaper commented in exasperation in late 1984 when the last of the Borghese plotters had been found not to have plotted and the plot not to have been a plot. While right-wing terrorism is no danger to Italy's social and political stability, the failures and coverups by governmental and intelligence authorities are one of the enduring mysteries – and scandals – of the republican state.

The left's attack on "the heart of the state"

As "black" terrorism was becoming a major threat after 1969, "red" violence was just beginning to take shape. The transformation of elements of the radical left into an organized urban guerrilla movement was an incremental but swift process. The first definite act occurred in September 1969 when a number of dissident Catholics and Communists of the extraparliamentary left, led by Renato Curcio and Margherita Cagol, formed a "metropolitan political collective" in Milan. Their announced aim was to radicalize the struggle for workers' rights and carry it into the factories. Some weeks later members of the collective met in the Ligurian town of Chiavari and there went a step further, agreeing to engage in armed clandestine action. In July 1970 the group evolved into a still more radical organization called "proletarian left" and began to develop concrete plans for an "armed struggle" against the enemy – namely, the entire political, economic, and social structure.

In this way evolved in the course of about a year an organized clandestine group committed to armed terrorism, the Red Brigades. For a number of years – presumably while they were concentrating on organization, training, and infiltration – the Red Brigades' operations were symbolic and relatively harmless. The "armed struggle" began in September 1970 with the firebombing of the garage of the head of personnel in Sit-Siemens. Sit Siemens, a large electronic concern in Milan, was a prototype – like Fiat, Pirelli, and Alfa Romeo – of the capitalist enemy and as such a focal point of terrorist infiltration and violence. A number of similar actions followed, perhaps carried out as the "entrance fee" into the Red Brigades.

In 1972 the Red Brigades initiated a new tactic: the impeccably executed kidnapping. In a two-year period they seized, held for a brief "proletarian trial," and then released four "symbolic" officials: a director of Sit-Siemens; a provincial secretary of the right-wing union, CISNAL; a director of Alfa Romeo; and the personnel director of Fiat. The kidnappings culminated in Genoa in April 1974 with the first abduction of a state official, a deputy state attorney, Mario Sossi, a magistrate with a reputation as very conservative and very tough on radical leftists. Sossi, too, was released unharmed after thirty-five days. The propaganda effect was enormous, and by now the Red Brigades were a major national phenomenon.

At that point the Red Brigades suffered a brief setback. During the fall of 1974 the police ran a number of successful antiterrorist

actions, partly thanks to their infiltration of the Red Brigades'
ranks. Curcio was entrapped and captured, and by the end of the
year some half-dozen of the original founders had also been
caught. The following year Margherita Cagol was killed – shot
while running away, according to the police; gunned down in cold
blood while unarmed, according to the Red Brigades. Up to that
time the Red Brigades had never deliberately killed; the only death
had been that of a policeman, shot when the terrorist was trying to
escape arrest. With Cagol's death the cry went up from the Red
Brigades: "Never again without a gun." From then on the war
against the state was bloody.

It began in 1976. In June of that year in Genoa the Red Brigades
shot down the state prosecutor, Francesco Coco, who had advocated a firm stand against the terrorists in the Sossi case. In Turin in
April of the following year, just before the start of the trial of Curcio
and the other captured Red Brigade leaders, the president of the
bar association, Fulvio Croce, was killed. For a time it was impossible for the court to find anyone willing to serve on the jury at
Curcio's trial. In November, again in Turin, the assistant editor of
La Stampa was murdered at the door of his apartment. Throughout
this period and the next several years, the Red Brigades also carried
out a campaign of brutal intimidation – assassinating judges, police officers, and state legal officials; shooting in the legs dozens of
industrialists and Christian Democratic functionaries; and bombing carabinieri barracks, police stations, and Christian Democratic
party offices.

Red Brigade terrorism reached its zenith on March 16, 1978,
with the abduction of Aldo Moro. In the eyes of the left terrorists
Moro was de facto leader of the political establishment, the epitome of the politico who kept a corrupt political system going,
cynically handled politics as a power game rather than a means of
working for social justice, and above all enticed the Communists
into collaborating with the party responsible for the evils of the
detested power structure. On May 9 Moro was executed and his
body left in the center of Rome, at a point equidistant from the
headquarters of the Communist and Christian Democratic parties.

In the following months and years the killings, kneecappings,
and firebombings by the Red Brigades went on at an increasing
rate. Judicial officials, police, and carabinieri were the prime targets of assassination, industrialists and politicians of kneecappings.
The number of assassinations steadily rose: two in 1976, sixteen in
1978, twenty-four in 1979, and twenty-nine in 1980. In addition
there were over 100 other left-wing terrorist organizations, and

some of these – Front Line, Armed Proletarian Nuclei, Armed Proletarian Power – engaged in similar acts of murder and violence. Almost more frightening to the public than the number of killings was the seeming impunity of the terrorists' actions. In December 1981 there was a novel and sensational twist to their operations when the Red Brigades abducted and held for forty-two days an American general, James Dozier, deputy chief of NATO ground forces in Southern Europe. But that kidnapping, far from marking a new peak of their success, was in fact the last gasp of the original Red Brigades.

It was in the summer after the Moro assassination that the police began to mount an effective and coordinated antiterrorist operation directed by a carabinieri general, Carlo Alberto Dalla Chiesa. By fall most of the "second generation" of Red Brigade leaders followed the founders to prison and in the next two years a total of 650 terrorists were arrested. By that time the Red Brigades were beginning to break up. The antiterrorist legislation of 1979–80, which offered lenient sentences to terrorists who cooperated with the police, was the critical factor. In the spring of 1980 a number of leaders, including Patrizio Peci, the head of the Turin group, were rounded up; unlike any of the older generation, Peci and six others talked. It marked a turning point. A wave of arrests and the discovery of a number of important hideouts and weapons caches followed. As a consequence the terrorists not only lost their myth of invincibility but their own faith in the inevitability of revolution.

In the urgency to recruit new members, the Red Brigades took in a number of drug addicts, further weakening the organization. The old split in the ranks deepened between those who regarded killing in itself as a political instrument and those who aimed at longer-term social turmoil. When Patrizio Peci's brother was kidnapped and murdered in retribution, the public knew that the Red Brigades were no longer the organization it once had been. What began as killing for an ideal had become killing as an ideal. Police successes before and after the Dozier kidnapping and the growing number of Red Brigade members who cooperated with the police resulted by the summer of 1982 in the effective destruction of the original organization. The smaller groups had by this time already been wiped out. By early 1983 there were 1,350 Red Brigade suspects and accomplices in police hands.

Subsequently, remnants of the Red Brigades have continued to carry out an occasional terrorist act – such as the assassination of an American government official in Rome in 1984 – and have apparently had some success in recruiting new members. But it had become a new organization, with links to the mafia, the criminal underworld, and possibly to terrorist elements outside Italy. Few doubted that however it might reconstitute itself and whatever random acts of terrorism it might in the future commit, the radical left as an agent of social destabilization was a spent force.

The causes, aims, and possible international connections of the left terrorists have been the subject of endless conjecture. Beyond doubt an essential catalyst was a violent rage that boiled up in the radical left against the Communists for, in their view, having abandoned the revolutionary struggle against the existing economic and social order. Sociologists such as Sabino Acquaviva go on to trace their origins more broadly to the disintegration of the family and of traditional values as well as to the crisis inside the twin "churches" of Italian society, the Catholic church and the Communist party. With the need to believe and nothing to believe in, the terrorists created their own institution and ideology to replace those that were lost. And in fact the members of the original group were converted – through the intermediate stage of extraparliamentarism – from Catholicism and Communism to, in Ronchey's words, "that post-religious ideolgy in which absolute values are transferred from transcendental faith to sanctified social conflicts." It is therefore not surprising that as leftist political groups bear some of the traits of sects, the left terrorists individually should resemble a priesthood in their fanatical devotion to an absolute faith. Antonio Negri, a leading theoretician of revolutionary violence, indeed referred to his own original group, Workers' Power, as a "combatant religious order."

Another widespread theory finds the cause more simply in everyday social problems – youth unemployment, scandalous conditions in universities and hospitals, woefully inadequate urban housing, and ubiquitous corruption – and the deepening conviction that reform was not possible through existing political institutions. Interestingly enough, the Communist party itself has contested this view. A lengthy commentary on the subject in 1978 in the party's weekly, *Rinascita,* pointed out that organized terrorism was most widespread in developed areas of the country where there was no unemployment rather than the South where economic and social problems have been particularly acute. It also observed that nearly all the founders and leaders of the groups were themselves of middle-class backgrounds and that marginal social groups were not the direct cause of Italian terrorism but rather its strategic choice to serve as the springboard for an attack on society.

Some of this theorizing came to appear rather overblown at least with regard to the younger and newer members who had fallen into police hands and began to explain their motivations. By and large they came through as immature young people on a reckless binge of destruction. ". . . Just like pure adventurists, representatives of the most infantile extremism," was the self-description of the person who masterminded the Dozier kidnapping. Peci himself eventually wrote memoirs that revealed that he was capable of deep cruelty but not of deep thought and that the Marx he followed was closer to Groucho than to Karl. Perhaps the brilliant execution of their operations had led to the assumption that terrorists were intellectual giants.

The specific, immediate aim of the Red Brigades has most often been understood to have been the creation of instability sufficient to produce an authoritarian reaction, which would in turn spark a mass proletarian uprising that would devour the capitalist state. Hence their tactic was to "strike at the heart of the state," in their phrase, by killing or maiming its actual or symbolic agents. The gun was their medium; industrialists, journalists, and lawyers no less than politicians, policemen, and judges were their targets.

Like their rightist counterparts, the terrorists of the left succeeded for a time in "creating a climate," but they failed to achieve any positive goal. The premise of their actions – their social analysis – was totally erroneous. Italy was not on the verge of economic collapse, bourgeois society was not disintegrating, and the working masses were as far as ever from a general insurrection. There was never any chance they could trigger a class war that would produce a primitive communist society. Even their tactics were counterproductive. Far from stimulating the workers to "revolutionary solidarity," the Red Brigades increasingly isolated themselves. No one opposed them more firmly than the Communist party and the trade unions. As late as 1978 some young people retained a sneaking sympathy for Curcio and the Red Brigades, seeing them as lethal but well-intentioned Robin Hoods. By the end of the decade that attitude had evaporated. By then the continued arbitrary killing of judges and police caused even the extraparliamentary left to renounce any form of violence.

The most controversial issue about left terrorism is what caused this critical mass of discontent to take shape in an organized, clandestine armed force. Italian police officials and most Italian journalists and politicians are convinced that the impetus has been purely indigenous and subjective. A widely held view, for instance, considers terrorism on the right to have been the detonator of terrorism on the left. What set it off was a combination of disappointment and fear: disappointment that the unrest of 1968 and 1969 did not lead to deep social change and that there was no longer a revolutionary left; fear that a right-wing backlash might result in the sort of ultraconservative coup prefigured by De Lorenzo and carried out by the Greek colonels in 1967. The Red Brigades and other groups – inspired by Lenin, the Chinese revolutionaries, and Latin American guerrillas – were formed to defend worker interests and promote social revolution. Although they exchanged arms and information with other terrorist groups, such as the German Red Army Faction, and received some weapons and explosives from the Palestinians and money from the Libyans, they acted without foreign direction. Hence left terrorism in Italy has always been Italian terrorism.

Others are equally convinced that there must be some "external" element that has impelled or directed the left terrorists. The American Central Intelligence Agency, the Libyans, the Palestinians, and even domestic fascists and Communists have been proposed as the guiding hand. But most often Soviet and East European intelligence services are alleged to be behind them. According to this theory, Italy's key geopolitical position makes it a prime target for a destabilization process that would eventually encompass the entire West. Socialist leader Craxi maintained for years that left-wing terrorism was centrally directed. President Pertini on several occasions publicly articulated his belief that the Soviets or one of their allies were responsible. Prime Minister Spadolini, in a speech to the Chamber of Deputies in January 1982, acknowledged that there was no evidence of foreign intervention but insisted that Italy's position in the Mediterranean and its nearness to the Middle East made it an obvious target for destabilizing actions. Life was breathed into these conspiracy theories when the attempt to assassinate Pope John Paul II was alleged to have been organized by Bulgarian intelligence agents acting as a surrogate of the Soviets.

Between 1969 and 1983 more than 14,000 acts of violence were committed by terrorists of both the left and right, causing the death of 409 persons and injuries to 1,366. No other Western democracy has experienced terrorist violence at such a level over so long a period. Yet the country's social cohesion was not damaged, democratic institutions and procedures were not compromised, and legal repression did not set in. Although terrorism was a vastly greater menace in Italy than in Germany, parliament enacted no *Berufsverbot*, banning from government employment persons considered disloyal to the constitution. Antiterrorist legislation

opened the door to some cases of legal abuse but led to no political
infractions. The public's calm and firm response to the terrorist
challenge demonstrated better than anything since 1945 the underlying stability of Italian society and the tenacity of the country's
commitment to democracy and a government of laws.

The mafia

Far more lethal and far more a threat to the legal order are the three
criminal organizations, the mafia in Sicily and Calabria and the
camorra in Naples. They control wholesale agricultural markets;
maintain protection rackets over large and small commercial enterprises; manipulate bids on public-works projects and extort
kickbacks on their construction; fiddle interest rates; fix sporting
events; operate prostitution rings; smuggle cigarettes, jewels, and
weapons; and kidnap for ransom. Together they operate one of the
major world centers of heroin trade. In these ways they have
amassed fortunes that are "laundered" and invested in legitimate
businesses. As a result they have become a great economic power.
That is the first aspect of the mafia danger.

The mafia's methods are blackmail, extortion, and rake-offs.
Murder is the ultimate instrument for maintaining authority and
settling internal disputes. Passive adversaries are of no concern.
The persons the mafia does not tolerate are businessmen and public officials who refuse to cooperate, journalists who are too inquisi-
tive, trade unionists who try to organize or protect workers, and any
political, police, or judicial official who seeks to interfere with their
activities. Usually a threat or bribe is enough to ensure silence or
compliance. When it is not, murder is automatic and serves as an
example to others. Assassination was relatively rare in the old days;
since the war it has become increasingly common. After running at
a rate of approximately 50 a year, it reached bloodbath proportions
at the end of the 1970s with the killing of over 500 persons every
year after that. Most were victims of mafia gang wars but they also
included the prefect of Palermo, the president of the Sicilian regional government, the head of the Sicilian Communist party, the
head of the Palermo Christian Democratic party, the deputy police
chief of Naples as well as less prominent police, carabinieri, and
judicial officials. Being able to murder at will and with impunity is
the second aspect of the mafia threat.

Financial power and assassination on such a scale are a far cry
from the mafia's modest beginnings. Taking shape early in the
nineteenth century, the mafia was originally less a criminal organi-

zation than a complex social phenomenon resulting from centuries of bad government. Traditionally limited to the west of Sicily and the south of Calabria, it was a force for law and order that the governing authority in Naples – and after 1870 in Rome – could not ensure. Power belonged to certain bosses who ruled precisely defined territories. Often they helped the poor and cooperated with the police in combating ordinary crime. They did not think of themselves as criminals and were regarded by the populace as protectors. As a result the mafia was deeply ingrained in the social fabric of the area, a fact that explains its tenacious roots.

The old mafia was essentially a rural phenomenon, engaged in cattle thievery, control of water supplies, smuggling, protection rackets, and blackmail. As the effective authority in the area, its power was absolute and whoever challenged it had to reckon with the most primitive form of reprisal – destruction of property, kidnapping, or murder. Almost always a threat was sufficient to keep everyone in line. Power therefore rested on a continuous reign of intimidation. The code of *omertà*, "silence," guaranteed that no one would talk to the police or magistrates. Anyone who did, paid with his life. The saying *"Chi parla muore, chi tace campa"* – "Who talks dies, who is silent lives" – was bred into every Sicilian from the time of childhood. Ultimately the mafia was a state of mind and a way of life that pervaded everything. The atmosphere of living under mafia terror has never been better described than in the novels of Leonardo Sciascia.

That mafia is a thing of the past. Although largely suppressed by Mussolini, the mafia was revived by the American army in 1943 to help fight the Germans. After the war, as the island was industrialized, the mafia left the countryside and moved into the cities. There it became massively involved in land speculation and building construction while extending its protection rackets over the entire range of trade and commerce. Mafia power in Sicily was so systematized by the early 1980s that business contracts normally allowed 15 percent of costs to cover payoffs. Moreover, passive acceptance of the mafia allowed the organization to infiltrate the public administration on the island. If the old mafia had stayed away from drugs, the new one became a major participant in the international drug trade in the seventies. By 1980 Palermo was probably the world center for the production and sale of heroin. During the same period the mafia developed into an important conduit in the illicit sale of arms to the point where Italy was, according to some estimates, the world's largest center of illegal arms transfers. The sums of money were so vast that gang wars escalated to the point that in 1983 266 persons were killed in Sicily alone.

The contemporary mafia is characterized by two important and novel developments. On the one hand it has burst its old geographical boundaries. As its operations expanded, the mafia spread into eastern Sicily and by the early 1980s Catania ranked almost with Palermo as a locus of mafia crime. Having already gained a foothold in northern Italy in the 1950s as droves of Sicilians went North in the search for work, mafia operations spread throughout the whole of the country.

More sinister still has been the mafia's infiltration of legitimate business activities. By the 1970s its income from drugs and arms trafficking, kidnappings, and extortion was enormous. In the late seventies and early eighties drugs alone brought in staggering sums, estimates varying from $750 million to $10 billion a year – income which, in "*Fortune* 500" terms, would rank the mafia with ITT in the case of the lower figure and well above the biggest American corporation, Exxon, in the other case. During the 1970s the number of banks increased by 400 percent in Sicily, by 80 percent elsewhere in Italy. Some of these so-called narcodollars have been channeled into such legitimate enterprises as vacation resorts, restaurants, construction firms, and transportation companies. Businesses controlled by the mafia have then been run by mafia methods to drive competitors out of business. As a result the mafioso boss was transmogrified in the course of the 1970s from a simple gangster into a big-time businessman and financier.

The Calabrian mafia, traditionally known as the 'ndrangheta, has gone through an equally startling change. Originally it was a loosely organized agrarian phenomenon that never amounted to much because the peasants were too impoverished to be exploited except at harvest time. Around 1960 the Sicilian mafia found the Calabrian coast ideal for the smuggling of drugs, gems, cigarettes, and arms. In short order the local mafia took over these operations, organized itself, and established its own contacts in northern Italy and the United States. By the time the huge economic-development projects for the Mezzogiorno arrived, it had the skill and apparatus to exploit them and make itself an important economic influence in the area.

The construction of *autostrade* was the catalytic event. Bribery, protection money, and rake-offs soon became such an accepted feature of life in southern Calabria that the government eventually allowed for them in its budget allocations for construction projects while firms bidding for contracts have regularly added 15 percent to their cost estimates under a line labeled "the Calabrian risk." Everyone understood that no factory could be built or road laid without mafia agreement. Soon the mafia controlled all economic activity in southern Calabria and began to extend its operations up the coast to take over tourist hotels and facilities. It lobbied the government to develop a port and steel-manufacturing plant at Gioia Tauro and then mercilessly exploited their construction until the project was abandoned when the government decided there was no economic base for it. In the meantime approximately 1,000 persons were killed in mafia gang wars over construction contracts. For a time the homicide rate in Gioia Tauro – population 17,000 – exceeded that of New York City.

Mafia extortion is devastating for small and middle-sized firms. Finding it difficult to pay up, owners either look on helplessly as their factories are destroyed or they leave the area. In alarm over the mafia's growing stranglehold over the Calabrian economy, a group of businessmen wrote to Prime Minister Rumor in 1970, pointing out that it was becoming impossible to resist mafia de-mands for bribes and protection money. A full decade later at a meeting organized by the Communist party in Reggio Calabria, business leaders declared that the situation had steadily deterio-rated and, though the economic damage was worse every day, political leaders refused even to talk to them about the problem. The situation became so bad that in 1984 the Communist party formally proposed that the Calabrian parliament should be dis-solved as a result of gross irregularities in its activities.

The camorra, historically little more than unorganized mobster-ism, today has the local reputation of being "Naples' biggest in-dustry." It originated in the early nineteenth century in the city's prisons. Although not much more than organized petty crime, in the chaotic conditions of Bourbon Naples, the camorra was at times the city's only force for order. Almost everyone, from govern-ment and church officials to bums and prostitutes, was involved with it; and in a city where the line between legal and illegal – moral and immoral – was and remains ambiguous, the camorra was not a particularly sinister association.

At the end of the war the camorra, like the mafia, was relaunched with the help of a number of American military officers, some of whom – such as Vito Genovese – were themselves mafia gang-sters at home. Since then it has become steadily better organized and more professional in its operations. According to a 1982 report of the Naples attorney general, the camorra had about 5,000 members organized into some thirty "families" with no fewer than

100,000 collaborators. Since the late 1970s two groups have pre-dominated, the "Organized New Camorra," run from prison by Raffaele Cutolo, and the "New Family," an umbrella organization for eight other camorra gangs.

Centered in Naples and the surrounding area of Campania, the camorra runs a variety of activities, which are reported to bring in several billion dollars annually. It controls the fruit and vegetable trade and has a hand in the area's "underground economy," which is probably the world's biggest single producer of gloves and shoes. It operates protection rackets over almost every sort of commercial activity, extorting payoffs from some 10,000 large and small enterprises. Its smuggling of contraband, in particular American cigarettes, was such a big business that as of 1980 at least 30,000 persons were reported to be directly and 270,000 indirectly involved in the various aspects of this activity. In that year some 30,000 cases of cigarettes were handled, with a value of $40 to $50 million. Cigarette smuggling was in fact a pillar of the Neapolitan economy and for a long time neither the customs police nor the carabinieri interfered with it.

In 1980, however, the police confiscated the major part of the smugglers' fleet at about the time the bottom fell out of the cigarette market following a drastic change in the dollar–lira exchange rate that made smuggling uneconomic. As a result the camorra began forcing its way into the international trade of arms and drugs, particularly cocaine. About the same time several earthquakes occurred, leaving 60,000 persons homeless in Naples. The flood of goods and money for relief that flowed into the area became an object of ruthless plunder by the camorra. Government aid was directed to construction – a prime area of camorra control. No sooner indeed was the first project begun than the engineer in charge was shot and wounded for refusing a payoff. All the while the homeless had to pay the camorra protection money for the temporary shanties in which they lived.

The existing agreements among the camorra gangs dividing up areas and types of operations broke down under the strain of these changes and the infusion of vast funds. Before then the camorra murdered about fifty persons a year, mostly those who refused to pay extortion money. With the outbreak of gang wars, the number of homicides rose to 133 in 1980, 295 in 1981, and 373 in 1982, when it began to decline.

Even the briefest sketch of the mafia and camorra make clear that although the mafia has no ideology or revolutionary intent, it is vastly more integrated into society and far more a threat to the state and society than was political terrorism at its height. The economic consequences are incalculable. In 1984 the principal body representing traders, Confcommercio, estimated that protection rackets extorted around $500 million a year from 146,000 businesses throughout Italy. That there has been disinvestment in areas where it operates is beyond question. How much foreign and domestic investment never takes place because of the prospect of having to deal with the mafia is impossible to know. But the mafia as an economic power in its own right has even more obscure and sinister implications. A big business with enormous funds at its disposal, it has already bought legitimate firms – especially in tourism, housing, construction, and transport – and has sought to infiltrate important national and international enterprises and banks.

Worse still, the mafia is the number one threat to law and order. Its key role in the trafficking in hard drugs is a grave menace for the United States no less than Italy. Its ability to operate beyond police control makes it a serious subversive threat to the authority of the state. In each year of the early 1980s it murdered more persons than did all the political terrorists by bullet or bomb in the whole of the postwar period. Almost without exception, mafia assassins are never found.

"This frightening state of affairs, however, meets with general indifference as if the events were taking place in another country, far from the interests of the Italian people." So wrote a noted authority on the mafia, Michele Pantaleone, in 1962 in *Mafia e politica;* his words remained just as true two decades later despite a palpably worsening situation. A key to the problem has always lain in the attitude of the government and the parties, which Pantaleone provocatively described as "political *omertà.*" Until 1982 no serious effort had been made to fight the mafia since Mussolini sent Cesare Mori to be prefect of Palermo in 1926 with authority to fight the mafia with mafia methods. The question inevitably arises whether this inaction was due to mafia influence in the government.

The mafia's own political aims are simple: a state that is too feeble to enforce the law against it, a government that will not interfere with its activities, and a public administration that will connive in its operations. By political temperament and interest, mafia leaders have always been deeply conservative and strong defenders of the social status quo, which they have so profitably exploited. In Sicily for a time after 1943 mafia leaders supported an independence movement, in the hope of maximizing their influence on the island. When separatism became a lost cause, most of them shifted their support to the right wing of the Christian Democrats. But they have felt no commitment to this party; in the 1972 national election they backed the neo-Fascists – whose vote increased by 8 percent – and have long given support to some local Republicans. In fact nothing would please them more than to have links with all the parties. The Communists have the best record in opposing the mafia, though they have at times treated the problem polemically and ideologically as an inevitable aspect of the capitalist system.

The mafia and camorra have been repeatedly investigated by parliament for over 100 years. Nothing has ever come of these inquiries. The latest parliamentary commission was established in 1962; its final report in 1976 contained a mass of information on the mafia but offered no suggestions on how to deal with the problem and stayed clear of implicating the political parties. In 1965 parliament enacted laws to combat the mafia; but the legislation had no political will behind it and did nothing whatever to halt the mafia's spiraling wealth, influence, and killing. As Pantaleone observed, the government has always tended to minimize mafia crimes as a way of defending itself from charges of doing nothing to combat it.

By 1980 the mafia threat was so obvious that Interior Minister Virginio Rognoni had to acknowledge in a speech to the Chamber of Deputies in July of that year that the mafia was running out of control. Yet he was thoroughly evasive about measures to combat the criminal underground and exculpated the government by attributing its inaction to persistent government instability and social conditions, including the Italian lack of respect for the state. When the question arose in the ensuing debate of special legislation – comparable to the antiterrorist laws that had recently been enacted – representatives of various parties spoke against such measures.

Obviously the government in Rome was unwilling to take any serious action against the mafia. Even the number of police and magistrates dealing with the problem was left essentially as it had been when the mafia was a band of cattle thieves. Authorities in Palermo were given no properly trained personnel and little or nothing in the way of equipment – computers and data banks – that would assist their operations. Resistance was heroic but isolated. Cardinal Pappalardo of Palermo and some diocesan priests regularly denounced the mafia. As in the past a few individual Sicilians – police, magistrates, party officials, and journalists –

were even willing to risk their lives to combat it. Most were sooner or later murdered. In 1980 the president of the Sicilian regional government, the Christian Democrat Pier-Santi Mattarella, who had evidently been trying to break mafia control over public-works projects, was gunned down. In 1982 Pio La Torre, the head of the Sicilian Communist party and an expert on the mafia, suffered a similar fate. None of the assassins was ever found.

Even as the number of martyrs grew, Prime Minister Spadolini and Interior Minister Rognoni dithered. Finally, after La Torre's murder, they sent Carlo Alberto Dalla Chiesa, the carabinieri general who had directed the campaign against the Red Brigades, to Palermo as prefect but then balked at giving him the authority and personnel he wanted. At the same time anti-mafia legislation remained bottled up in parliament. Spadolini's statement to parliament in August 1982 laying out the program for his second government spoke of the continuing danger of leftist terrorism but had little to say about the mafia.

A few days later, after but four months in Palermo, Dalla Chiesa and his wife were brutally murdered. Only then and in the wake of a storm of public protest over its inaction did the government at last take a forthright step. It created the position of commissioner to combat the mafia and gave him sweeping powers, much of which had been denied to Dalla Chiesa, to investigate mafia leaders and their operations. Shortly afterward parliament enacted legislation, originally drafted by La Torre, that for the first time made it illegal to belong to the mafia, permitted investigation of the business and banking activities of mafia suspects, and authorized the confiscation of property and bank accounts. The measures had some results. Property was impounded, including well-known hotels in Rome and Milan. Police put impressive numbers of mafia and camorra members behind bars.

But it was still too little and too late. By now the main problem was tracking down the enormous sums accumulated by the mafia and discovering how they were being "laundered." In some cases banks resisted the government's attempts to investigate suspicious accounts. In other cases the mafia withdrew their deposits – hundreds of billions of lire – to avoid detection. Eventually the casinos of northern Italy became major places for recycling mafia funds. In his annual report for 1983, the attorney general of the republic stated that the mafia was everywhere in Italy and comprised a vast conspiracy involving above all drugs but also arms trafficking and the traditional forms of criminality for which it was known. The government, however, was unmoved. The view of the new interior minister was the same as that of his predecessors: no "exceptional legal measures" but rather an effort to combat the root causes, which he identified as unemployment and the economic crisis in key industries.

Not long after the attorney general had issued his report, a Sicilian journalist appeared on national television with a different explanation of mafia power. For a parliamentarian, he stated, mafia support meant not only personal riches but also 150,000 to 200,000 votes in an election. He added: "Mafia members are in parliament, they are sometimes ministers, they are bankers, and they are those who at this moment are at the top of the nation." A few days later the journalist was murdered.

In late 1984 an arrested mafia leader, Tommaso Buscetta, confessed and turned state's evidence – naming names, describing the structure of the Sicilian mafia, and exposing the operations of the mafia's international drug trade. Buscetta was the first mafia boss to cooperate with the police, and his collaboration not only opened the way to one of the police's most effective anti-mafia operations but at long last "ripped a hole in the code of omertà," in Leonardo Sciascia's words. Equally important, the follow-up actions of the police, magistrates, and Interior Ministry signified a substantial change of attitude on the part of state authorities. In Naples alone in 1985 over 600 camorra suspects were put on trial. Although the mafia had suffered only a setback rather than a mortal or even a grave defeat, a serious start in combating it appeared at last to have begun.

10. Economic and social transformation

Italian economic development in the postwar era has been prover-bial, excelled only by that of Germany and Japan. In 1945 Italy was one of the poorest countries in the West. A land bereft of natural resources and with only a quarter of its soil suitable for farming, the country had suffered more from the war than any other Western nation but Germany. At the end of hostilities, destitution was widespread, with the population suffering the classic earmarks of poverty: high illiteracy and infant mortality, poor diet, and limited education. Most housing lacked baths and much of it even running water. Unemployment and underemployment were high; inflation was rampant and taxation regressive. A late industrial developer, Italy had only a modest manufacturing sector, which was centered in a narrow area of the Northwest and depended heavily on tariffs and state assistance. Merely a third of the labor force was employed in industry; more than half was engaged in small-scale agriculture. Per capita income was lower than at any time since unification and half what it had been in 1938.

By 1970 Italy had become the world's seventh-ranking industrial state, was a leading international exporter, and held some of the most substantial gold and foreign-exchange reserves in Europe. During the intervening period the country's gross national product had increased by 568 percent while per capita income had risen, at constant prices, by 464 percent – which worked out to an increase well exceeding that of the entire preceding hundred years. Whole new industries – such as steel, chemicals, and oil refining – had been established with the most advanced technology and were able to compete with the best in Europe. Old private firms – like Fiat, Pirelli, and Olivetti – had revived to become European leaders in their fields. Unemployment had dropped from over 10 percent to half that figure. More than 5 million agricultural workers had moved into industry, reducing the farm population to less than 20 percent of the total working force and converting Italy from an essentially peasant society into a largely urban one. Social security coverage had been made comprehensive and relatively generous. The material standard of living had vastly improved for the great majority of the population. (See Appendixes E, F, and G.)

Few, if any, poor and backward European countries had advanced so far so fast. Few, if any, economies had changed character so drastically – from virtual autarky to transformative industries thriving on exports. For the first time in centuries Italians were again in the forefront of world commerce. This amazing progress not only manifested the Italian capacity for hard work and innovation but also gave the people, for all the country's problems, a strong sense of progress and self-esteem. The benefits of this advance were evident in almost every sphere of national life.

Amazing growth

Italy's economic development has evolved in several phases. Recovery began in 1947 when Luigi Einaudi was given full powers to manage the economy. Einaudi's harsh deflation policy, with its tight credit and cuts in government spending, was bitter medicine but is generally credited with having brought inflation under control, stabilized the lira, and won international confidence. Marshall Plan aid followed with a large infusion of funds to finance vital imports. In 1949 natural gas was discovered in the Po Valley, giving Italy its first indigenous energy source. These factors, in addition to a great reservoir of cheap and highly mobile labor, laid the foundation for a broad economic advance. Already in 1950 industrial production and per capita income were roughly back at the prewar level.

The years between 1950 and 1963 were a time of economic growth so remarkable that it has appropriately been called an economic miracle. During that period the gross national product rose at an annual rate of 7 percent, against a European average of 4.5 percent. In 1960 alone industrial production went up by 20 percent. Steel production increased from 2.3 to 10.2 million tons; the output of motor vehicles went from 118,000 to 1,105,000; electric energy production trebled; gasoline production went up by seven times. Exports in these years trebled.

Economists are in broad agreement that the basis of this growth was the low and stable labor costs that resulted from the excess supply of labor during this period. The continuing high level of unemployment was largely due to the massive shift of population from rural areas to the cities, from agriculture into manufacturing and services. Between 1950 and 1963 the number of workers in agriculture declined by 50 percent. The resulting low labor costs also helped to make Italian goods highly competitive in world markets. In this situation profits were high and, reinvested in capital stock, produced rapid industrial growth. With the Italian entry into the European Economic Community in 1957, the country not only gained an expanded market but also was forced into free-market competition in which its products surprised everyone by selling extremely well. It was in fact exports that led the economic miracle to its heights between 1958 and 1962. Hence, behind Italy's remarkable performance lay three essential elements: the low wages and hard work of the labor force, the energy and imagination of entrepreneurs, and the courage of the government to break with the strong protectionism of the past and take the plunge into free trade and open competition in the world market.

The first blip in the country's steady economic advance occurred in 1963. By then the labor market had begun to tighten and wages to rise, driving up production costs and reducing profit rates. Moreover, the establishment of the first center-left government created a climate of apprehension among entrepreneurs and the rich, leading to a decline in investment and the illegal export of currency. Though the economic miracle was at an end, there followed a period of erratic if still impressive growth. Industrial investment never recovered its previous level and inflation set in for the first time since the early postwar years, but exports boomed. The growth rate, though fluctuating widely, was still an impressive 4 percent a year over the whole period.

A turning point came with the "hot autumn" of 1969, when workers set in motion a revolution in industrial relations. The resulting wage and benefit increases, labor restrictions, and strikes reduced the growth rate to a postwar low of 1.6 percent in 1971. Scarcely had the economy begun to recover when the quadrupling of oil prices beginning in 1973 dealt the Italian economy a tremendous blow. Being 85 percent dependent on foreign energy sources, Italy was hit harder than any other Western country. Its energy import costs went from $1.6 billion in 1972 to $20 billion in 1980. In the former year oil purchases amounted to 14 percent of the value of total imports, in the latter 23 percent. Between 1973 and 1976 a current-account deficit developed of $11 billion. The government was forced to arrange emergency international financing and to devalue the lira. The combination of wage and oil price increases badly hurt industrial profits and drastically reduced the competitiveness of many public and large private enterprises.

In the decade after the mid-seventies the Italian economy went through a series of ups and downs that at times defied economic logic. The overall growth rate reached the highest level in the European Community in 1979 and 1980, then slipped in the following three years – the poorest sustained performance in the country's postwar record – but by 1984 was again the highest in the Community. In the foreign-trade sphere the adroit policies of the Bank of Italy under Paolo Baffi had effected such a dramatic turn-around in the trade balance that the international loans had been repaid by the end of the decade and exchange reserves were built up to an unprecedented $40 billion. Then in 1980 exports failed to expand for the first time in the postwar period and the balance of trade registered its worst deficit ever. Two years later exports rebounded; however, imports now grew still faster to leave an even worse trade deficit in 1984. Damaging trade performance were the strikes, absenteeism, and high labor costs that rose continuously throughout the seventies – accounting for a 40 percent increase in the price of Italian manufactures between 1977 and 1979 alone. After 1980 strikes and absenteeism dropped, productivity and capital inflows improved, and profits in many industries soared. Unemployment went from 6.4 percent in 1977 to 14.2 percent in 1985, with some three-quarters of the unemployed estimated to be persons under the age of thirty.

Since the political convolutions during most of this period left governments too weak to pursue any coherent economic policy, the deepening systemic economic and social problems had to be concealed behind even greater outlays from the treasury. Public spending rose from 38 percent of GNP in 1974 to 58 percent in 1983, as subsidies for ailing public-sector enterprises and indexed transfer payments – for augmented pension and health benefits – steadily grew. Income from taxes in these years expanded only from 31 to 42 percent. The government budget deficit consequently climbed from 10 percent of GNP at the end of the 1970s to 15 percent by 1983 – more than double that of any other Western country – and the national debt soared to the point that in 1984 it equaled the country's GNP. The amplitude of government spending helped to minimize the impact of the international recessions of those years but fired inflation, which fluctuated at around 15 percent between 1975 and 1980 and exceeded 20 percent in the latter year – the highest level in Europe. Only after 1983 was inflation reduced to 8.5 percent, though that was still a higher rate than in most of Italy's trade competitors.

In the mid-eighties the Italian economy presented, in short, a bewildering spectacle. It continued to be plagued by high unemployment, high interest rates, high labor costs, high inflation, a vast public expenditure, and a staggering public deficit. At the same time exports were back at an all-time record, some state industry was being restructured and modernized, large private firms were once again European leaders in their fields, the performance of small and medium-sized companies bedazzled observers, and a general sense of prosperity pervaded the country. These bald trends were, however, merely the surface outlines of startling changes that took place throughout the postwar period in the position of the labor force, the fortunes of entrepreneurs, and the shape of industrial life in Italy.

The role of the trade unions

Of Italy's 20 million workers, around 45 percent are union members – the highest level of unionization in Europe after Britain. The proportion of organized workers is greater in agriculture and the public-service sector than in industry, even though the 1.5-million-strong Confederation of Small Farmers is not affiliated with the trade-union movement. Unionized agricultural workers are concentrated in the South and strongly influence the labor movement there. Most organized industrial workers are in the North, especially the large firms in the "industrial triangle" – the area between Turin, Milan, and Genoa – and are the most militant segment of the union movement. Unions are extremely weak in the small plants, which have been steadily growing in number throughout the postwar period. The country's 1 million foreign workers, many without work permits, are entirely outside the unions, as are the millions engaged in the small firms of the "underground economy."

Most organized workers belong to one of the three large confederations. The biggest, with nearly 4.5 million members, is the CGIL, the Italian General Confederation of Labor. The best organized, most efficient, and most disciplined of the unions, the CGIL strongly influences the labor scene. It enjoys the support of most industrial workers and is therefore strongest in the North. Its greatest single center of power is in Communist-governed Emilia-Romagna, where 96 percent of the workers are organized, with 73 percent of them belonging to the CGIL. Communists comprise 60 percent of the members and hold the top position of general secretary and other key jobs. The union's first head, Giuseppe Di Vittorio, was the outstanding trade union figure of the postwar period; the leader from 1970 to 1985 was the able and moderate Luciano Lama. Both leaders tried to push the Communist party toward the center on various issues; both had at times to be brought to heel by the party. Thirty percent of the CGIL's membership and executives are Socialists, with the remaining 10 percent of the members coming from the ultraleft. As a result of the growing hostility between the Communist and Socialist parties since the early 1980s, relations between the two segments of the union have been increasingly strained.

With nearly 3 million members, the Italian Confederation of Workers' Unions, or CISL, is the second largest federation. Although a union of Catholics and until the mid-sixties linked to the Christian Democrats, it has become somewhat more ecumenical in its membership. During much of its history it has been wracked by tensions and conflicts between moderates and a radical group of left Catholics. At times it has been passive, at times militant; on occasion it is to the right, on occasion to the left of the other unions. Not surprisingly CISL is considered by employers, the government, and the rest of the union movement to be unreliable and difficult to deal with. Relatively strong in the South, the CISL's greatest power is among the country's civil servants. Pierre Carniti, who became secretary in 1979, was the first non–Christian Democrat to head the union.

The smallest of the three confederations is the UIL, the Italian Union of Labor, with 1.25 million members. Its members come from the service sector, public administration, and large industry. For many years an uneasy amalgam of Socialists, Social Democrats, and Republicans, the UIL has been dominated by the Socialists since 1976, when Giorgio Benvenuto was elected secretary, the first Socialist to hold the position.

The percentage of the working force belonging to the three confederations has fluctuated drastically over the years – from a high of 60 percent in 1947 to a low of roughly half that figure two decades later. Since the late seventies the number has averaged about 45 percent, although this figure includes 2 million pensioners, camouflaging a loss of workers.

The neo-Fascist union, CISNAL, the Italian Confederation of Workers' National Trade Unions, with which the other unions and the government refuse to deal, is estimated to have about a half-million members. CISNAL is strongest in the South and among public-service workers. Of steadily increasing importance have been the "autonomous" unions, which are particularly strong in the railroads, air transport, schools, civil service, and banks. They themselves estimate their collective membership to be over 1 million.

Originally, upon the fall of Fascism, there was only a single trade union, the CGIL. It was founded by Socialist, Catholic, and Communist trade unionists in 1944 in a deliberate attempt to subordinate ideological differences and in that way maximize working-class strength and reinforce the new democratic order. Solidarity was at first easily maintained since all unionists and workers had the supreme goal – never subsequently relinquished – of achieving the maximum level of employment and, beyond that, protection of wages. For a brief time they succeeded, securing a freeze on employment levels and building an escalator clause, *scala mobile*, into wage contracts.

But the seeds of discord were present from the start and rapidly grew. Since union leaders were closely linked to their parties, they were inevitably dragged into the competition among the parties and their ever more divergent views. Although the trade union leadership accepted the capitalist structure of the economy, the Communists and left Socialists wanted substantial changes in the system, including some nationalization. Others supported in varying degrees the classic liberal economic policy of the De Gasperi governments. By 1947 unity was shattered, victim on the one hand of the Communists' having gained control of the confederation and on the other of the expulsion of the left from the government and the commencement of the cold war. Non-Communists started pulling out in 1948 and by the spring of 1950 had formed the other unions. The split was a blow from which Italian trade unionism has never recovered.

As Alessandro Pizzorno remarks in *I soggetti del pluralismo,* the Italian working class has at times been strong politically but weak economically (1945 to 1948), at other times weak in both respects (1948 to the early 1960s), and at still other times strong economically but weak politically (early 1960s to 1968). Only in the decade after the "hot autumn" was it strong in each regard. Since then it has lost influence in both spheres.

In the first decade and a half after the war, almost everything was ranged against the workers. The labor market was extremely unfavorable – demand for labor was limited while unemployment was high. Even as the economy expanded the labor force was continuously replenished by workers from the farms. Employers were politically influential, conservative, and untouched by any feeling of paternalism. The government was generally in the hands of a center-right coalition that followed a course of strict fiscal austerity. The two preeminent workers' parties were politically isolated.

Wage earners were therefore at the mercy of employers. New workers, in particular southerners desperate for a job at any salary, were especially vulnerable. Many employers paid illegally low wages, stretched working hours beyond their normal limits, and sometimes cheated workers of their social security benefits. When there were reductions in force, the unionized workers were the first to be fired and the Communists and Socialists among them were let go before anyone else. This cheap and exploited labor was a major element of the economic miracle. When the Common Market was formed in 1957, Italy had the lowest wage rate of any of its six member states.

After 1947 the unions were no help to their members. The very weakness of the confederations forced them into dependence on the parties to which they were linked, and that dependence in turn required them to support party positions even when these were irrelevant or hostile to the workers' interests. In the late 1940s the CGIL tried to disrupt the delivery of Marshall Plan aid and to prevent Italy's adhesion to NATO. The CISL accepted mass layoffs, refused to join the other unions in actions for higher wages, and was rarely willing to call its members out on strike. For their part entrepreneurs and the government throughout the 1950s were hostile to the entire union movement, singling out the CGIL for particular repression – interfering with its activities on the shop floor, excluding it from wage negotiations, and the like. By the mid-fifties the unions were in deep crisis. Workers – intimidated by employers and out of step with the confederation leadership, which was at a loss to explain the success of the capitalist system – left the unions in large numbers. This was especially true of the CGIL, whose membership declined from 5.7 million in 1947 to 3.1 million in 1957 and eventually to a low of 2.5 million in 1967. During this twenty-year period Italian trade unionism was probably the weakest in the Western industrial world.

With the tightening of the labor market and the entry of the Socialists into the government in 1963, wages began to improve and the unions became more aggressive. But what transformed the labor situation was the wave of worker militancy following the student and labor unrest that overran Western Europe in the late 1960s. In Italy the effects were deeper, broader, and more lasting than anywhere else. Although a few extremists thought the revolutionary hour had struck, most workers simply wanted a share of the enormous economic growth of the preceding fifteen years and protection against exploitation. The ferment, which took the form of strikes, slowdowns, plant occupations, and the disruptions of production, extended into the early 1970s but achieved its initial great success at the turn of the year 1969–1970, when a large number of labor contracts – which normally run three years –

expired and had to be renegotiated. Now the workers insisted on better pay and working conditions and more substantial social benefits. Impatient with the feuding among the confederations, workers forged their own links on the shop floor, in some places forming factory committees outside the control of the unions. At the same time a number of craft unions from the three confederations, in particular the *metalmeccanici*, the 1.5-million-strong union of engineering workers and metalworkers, developed a de facto unification. The confederations were carried along. Not only did they take over the negotiation for improved wages and working conditions but they also for the first time closed ranks in a common cause.

From the early 1970s on, wages rose by an average of about 25 percent a year. Various fringe benefits were increased to the point where they amounted to an additional 50 to 60 percent on wages, the highest in any Western country. Working hours were reduced so that by the end of the decade they were shorter than anywhere but Belgium. Some categories of workers who were laid off received unemployment compensation at little less than full wages, often for years beyond eligibility. At first these benefits were primarily enjoyed by industrial workers in the North where the "hot autumn" had its strongest impact, but they soon spread to other types of workers in other areas. In 1975 the escalator clause was strengthened in wage contracts to give a high proportion of workers nearly 100 percent indexing, with quarterly revisions, thereby raising wages nearly as fast as prices.

The impact of this dramatic increase in wages and fringe benefits as well as shorter hours – along with strikes and absenteeism – is saliently reflected in a few statistics. Between 1969 and 1978 real wages rose by 72 percent. However, since GNP rose by only 32 percent, the increase in wages greatly exceeded output. Output itself declined because employees worked less and produced less on the job. Labor costs in this period went up 450 percent while productivity increased by 337 percent. By 1982, according to the *Financial Times,* Italian unit labor costs were accounted to be the highest in the world. To lighten the burden on entrepreneurs – at the expense of taxpayers – the costs of the various social security payments were increasingly shifted to the state. It was this outlay in combination with the rising subsidies during this period to the troubled state enterprises that was largely responsible for the increasing budget deficits after the mid-1970s.

A no less notable and controversial consequence of the "hot autumn" was a statute of workers' rights that was drafted and pushed to enactment in 1970 by the Socialist labor minister at the time, Giacomo Brodolini. The law on the one hand greatly strengthened the authority of the unions in the factories – to an extent disquieting not only to factory owners but also to ultraleft workers. On the other hand, to end the injustices of the past, it outlawed dismissal without just cause, prohibited hiring except through the state employment office, forbade employers to keep records of employees' political or union affiliations, and guaranteed freedom of assembly and speech on the shop floor. For all its good intentions, however, the law made it nearly impossible to dismiss employees for almost any reason short of demonstrable felony, undermining discipline in the factories. The ease of taking sick leave resulted in a spread of absenteeism that was a joke throughout Europe. As a result employers lost much of their control over their work forces, and labor mobility was for all practical purposes at an end. In 1979 when Fiat dared to dismiss sixty-nine workers for having committed acts of outright physical destruction in its Mirafiori plant, the firm's action caused a national sensation.

The workers' militancy did not dissipate for many years after the "hot autumn" and was manifested in a steady increase in strikes. At first these reflected an unrelenting push for wages and other benefits on the part of organized workers. As time passed the confederations' policy of uniform wage scales and, later, of wage restraint gave rise to a great expansion of autonomous unions, which opposed across-the-board wage hikes on the one hand and wage moderation on the other. These independent unions have in subsequent years regularly tied up the country in wildcat strikes, particularly in transport – railways, airlines, ferries to the islands, and urban buses – but also in hospitals and public administration. Such strikes, organized in ways and at times to amount to social and economic blackmail, have emboldened radicals in the major unions to organize strikes in their own sectors, which the confederations often have no choice but to sanction.

Between 1970 and 1977 Italy was at the top of the European strike record, normally ahead of Ireland and Britain. In 1975, for example, for every thousand workers, Italy lost 1,730 workdays because of labor strife, Britain 265, and Ireland 403. Even in 1980 when Ireland rose to the head of the list, Italy still lost 919 workdays, Britain 531, and Germany 4. Moreover, official statistics as a rule did not take into account either political strikes or the frequent "ministrikes" – as when a conveyor belt was turned off, a car painter deliberately bungled, or airline stewardesses brought air travel to a halt. Eventually there was a backlash among some workers. In October 1980 Fiat was closed by a strike protesting the company's planned layoff of 23,000 workers because of the worldwide crisis in the automotive industry. After several weeks, 40,000 Fiat employees held an unprecedented demonstration against the strike, causing its collapse.

The "march of the 40,000" was emblematic of the changing climate of industrial relations after merely a decade. The workers' statute and union regulations, backed by the power of the strike, made it difficult to restructure Italian industry at a time when it was in the throes of crisis and change. Fiat demonstrated a determination to bend these restrictions and went on to prove that by scaling back its labor force and introducing robots into the assembly line for automated production, it could turn itself around. By 1983 the company was producing some 4,000 cars daily and was again the biggest single automaker in Europe. Olivetti and many smaller firms followed suit and, in some cases after discreet discussions with the unions and the Communist party, reduced their labor forces, introduced new production techniques, and revived to become competitive – Olivetti to become the world's eighth largest producer of office equipment. Often the government helped out by agreeing to foot the bill for unemployment compensation for the laid off workers. So with an Italianate sleight of hand, many of the restrictive provisions of the workers' statute were by the early 1980s being quietly ignored with the unions' tacit agreement. These changes were often more difficult to introduce in state industries because of their sensitivity to political pressure. Some of these enterprises as a result went into deep crisis. In 1983 IRI's steel sector, for instance, lost $1.2 billion, or more than half of IRI's total deficit that year.

If the "hot autumn" transformed wages and industrial relations, it also had a tremendous impact inside the trade union movement itself. The old hostility and rivalry among the confederations gave way to cooperation and a desire for unity. The first concrete obstacle on the path to unification was the tight links between the parties and the unions, especially the CGIL and CISL. In fact CISL had already begun in 1965 to distance itself from the Christian Democrats. It stopped supporting the party in elections and forbade its officials to accept government office. But question inevitably arose whether union officials should also give up their seats in parliament. By the late 1950s nearly 100 deputies – 20 percent of the Chamber of Deputies – were union officials. The controversy over this question has been well recorded in Joseph LaPalombara's *Interest Groups in Italian Politics*. It is an issue that goes to the heart of Italian trade unionism: how to balance political power and responsibility with partisan independence to defend workers' interests. The matter was finally resolved in favor of giving up parliamentary representation. In 1969 each of the three confederations adopted an "incompatibility rule" forbidding union officials from holding a seat in parliament or a position in a party or in government.

These developments opened the way to joint action, and throughout the 1970s the three unions did their best to tread a common line. As often as not this left CISL out of step with the Christian Democrats while the CGIL took a different stand from that of the Communist party on a number of important issues. Efforts to amalgamate into a single union failed, however, both because the CISL and UIL feared that the Communists would dominate the new organization and because the Christian Democrats resisted any move that would attenuate their links to Catholic workers. A loose federation was formed in 1972, and in the years that followed there were few deviations from joint positions. But the cooperation that was possible in the lingering warmth of the "hot autumn" and the period of steady integration of the Communists into the governing system after 1976 gradually came apart once the Communists went into the opposition in 1979. In 1984 the unions disagreed over the ultrasensitive issue of wage indexing. UIL and CISL supported the Craxi government's effort to reduce the rate while the CGIL, which in 1978 had led the way in advocating wage restraint, echoed the Communist position of unequivocal opposition. Although a compromise measure was eventually enacted, the old cooperation was shattered.

If organizational disunity has been a major cause of the weakness of the trade union movement during much of the postwar period, another reason lies in the flawed relationship between the confederations and the workers. Institutionally the unions have always been strongly hierarchical and highly centralized, with power concentrated at the top so that it could be brought more effectively to bear on employers and the government. Until the 1960s union organization and activities in the factories were weak. This problem was aggravated by the fact that category unions, which organize workers by craft and which in the United States, Britain, and Germany are the most important form of union, are not very strong – except for the metalworkers – and too subordinate to the confederations to have much autonomy. The result in practice was that the union leadership often lost touch with the rank and file and misassessed or was unaware of the mood on the shop floor.

Although this situation changed somewhat in the 1960s when the CISL and UIL established more of a presence at the workshop level, it was only with the "hot autumn" that the confederations came down from the heights and went into the factories. For the first time the plants themselves were the focus of union activities. Workers' councils were set up, union assemblies met, and wage agreements were negotiated at the workplace level. Craft unions became stronger, with the metalworkers in the forefront of collaboration. Not since the early postwar period had union leaders and employees been so in tandem. Union membership revived dramatically. The number of CGIL members, which stood at 2.6 million on the eve of the "hot autumn," went back up to 3.4 million in 1973, and eventually increased to its 1984 figure. Total membership in the three confederations rose from 4.7 million in 1968 to almost 9 million in 1980.

The "hot autumn" introduced a third major change in the trade union picture. As workers gained better wages and working conditions and as the union became stronger, the confederation leadership shifted focus toward social goals. The approach was not entirely new. Italian trade unions have traditionally regarded themselves not just or not even primarily as workers' representatives in wage negotiations but as a codeterminant of broad national policies and an agent of social reform. Having lost any chance of playing this role after the schism of 1948, the unions suddenly found that in the circumstances of the 1970s they were as strong as any other social institution and even most of the governments of the day.

The unraveling of the center-left governing formula during the first half of the decade lamed the country politically. The economic crisis after 1973, on top of the change in industrial relations after 1969, left the business community vulnerable. Social and political tensions were growing and no one wanted union–management conflicts to add to the strains. For their part union leaders felt that longer-term social reforms were now necessary to consolidate the gains in wages and working conditions. Moreover, they were coming to acknowledge that the huge and continuing wage increases were a cause of runaway inflation that nullified wage benefits and priced Italian exports out of the market. They insisted, however, that they would be able to work for wage restraints only if they could demonstrate that the interests of wage earners were directly represented by the unions in the councils of government and that their longer-term concerns – pensions, health care, rent control, housing, and so on – were being taken into account.

Welcoming this moderating influence, the government, the Confederation of Industry, and some leading industrialists were by the mid-1970s loudly proclaiming that only with the cooperation of the unions and the Communist party could wages be controlled and industrial peace restored. Once the Communists were in effect brought into the governing majority in 1976 and supported an austerity policy, the CGIL took the lead in advocating trade union moderation.

In the so-called EUR line of February 1978, the confederations advanced what amounted in effect to a social contract. They would support a policy of wage restraint and fiscal austerity while the government would promote programs for increased employment, especially in the South, and a variety of social reforms. In the following years the unions tried to keep a check on wage claims – agreeing to cuts in the wage escalator in 1983 and 1984 – generally sought to maintain industrial peace, and eventually went along with some reductions in force to allow industrial restructuring. Although private industry pressed for a basic change in the wage escalator and began declaring some workers redundant, they clearly preferred cooperation to confrontation. For its part the government followed a conciliatory approach and did not insist on manpower reductions in unprofitable state enterprises, keeping loss-making industries going – at government, or taxpayer, expense – as a way of maintaining employment. The government also endowed the unions with the institutional status they claimed by consulting them on its economic program, negotiating with them for new wage accords, and incorporating them into various agencies responsible for implementing social and economic policies. Trade union representatives were appointed to hundreds of public agencies and given effective control of such bodies as INPS. They were also allowed a voice in programs dealing with economic development in the South, youth unemployment, and pension reform.

But by the early 1980s it was clear that the attempt at "institutionalized collaboration" was breaking down. The main economic program of those years, the Pandolfi plan, was never carried out. Unemployment and inflation ran out of government control. Few social reforms materialized and some that did, such as rent control, largely failed in practice. Industry tried to take back control over work practices and reinstate labor mobility. By the same token workers were interested in wage increases and the unemployed in jobs, not in wage restraints and long-term social changes. In the eyes of the union rank and file the ritual policy consultations with the government achieved nothing of tangible value. Some workers turned to the independent unions and some unemployed turned to the extreme parties – in the South often to the neo-Fascists – for political support or at least as protest. Inside the unions a radical fringe took shape and advocated an "unceasing attack" on the existing economic order.

The dispute over wage indexing was symptomatic of the differences among the confederations, leaving them unable to present a united front or to speak with authority for the workers and therefore in no position to play the political role they sought or even to make policy proposals. It was an astonishing reversion. Union cooperation and power had again been sacrificed to partisan politics, with the Communist element in the CGIL once more unwilling to follow a line independent of the Communist party. But there was a deeper problem. In a way the unions were victims of their own success. Having accomplished their concrete objectives, they lost much of their purpose. They became disillusioned and at times scathingly self-critical. Asked in an interview in 1981 to characterize the union movement, Benvenuto replied: "A paralyzed force. A conservative force. A force that lives on memories of the past and that will not tolerate renewal." However that might be, in arriving at that point the unions had transformed the lives of Italian workers and in so doing they had made a major contribution to social justice and political stability. And despite the decline in their power in the course of the 1980s, they remained a major guarantor of the country's democratic order.

The role of employers

Like the trade union movement, the business community has gone through periods of strength and weakness, relative unity, and sharp division. Differences among industrial firms – large or small, new or mature, export or domestic-market oriented, labor or capital intensive, low or high technology, private or state-owned – have led to strongly competing and contradictory positions on the whole gamut of economic issues, from labor relations to the government's role in economic affairs, the relations of business to the parties, and the scope for economic planning.

In the first decade or so after the war there was sufficient unity of purpose to mask these differences. Because of Italy's retarded industrialization, the business sector was traditionally weak and, though adamantly opposed to government interference in business, it had always looked to the state for protection in the form of high tariffs and other assistance. This client-type relationship continued after 1945 when the major form of competition among Italian entrepreneurs was one less of commercial rivalry than of competition for government support. Some leading industrialists saw in the Liberals a party precisely attuned to their outlook and therefore the ideal representative of business interests in government. But the majority turned to the Christian Democrats, particularly as the party relinquished its Catholic social doctrines and extended its control over the state. The leading spokesman for business interests was Confindustria, the Confederation of Industry, which had been founded after World War I. It supported the Christian Democrats financially and in return was given, in Alberto Martinelli's words, "governance of the economy, either directly, through its own staff, or, more often, indirectly, through political leaders and government officials. . . ." During this period Confindustria and the government marched step in step to a tune of fiscal austerity, low wages, and union repression.

The unity of the business community began to come apart after the mid-fifties as industrial and political interests diverged. The large, mature private firms were powerful enough to manage increasingly on their own. Fiat, for example – which in the last two years of the war had simultaneously placated the Fascists, the Germans, the resistance, and the Allies – needed little help in taking care of itself. The state enterprises, with their counterpart to Confindustria called Intersind, promoted state planning and government involvement in the country's economic development. As the state sector grew in importance, it became more powerful than Confindustria and established ever tighter clientelistic ties with the Christian Democrats. The newer and smaller firms, which were as hostile to the unions as they were to government intervention, felt that their interests were not being protected. They eventually broke away to form their own organization, the Confederation of Small Industries, Confapi, which was closely bound to the Christian Democrats. Merchants formed their own body, Confcommercio, and the landowners already had theirs, Confagricoltura. Hence, as Martinelli points out, the old relationship "between a unified party and a rather homogeneous business class became a fragmented network of influences in which different party factions were related to different centres of economic power."

In the course of the 1960s the Christian Democrats gained such a hold on the economy through the state enterprises and banks that Confindustria progressively lost influence. For a time Intersind rather than Confindustria was the pacesetter in wage negotiations.

Small enterprises had to fend for themselves and, increasingly dependent on the banking sector for loans as the economic miracle wound down, were more than ever at the mercy of the Christian Democrats, who controlled the banks. Eventually the private business community woke up to the fact that the Christian Democrats, far from being the friend of business interests and free-market principles, were in reality their nemesis.

By the end of the 1960s the leaders of giant private industries took steps to defend the autonomy of the business community from the party and the ever-increasing power of the ever more politically directed state enterprises. In 1972 Agnelli forced himself in as head of Confindustria and in 1976 arranged to be succeeded by his confidante Guido Carli. Throughout the seventies Confindustria was therefore in the hands of big business. It followed a strategy of disengaging the private sector from Christian Democratic control, of reversing the trend toward expanding state intervention for political purposes, and of promoting entrepreneurial interests more through the lay parties. It was at this point, for instance, that Agnelli associated himself with the Republicans. In the mid-seventies some in this group, led by Agnelli and Carli, came to the view that the country's economic problems could only be dealt with if there were a broad political consensus and specifically a modus vivendi with the Communist party and the unions.

This whole approach left many small industrialists – who represented a majority of the business community – if not disgruntled, in P. G. Wodehouse's phrase, certainly not gruntled. In what amounted to a counterrevolution at the time, they managed to elect a conservative, Vittorio Merloni, as Carli's successor in 1980. In the years immediately following, divergencies narrowed as the unions and the Communists went on the defensive and almost the whole of private industry thrived. The entire business community was then able to unite on a policy of reducing labor costs and increasing labor mobility, differing mainly on how militant to be in resisting the unions. But even as Confindustria's influence increased, the organization kept its distance from the parties and the government. It made few proposals and had little impact on the government's economic policies. Free-market principles were triumphant. The distance traveled from the corporatist days of the early postwar period was vast.

The changing face of industry

As a result of the dominant position achieved by the state enterprises since 1945, the purely private-sector economy is proportion-

ately the smallest of major Western industrial countries, account-
ing for 35 to 40 percent of Italy's industrial production. This private
sector is remarkable for its large number of small producers and its
small number of large producers. At least 90 percent of Italy's
industries employ fewer than a hundred workers; behind them is
the largest number of shopkeepers in Europe. The major industries
at the top of the pyramidal structure of the private sector are, and
have traditionally been, concentrated in remarkably few hands – a
narrow cartel of northern entrepreneurs (see Figure 2).

Chief among them is Gianni Agnelli of the family that founded
Fiat and that has maintained its primacy ever since. Italy's dominant private firm, Fiat is Europe's biggest producer of cars and an
important manufacturer of other vehicles, aircraft and aircraft en-
gines, railroad stock, turbines, farm equipment, and much more.
The other industrial superstar is Carlo De Benedetti, who took
over Olivetti in 1978, brilliantly resuscitated it, and went on to
become one of Europe's most dynamic business leaders. The Agnelli family, De Benedetti, Leopoldo Pirelli, Carlo Bonomi, and
Attilio Monti all control large holding companies with a wide array
of interests. Essentially outside dynastic control are Montedison,
the largest private firm after Fiat and one of Europe's major producers of chemicals, and Zanussi, a leading manufacturer of home
appliances. Although private banks represent merely around 20
percent of the country's banking facilities, the leading merchant
bank, Mediobanca, is almost half privately owned and is managed
as though it were entirely so. The close interweaving of shareholdings keeps these corporations linked and helps to maintain their
financial autonomy.

A striking feature of Italian private industry is its role in the
media. Virtually all the major daily newspapers are owned entirely
or in part by these corporate powers: *La Stampa* by Agnelli; *Il
Messaggero* by Montedison; *Il Giornale Nuovo* by Silvio Berlusconi;
Il Sole 24 Ore by Confindustria; *Il Tempo* by Italmobiliare; *La
Nazione, Il Resto del Carlino,* and *Il Piccolo* by Monti; and the
Corriere della Sera by a consortium controlled by Agnelli, Pirelli,
Bonomi, and Montedison. *La Repubblica* is owned in part by *L'Espresso,* a weekly in which Mediobanca and De Benedetti have
interests. Agnelli, Monti, and Confindustria have absolute editorial control over their papers; the others have varying degrees of
influence. There are also a number of private media empires that
are linked to these corporate circles. Berlusconi has built up a
television conglomerate that not only dominates private television
but that also has overtaken the state network in advertising reve-
nues and possibly in viewers. Edilio Rusconi and Arnoldo Monda-

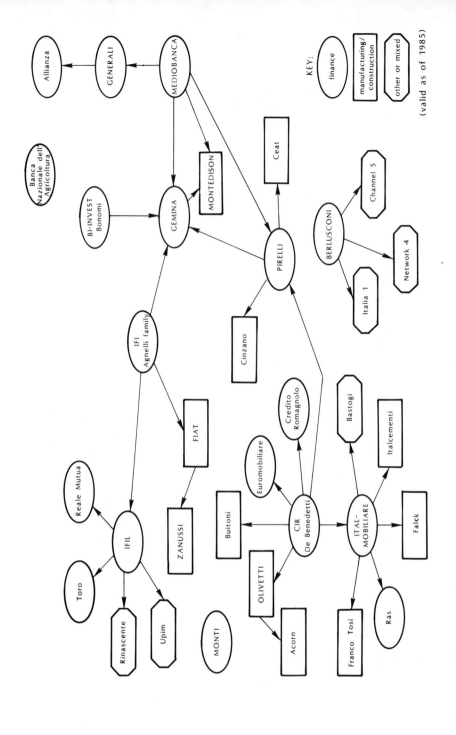

KEY:

finance

manufacturing/
construction

other or mixed

(valid as of 1985)

dori publish most of Italy's weeklies and monthlies. Carlo Caracciolo is the principal owner of *L'Espresso, La Repubblica,* and seven local dailies. In a country where political influences are omnipresent, the corporate-controlled press is an important weapon, providing entrepreneurs a means of influencing public opinion and the parties.

In the course of the 1980s several dramatic developments took place that altered the internal and external relationships of the private sector. Small and medium-sized enterprises grew ever more numerous and productive. Large industries, having declined to the point by the end of the seventies where they had to restructure to survive, undertook drastic reforms and, with a large infusion of foreign investment, became stronger than ever. The state sector, on the methadone of government subsidies, did not kick its bad habits and became more than ever dependent on huge injections of funds. As a result the private sector replaced the state sector, vital though it remained, as the really dynamic segment of the Italian economy. At the same time the so-called Catholic area of the private financial world – led by Michele Sindona, Roberto Calvi, Carlo Pesenti, and the Vatican Bank – sank in failure and corruption, resulting in some redivision of corporate holdings and leaving the lay area once again supreme. Both developments were politically significant. The private sector became more independent than ever of the government and therefore better able to withstand party influence, a development particularly at the expense of the Christian Democrats. The private-sector economy was thereby reinforced as one of the most important segments in Italian society able to remain outside the system of *partitocrazia.*

Over the years the Italian economy has developed a number of striking peculiarities that explain its unusual performance and ability to ride out international business cycles. One of these traits has been the remarkable strength of the export sector, which in some ways is a paradigm of Italy's economic performance – uncoordinated, often brilliant, sometimes slapdash, largely based on individual improvisation, and usually best when the government is not involved. Because of their exceptional ability to sense changing consumer demand and to produce attractive goods at reasonable prices, Italian exporters have been highly agile in shifting into new markets and alternative products. Year after year Italy was able, as *The Economist* wrote in 1981, "to export its way out of trouble with a style and panache that left its critics gasping and its admirers breathless."

The postwar record has been impressive. Italy's share of manufactured world exports has more than doubled in the postwar period, from 3 percent in 1950 to 7.5 percent already by 1972. The rate of export expansion has generally exceeded that of the average of world exports; in the 1950s it was excelled only by that of West Germany and Japan; in the 1960s only by Japan. Italian exports have increased every year since 1945 except for 1980 and since the latter year have nearly doubled in value.

An achievement of this order is all the more impressive since exporters have rarely received help from the government, either through assistance in penetrating world markets or through export credits. Although there has been some marked improvement since the late seventies, the government still lacks a coordinated export strategy. The Foreign Ministry claims authority over all aspects of external relations but lacks economic expertise; the Foreign Trade Ministry has bureaucratic primacy but little professionalism. The Industry and Agriculture Ministries have their own conflicting interests while the Bank of Italy and the Treasury Ministry compete over control of international monetary matters. The prime minister's office – whose role even in preparing for the Western economic summits has been essentially nonsubstantive – makes no effort to be a referee among rivals. Trade policy is as a result a free-for-all.

If the government helps only rarely, it at least never hinders Italian exporters. Sometimes very large firms carve out an area of interest and operate there with complete independence. At times these business activities forge an economic relationship that preempts the country's foreign policy in that part of the world. The most famous example was the operations of ENI under its swashbuckling chief, Enrico Mattei. Not only did Mattei break into the Middle Eastern oil market, he changed the pattern of contracts that had been established by British and American oil companies and substantially altered Italy's political position in the area.

All Italians agree that ideological and political considerations must be ruthlessly excluded in the search for trade. At the height of the cold war, Italian businessmen did their best to establish markets in Eastern Europe and China. During the Korean War, Fiat sold vital manufactures to North Korea. In NATO the Italian government has resisted American-sponsored embargo lists of exports to Communist countries. Neither the Communists nor the Socialists have ever seriously objected to Italian business activities with right-wing regimes in Africa or Latin America.

Despite their impressive growth, Italy's exports have seldom matched her imports. The latter have generally expanded at an equal or greater rate not only because of the need for raw materials but even such commodities as food – startling testimony to the failure of Italian agriculture to keep up with the country's industrialization. Throughout most of the postwar period Italy has consequently had trade deficits. Thanks to two exceptional sources of income, however, the current account has generally been in surplus or at least in balance. One is the high and steadily mounting level of tourist spending, producing a net income in 1983, for example, of roughly $10 billion. The other source is the remittances of Italian workers abroad, which in the early 1980s averaged about $1.5 billion a year.

The Italian export industry is remarkable for its ability not only to move quickly into new geographic areas but also to change into the production of items for which demand is on the rise. It therefore shifted steadily into manufactured goods (84% in 1952; 96% in 1979) and within this category away from textiles and food products into cars, clothing, precision machinery, electronics, and household appliances. Italian companies are also major contractors of highways, tunnels, bridges, and hydroelectric installations. In the course of the 1970s the foreign-trade sector was badly damaged by its loss of price competitiveness and the oil price increases after 1973, which nearly destroyed certain industries and created a large foreign exchange deficit. Thanks to the innovative capacity of Italian firms, Italian exports to OPEC countries rose from $500,000 in 1970 to almost $10 billion a decade later. By 1978 the country's current account was in surplus by $6 billion, an astonishing reversal in the face of the steadily rising oil bill.

Not surprisingly, there has been a striking proliferation of export firms, from 16,000 in 1967 to 100,000 in 1980. Behind this development lies another outstanding trait of the country's current industrial structure – the rise of a sector of small and medium-sized firms that *The Economist* in 1981 described as the most dynamic anywhere in Europe. Originally most of these companies were set up to escape the trade union regulations that followed the "hot autumn," since firms with fewer than fifteen workers need not to be unionized or pay standard wages and social benefits. They therefore operated at great cost efficiency and high productivity and without risk of strikes. There was still another impetus. Firms with annual incomes below approximately $75,000 were not required to make their books available to income-tax authorities. The astonishing consequence of this has been that as of 1984 fully 95 percent of Italian firms declared incomes of less than that figure. Smaller was better, indeed.

As a result there has developed on top of the economic division between North and South and between successful private enterprises and loss-making, politically corrupted state enterprises an additional layer to the Italian economy. Today there are over a million such firms, ranging from small factories to tiny workshops in garages and cellars. Sometimes they are subcontractors of huge, sophisticated industries such as Fiat. Often they are simple individual enterprises, operated by a family or as a second job. In either case their flair for design is equaled by their savvy for business promotion. They are the most profitable sector of the Italian economy. Particularly proficient in the export area, they are largely responsible for the buoyancy of Italian exports after the mid-1970s. In the fashion world Italian clothing, furniture, and textiles have emerged as a world leader, while in some industrial areas, such as machine tools and robots, Italian products have earned an outstanding reputation for quality and won a growing share of the world market. In 1983 the value of Italian clothing exports was larger than that of France, Britain, Germany, or the United States.

Some of these firms shade into the *industria sommersa,* the "underground economy." This is an intricate network of small firms and cottage industries that do business in such a way as to escape not only trade union regulations, taxes, and export regulations but also any official recording of their activities. Although most of these concerns are concentrated in the North, an often-cited example is the glove industry in the Naples area. Official statistics record not a single glove factory; in fact, some 30 million pairs of gloves are estimated to be produced there annually, making the region the world's largest glove manufacturer. Since the production of these small firms escapes official records, the country's GNP and export statistics are appreciably undervalued. It is generally thought that the "underground economy" employs anywhere from 2 to 4 million persons and produces fully 20 to 30 percent over the official GNP. Presumably the country's true GNP would push Italy a notch or two above its place as seventh in the world economy.

This small-business sector has changed the industrial map of Italy. No longer does the Italian economy entirely hinge on the old industrial triangle. The new firms are not in large cities but in provincial towns in former agrarian areas. And they have spread from Emilia-Romagna, the Veneto, and Tuscany into the Marches and on to Umbria, Abruzzi, Puglia, and the area below Rome. They produce clothing, leather products, shoes, furniture, textiles, toys, car parts, jewelry, machine tools, and agricultural machinery.

Thanks to the low price, innovative nature, and high quality of their products, these firms are remarkably resistant to the ups and downs of the international economy. Some of the most profitable of them lie in the heavily Communist Tuscan countryside and have produced a remarkably successful "Communistic capitalism."

This small-business sector is an excellent example of how Italians have managed, by dint of ingenuity, to solve certain economic problems, which in some cases they created themselves. The practical situation was once graphically summed up by a former *La Stampa* editor, Arrigo Levi: "Italians, like Houdinis, tie their hands daily with incredible union and state regulations, but they untie them each afternoon and start working like mad, with great success, zest, and considerable achievements. My pet solution for Italy's economic ills was to pass one law, consisting of one clause, saying that all the other economic laws and regulations apply between midnight and 2 P.M., while between 2 P.M. and midnight there can be a happy anarchy. This, by the way, is what already happens."

In the development of these distinctive and highly regionalized manufacturing sectors, Arnaldo Bagnasco perceives "three Italies" – one centered in the Northwest, comprising large modern industries; a second in the Northeast of small enterprises of low technology but high craftsmanship; and a third, in the Center and South, where extreme forms of the other two exist side by side. Some Italians regard their country's position in the international economy in somewhat comparable terms: in an uneasy position between the industrial leaders of the world, with which they have difficulty keeping up, and the advanced Third World, which is catching up. They note that Italy devotes less to research and development than other industrial countries and fear that the country could slide into a semideveloped status with only a few firms, such as Olivetti, in tandem with modern developments through links with American industry and technology.

Twentieth-century baroque

Italy's postwar economic development unleashed the country's native energy and talent, erased the long centuries of poverty, and gave the mass of Italians a standard of living that none would have dreamed possible in 1945 – or before. Levels of health and diet rose; education became more widespread and illiteracy vanished. A social safety net, scarcely extant at the end of the war, was gradually extended to provide almost everyone with health benefits, and a pension. With the movement of the population from the land to the cities and from South to North, social and regional differences diminished. In the wake of these changes, class divisions, traditional mores, and the church lost some of their hold. Hence it was not just the rate of growth and its profound consequences but the contrast between the starting point and the destination that made Italy's economic miracle the most dramatic in Europe. Although the economic advance and resulting social changes created new problems and tensions, the overall steady movement from mass poverty to mass prosperity along with the gradual but sweeping social improvements made the country's manifold problems manageable and helped to prevent alienation of all save a tiny minority from the political order.

Nonetheless this veritable revolution has left great gaps, distortions, and inequities. Economic development took an independence course and, apart from the expansion of the state enterprises and the programs for the South, there was no overall concept much less developed program for economic advance, as was at least attempted in other European states. Political will always failed. It was everyone for himself.

At the end of the war a ruinous inflation badly hit the established middle class. Shortly afterward Einaudi's deflationary measures were so strong that, in H. Stuart Hughes's words, they "placed the bulk of the Italian people in a stationary situation of well-ordered misery." By contrast, the rich, the great landowners, and the aristocracy managed to hold on to their wealth. As prosperity gradually spread throughout society, the benefits were unevenly divided. Those unfortunates who were not organized in trade unions and could not strike were overlooked amid the broad increase in national wealth. So as the standard of living rose for the country as a whole, disparities remained among social groups as well as between North and South. Moreover, with the national economy focused on exports and the production of nonessentials for domestic consumption, little attention was given to health care, education, transportation, housing and other social needs.

It was a deepening sense that major elements of national life were out of sync and that Italy was out of sync with other industrially advanced countries that was in part the catalyst for the wave of ferment that began among students in 1968 and continued to spread throughout society in subsequent years. There was a spontaneous unleashing of sentiment to take Italy out of the past and into the late twentieth century. The result was an unprecedented challenge to prevailing social values and established institutions. The wave of protest eventually swept the parties along or swept them aside.

The changes, tangible and intangible, set in train during this period constituted a turning point in postwar Italy and have deeply marked contemporary Italy. It was as a result of this turmoil, for instance, that parliament enacted the labor statute as well as divorce, abortion, and family legislation. As the new mood infected the judicial system, courts took more liberal stands on civil liberties, social causes, and employees' rights. Regional devolution of central government powers was finally carried out in full. The new libertarian spirit found political expression in the refoundation of the Radical party and the formation of new left groups as well as in the establishment of politically iconoclastic newspapers such as *Manifesto, Lotta Continua,* and *La Repubblica.* Eventually the formation of new types of social action was taken up by other circles, with the establishment of local school committees and, on the conservative side, by groups such as Communion and Liberation.

Social attitudes changed remarkably fast. The position of the church, for example, was undermined in the course of a single decade. The role of the sexes was altered. As women moved into the cities, were better educated, and drew away from the church, they began to challenge the notion that their place was in the home, at the center of the family. In the ferment of the late sixties a women's liberation movement was launched with the aim of achieving in practice the equality of rights women were guaranteed in Article 3 of the constitution. It made itself felt not only in divorce and family legislation but also in a law for nursery schools in 1972, the establishment of women's health clinics with birth control counseling in 1975, and an equal pay for equal work law in 1977. But it was the abortion issue that acted as catalyst in creating an active feminist movement. Taking shape in 1974, feminist groups demanded the right of abortion on demand, free of charge in state hospitals. At issue was not just freedom of choice but equality of status. Lay party circles were not unsympathetic, but parliament would not go so far. "A situation thus appeared," Yasmin Ergas has written, "in which the male political system appeared to deny a women's demand that had already aroused widespread support." Although the legislation that was finally enacted in 1978 did not fully accept the principle of female self-determination, it was in practice liberal and received overwhelming support in the 1981 referendum.

Some of the reforms of the 1970s were, if well-intentioned, ill-conceived and often resulted in notorious failure. Despite repeated attempts to provide better housing and fair rent-control laws, a situation resulted that was marked by widespread illegal construction, a paucity of subsidized, low-cost housing, and a massive shortage of apartments in cities where tens of thousands of housing units remained vacant. Reforms in health services improved coverage over the years, but even the new system adopted in 1979, which was intended to correct the deficiencies of the past, produced a siuation where, in the words of one expert, "The doctors are dissatisfied, the people are dissatisfied, the nurses are dissatisfied, and the budget is broke."

Another example is education. Over the years successive governments have tried to bring the Italian system up to the quality of its European equivalents. But schooling is still obligatory only up to the age of fourteen, and in the 1980s roughly 18 percent of the population had learned nothing more than to read and write. Although teaching is often of high quality, the conditions of higher education are chaotic. In 1969, in a spirit of egalitarianism, universities were opened to all high school graduates free of charge. Enrollment immediately soared. At Rome University, the most severely affected, it rose from 20,000 to 150,000 in 1980 and throughout Italy went from around 200,000 to roughly 1 million in the same period. Teaching staff and facilities were not appreciably increased, however, and the resulting conditions of study were appalling. In an era of high youth unemployment, universities became way stations for those without jobs. According to some estimates, fewer than one-third of the registered students attended class, and in 1977 only one student in ten took a degree. Appointment to university rectorships and professorships is heavily influenced by a candidate's political credentials. Although there are some areas of higher education and research where Italy excels – such as engineering, theoretical physics, some branches of science, and the fine arts – the general level of higher education and the facilities for research and advanced study are, with a few notable exceptions, inadequate so far as they exist.

All in all Italy has undergone as profound a social change as any country in the West. Although the transformation has on the whole left the country more modern, efficient, and humane, great pockets of obsolescence, backwardness, and underprivilege remain. Italy consequently presents a mixed face: development and underdevelopment, modern and baroque, Northern European and Mediterranean. But the most important fact is that trends have always been upward, giving the broad mass of people a feeling that life had improved and would probably continue to improve. The economic advance was great and broad enough and social change deep and timely enough to contain any underlying discontent with the political system and to strengthen the country's underlying social cohesion and remarkable political stability.

11. Regional devolution and the problem of the South

The astonishing diversity of the country is one of the first impressions of any traveler to Italy. On a relatively small stretch of land – not much more than half the size of France – are a hundred different worlds. They range from the pastures of the Alps and Dolomites on whose slopes French, German, and a form of Latin are the first language to the olive and orange groves of the South where ancient Greek, Arab, and Norman influences are everywhere visible. Sardinia and even Sicily retain a sense of isolation that modern transport only slowly diminishes.

Behind these geographic contrasts are even deeper social and cultural differences. The individual Italian commonly characterizes himself first as a Piedmontese or Sicilian, as a Florentine or Neapolitan, and by this he means not an address but a historic, almost ethnic identification. Only gradually has unification broken down centuries-old regional identities and local pride. At the same time Milan and Turin with their modern industries are closer in appearance and outlook to Frankfurt and Brussels than to Naples and Palermo with their almost oriental color and turmoil. An intense provincialism is – logically perhaps – coupled with an exceptional lack of nationalistic feeling. Overcoming the country's divisions and diversity was the foremost aim of the nineteenth-century Piedmontese unifiers of the country. In the famous epigram of one of them, Massimo d'Azeglio, "We have made Italy, now we must make Italians." The success has not been complete. Italy remains a country of countries, a land of contrasts far greater than that of any other European nation.

In the unsettled conditions at the end of the war, the sense of separate identity became so strong around the periphery of the country that it flared into demands for outright separation or at least a degree of autonomy. In Sicily parliament declared the island semiautonomous in May 1945, and the Sardinian parliament followed course in February 1948. In French-speaking Aosta on the French-Swiss border, the regional council that was independently established in 1946 enacted an autonomy statute two years later. The German-speaking population of the South Tyrol, or Upper

Adige, which Italy won as a result of the First World War, wanted to secede and join Austria, a move that was fully supported by the Austrian government, which formally claimed back the area after 1945. De Gasperi and Austrian Foreign Minister Karl Gruber reached a compromise agreement in 1946 that left the area in Italy while granting it administrative autonomy.

Therefore by the time the constitution came to be written, regional autonomy was already an established fact in certain areas. Although there was no appreciable interest elsewhere in Italy in local self-government above the communal level, the Constituent Assembly, with the strict centralism of the Fascist state in mind, gave much thought to a devolution of authority that would limit power at the center and bring government closer to the citizen. Ultimately it decided, in one of its major departures from Italian tradition, to create a regional system. It recognized the existing situation around the periphery by establishing five "special regions" with unique powers and created in the remainder of the country fourteen – later fifteen – "ordinary regions" with less authority. Statutes passed in February 1948 granted the five special regions legislative and taxing rights along with the power to alter national laws to meet regional conditions. This exceptional grant of autonomy appeased separatist fervor elsewhere except in the South Tyrol.

Austria irredenta

Between the Brenner Pass and the Gorge of Salorno there now exists a virtual country within a country, an area almost entirely self-administered. With privileges exceeding those of any other region, the 280,000 German-speaking South Tyrolese have developed their own nation. In its architecture, way of life, values, dress, language, and culture, the South Tyrol is completely Germanic. The press and radio are in German. The school curriculum – including history and literature – is almost entirely German-Austrian in orientation. On graduation most students go to Austrian universities on Austrian scholarships. Economic life is focused on Austria and there are special trade agreements between it and South Tyrol. The area has its own trade unions and political parties – the South Tyrol People's party being the largest. As a result of a 1979 Austrian law they even enjoy certain of the rights of Austrian citizens. Most South Tyrolese frankly acknowledge that they feel themselves to be Austrian and think of Austria as their homeland. But they recognize that the border is not to be redrawn and they therefore simply minimize their links with the rest of the country. They normally refuse to speak Italian, pretending to outsiders not to know the language. They resent the presence of non-German-speaking Italians, particularly if they are government officials or police, and do their best to make them feel unwelcome. For these and other reasons, Italian residents of the area are consequently moving away. According to the 1981 census, the Italian-speakers in the area declined from 33 percent in 1953 to 29 percent, while the German-speaking population rose to 66 percent, with the Ladino-speaking group remaining at 4 percent.

This delicate situation is the result of a long struggle between the South Tyrolese and the Italian state. Although the De Gasperi–Gruber agreement was incorporated into the 1947 Italian peace treaty, the Italian government feared that autonomy was merely the first step toward separation and therefore amalgamated the South Tyrol with the predominantly Italian province of Trentino to form a region in which German-speakers were a minority. That act was the central cause of the legal frictions and the sense of grievance that the South Tyrolese have subsequently felt. "Free from Trent" became the cry of the South Tyrolese, and it was fully endorsed by the Austrian government. De Gasperi himself came from Trentino; for nearly forty years he had been an Austrian citizen and had served as a deputy in the Austrian parliament before 1914. He therefore well knew what it was to be national minority in another country. But a settlement agreeable to the two sides proved elusive. The dissatisfaction of the South Tyrolese eventually took the extreme form of terrorism, until an accord was reached between Rome and Vienna in 1969.

By the terms of the agreement a new autonomy statute went into effect in 1972 that created within the region of Trentino two autonomous provinces – Bolzano and Trent – with the German-speaking area enjoying full cultural autonomy and complete authority to administer local affairs. Since then a "package" of 137 measures to implement this autonomy has been slowly implemented. By the mid-1980s only a few Italianate vestiges, such as the use of Italian in court trials, were left and the South Tyrolese were agitating to eliminate them as well.

Even these concessions, however, have not finally settled the question. Social housing, positions in public administration, and similar matters are divided according to ethnic strength. To enter the local civil service, a command of both German and Italian is required, thereby eliminating many Italians. Hence Italians have a sense of being a minority in their own country. This sentiment reached such a pitch that in the local elections of 1985 there was a "nationalistic" backlash in the form of a huge protest vote for the neo-Fascists, who in Bolzano quadrupled their electorate to reach nearly 23 percent. At the same time the German-speakers continue to suffer from a sense of being a beleaguered minority in a state they do not respect. Tensions consequently remain, endangering the settlement agreed in the autonomy statute.

Delayed devolution

Implementing the constitutional provisions for the ordinary regions was postponed for many years. There was a general reluctance to establish yet another level of government between Rome and the provinces and communes. Regional government as practiced in Sicily had proved so grossly ineffective that there was doubt about risking it elsewhere. However, the controlling factor was the competing partisan interests of the Christian Democrats and the left. This situation was a double paradox. The Christian Democrats had a tradition of favoring regional decentralization. When they became the dominant party on the national level in 1948, however, they did not want their control weakened by regional administrations that in some cases were destined to fall into the hands of the Socialists and Communists. The left, which had been generally committed to centralization, obviously reasoned to the opposite conclusion and became strong supporters of increased regional power. Not until 1963 when the Socialists made it a condition of forming a center-left coalition did the Christian Democrats allow the enabling legislation to pass. Even so it was only in June 1970 that elections for regional councils were held and in April 1972 that regional constitutions were approved in Rome. The transfer of governing authority occurred in two stages, some in 1972 and the remainder in 1977, at which point the constitutional provisions on the ordinary regions came into full effect.

Regional authority lies primarily in two areas, economic activities of an essentially regional nature and social services. Within the limits established by parliament, the regions may accordingly legislate on such matters as community boundaries, police regulations, welfare and health services, professional and trade schools, town planning, tourism, local transport, fishing, agriculture, and forests. They are also responsible for administering these matters, though the constitution states that the regions should delegate this authority to the provinces, communities, and local public agencies. The regions also enjoy modest financial authority both through the right to assess some local taxes and through guaranteed state financial grants. To carry out these responsibilities, each region has an assembly of thirty to eighty members, depending on the region's population. The body is elected for five years and in turn elects an executive, or *giunta,* as well as a regional president. In each regional capital there is a commissioner, appointed by Rome, who approves regional legislation and who chairs a regional "control commission" that oversees the legality of regional administration. In the case of Calabria, to allay local jealousies within the region, parliament was situated in Reggio Calabria and the executive offices in Catanzaro.

Such devolution of power is unprecedented in Italian history. The authority transferred to the regions is, however, by any standards extremely modest. Moreover the principle behind devolution is less one of certain powers residing in the regions than one of authority being delegated from the center, and a jealous center at that. With the line of jurisdiction between the state and the regions ambiguous, regional powers have been an object of continuing dispute. Italian regionalism therefore faces two continuing problems: the amount of authority to be wielded and the efficiency of regional authorities in discharging their responsibilities.

Regionalism in practice

In establishing regions it had been thought that bringing government closer to the citizen would awaken a greater sense of popular involvement and would stimulate local interest in the development of the region. It had also been expected that the regions would be able to coordinate policies and deal with local problems more pragmatically and effectively than either national or communal governments. And it had been anticipated that regional administrators would be willing to experiment and innovate. In general these hopes have been disappointed.

Since their establishment the regions have not animated greater popular participation in regional affairs, indeed have not taken hold on the public consciousness. According to a 1979 poll by the Doxa Institute, eight out of ten persons in Tuscany knew nothing about the functions and powers of the regions. This finding is confirmed by the experience of anyone who travels around Italy and inquires about the activities, influence, and authority of the region. The average citizen appears to regard his regional government simply as another layer of administration between Rome and the community but not as a vital institution with its own character and functions. The hope that regional government would stimulate local elites to play a role in the governing process has also not been realized. Although regionalism has been important in allowing the Communists, Socialists, and lay parties to play a role largely denied them on the national level, regional government has generally been used less to demonstrate a capacity to govern effectively than to gain patronage. In a study of the operations of communal government, Sidney Tarrow drew a number of general conclusions that apply almost equally well to contemporary regional administration: that local authorities circumvent formal links to the central government and deal directly with party contacts in Rome, that they devote much or most of their time to cultivating political contacts, and that the resources they acquire are allocated by mass clientelism rather than functional logic.

Regional governments have demonstrated little of the hoped-for innovative and pragmatic spirit of administration. The notion that it would do so was to some extent undercut from the start inasmuch as 80 percent of the 60,000 regional officials came from the central civic service. These officials have largely maintained their old bureaucratic mentality as well as their reputation for being under-qualified and overpaid. They have created a regional bureaucracy and have resisted the constitutional directive to delegate authority to the communities. Mayors complain bitterly about autocratic regional "ministers" whose primary interest is patronage and building administrative empires. So instead of more participation, there has been more bureaucracy.

The problems are epitomized in the issue of finance. Since their own taxing authority, based essentially on property, brings in less than 10 percent of their total budget, the regions are dependent on Rome for the lion's share of their income. Moreover they have little discretion in dispensing these funds. Most regional expenditures are fixed, earmarked for specific services – the largest part for a region's ordinary administrative costs, and the remainder for regional development programs. Other state funds go to the regions simply for transmittal to communities and local government agencies for such programs as national health services. Altogether less than a third of a region's income, according to a 1979 report of the Censis Foundation, can be spent as decided by regional authorities themselves. Consequently the regions are deprived of much of the flexibility and scope for coordination that was a large part of their purpose.

If dependence on Rome is one aspect of the financial problem, another is the converse. Sometimes the regions fail to use the authority they have to spend the funds, both fixed and discretionary, that are at their disposal. Roughly a third of a region's earmarked funds regularly go unused. Authorities in Rome attribute this fact to the dilatoriness of regional legislatures and executive officials. Regional authorities blame the problem on the central government and on contradictory or inadequate legislation. In fact it is difficult to fix responsibility. In a case, for instance, of a region that receives funds for a vocational training center but fails to carry through with the project and forfeits the money, the failure could result either from ambiguous laws and regulations of the central government or from a failure of the community in question to provide a site for the center or simply from a lack of interest in the project by regional officials. By and large, however, most observers incline to the view that primary responsibility for the huge amount of unspent funds lies with the regions. There are some exceptions, such as Tuscany, Emilia-Romagna, and Lombardy. But it is a sad fact that the least developed of the regions, those in the South and Sardinia in particular, have spent the smallest proportion of the funds available.

Nor have regional parliaments borne out hopes. There are large areas where they could legislate independently but do not. Instead they tend to take over laws enacted in Rome, at most adapting them slightly to suit regional conditions. All too often the region's problems are ignored, patronage becomes an overriding interest, and party politicking replaces serious governing. They themselves become bogged down in the same partisan maneuverings that occur on the national level, making regional assemblies merely bad copies of the Roman parliament.

Some regional governments, especially in the South, are even more unstable than those on the national level. Sicily and Calabria are regularly without governments for months on end largely as a result of factional struggles within the dominant Christian Democratic party. In Sardinia as well coalitions are constantly shifting for the same reason.

As in any system of shared powers, there are jurisdictional problems. In providing for regions, the constitution left intact the ninety-four existing provinces, each with its prefect from Rome and its own parliament and executive, even though many of their functions were transferred to the regions. It has long been recognized that this situation should be tidied up because of the confusion of competencies. Although the Socialists and Republicans would abolish the provinces, there has been growing sentiment for retaining them in some form. Following the earthquake in southern Italy in November 1980, for instance, the prefects in the affected provinces, with their local authority and direct links to Rome, demonstrated a greater ability to respond to the disaster than did regional authorities, who had difficulty setting emergency services in motion. At the same time, municipalities – once proud and famous cities – see their autonomy slipping away. With expenditures skyrocketing and their incomes reduced by a tax reform in 1971, they are increasingly dependent on other governing levels for their financial survival and are turning to Rome rather than the regions for help.

In assessing local self-government, Italian experts and political scientists tend to be critical of the overall record even while acknowledging that devolution is a worthy goal and has become an accepted principle of the political system. A voluminous study of the performance of local administration in the decade and a half up to 1985, conducted by scores of specialists under the auspices of the Institute for the Science of Public Administration, concluded that Italy is the most centralized country in the West – without strong government either in the regions, as in Germany; in the provinces, as in France; or in the cities, as in Britain and elsewhere. The analysis found that by and large the regions are 90 percent dependent on the central organs of the state, that provinces serve almost no legitimate purpose, and that communal government not only is generally weak but also has failed to develop an indigenous governing class. At every level autonomous administration had been compromised by the narrow interests of the parties, which use local government institutions for patronage and jobbery rather than as instruments for dealing with local issues.

One of the results of this *partitocrazia,* according to the study, has been to create and perpetuate a proliferation of government. For instance, although the populations of Lombardy and Sweden are the same size, the former has six times the number of communal governments – with that many more administrative positions to be dispensed by the parties. The maintenance of provinces is also largely to be explained in this way. Another consequence has been to subordinate every aspect of local government to party interests. In examining the 1980 round of regional, provincial, and communal elections, the study found that the national headquarters of the parties imposed their own candidates on election lists and, after the balloting, sent out party functionaries to be mayors and administrators of places where in many cases they had not previously set foot. As the director of the study commented: "The parties engaged in complex diplomatic games, dirty tricks, surprise moves and veiled bribery. The big parties tried to dominate, the small ones to exploit their pivotal positions. Everything was legitimate but could not have been further from the real problems of the area."

This bleak picture demonstrates how genuine self-government in the local sphere is to some extent thwarted and the objectives of devolution are compromised. The separation of the citizen from his government is as wide here as on the national level. Given the nature of coalition politics, voters cannot determine who is to be mayor of their town, president of their province or region, or even the makeup of the governing coalition. Regional and other local governments are formed and remade as a function of partisan politics with little or no relation to election results and the performance of the incumbent administration. In the course of 1984, for instance, Naples had, in addition to one provisional government, five different mayors – one Communist, one Social Democrat, two Christian Democrats, and one Socialist.

The differing results of local self-government have had the effect of exposing an unintended result of devolution. As such political scientists as Sabino Cassese have observed, regional government has by and large been more of a success in the North than in the South. In this very disparity of results comes to light one of Italy's oldest and most intransigent problems, the division between North and South.

The sad face of the South

Although Italy is normally divided into North, Central, and South, the essential division is between the North and the South. Whether the dividing line is just north or south of Rome is a matter of popular debate. But wherever it precisely lies, it demarcates a gulf between the two areas that is historically, physically, culturally, and even psychologically so deep as to create almost two countries.

The South of Italy, an area the size of Greece with a population of 20 million, is popularly known as the Mezzogiorno, or land of the midday sun. The very word conjures for the foreigner an image that has prevailed since the era of the grand tour: the South as a lush and sunny garden, dotted by romantic, decaying monuments, all under a boundless blue sky. The reality, however, is one of blazing, rainless summers and freezing winters, of barren mountains and arid valleys that in spring and winter are devastated by violent rains, flash floods, and landslides.

In ancient times the South was the most prosperous part of Italy; by the Middle Ages it had fallen behind the rest of the country, and the disparity steadily widened in succeeding centuries. With the unification of the country, the Bourbon monarchy was deposed, the power of the church reduced, and some modernization introduced. But the local barons retained their influence and the new Piedmontese bureaucracy behaved more like another in the long line of foreign invaders than liberators from the North. The new institutions, laws, and economic policies were generally alien to the customs and contrary to the interests of the South. Taxes became ruinous, the area's economic base was undermined while the industrialization of the North perpetuated and even deepened the division. Economic conditions were so hard that in the fifty years before the First World War roughly half the southern population – 5 million people – left their homes to start new lives abroad. When the Fascists came to power they announced ambitious development plans for the area, mostly land-reclamation projects. Apart from the much-touted draining of the Pontine marshes, these projects never amounted to much and the emigration continued, now to the African colonies as well.

Well into the present century the South consequently remained, in Carlo Levi's words, "that land without comfort or solace, where the peasant lives out his motionless civilization on barren ground in remote poverty, and in the presence of death." Following unification a few humane and heroic voices were raised in indignation and pity. Two northerners, Leopoldo Franchetti and the later prime minister, Sidney Sonnino, investigated conditions in the South and wrote courageous exposés. By the turn of the century several southerners – most prominently Giustino Fortunato, Gaetano Salvemini, and another subsequent prime minister, Francesco Saverio Nitti – joined in with specific proposals on how conditions might be improved. Although concern revived at the end of the Second World War, the governments of the day were more interested in overall reconstruction and did nothing. But the mood was now changing. Some of postwar Italy's leading writers – Ignazio Silone, Carlo Levi, Domenico Rea, and Leonardo Sciascia – were publishing eloquent novels on the plight of the South. These authors understood better, felt more deeply, and conveyed more powerfully than the politicians what life there was really like. With a cool eye but deep compassion, they illuminated the remorseless cycle of privation, resignation, and feelings of inferiority. Such classics as Silone's *Fontamara* and Levi's *Christ Stopped at Eboli* awakened and discomfited millions of Italians, creating a widespread feeling of shame if not guilt. Within the South itself, pent-up anger was reaching the boiling point. Finally the government had no choice but to act.

Regional social-economic differences exist in every country, particularly when one area is relatively industrialized and the other essentially agricultural. The unusual nature of Italy's North–South problem is the depth of the division and the breadth of its causes, combining both material and psychological factors. Life in the South, Fortunato once wrote, was "a savagely bitter struggle between man and nature which has left painful and indelible scars on both." Over the years the "southern problem" has been defined in a dozen different ways but in objective terms comes down to a matter of overpopulation in relation to economic resources and development. Its symptoms have been all too obvious: poverty, unemployment and underemployment, illiteracy, poor health, high infant mortality – and hopelessness. This is the vicious circle that successive postwar governments have tried, or been goaded into trying, to undo. They have followed three courses of action – land reform, infrastructure development, and industrialization.

The problem of land

It was in 1949 when southern peasants started occupying some of the *latifondi,* or large estates, that the government was forced to deal with the problem of the South. At that time over half the population of the Mezzogiorno – compared to a third in the rest of Italy – earned its livelihood from the soil as small holders, tenant farmers, or day laborers. These peasants barely eked out a subsistence living. In the face of the spreading discontent, the government enacted a modest land reform program in 1950 to buy out some large estates and sell the land to the peasants. As a result of the resistance and ruses of the large landholders, at most half the available land – and the poorest at that – was in fact distributed. When the program was largely completed in 1962 a mere 1.5 million acres had been transferred to some 85,000 peasants. For many, especially in the mountainous areas, the redistribution amounted to no more than a small plot of poor soil, insufficient to maintain a family. So the flight from the land into the cities and to the North intensified. And in the South as a whole, land holdings – half the average size of those in other Common Market countries – were too small to achieve fully modern and low-cost production.

As its institutional arm for dealing with the South, the government established in 1950 what developed into the biggest regional development agency in Europe, the Cassa per il Mezzogiorno, or Development Fund for the South. It was given an initial grant of

$125 million to be dispensed throughout the South – which was defined as the entire peninsula south of Rome, part of the Marches, and Sicily and Sardinia. During its first dozen years the fund concentrated its attention and roughly 78 percent of its money on agriculture, with most of the remainder going to related infrastructure. Land reclamation, irrigation, aqueducts, and a vast extension of the road network gradually changed the face of the South. With the construction of dams came both electric power and water for towns and farms. Malaria, which before 1945 had afflicted Italy, in particular the South, more severely than any other area of Europe, was finally eradicated, making it possible to cultivate lowlands for the first time in well over a millennium.

The impact of these advances on agriculture was beneficial if limited and was marked by sharp regional disparities. Technical experts introduced new farming and marketing methods but the sizes of farms and the strength of peasant traditions frustrated hopes of modernizing agriculture except in the plains – notably in the area of Metaponto on the gulf of Taranto and the coastal strip of Puglia – where the combination of land reform, land reclamation, and modern farming techniques meshed with much success. Gisele Podbielski estimates that gross agricultural production in the South rose by 78 percent between 1950 and 1976.

However, the real income of the average farmer increased but little. Tens of thousands continued to leave the farms and poured into the labor market in the North. In the course of the postwar years the share of agriculture in total employment in the South declined from 57 to 27 percent. As time passed southern farmers could neither meet growing domestic needs nor match increasing foreign competition. By 1960 a preeminently agricultural country had become a net food importer.

The problem of capital

Soon enough it became clear that efforts to improve agriculture had not reduced unemployment, raised incomes, or narrowed the overall gap between the South and the rest of Italy. Many experts had insisted all along that only rapid industrial development would create the jobs and prosperity needed to break the vicious circle of unemployment and poverty. Put simply, industry was to be moved to the area of surplus labor rather than labor's moving to the area of industrial activity. Since there was no southern capital for such industrialization, legislation was enacted in 1957 shifting state investment funds from agriculture to industry. Special "development poles" were designated – the Naples-Salerno area and the Taranto-Bari-Brindisi triangle – where giant basic industries were to be established. It was anticipated that these would in time attract further, secondary industries and create a broad and diversified industrialization. The South would then be on its way to autonomous and self-sustaining economic development.

The fund's spending on infrastructure was therefore cut from 42 percent in 1957 to 13 percent in 1965 while assistance to industrial enterprises was stepped up from 48 percent to 82 percent. To encourage private investment the government offered generous credits and tax incentives. It also required the state holding companies, IRI and ENI, to place increasing amounts of capital in the South. IRI, the major investor, injected over $20 billion into the Mezzogiorno between 1963 and 1978. In this way came about a steel industry (at one time the most modern in Europe) at Taranto, an Alfa Romeo plant near Naples, and giant petrochemical factories in Sicily and Sardinia. The volume of industrial development in the South during this period was remarkable. Podbielski calculates that it increased over seven times between 1951 and 1975, while only doubling in the Center and North.

Even though some of these investments were productive and profitable, the all-out heavy industrialization program did not turn out to be the magic solution to the South's problems. The new industries were not labor intensive and created relatively few jobs. The managerial and technical personnel were seconded from the North and returned there, leaving the South without an indigenous managerial and technical class. And the industries themselves were subsidiaries of northern companies which never developed links to the local economy.

Laws were therefore enacted in 1971 and 1976 requiring the Development Fund to concentrate on a new range of intersectoral and interregional projects. These included the further development of industrial infrastructure, the exploitation of natural resources, social projects in metropolitan areas, water-reclamation projects, cleaning the Gulf of Naples, extending the road network into remote mountainous areas, reforestation, and promotion of citrus fruit production. Many of these programs had to be scaled down or scrapped as a result of the economic crisis following the oil price increase after 1973. Some of them were gigantic fiascoes. Over $800 million was spent on cleaning the Gulf of Naples without producing a pint of unpolluted water. By the end of the decade the era of big infrastructure projects was over. Emphasis then shifted to the selective encouragement of small and medium-sized firms, which in the early 1980s accounted for over 90 percent of the projects and 85 percent of the investment of the Development Fund.

The fund, originally established for fifteen years, was extended year after year until 1984, when it was finally terminated. During the first 30 years, between 1950 and 1980, it spent about $20 billion of the total $30 billion allocated to it. The European Community's regional fund added over $2 billion of its own, making the Mezzogiorno its single main beneficiary.

Industrialization without development

Even before the fund was phased out, it was impossible to deny that southern development had fallen far short of all its original goals and that the single most important objective, industrialization, had manifestly not been met despite a number of isolated successes. Development had been the victim of bad planning, bad economics, bad politics, and bad luck. Most observers agree that, even leaving aside political distortions, the most basic error was the failure to develop a long-term, coordinated investment policy or comprehensive economic program. Instead there was a jumble of laws and policies that were often inconsistent and undirected. Emphasis shifted from agriculture to infrastructure development, to large industry, to small and medium-sized industry, and back to agriculture. The whole development process went ahead, Gianni Agnelli remarked at a conference of southern experts in 1980, either in "the good faith of error" or in "the bad faith of political 'necessity'."

"Political necessity" at times took the form of rank political expedience. In a study of the Mezzogiorno, Judith Chubb found that although the Christian Democrats had at first resisted industrialization in fear that it would upset the established social and economic order and therefore undermine their political dominance, they quickly learned that capital investment could be a wondrous opportunity for political alchemy. In no time they transformed the Development Fund into a fountain of clientelistic gold, which they ladled out for partisan benefit. Projects were designed less to secure long-term economic development than to reinforce local networks of clientelism. The monies were not necessarily wasted. Nor were the Christian Democrats the only offenders. But since they usually controlled the fund and held the throttle on investment by state enterprises, they are primarily responsible for the fact that a high proportion of the monies were dispersed, as one Italian observer phrased it, "in a thousand undirected rivulets."

Good intentions and political expedience sooner or later ran afoul of economic facts. Industrialization and employment were not entirely compatible goals. Large enterprises lacked the requisite economic hinterland to support them and failed to act as the anticipated catalyst for follow-on private investment. So the new plants came to be known as "cathedrals in the desert" – great isolated structures with few economic worshipers. Because it was politically unthinkable to close them, the giant loss-makers continued to operate and were an important cause of the financial crisis that plagued the state holding companies after the mid-1970s.

Often these southern industries could not compete in the international market or withstand structural economic trends. The steel works at Taranto and Naples-Bagnoli were dragged down by the decline of the entire European steel industry in the 1970s. The huge petrochemical plants on the coasts of Sicily and Sardinia were based on cheap petroleum supplies; after the oil price increase in 1973, they went bust. The most notorious case of all was the steel plant and port facility in Calabria, planned when the Italian steel industry was already producing at only 65 percent of capacity. The project was conceived following a burst of civil violence in Reggio Calabria in 1970, signaling southern frustration over neglect of the area's problems. The purpose was to develop an industrial complex that would bring income and jobs to the region – a facile political solution to a deep social and economic problem. The site chosen was Gioia Tauro, a beautiful and agriculturally productive area on the Calabrian coast. Profitable farms and olive groves were expropriated and demolished. With the enormous funds for construction came the mafia, and with the mafia came bribes, rake-offs, and murder. Then in 1979, when the crisis in the steel industry was too glaring to any longer be ignored, the entire project was scuttled. Gioia Tauro was a grand example of a failure so broad as to give rise to a derisive slogan that characterized much of the investment in the South, "industrialization without development."

As a result, the private investment that was to follow the development initiated by the state enterprises never came. Private investors faced not only what Agnelli described as "the Italian risk," which he defined as "terrorism, the dark interstices of public life; the kidnappings; the Mafia; the Camorra; the payoff." In addition they had to cope with "the southern Italian risk," which Agnelli described as worker absenteeism, low productivity, labor unrest, and low labor mobility. A concrete example of "the southern Italian risk" was the Alfa Romeo plant constructed near Naples in 1972. In its first eight years of operation it was so afflicted by labor strife and absenteeism that it ran up losses of $700 million, which had to be covered by the parent company in the North. For a time every "Alfa Sud" car that went on the road was sold at less than its production costs.

Potential investors, Italian and foreign, consequently investigated prospects in the South and at times decided that the hazards were too great. Up to the mid-1970s some 200 foreign companies invested about $3 billion in the South. During the next half decade, foreign firms that abandoned the Mezzogiorno outnumbered those that came to establish themselves there. The South therefore lost ground in the competition for domestic and foreign investment.

Under its own steam

In private a Milan business leader might bitterly lament that the South had been included in a unified Italy. But in public he neither questioned that the South could be transformed into a general copy of the North nor suggested that heavy industrialization was as economically unnatural for the Mezzogiorno as it would be for Brittany, Schleswig-Holstein, or Nebraska. By and large policymakers were still in thrall to the nineteenth-century notion of an industrial machismo that considered steel mills a mark of economic virility and the production of leather goods and oranges its opposite.

Since the late seventies, however, a few observers have looked at southern development from another angle and have reached more positive conclusions. The Censis Foundation's 1979 report devoted a chapter to "The Rising South," and its analysis showed that employment had been increasing in certain southern industries at a faster rate than in their counterparts in the North. The sectors were identified as manufacturers of clothing and furniture in Abruzzi, miscellaneous small enterprises north of Bari, and the electronics industry in the area of Caserta, north of Naples.

A prominent expert on the Mezzogiorno, the late Francesco Compagna, whose journal *Nord e Sud* has long been an important and enlightened voice in the South, carried the point further in his book *Mezzogiorno in salita* (Mezzogiorno on the rise). Industrialization had genuinely taken hold, he pointed out, in the area between Rome and Naples, in the southern Marches, and along the Adriatic coast from Pescara to Bari. Moreover the impetus for this surprising industrial vitality was coming from a new generation of young entrepreneurs who themselves were from the South and who were making it on their own – without the state and without the North. The notion that the southern Italian is not adept at business but rather interested only in the security of a job in the civil service could therefore not be sustained.

Compagna consequently replaced the usual black and white picture of the South with a more nuanced one. While acknowledging that much economic intervention had been mistaken, he insisted that the government's efforts through the fund had not been the massive squandering of state monies that had sometimes been charged. For all its errors of planning, industrialization had not been a failure; for all its inadequacies, the fund had sponsored dams, irrigation, and land-reclamation programs that had greatly improved southern agriculture. Compagna acknowledged that the gulf between North and South had not diminished to the extent hoped but he insisted that this fact should not detract from a recognition that in many areas real progress had been made.

Beyond any doubt the South has been transformed. Poverty and what accompanies it were still widespread in the 1950s. At that time there were whole provinces where half the population could neither read nor write. Giorgio Amendola, long the Communist party's expert on the Mezzogiorno, recalled in his *Intervista sull'antifascismo* (Interview on anti-Fascism) that in the early postwar women and children were still going barefoot in much of the South and that in Basilicata the per capita meat consumption was three pounds a year, meaning that there was meat only on a few holidays. That sort of poverty had disappeared, Amendola noted, and with broader compulsory schooling, illiteracy had almost been eradicated as well. There have been other marked advances. With a manifold increase in personal income, health and housing have greatly improved, life expectancy has risen, and infant mortality has declined by two-thirds.

The social changes are no less striking. The Mezzogiorno is now linked as never before to the rest of Italy not only through better roads and the web of economic relations but also through television, ties with relatives in the North, and the ever-growing number of tourists. The long isolation of the South has been broken. Southerners have gradually adapted themselves to the mores and outlook – the secularization, the standards of a consumer society, and the social values – of their conationals in the North. Objective and subjective differences remain. But in most ways Italians are more closely knit than they have been in over a thousand years.

The gap that remains

Although the differences can easily be overdone, Italy remains, despite everything, a divided country – divided in outlook and in material well-being. After thirty years of attempts to deal with the problem, the South's portion of the gross domestic product is virtually unchanged, averaging 24 percent of the country's total. The number of persons employed was lower in 1975 than in 1950, the creation of new jobs having been more than offset by a high birthrate, the decrease in infant mortality, and the exodus from the farms. In recent years unemployment in the South has generally been double that in the North. Incomes are still appreciably lower; during most of the postwar period they were 50 percent and in the early 1980s 40 percent below the national average. Regional disparities are even greater and follow an almost perfect North – South correlation. In 1979 the per capita income in Lombardy was 33 percent above the national average; in Sicily it was 29 percent below; and in Calabria, at the bottom of the scale, 42 percent below (see Appendix H). Illiteracy is 0.6 percent in the North, 6 percent in the South.

This combination of high unemployment and low comparative income has been the scourge of the South. Between 1945 and 1970 over 4 million southerners left their towns and farms to seek work in northern Italy, Switzerland, the Common Market countries, or overseas. The migration, the largest in postwar Europe apart from that of the Germans from east of the Oder-Neisse, not only created problems for the northern cities but also deprived the South of much of its younger working force. The migration did at least alleviate some of the social and economic problems that might have exploded in serious violence. But in the 1970s, with the economic recession and the disappearance of job opportunities in the North, unemployed rural youth moved into the cities of the South where they were prey to drugs, the mafia, and common criminality. As the South has been transformed from a rural to an urban society, its overpopulation has been changed from an impoverished peasantry to urban unemployed.

Today, as in the past, travelers to the South therefore find themselves in a world of sharp contrasts. The rugged, often desolate mountain country that occupies most of the Mezzogiorno remains poor and underdeveloped while the fertile but narrow coastal plain generally flourishes. The "flesh" of Giustino Fortunato's famous metaphor of the South is fatter but the "bone" still protrudes.

Along much of the coast travelers find well-irrigated, productive farms; in Puglia they also discover prosperous, modern cities and some heavy and medium industry. In Campania they encounter – in addition to the awesome squalor of Naples – some impressive industry and the thriving tourism of the opulent Amalfi coast. But as they go into the interior, they observe that the land is now, as it has been for centuries, mostly arid and unproductive and that the villages are often half-abandoned and largely inhabited by women and the aged.

Faulty economic programs, tainted by patronage and corruption, seem to be inseparable from southern politics. Some southern politicians, such as Aldo Moro, Emilio Colombo, and Giovanni Leone, have played important roles in the republic, and most of the positions in government administration in Rome are held by southerners. But the area itself lacks a stable political group and an effective administration that might help it pull itself out of its passivity. The Christian Democrats have been the dominant power in the South and must therefore bear most responsibility. But southern voters are indifferent. Or they care less about the development of the area than about receiving a dollop of patronage or a double or triple pension.

In the end the South – like comparable areas in other countries – is no doubt destined to be less economically developed and less prosperous than the North. But southern shame and northern guilt warp judgment. Until the disparities of nature are acknowledged, expectations will continue to exceed reasonable possibilities, development will risk being distorted, and "the problem of the South" will continue to elude solution.

12. The changing relations between church and state

In October 1978 the college of cardinals of the Catholic church elected as pope Karol Wojtyla, archbishop of Cracow. With that vote a non-Italian ascended the throne of Saint Peter for the first time since 1522. The outcome was a surprising and dramatic break with tradition. For centuries Italians had a presumed right to occupy the position. The curia, the church's governing body, was almost entirely Italian in tradition, membership, and language. And though Italians had recently lost their majority in the college of cardinals, they remained the largest bloc in it and failed to elect one of their own number on this occasion only because they could not agree on who it should be. Inevitably the election of a "foreign" pontiff was therefore a greater shock in Italy than anywhere else.

Under the circumstances the adjustment of the Italian people was remarkably quick and easy. But did the installation of a Polish pope herald a fundamental change in the traditional relations between the Vatican and the Italian state? There were many that autumn who said that the Tiber, separating the Holy See from the Eternal City, was sure to become wider than ever before. A foreign pope without personal ties to the country and its political leaders was bound, it was thought, to play much less a role in Italian affairs than his predecessors. The way might then be open for a harmonious separation of church and state for the first time since Constantine.

How close church and state could be in human and political terms had been illustrated only a few months earlier by an unusual event. Brushing aside papal protocol, the aged Paul VI, himself near death, conducted a memorial service for a secular figure – Aldo Moro, the Christian Democratic leader slain by the Red Brigades. Friendship between the two men went back to the war years, when Moro was president of the Catholic University Federation, a body in which the pope had a deep personal interest. Their association was close throughout the years that followed, epitomizing a period of Italian history when contacts between the pope and politicians were continuous, intimate, and touched almost every aspect of public affairs. In retrospect the religious service that

afternoon turned out to be a symbolic requiem for a remarkable era
in the long, troubled relationship between Italy and the church.

The solution of the "Roman question"

The formal basis of church – state relations is the three Lateran
Treaties of 1929, one of which – a concordat – was amended in
1984. Those accords, a diplomatic triumph for Benito Mussolini
and Pope Pius XI, brought an end to the ideological and legal war
that raged for sixty years between the Holy See and the Italian state.
Italy had been unified on liberal, secular principles and, in keeping
with Cavour's famous phrase of "a free church in a free state," most
of the church's legal privileges had been abolished. When Italian
troops entered Rome in 1870 the pope ceased for the first time in
centuries to be a temporal sovereign. In anger he shut himself into
the Vatican as a self-proclaimed prisoner. The church refused to
recognize the new state, excommunicated its monarch, and forbade the faithful to hold public office or vote in national elections.

In depriving the newly unified country of the loyalty of the
Catholic faithful, the church bore heavy responsibility for the division between "the legal Italy" and "the real Italy," between the
forces creating a modern Italy and the backward, rural Italy of the
past. It not only fostered a widespread popular alienation from the
state but also isolated itself and its faithful from the vital forces of
society. Consequently Italian political, economic, cultural, and
scientific life was largely in the hands of persons who were not
practicing Catholics and who indeed were mostly antipathetic to
the church.

Although a modus vivendi gradually evolved after the turn of the
century, the "Roman question" was not settled until Mussolini saw
advantage in gaining church support and was willing to pay a
significant price for it. The Lateran accords were in three parts.
One was a treaty creating an independent Vatican city-state of 108
acres and giving the Holy See possession of a number of churches
and palaces in Rome, a papal summer residence at Castel Gan-
dolfo, basilicas at Padua, Loreto, and Assisi, and custody of all
catacombs in Italy. The pope was recognized as juridically sovereign and the Vatican was accorded the attributes of a sovereign
state, with authority to maintain its own police, postal system, bank,
and radio sender. In return the pope recognized the Italian state
and renounced the Holy See's claim to the former papal territories.
With mutual agreement, crimes committed on Vatican soil would
be tried in Italian courts and be subject to Italian legal penalties.

A second agreement was a concordat that established Catholicism as "the sole religion of the state" and gave the church sweeping privileges in civil affairs. Catholic religious instruction was compulsory in both elementary and secondary schools. Religious marriage was valid in civil law; dissolution of marriage was solely the responsibility of ecclesiastical courts. Religious institutions were authorized to hold property and were exempted from taxes. Persons expelled from the priesthood were banned from teaching, government employment, and indeed any position that brought them into contact with the public. Non-Catholic religions were relegated to inferior legal status and placed under certain restrictions. Priests were banned from party membership and political activity. The state was given the right to approve the appointment of bishops.

To compensate the papacy for its loss of property at the time of unification, a third accord was a financial settlement that gave the Holy See a huge indemnity, which in time became the basis of a financial empire, first in Italy and then abroad.

Although the Lateran Treaties finally settled the "Roman question," they did so at the expense of the separation of church and state that had been a central precept of the *risorgimento*. But for all their legal concessions, the Fascists sharply circumscribed the activity of the church in civil life with the result that relations between the church and the government were at times uneasy. Paradoxically it was with the return of democratic government that the boundary between church and state was systematically undermined. For now the dominant political force was a party of practicing Catholics with close connections to the church. And the incumbent pope, Pius XII, an authoritarian prelate of almost theocratic views, was in a militant phase of his pontificate. The pope's pronouncements in those years made plain that the church would not confine itself to strictly religious matters but expected obedience on any political and social issue that, in its view, touched on moral questions. With a new constitution to be written at the end of the war, the church and the Christian Democrats had a common point of departure and a strong impetus for a working partnership.

Apart from its general objective of combating Communism, the church's primary concrete aim after the fall of Fascism was to buttress its legal position. As with the Reichskonkordat in Germany, Pius was obsessed with the preservation of the 1929 concordat. He achieved his objective with unexpected ease. Given the overwhelming problems of national reconstruction, none of the members of the Constitutional Assembly wanted to reopen an issue so sensitive as church – state relations and provoke a fight with the church. Nenni summed up the mood even on the left when he said, "The smallest of agrarian reforms is of greater interest to me and to my colleagues than the revision of the Concordat." The question consequently was not whether to renounce the pact but whether to enshrine it in the constitution as part of the foundation of the new state. The Christian Democrats and, to general amazement, the Communists supported its full integration. Only the Socialists and lay parties were opposed. By a vote of 350 to 149, the Lateran Treaties were incorporated as Article 7 of the constitution.

That act set the tone for the subsequent course of church – state relations, initiating what the noted Catholic scholar Arturo Carlo Jemolo called a "confessional phase" in Italian history. The key to it, however, was less the juridically privileged position of the church than what lay behind it: a nearly organic relationship between the church and the Christian Democrats.

On the party side, functionaries at all levels came out of an orthodox Catholic subculture and had close ties to ecclesiastical officials. For its part the church was determined not only to combat Communism but also to create a civil society consistent with Catholic doctrine. In the Christian Democrats, Pius saw an instrument to achieve these objectives. The Vatican, the hierarchy, and the laymen's organizations worked together to mold Catholics into a political bloc and to tie that bloc to the party. At election time the church, from the pope down to the parish priest, pronounced it a religious duty not only to vote but to vote for the Christian Democrats. These were the days when parishioners were solemnly warned: "Stalin cannot see what you do in a voting booth but God can." In 1948 it was declared to be a sin to vote for the Socialists or Communists and the following year anyone who did so was excommunicated.

In return the church demanded the fullest cooperation of the party. Ecclesiastical officials asserted a voice in personnel appointments at every level of the public administration, from the humblest provincial school up to the ministries in Rome. Bishops vetted, proposed, and vetoed candidates for election. The pope insisted on being consulted in the fall and formation of governments, the selection of coalition partners, and the choice of cabinet ministers. Once a government was installed, the church made its views known on policies to be followed, legislation to be enacted, and even matters before the courts.

Such clerical influence was pervasive and potent. It was carried further by Catholic Action and other Catholic groups whose activities have been described in Joseph LaPalombara's study of Italian interest groups. An example of their impact can be gleaned from a statement quoted there by a high Treasury official: "The only groups that count in Italian public administration, as long as the Christian Democrats hold governmental power, are the Catholic groups. The Catholics, because they have direct access to the ministers, are likely to get anything they wish from the ministries."

Yet it was the judiciary, according to Jemolo, that was the most submissive of all the state organs. Under both the Italian criminal code and the concordat, statements considered defamatory of the pope and critical of the church were subject to severe punishment. The courts were at times ruthless in implementing these provisions. Books, newspapers, and films considered to offend Catholic moral teachings were often banned. Rolf Hochhuth's noted drama about Pius XII, *The Deputy*, was prevented from being performed in Rome on the ground that it violated a concordat provision on maintaining the holy character of the city. Although legal obstacles and occasional police harassment of Protestants went unredressed, Catholic ecclesiastics were usually held to be immune from prosecution. In a notorious case in 1956 the bishop of Prato publicly condemned two of his parishioners, who had been married in a civil ceremony only, as "public sinners" and labeled their marriage a "scandalous concubinage." The couple sued for slander, won their case but later lost on appeal when the court decided that religious figures were not subject to the authority of the state when exercising their religious function.

All this had a deep social impact. By injecting itself into every aspect of civil life and dividing the political world into saints and sinners, the church reinforced the country's historic problem of social division. As LaPalombara commented, the church's massive political intervention had the same effect after 1945 as after 1870 by separating "loyal Catholics" from other Italians. In his judgment, the way the church intervened – demanding obedience to authority and creating a Manichaean world of good and evil – lent politics an authoritarian character, intensified the fragmentation of the political system, and tended to undermine public confidence in the country's political institutions. Other observers were equally disturbed. In 1957 Gaetano Salvemini called for a repeal of the concordat and the ouster of the Christian Democrats from government on the ground that the party and the Vatican were transforming Italy into a totalitarian state.

After the death of Pius in 1958, this unabashed clericalism went into gradual decline. John XXIII had less interest in Italian politics, and where Pius had tried to erect barriers he sought to open doors. The excommunication of Communists quickly fell into disuse. Pope John's meeting with Khrushchev's daughter and son-in-law was symptomatic of the new mood. In his brief papacy he dedicated himself to an *aggiornamento,* a modernization of the church. He introduced a vastly different tone into ecclesiastical affairs and, with his encyclicals *Mater et Magistra* and *Pacem in Terris,* he directed the church toward the problems of the poor and the Third World, inaugurating an attitude of tolerance toward differing ideologies and religions. Pope John's espousal of international conciliation eventually evolved into a Vatican *Ostpolitik.* His successor, Paul VI, was deeply experienced in Italian political affairs but – or perhaps for that very reason – sought to separate the affairs of church and state more clearly than in the past. The Second Vatican Council of 1962–65 applied this disengagement to the church as a whole by promulgating a new approach to church–state relations, relying less on a formal set of legal obligations than on the tolerance of a pluralist society to ensure the church's freedom to pursue its mission. By this time, however, Italian society was being transformed in a way that would soon undermine the church's role in the state and give a new answer to the "Roman question."

Farewell to "Catholic Italy"

Throughout Europe, as the postwar period advanced, there was a steady attenuation of the ties between church and state – religion and politics – as secular attitudes spread throughout society. In Italy the drastic population shifts from the land to the cities and from the South to the North destroyed a centuries-old social order. Italian Catholicism was rooted in a peasant society and culture. The transformation of the country from being largely rural, illiterate, and impoverished to being urbanized, technologically advanced, and prosperous caused a revolution in social attitudes. Membership in the European Community intensified these changes by bringing Italians into the mainstream of Western European intellectual and social trends. As a result the tenor of life and values changed. In the ecclesiastical sphere ties to the church weakened, priests lost their central place in the community, and religious beliefs relaxed their hold. Generally speaking, the further south the less pronounced these tendencies. But by the early 1970s in most of Italy the traditional Catholic world was a thing of the past.

This secularization process was stronger and more remarkable in Italy than elsewhere in Europe. Italy was the geographic center of the Catholic world. The Vatican was an Italian institution and the pope himself was bishop of Rome, metropolitan of the Roman province, and primate of Italy. By the terms of the constitution, the church enjoyed privileges unique among democratic countries. Catholicism formed a deep and natural part of the social fabric of the nation. For the average citizen church ceremonies were at least as much social as religious events. Even in the days of the bitterest ideological confrontation, many a nonbelieving Communist insisted, often against ecclesiastical resistance, on being married in church and having the children baptized. This was the world that largely vanished in the course of a decade or so.

A few statistics illustrate the extent of the change. In 1956, 69 percent of the population attended mass regularly; twenty years later, the figure was down to 37 percent; by 1985 it had fallen to 25 percent. In a 1974 poll, 59 percent of those questioned characterized themselves as "indifferent" to the church and 11 percent "in opposition" to it. Only about 30 percent described themselves as practicing Catholics and those taking part in church lay activities numbered an exiguous 1 percent. Another indicator was the number of couples who had only civil marriages. Before 1970 these were almost unheard of; by 1980 the figure reached 10 percent and in Rome 25 percent. The number of abortions soared during this period. A 1980 survey by the diocese of Rome on sexual morals, abortion, and divorce showed that even among practicing Catholics, 60 percent approved of divorce, 47 percent of abortion, and 52 percent of birth-control methods condemned by the church. Even more startling was the result of a poll by the Regional Episcopal Council in Piedmont conducted in 1984. This found that a mere 9 percent of Catholics in the region attended mass every Sunday, with another 21 percent going to church at most once a month. Although 89 percent had had a religious wedding and 92 percent had had their children baptized, only 12 percent shared the views of the church on sexual morals and a mere 6 percent opposed abortion. Implicit in these various figures was the practical lesson of secularization: ever fewer Catholics listened to the church and of those who listened, ever fewer obeyed.

Secularization has created problems in the church's ordained ranks as well. Between 1961 and 1981 the number of priests declined from 43,500 to 40,600. In 1961, 601 persons took holy orders; in 1980, the number was down to 347. The number of seminaries declined in roughly the same period from 375 to 259.

These social changes went hand in hand with the deep political changes of the late sixties. In 1970 a parliamentary majority formed of the lay parties and the left enacted Italy's first divorce law. Later in the year the Constitutional Court annulled a law making adultery a crime and several months after that canceled a prohibition of contraception and public dissemination of birth-control information. For the first time in the history of the Italian republic actions were being taken in defiance of the church. It was the year of the centenary of unification and the wheel was turning full circle.

The Vatican's dismay was understandable. Not only were key church positions being overridden, the concordat had been unilaterally altered with the passage of the divorce law. The Holy See protested to the Italian government and an appeal was subsequently made to the Constitutional Court with the argument that changes to the treaty required mutual agreement. Both the protest and the appeal were rejected. However, Catholic lay groups, supported by most bishops and Christian Democrats, decided to seek an annulment of the law through a national referendum. The outcome, which upheld divorce by a 60 percent majority, marked a watershed. As Giacomo Martina, a historian at the Jesuits' Gregorian University in Rome, observed, for many in the church the event was psychologically comparable to the fall of Rome in 1870. And, in truth, it was not only an unprecedented repudiation of the two institutions that had dominated postwar Italian society – the church and the Christian Democratic party – but also a declaration by a decisive majority that religious doctrine was not to be the basis of the country's laws or social life.

A second and perhaps even more crushing blow occurred over abortion. Not only did parliament enact a liberal abortion law in 1978, the Christian Democrats did not prevent its passage. Despite a Catholic counteraction, with some doctors and nurses refusing for reasons of conscience to perform the operation, abortion became widespread. In 1980 – and in the following several years – around 240,000 women had legal abortions while roughly an equal number, particularly from rural areas and in the South where they faced a variety of practical and social restrictions, had illegal ones. These figures worked out to an abortion rate of over 800 for every 1,000 live births.

As in the case of divorce, a number of Catholic lay groups, with the strong backing of the hierarchy and Pope John Paul but not this time of the Christian Democratic party, forced a referendum on the issue. Despite the pope's aggressive intervention in the campaign and a possible sympathy vote resulting from an assassination attempt against him four days before the balloting in May 1981, merely 30 percent voted for repeal. In only one province, the South Tyrol, did the proposal to annul the law gain a majority. To wide surprise women in the conservative South voted to retain abortion in roughly the same proportion as those in the North. The fact that 21 million Catholics voted contrary to the admonitions of priests, bishops, and the pope was a profound shock to ecclesiastical leaders.

The inexorability of the trends reflected in the referenda results and the political impact of these changes came to light in a 1985 study based on data collected by the Doxa polling agency. In global terms this showed that the number of practicing Catholics had declined to a quarter of the population and that little more than a third of them supported the Christian Democrats (see Appendix I). Nothing could better have illuminated the extent of secularization, the shrinkage of the Catholic subculture, and the growing political autonomy of practicing Catholics.

A new modus vivendi

Nor could anything have formalized the church's now circumscribed position in Italian society better than the signature in February 1984 by Prime Minister Craxi and Vatican Secretary of State Agostino Casaroli of a revised concordat. The treaty – which left untouched the other two Lateran accords – concluded sixteen years of effort by the government and the Holy See to work out a new church–state arrangement.

Even prior to the divorce and abortion legislation, the 1929 concordat had become a relic of a bygone era. Some of its terms were obsolete at the time it was incorporated into the constitution. The provision for prayers for the king was obviously a dead letter. Special guarantees for the activities of Catholic Action, framed for a Fascist government, were as meaningless as was the ban on political activity by the clergy. With the passage of time more and more of the terms became archaic. The legal disadvantages for non-Catholics became unacceptable to a people as instinctively tolerant as Italians. With the legalization of divorce in 1970 a main part of the concordat was amputated, making an operation on the torso unavoidable.

In 1971, after several years of parliamentary study, a joint Vatican-Italian commission was formed to work out modifications. In the dozen years that followed, six draft treaties were tabled; but in the end negotiations always broke down over the three issues that constituted Mussolini's main concessions to the church – compulsory religious instruction in public schools, the validity in civil law of an ecclesiastical annulment of marriage, and the tax exemption of church organizations. Although two prime ministers – Andreotti in 1978 and Spadolini in 1982 – had been close to striking a deal with the Vatican, it was Bettino Craxi who pushed the negotiations to a hasty and successful conclusion.

The fourteen articles signed by Craxi and Casaroli demonstrated how little substance was left in the legal relationship. Although technically a "modification" of the 1929 concordat, in the letter and spirit the 1984 treaty established a fundamentally new arrangement. The preamble and first six articles – regarding the autonomy of church and state, religious liberty, ecclesiastical organization, and the status of the clergy – essentially took note of the changes in Italian society and the precepts of the second Vatican Council. Another article formalized cooperation between church and state in maintaining works of historic and artistic importance and gave the Jewish community right of access to Jewish catacombs.

The articles of importance were merely three and they marked nearly complete capitulation on the part of the church. In two of the most controversial points in the long years of negotiations – marriage law and religious instruction in public schools – the church retained almost nothing. Although a religious wedding retained its validity in civil law, the ceremony had to conform to the legal standards set by the Italian state. Marital annulments by ecclesiastical courts were subject to Italian courts. Religious instruction in public schools was made purely voluntary. This provision was the most important concession by the church, which during the years of negotiations had insisted that instruction should be the norm and exclusion possible only at specific request.

The third issue of importance concerned the state stipend to priests and the taxability of church property. The Holy See had for decades claimed exemption from taxes both on the property of church organizations and on the Vatican's shareholdings in Italy. With the tacit understanding of successive Christian Democratic governments, the Vatican long abstained from paying taxes on dividends earned on its Italian stocks. Under parliamentary pressure, the government declared in 1968 that the church was in fact liable for the tax. After protesting in vain, the Vatican started selling off its Italian stocks, though it never paid the back taxes. The more difficult issue concerned the tax status of some 50,000 ecclesiastical organizations and properties that were used at least in part for commercial purposes – such as monasteries that rent rooms to tourists. In the end, these matters were regulated in a complex supplementary protocol that divided church properties into two categories, with only those of a strictly religious nature retaining their tax exemption. The stipend to the clergy (which amounted to $175 million in 1984) as well as funds for the construction of churches would be phased out by 1990, leaving the church dependent on voluntary contributions.

Another area of church – state contention that moved at the same time toward solution was the Vatican's financial affairs. The activities of the Vatican bank in particular had caused serious problems for the Italian government. Not being subject to Italian exchange controls or banking regulations, the bank had at times been used as a conduit for smuggling money out of the country and had itself been party to financial deals that had in some cases proved fraudulent. The Italian financial system had been directly damaged as a result.

The Vatican bank operates as a normal commercial bank except that its depositors are limited to religious orders and institutes, residents of the Vatican, and a small number of Italians. Organized in its present form in 1942, the bank is officially called the "Institute for Religious Works" – or IOR in its Italian acronym – inasmuch as its earnings are supposed to support religious activities. Like the Holy See itself, it issues no public balance sheet and is obsessively secretive about every aspect of its affairs. Although the "Holy See patrimony" – the funds flowing from the 1929 financial settlement – is formally administered separately, it apparently came under the bank's control in the 1960s or 1970s. Because of the secrecy and confusion, estimates of the bank's assets vary wildly, running from $1 billion to $25 billion, the low figure being widely considered the most plausible. In managing these funds the bank might have been expected to be among the world's most cautious. Something like the reverse was the case.

Until the end of the 1960s the bank's funds were invested in a broad range of Italian industries and in vast property holdings in Rome and beyond. With the affirmation of the tax liability on its stock dividends in 1968, the bank shifted its assets into financial shareholdings outside Italy. It bought heavily into American industry, finance, and property – holding a major interest, for instance, in the firm that developed the Watergate complex in Washington. In transferring these funds, the bank's president, Archbishop Paul Marcinkus, an American with no financial experience, leaned heavily on the assistance of two Italian bankers, Michele Sindona and Roberto Calvi.

Marcinkus could not have chosen more unwisely. Sindona, one of the biggest financial swindlers of the century as it turned out, impressed the Vatican with his financial skill in selling the church's Italian stocks at a profit in a difficult market and in investing its capital overseas, partly in his own banking operations. In 1974 Sindona's American bank, the Franklin National, became insolvent and his whole financial empire fell apart soon afterward. The Vatican lost tens, possibly hundreds, of millions of dollars in the collapse. Some years after Sindona had been sentenced by a New York court to twenty-five years for fraud and grand larceny, the Vatican bank's second-ranking official as well as his predecessor and the bank's chief accountant were all indicted by Italian magistrates for complicity with Sindona.

Marcinkus's other adviser was a freewheeling banker whose ties to the Vatican were so close that he was known in the international press as "God's banker." Calvi was head of Italy's largest private bank, the Banco Ambrosiano, and throughout the 1970s was involved in complex and fraudulent transactions in Latin America and the Bahamas. The Vatican bank worked closely with Calvi and appeared to have been a de facto partner in some of Calvi's Latin American operations. It owned ten of Calvi's "shell" companies, and Marcinkus himself was a director of the Ambrosiano's operation in the Bahamas. It has been hypothesized that the archbishop was drawn into collaboration with Calvi in his speculative deals as a result of the heavy pressure he was under to produce high bank profits. In the 1970s the Holy See had begun running annual budget deficits of $20 to $30 million. Evidently it was the Vatican bank's profits that were needed to cover the gap. How those earnings were made was apparently of little or no concern. Marcinkus himself was quoted as saying simply: "We place our money where it earns the most."

Eventually the Ambrosiano's operations caught the attention of the Bank of Italy. In 1978 the central bank initiated an investigation, which immediately aroused ferocious resistance, Calvi having been generous with a number of powerful politicians. The upshot was the notorious Baffi-Sarcinelli affair, which saved Calvi for a time. In 1981, however, Calvi was convicted of illegal currency dealings, and the following year the Bank of Italy renewed its investigation with more determination. Taking fright, Calvi fled the country and was found hanged in London. His elaborate financial structure was now in ruins and the Ambrosiano bankrupt. The collapse resulted in debts of about $1.3 billion, which the *Financial Times* said had to rank "almost certainly as Europe's largest and gravest post-war banking scandal."

The Italian government was concerned not simply about compensation for the losses in this case, losses for which it considered the Vatican bank in part morally and legally responsible. In addition, as the Christian Democratic treasury minister, Beniamino Andreatta, told parliament at the time, the Vatican's persistent violation of currency regulations and its collusion in tax evasion were damaging the Italian economy and had to be stopped. The Ambrosiano scandal offered the Italian government the necessary leverage to force the Holy See to halt the illegal movement of capital into and out of Italy through the bank. In the end the Vatican, though refusing to acknowledge any legal responsibility, paid Ambrosiano creditors $244 million in "recognition of moral involvement" in the bank's failure. It further agreed to submit disputes to Italian courts for arbitration, for the first time making itself subject to Italian law.

The new concordat and the financial controls on IOR demonstrated how much wider the Tiber – the gap between church and state – had become during John Paul's pontificate. Yet for obvious reasons the Vatican cannot treat Italy as a country like any other. It therefore remains an open question whether the church, especially under a pope as firm on certain social issues as John Paul II, can be a silent observer of what happens on the other bank.

The postconciliar church

The Italian hierarchy has had to absorb in a brief time changes of historic – even epochal – dimensions. France may be the church's eldest daughter, but Italy is its birthplace and home. Suddenly to find that its position had declined so far so fast has been a bitter blow. The adjustment has been the more difficult because the Italian church had a long record of implacable resistance to social and intellectual change. The bishops were traditionally extremely conservative and with few exceptions took fright at the *aggiornamento* of Pope John and joined the curia in slowing down or thwarting change during the Second Vatican Council.

If secularization swept away the church's political and social position, ecclesiastical changes destroyed the centuries-old primacy of the Italians in the worldwide church. Several institutional reforms of great importance flowed from the decisions of the Vatican Council and Pope Paul's determination to give the church as a whole a more international character by reducing the influence of Italians and other Europeans. The most important change was in the college of cardinals. When Paul became pope in 1963, 52 of the 80 cardinals were Italian. After the mid-sixties the size of the body was expanded and the number of Italians in it declined through attrition. By 1971 there were 120 cardinals, of whom only 28 were Italian, for the first time bringing an end to the Italian majority.

At the same time Paul reduced the weight of the Italian church in other ways. Beginning in 1966 the Italian dioceses were consolidated and the number of bishops reduced to 270 from 315 – a still disproportionate figure when compared to France's 88 and Spain's 65, for example, but now exceeded by the number of American and Brazilian bishops. By the same token Paul sought to place some distance between the Holy See and the Italian hierarchy. With the pope as primate of Italy and the curia essentially Italian, the Vatican and the Italian church had always been inseparably intertwined. Pius XII had created an Italian Episcopal Conference, but it was a grouping without any autonomy. Finally, in 1966 – for the first time in history and 100 years after similar bodies had been established in other countries – an independent conference of bishops, the Conferenza Episcopale Italiana (CEI), was established.

In the face of these deep social and ecclesiastical changes, the bishops have shifted their attention away from the public sphere to concentrate on pastoral matters, in particular religious renewal at the diocesan and parish level. Behind this change lay not only the approach laid down by Vatican II but the growing conviction that the past obsession with anti-Communism had led to a fundamental misassessment – that it was not Marxist materialism but the materialism of the consumer society that, in the wake of secularization, had weakened the church's position. The bishops have become cautious, compromising, and anxious to avoid controversy.

Changes in the church have also resulted from Paul VI's fostering a new generation of bishops – Carlo Maria Martini of Milan, Anastasio Ballestrero of Turin, Marco Cè of Venice, Mariano Magrassi of Bari, and Luigi Bettazzi of Ivrea. They are persons open to new ideas, who want the church to be more understanding of social change and who seek to reach political and social forces beyond the church. In northern Italy, where ecclesiastical renewal is most active, Cardinal Martini has followed such a course in his diocese, the largest in Italy, making himself in a short time one of the commanding figures of Italian Catholicism. The approach of these new leaders is evident in a document, "The Italian Church and the Perspectives of the Country," approved by the Episcopal Conference in 1981, which forswears direct political engagement in favor of indirect social action.

Contemporary Italian Catholicism therefore presents one more paradoxical element in an overall picture of contradictions in Italy. On the one hand the church is still the country's most omnipresent institution and, with the revised concordat, retains a special legal position in the state. On the other hand – as ecclesiastical leaders are the first to affirm – the church has become a minority institution in a diaspora, leading its own life, ever more without influence either on the values of society or on those who wield political and economic power. In a report to the permanent commission of bishops in 1983, Cardinal Ballestrero spoke of a "profound chasm between the realities of the church and the realities of the country." He lamented that the church was popularly regarded "as a reality extraneous to the world and to the country." "The church will never accept being a stranger in this our own nation," Ballestrero insisted. He frankly acknowledged, however, that he had few ideas on how it could recover the place it had lost.

The laity in a changing environment

The political and pastoral changes faced by the hierarchy have been paralleled by a transformation in the world of the Catholic laity. The official laymen's movement, once probably the most formidable in the entire Catholic world, has long been in decline. The major group, Catholic Action, was founded at the turn of the century and was one of the very few organizations to maintain a degree of autonomy during the Fascist period. After the war it developed rapidly in size and militancy and by the 1950s had some 3 million members. Catholic Action was the main pillar of Christian Democratic political support. In deference to the concordat's ban on political activities by priests, so-called civic committees were established as thinly veiled front organizations. Organized and headed by Luigi Gedda, a genetics professor of reactionary political views, the civic committees conducted a political crusade against the Communists while at the same time trying to push the Christian Democrats to the right and into alliance with the neo-Fascists. At their height in the fifties, the civic committees counted about 2 million members.

Gedda was head of Catholic Action from 1952 to 1958. Being

more in sympathy with the clericalist views of Pius XII than were most Christian Democratic leaders, Gedda had a close and confident relationship with the pope and was at times emboldened to run his organization almost as an autonomous political force, causing great strains between Catholic Action and the party. By the 1960s, however, Gedda's blatant political agitation was incompatible with the mood of the country and the trend of developments in the Vatican of Pope John. The group lost focus, a sense of purpose, and a clear political orientation. The civic committees went into a decline from which they never recovered.

In the wake of the Vatican Council and the student and worker unrest at the end of the sixties, membership in Catholic Action fell off drastically to about 1.6 million. The organization abandoned its political activism on behalf of the Christian Democrats and in 1969 adopted a new statute that committed it to political neutrality. In the years that followed it was drastically decentralized and withdrew so far from public affairs as to refuse to organize an anti-divorce campaign or take much part in the abortion referendum. At its triennial conventions in 1980 and 1983 the organization defined its objectives in religious and social as distinct from political terms. Despite its effort to be relevant to the times, Catholic Action has been unable to stop the drastic loss of members, down to 600,000 in the early eighties, and remains very much in the shadows of public life.

Similar difficulties have characterized the evolution of the other important laymen's organization, the Christian Workers' Associations, ACLI. Established in 1944, the body was intended to protect the interests of Catholic workers in the united trade union movement, CGIL. When the latter came under Communist control in 1948, Catholic workers, guided by ACLI, withdrew and formed their own union, the Italian Confederation of Workers' Unions, CISL. Having thereby lost most of its own original purpose, ACLI became increasingly involved in politics on behalf of the Christian Democrats, with many of its leaders and functionaries holding positions in the party and seats in parliament.

By the end of the 1950s this close alliance with the Christian Democrats came to be seen as compromising the association's autonomy, and ACLI dissolved most of its organizational links with the party. In 1970 the association disassociated itself from the Christian Democrats – forbidding its officials from running for parliament on the party's list – and adopted an anticapitalist and prosocialist stance. The church withdrew its financial support and its religious counselors; pro–Christian Democratic groups seceded; and roughly half its 1 million members quit. Several years later the association went through another convulsion; this time its leftist leadership was replaced, some going over to the Socialists and forming an important Catholic component of that party. Since then ACLI has followed an independent course on the fringes of the Christian Democratic left, although some young "Aclisti" are close to the Communists and Socialists. The organization, with 500,000 members as of 1984, has at the same time gradually improved its relations with the church. For the first time in over a decade a bishop spoke at the 1981 ACLI congress; two years later the pope received the organization's leaders.

The Catholic scene presents still other facets of decline, revival, vitality, and turmoil. The once-important Catholic professional organizations – for teachers, women, artisans, business executives, university students, university graduates, and so on – have all experienced a drastic decline in members and influence. At the outset of the 1980s there emerged a variety of new movements dedicated to religious revival. They reflected – in the wake of a general crisis of revolutionary ideologies, a disillusionment with Marxism, and a weariness with political struggles – a new type of religious sensibility. Pope John Paul's charismatic appeal has helped to evoke this spirit, and he himself has made a conscientious effort to reach these groups in his general audiences and his Sunday appearances in Saint Peter's Square.

The most conspicuous and dynamic of them is Communion and Liberation, essentially a youth organization of some 70,000 members that extols conservative Catholic views in every sphere. Founded in 1969 by a Milanese priest, Luigi Giussani, it subsequently developed a political wing, known as the Popular Movement, which has been active at every electoral level, from local school councils to national politics. In universities, where CL is strongest, it has combated leftist influences; in elections it has been an important force for the Christian Democrats, particularly in the North; and in the abortion referendum it took the lead in campaigning for repeal. In the latter half of the 1970s it spearheaded a reform movement within the Christian Democratic party with the intent of stopping the party's cooperation with the Communists and of giving the party a more ideological and moral image. The Popular Movement has put up some of its own young leaders in national elections, a few of whom had some success. Communion and Liberation enjoys the support of Pope John Paul, who esteems its combative and disciplined action on behalf of traditional political and religious causes.

There is also a broad spectrum of Catholic groups on the left. The lot of left Catholics – caught as they are between Communist and ecclesiastical monoliths – has never been easy. In the early postwar period most of them remained inside the bounds of the church and Christian Democracy. A notable example was the group around Giuseppe Dossetti, a professor of church law and a vice-secretary of the Christian Democratic party in the early postwar period, whose ambition was to give political substance to Catholic social doctrines. The movement eventually foundered against the hostility – for different reasons – of both De Gasperi and Pope Pius. Although Dossetti abandoned the struggle and retreated into the priesthood, one of his protégés, Giorgio La Pira, kept his ideals alive in messianic form as mayor of Florence from 1951 to 1964.

It was not really until the "hot autumn" that the long-repressed sentiments of left Catholics burst out, and then they did so with angry vehemence against the hierarchy and the Christian Democrats in equal measure. Both were considered to be in collusion with the power establishment; both were considered to have betrayed their mission. Talk was in the air of a "conciliar republic" of Catholics and Communists. Small groups of dissenters sprang up throughout Italy – in churches, in Catholic intellectual and journalistic circles, and in time even in theological faculties. In working-class districts of many cities, parish communes developed among social-minded parishioners. Influenced by the Latin American "liberation theology," a "Christians for Socialism" movement was founded in 1973.

From the start this *cattolicesimo del dissenso* encountered stiff ecclesiastical resistance. As early as September 1968 Pope Paul denounced the dissenters in global fashion. In some cases the church took action against the leaders. Don Enzo Mazzi, a priest who formed a commune in the Florentine parish of Isolotto, was first transferred and later legally stripped of his ecclesiastical authority. The noted writer Raniero La Valle was eased out of the Catholic newspaper *Avvenire d'Italia*. Giovanni Franzoni, former abbot of Saint Paul Outside the Walls in Rome, was suspended for opposing the referendum against divorce. Although the hierarchy succeeded in dividing and isolating the dissenters and reformists, it did so at the cost of shutting out of church life persons whose very religious convictions drove them to advocate social reform.

The church and the parties

Secularization, defection of the laity, and virtual disestablishment by the state have left the church adrift in Italian society, more so perhaps than at any time since early in the century. In searching for a proper place for the church in the country's rapidly changing social and political environment, most bishops have concluded that a discreet role acknowledging the changed situation is the most appropriate to the times and circumstances. The bishops have continued to speak out, individually and collectively, on public issues that in their view impinged on matters of faith and morals. But their pronouncements were ever fewer and ever less exigent. On the whole they adjusted gracefully to the new situation, concentrating on their pastoral mission. The rub has come as the hierarchy has sought to square this broad disengagement with its long-standing relationship – friendly or hostile – to the political parties.

During the early postwar period Pope Pius, in his fear of Communism and desire to create a "Catholic Italy," recognized virtually no limit on the church's political involvement; he declared it a matter of religious duty to vote for the Christian Democrats, excommunicated Communists and Socialists, and tried to use the Christian Democratic party as the church's political arm. With John XXIII the attitude and priorities changed; the pope's veto of a center-left government in the late 1950s and his approval of it a few years later marked the last time the church intervened in cabinet building. By the end of his papacy the ecclesiastical statements at election time no longer asserted it to be a "duty" to vote for the Christian Democrats but merely made an "appeal" to the faithful to remain politically united. Although "unity of Catholics" was understood code for "vote for the Christian Democrats," the days of open partisan commitment were over. In Paul VI the church had a leader with an intimate knowledge of Italian politics and one who never doubted that the church's interests were intimately linked to "the Christian party." He did not interfere in the party's internal affairs, however, and the Christian Democrats could count on full ecclesiastical support without receiving much clerical direction. From 1968 on election appeals were diluted even further and amounted to bland exhortations to make political decisions consistent with Catholic moral teachings. Only in 1976 – when it seemed possible that the Communists might overtake the Christian Democrats in the national election – did the church again overtly intervene. Reiterating that the Communist party remained unacceptable, Pope Paul sharply reproved a number of prominent Catholics for running as independents on the PCI election lists and appealed to the faithful to cast their ballots for the defenders of the faith, the Christian Democrats.

At the time of the 1979 and 1983 elections the Episcopal Conference issued statements reverting to the formula that "not all choices are compatible with Christian principles" but qualified this emollient position with a strong dose of *doppiezza* by ruling out parties whose social objectives or concepts of family and human rights were incompatible with Christian belief – in practice barring parties that had, for instance, supported abortion legislation and so excluding all but the Christian Democrats and neo-Fascists. Even so, these statements represented an unprecedented withdrawal from the political battlefield.

Ambiguity, conciliation, and passivity were not traits highly prized by John Paul II with his Polish experience, and in the course of the 1980s a change of style and direction became increasingly evident. From the start the hallmark of his papacy was the affirmation of a monolithic, authoritarian, and aggressive church. Appalled by Western secular and materialistic values, he pursued a mission of promoting traditional – and conservatively interpreted – social and ecclesiastical values.

John Paul's approach was first manifested in his strident intervention in the 1981 abortion referendum, which went well beyond the spiritual counsel offered by most Italian bishops. To many Italians the pope's "crusade" constituted rank intrusion in domestic politics; Craxi reproached him for "looking at Italy through Polish glasses." In subsequent years the pope admonished the Italian bishops to be more active in combating secularist trends with the church's own social teachings. It was not until 1985 at a meeting of bishops and laymen at Loreto, however, that John Paul publicly disclosed his view of the Italian situation. His assessment of contemporary Italy was withering: a secularized society afflicted by a "de-Christianization" of mentality and morals caused by a "practical materialism" abetted by atheistic ideologies. His response was to revive the old call for unity. In ecclesiastical affairs he pronounced it to be the duty of all Catholics to rally together; dissenters should return to the fold. In civic affairs he admonished the faithful to "stand united . . . for the supreme good of the nation" and not to shun a "public role." In a comment that was generally understood as support for the Christian Democrats, he praised the "tradition of social and political commitment of Italian Catholics." Absent from his remarks were any notions of reconciliation and dialog, which he warned could lead to "ambiguous compromise."

The substance and manner of John Paul's approach contrasted starkly with the conciliatory stance of the majority of the hierarchy and particularly such church leaders as Martini, Ballestrero, and

Pappalardo, as well as the pope's secretary of state, Cardinal Casaroli. The contrast marked, as the Italian press observed, the first time in modern history that substantial differences existed between a pope and most Italian bishops. Not only were the two sides not marching in step, they did not even see eye to eye much less speak the same language. A few prelates, however, led by Archbishop Giacomo Biffi of Bologna, shared the pope's outlook and favored an active "re-Catholicization" of the country.

Concretely the central disagreement was over both the content and extent of the church's political and social engagement. Some bishops and clergy were outspoken in condemning corruption, clientelism, and the misuse of political power – none more so than Pappalardo, who was renowned, in addition to his stand against the mafia, for his criticism of the Christian Democrats and the political games that had left Sicily and Palermo badly governed when governed at all. But most church leaders were convinced that there were no simple solutions to the oblique and intricate problems of the day and that overt commitment to the Christian Democrats could be counterproductive. Nonetheless the pope's approach found a welcome response in conservative circles among the clergy and such groups as Communion and Liberation, and his influence gradually made itself felt. Talk spread of the need to reinterpret the political content of the Second Vatican Council; reservations were expressed about the validity of political pluralism; and prior to the 1985 regional and communal elections the permanent committee of the Episcopal Conference strengthened a prior noncommittal statement by declaring, "Not all choices are compatible with the Christian faith nor consistent with the indispensable values of a just social order." When, during the same election campaign the bishop of Taranto declared that the alternative was "Either with God or without God," many were carried back to 1946, when Pius XII had defined the political choice as "between Christ or the anti-Christ."

Has everything changed only to remain the same? Despite the mutual disengagement, the church and the Christian Democrats retain a special relationship. It is with that party that the bishops and the curia still have the firmest links. And it is in that party that the church sees its last best hope of finding a defender of its worldly interests. The bishops know that the Christian Democrats need Catholic electoral support as much as ever but they recognize that each side can do less for the other. The church no longer has a phalanx of lay groups to do battle for the party, and its appeals to the voters – as demonstrated in the referendum campaigns – have so little impact as to leave the church humiliated. By the same token the party is less and less willing to buck the secularist trend and identify itself with positions that lack palpable public support. The party did not officially take a position on the abortion referendum and in the early 1980s even backed away from the Vatican on church–state questions.

As the church's interest in politics and its influence on them have declined, the relationship with the other parties has lost much of its significance. With the Socialists a fair degree of confidence has been established since the mid-1970s, a trend capped by the conclusion of the 1984 concordat with a Socialist prime minister. Although the era of excommunicating the Communists passed long ago and the church's opposition to the party is less overt, the bishops have left no doubt that the party is not acceptable for Catholics. Relations with the lay parties remain distant.

The deep social and political changes since the early 1970s obviously confront the church with novel and difficult problems. Not only has its own position been severely weakened, the church–state relationship has been revolutionized. Although remaining an important factor in national life, the church can no longer command the allegiance of the majority of Catholics on any issue of public life. Moreover, issues that it considers as moral-religious are regarded by an ever-growing number of Italians as social-political and not therefore properly matters of ecclesiastical concern. In practice the area where the church meets and interacts with the state has steadily diminished and is now quite small. With secularization, a revised concordat, strict rules for the Vatican bank, and a drastic reduction in the church's political involvement, causes for friction between church and state have almost entirely been removed. What has evolved is a church–state relationship of the sort Cavour intended, with each institution operating freely in its own sphere, without clericalism or anticlericalism. It was this harmony that the great majority of Italians hoped would not be disturbed by Pope John Paul's concept of a church militant.

13. Foreign and security policy

The maxim that every country seeks power, security, and glory has remarkably little application to Italy. Almost all Italians, political leaders and public alike, take for granted that their country has no appreciable role to play in international affairs and would be mistaken and frustrated if it tried to do so. They lack any desire to assert Italian influence in the world and feel little concern for their military safety. Even though Italy has a population of 57 million, lies in a strategic location, and has an economy among the world's largest, it takes a minor part in world politics. Italian diplomats and scholars not surprisingly complain that their country's foreign relations are singularly lacking in force, direction, and substance. Indeed, after forty-four years in the diplomatic service one of Italy's most distinguished ambassadors, Pietro Quaroni, concluded: "An Italian foreign policy in the real sense of the word does not exist."

In large part this withdrawal from the world is a natural reaction to the ignominy of Mussolini's foreign adventures and the inevitable consequence of a lost war. West Germany and Japan are also unwilling to occupy the role in international affairs to which economics and geopolitics would objectively entitle them. But the Italian diffidence is deeper and older. Ultimately it can be traced to the centuries of political division and foreign – as well as papal – meddling in the country's development. The long period of subordination to foreign powers, before and even after unification, has instilled national attitudes that condition the Italian approach to world affairs to this day.

Passive and pacific

These traits manifest themselves in a variety of interrelated ways. The general perspective of the people as a whole is inward-looking and essentially indifferent to the larger world. Although this ingrained provincialism is diminishing, Italians still have little interest in what goes on outside their peninsula. The press, universities, industry, trade unions, and political parties give only passing attention to international politics. Foreign affairs, to say nothing of foreign policy, is essentially a nonissue in Italy. By the same token there is a remarkable lack of nationalistic feeling. Italians have a keen sense of national pride and are extremely sensitive about the status accorded their country by others. But no European people is more devoid of the aggressive self-assertion that characterizes Western nationalism. As a result Italians settle their diplomatic problems with unusual dispassion and manage to take in stride actions by others that most states would consider an intolerable affront to national honor.

Behind this passive attitude lies another deep trait, a lack of self-confidence as a member of the international community. This timidity is apparent in the expressions of near powerlessness that pervade not only the writings of Italian scholars and journalists but also the statements of parliamentarians and government officials when addressing foreign affairs. It can also be observed in practice, in Italy's invariable impulse for mediation and compromise and a compulsive avoidance of confrontation and open dispute.

Lacking the interest, the will, and the self-assurance to play an active role in international politics, Italy defines and pursues its national interests differently than do other major and middle powers. The premise of Italian foreign policy is that Italy cannot stand alone and cannot follow an independent course. Foreign-policy goals are therefore stripped down to a bare minimum and implemented through multilateral institutions, in particular the European Community and the Atlantic Alliance. But even there Italy rarely takes a lead and never seeks to exert a determinative role. It is neither the first to articulate a divergent view nor the last to join a comfortable consensus. At most it tries to shape compromises congruent with the general lines of its narrow objectives. Although this minimizes friction with others, it also minimizes influence over events. And in merging its fate with the destiny of the European Community and NATO, it has gone further than most other European states in accepting military and political dependence. To some extent this is fatalistic submissiveness. To some extent it is also healthy realism and has saved Italy from the besetting sin of American, French, and British diplomacy in over-estimating a capacity to act alone and to alter world events.

Yet the passivity and deference, real as they are, mask a subtle form of self-defense that Italians have also learned from their history. By taking cover behind multilateral institutions, Italy protects itself from the direct blasts of international conflict. By turning over its security to NATO, it relieves itself of some of the heavy burdens of self-defense. Moreover, Italian diplomacy is more subtle than it sometimes seems. What appear to be concessions often turn out to be bills for later payment. Where others bluster and storm, Italy quietly maneuvers and finesses. While appearing to be manipulated, it may be manipulating. Such was its mode of survival in the past; such is its way of surviving in the contemporary world. Consequently, Italy's foreign policy accurately reflects the country's communal history and psychology.

Foreign Ministry officials from time to time debate among themselves whether Italy should break out of these self-imposed constraints and assert a more positive world role. In the end they always conclude that there is neither the support at home nor the scope abroad. A few Italian political leaders have on occasion been tantalized by the notion that Italy is in a uniquely favorable position – being geographically and otherwise peripheral to major disputes – to mediate various international issues. Sometimes their efforts are welcome and useful. More often the issues are not susceptible to mediation and the diplomatic forays are resented. Gronchi's interventions with the United States and the Soviet Union over Germany and Berlin, Fanfani's involvements in the Middle East and Vietnam, as well as Moro's attempts to conciliate Middle Eastern oil producers and Western oil consumers after 1973 all proved futile. More useful, though not always more successful, were Italian efforts to broker settlements in various Common Market disputes over the years. The one clear achievement of Italian good offices was the resolution in 1980 of a long wrangle between Britain, Malta, and Libya over Malta's neutral status.

Diffused authority

In view of the country's circumscribed ambitions and the popular indifference to international affairs, the Italian government should find it easier than most democracies to conduct its foreign relations. In one important respect this is so. Foreign policy can be made in a near political vacuum, uninhibited by domestic pressures. Public opinion as such scarcely exists. Occasionally some issue – political oppression in Poland and Argentina, American intervention in Vietnam and Central America, the nuclear arms race – arouses the public. But such occasions are rare and without lasting impact. Most of the time the press, the business sector, social-interest groups, and even the political parties make no attempt to sway the government's course. As for parliament, Ennio Di Nolfo has commented: "The history of the republican parliament of Italy is studded with debates on all the principal episodes which have made up [Italian foreign] policy, and also on the most significant moments of crisis in the international system. However, it would be difficult – if not actually impossible – to trace any link between the particular debates and the processes which have determined the decisions."

Yet Italy suffers an overwhelming disability in managing foreign relations: the perpetual weakness of the government itself. The dissent by one member of a delicately constructed coalition can bring a foreign-policy action to a complete halt. The De Gasperi era apart, frequent political crisis and changes of government make it almost impossible for Italian leaders to do more than keep afloat in the ebb and flow of international affairs. Since they are rarely in office for long, prime ministers and foreign ministers cannot usually gain a mastery of international issues or even form personal relationships with their European counterparts, as other European leaders have done with success throughout the postwar period.

Nor can the Foreign Ministry itself provide the necessary impetus and direction. Although some of its heads have performed creditably, only once in the whole of the postwar period has the ministry been led by a towering figure, Carlo Sforza, who presided from 1947 to 1951. Ministers are rarely chosen for their knowledge or interest in world politics but rather to satisfy factional requirements inside the Christian Democratic party. The incumbents themselves regard the position, as Henry Kissinger has written in his memoirs, "as a power base, never to pursue as a vocation." Kissinger further records: "In discussions with either Prime Ministers or Foreign Ministers, domestic politics remained the main preoccupation. . . . One could not sometimes escape the impression that to discuss international affairs with their Foreign Minister was to risk boring him."

To be fair, Italian foreign relations are in fact largely conducted by subcabinet officials who are on the whole highly expert, the equal of their counterparts in other countries including Kissinger's own. Moreover, the Italian diplomatic service, though still dominated by the aristocracy, is generally intelligent, able, and well-informed. The quality of ambassadors, as in every service, varies widely; but the best of them are the equal to the best of any country. In negotiations, Italian diplomats are skillful in defending and advancing Italian interests. The professionals cannot, however, compensate for the lack of leadership at the top and the prime minister's absorption in domestic and party matters. So the Foreign Ministry largely squanders its expertise and drifts placidly along until embroiled in a crisis, when it usually responds with outstanding agility and inventiveness.

These problems are intensified by the lack of effective institutional machinery to coordinate ministerial activities. There is no body similar to the U.S. National Security Council or the West German Federal Security Council to debate and decide foreign-policy positions and objectives. The historic supremacy of the Foreign Ministry has been undermined in important areas as a result of Italy's membership in the European Community and the growing importance of economic issues. Interministerial committees have been created, but they have not been very successful in reducing bureaucratic competition and policy differences. Key issues are handled in the prime minister's office and may be discussed in the whole cabinet. But the prime minister, who has but a single diplomatic advisor, cannot begin to supervise all aspects of the country's external relations.

The diffusion – and confusion – of authority is somewhat complicated by the ambiguous position of the president. Some chiefs of state have used their narrow prerogatives – receiving Italian and foreign ambassadors and visiting government officials; writing to foreign leaders; and making state visits – to assert an independent position on international affairs. Gronchi was the most notable case. He saw himself and his country as having a mission to mediate between the West and the Soviets and to improve the Western position in the Middle East and the underdeveloped world. All this culminated in statements in the late 1950s critical of the West's rigidity toward the Soviets and in a decision to visit Moscow contrary to the advice of his ministers. Nothing could have underscored his impotence better than the fact that when he arrived in Moscow, the Soviets snubbed him and his whole design collapsed.

No other president has gone so far, though his successor, Antonio Segni, sometimes gave specific advice to Italian ambassadors and tried to block certain diplomatic appointments. Alessandro Pertini at times acted independently, as in sending a message to Brezhnev in 1978 protesting the trials of a number of political dissidents in the Soviet Union. He also vented annoyance – making it a main point of his state visit to the United States in 1982 – over Italy's occasional exclusion from meetings and minisummits of Western leaders. French desires for exclusive groupings inside NATO and the close relations between France and Germany always aroused his ire, which he often did not try to conceal. In late 1983 Pertini created a stir when he called for the withdrawal of the Italian peacekeeping contingent from Lebanon, criticized the role of American troops in that country, and endorsed the establishment of a Palestinian state. Although the president reflected the views of most Italians and many Foreign Ministry officials, his statements were an embarrassment to the government, which let it be known that Pertini spoke only for himself.

Although every country has organizational difficulties in shaping its foreign policy, the extent of the problem for Italy – the lack of direction, coordination, and implementation – is deeper than in other major countries. "Who is it who makes foreign policy in Italy?" Ambassador Quaroni asked. His answer was: "No one."

Quiet success

In spite of these political and institutional deficiencies, Italy has been remarkably successful in achieving what it wants in international affairs. The initial and most important of its aims was to liquidate the damage of Mussolini's foreign policy, gain acceptance in the Western community, and secure aid for economic reconstruction. In working for these objectives, it had almost nothing to bargain with. Not only was it a defeated nation, it could not – as Cavour did brilliantly in the last century – pit one power against another for Italy's benefit. The Soviet Union had written it off to the West. Britain had more pressing concerns, and the United States was interested only to the extent that the Communist party seemed to threaten American interests. Faced with international isolation and domestic political difficulties, Prime Minister De Gasperi and Foreign Minister Sforza had to take advantage of whatever opportunities came along. The Marshall Plan they used not only as a source of material assistance but also as a means of gaining political acceptance by the victorious powers. The invitation in April 1948 to join the Organization for European Economic Cooperation, which administered Marshall Plan aid, marked Italy's formal entry into the Western community. But the critical step came with the invitation to join NATO.

The diplomatic background of Italy's accession to the Atlantic Alliance is a paradigm both of the Italian government's handling of foreign policy issues and of the nature of relations between Italy and the other Western states throughout the postwar period. During the initial explorations regarding a Western security arrangement in early 1948, it had been taken for granted that Italy would be included. As a first step it was encouraged to join the Brussels Pact, which had been founded some months earlier. The Italians refused. De Gasperi cited domestic political uncertainties; Sforza resented Italy's exclusion from the diplomatic explorations and feared that his country would be relegated to an inferior position in the proposed alliance. The Italian public, absorbed in its own affairs, was in a mood of neutralism, pacifism, and apathy.

Therefore when the concrete planning for NATO got under way in July 1948, there was strong doubt about Italy's intentions and Italy became, in Dean Acheson's phrase, "a perplexing problem." Militarily there was fear that it would drain scarce resources rather than augment them. Geographically there was reluctance to extend the definition of the Atlantic area to include the Mediterranean. And diplomatically there was concern that Italy would try to bargain its way into membership by demanding the return of its colonies and revisions in the peace treaty.

The Italian government, like the Italian public, was hesitant and divided. A military pact was of little interest because Italians felt no direct threat from the Soviet Union, especially after Tito's break with the Cominform in that year. The alliance aspect left them cold because they mistrusted treaty commitments. The great majority of Italians were unquestionably pro-Western, but they were pro-Western neutralists. Opposition was vehement from the Communists and Socialists and muted among left Christian Democrats and certain Catholic church circles, where there was a preference for nonalignment. Wholehearted support came from the Republicans, Liberals, and the bulk of the Christian Democrats. The Social Democrats were evenly split, with Saragat himself at first against entry. Within the government there was intense pressure in favor of joining by the diplomatic service, to avoid Italy's isolation, as well as by the military, to secure help in rebuilding Italy's armed forces.

Not until the eleventh hour – January 1949 – did the Italian government compose its differences and decide to join. But after months of Italian indecision and erratic and confusing diplomacy, there were doubts about both the genuineness of Italy's commitment and its value to the new alliance. The American government was in the end brought around by Dean Acheson, who argued that, if excluded, "Italy might suffer from an isolation complex and, with its large communist party, fall victim to seduction from the East." That fear broke the opposition, and Italy was invited to be a charter member of the alliance.

Paradoxically it was therefore the Communist party that was the key that opened the door to NATO membership. The Italian government as a result achieved what it wanted at the time: membership in the Western club, improvement in Italy's international status, and an assurance of continuing American political support. Far more easily and quickly than Germany or Japan, Italy was transformed from a defeated enemy into an ally. NATO membership was the most important international issue in Italy's postwar history and set the whole subsequent course of its foreign policy.

This episode in Alliance history is of interest because it exposes some of the lasting traits that have characterized Italy's foreign relations since then. On the Italian side there is evident the secondary place that foreign policy occupies in a government continuously embroiled in domestic concerns and the difficulty of formulating policies because of the inherent weakness of coalitions, where a single member can delay or prevent decision. Hence Italy usually looks on while others guide events, decisions are avoided until no choice remains, and Italian diplomacy often appears inept. Decisions are motivated more by narrow interests than by dedication to grand ideals, yet national pride is wounded by any sense of being slighted. On the part of Italy's allies, the narrowness of outlook is equally apparent. The critical issue is the Communist party and nothing more. In short, relations on both sides rest on a cynical base of ulterior motives.

Italy's participation in the movement for European economic and political cooperation reinforced the gains achieved through NATO membership. Although supranational idealism at first evoked less public enthusiasm than in Germany and the Benelux countries, there was in some circles – the lay parties and Christian Democrats – strong devotion to the idea of European federation. Sforza, a Republican, had been a renowned advocate of European cooperation when foreign minister in 1920–21, and his guiding objective when again foreign minister was a strong and united Europe. Italy therefore encouraged the integration movement as it developed from its beginnings in the coal and steel community in 1951 to its culmination in the European Economic Community in 1957.

But Italy was not a prime mover of the Common Market and in the negotiations had little to contribute. Its overriding interest was more pragmatic than idealistic and that interest was essentially economic. Italian leaders saw in an economic bloc an opportunity to boost exports, to facilitate the emigration of surplus Italian labor, and to secure funds for the development of the Mezzogiorno. Only the Communists and the Communist-dominated CGIL opposed Italian membership. The public was largely indifferent.

In the quarter-century since it was founded, the European Community has become the keystone of Italy's foreign policy. To the

Italians, association with Europe is more important than affiliation with the Atlantic Alliance. Foreign Minister Forlani was frank on this point in an interview with *La Stampa* in May 1978: "The most important aspect of our foreign policy is its incorporation into the European Community, which itself is largely economic; even military alliances, just to take the example of NATO, retain their validity only if they succeed in dealing with problems of economic cooperation."

The economic benefits were clear from the start. In liberalizing trade, the Treaty of Rome propelled the already buoyant Italian economy to its greatest prosperity in history. In the first decade alone Italy's trade with the Common Market countries rose by 500 percent and its share in world exports of manufactures nearly doubled. In the wake of this, the strong psychological pull of the Mediterranean was attenuated and Italy became a more genuinely Western European country.

There have been other advantages. Community membership helps Italy deal with its old and severe problems of overpopulation and unemployment. By opening borders and offering Italian workers job security and welfare protection in most of Western Europe, the Common Market has facilitated the emigration of surplus Italian labor. As of the 1980s, 1.7 million Italians lived and worked in other EC countries. Italy has also benefited from capital transfers as one of the least developed members of the Community. Although these funds have fallen short of expectations, they exceed those to any other member. Up to 1981 such institutions as the European Social Fund and the European Investment Bank paid out a total of 4.5 billion lire for use particularly in the Mezzogiorno. In one respect Italy has had to pay a price. The common agricultural policy has cost it dearly in terms of budgetary transfers to the Community and in higher costs of imported agricultural products, which produced a cumulative deficit between 1970 and 1978 of $26 billion.

The political accomplishments have been less tangible but of increasing importance. The expanding collaboration among the members, through the regular meetings of officials from the head-of-government level down, has given Italy the sense of participation, the prestige, and the point of reference that it seeks. Above all the association provides diplomatic cover for controversial political positions and reduces the need for independent policies. Italy supports American foreign-policy initiatives, for example, when other major European partners endorse them; when there is no European consensus it usually does not go along.

Popular support for the European Community has grown as well. "Among the major European countries," *The Economist* wrote in 1978, "Italy alone has cherished an idealistic vision of a genuinely united Europe, welcoming every step on the road to unification." To the average Italian the Community as a community has come to represent something more solid and reputable than his own government. After being the EC's weakest backers in the 1950s, the Italians have become its most loyal adherents. Today support for European cooperation is probably the only genuinely and universally popular element in the country's external policy.

Growing consensus

Throughout the years, partisan disagreement over NATO and the European Community – the only really contentious foreign-policy issues in the postwar period – has steadily diminished. What this means is that the parties of the left have moved toward the positions of the Christian Democrats and the lay parties. The Socialists were the first to shift. In 1957 they supported Italian adhesion to Euratom and, though demurring at first on the Common Market, soon became as strong proponents of European integration and Community enlargement as the lay parties. By 1958 they accepted Italian membership in NATO. Like the European sister parties at the time, the Socialists did their best to promote East–West détente and toyed with various disengagement proposals. But during center-left governments, when Pietro Nenni was foreign minister, the change in Italian foreign policy was one of tone rather than substance, and Nenni is perhaps best remembered as one of the early European advocates of normalizing Western relations with China.

The Communist change has been slower and more limited. By 1970 the party had accepted Italian membership in the European Community. In the following years it began to soften its opposition to NATO and in December 1975 Berlinguer declared at a meeting of the central committee that Italy's withdrawal from the alliance would not be in the interest of the East–West military balance and could cause a setback to détente. He added that Italy should follow a course that was neither anti-Soviet nor anti-American but one that was more autonomous. Subsequently his backhanded endorsement of NATO became more positive still when in June 1976 Berlinguer told the *Corriere della Sera* that he felt himself more secure with Italy in the Atlantic Alliance than on the other side because NATO offered a shield behind which socialism in freedom could be established.

The trend toward an agreed foreign policy has taken tangible form in a number of ways. In the policy declaration introducing his new government in August 1976, Prime Minister Andreotti declared that there existed "a broad measure of agreement among the political parties on the fundaments of foreign policy." Banal as this statement sounds, it was an understood code and marked the first occasion when an Italian prime minister could include the Communists in a common foreign-policy position. That event was capped in late 1977 and early 1978 when the Chamber and Senate each adopted resolutions, backed by all the major parties from the Communists to the Liberals, endorsing the basic tenets of Italian foreign policy and in particular detente, European integration, Community enlargement, and improved North–South relations. Although the point of the resolution was a domestic political one – to ease the way for increased Communist cooperation with the government of the time – it highlighted a clear advance toward a foreign-policy consensus. This accord was extended by a further Chamber motion in March 1980 when the same parties supported the European Monetary System, the West's need to maintain a military balance with the Soviet Union, a neutralized Afghanistan, and continued close links between Western Europe and the United States. In subscribing to these points the Communists took another step toward the position of the other parties.

Yet the Communists remain equivocal, rarely giving practical effect to their hortatory acceptance of NATO and the European Community. In 1978 they opposed immediate Italian accession to the European Monetary System. In 1979 they voted against the government's accord with NATO and the United States for the installation of new tactical nuclear weapons systems in Italy. In 1981 they were against Italian participation in the multilateral peacekeeping force in the Sinai. Although they no longer obstruct Italy's defense effort, they do not really support it. In the annual parliamentary consideration of the defense budget, for example, they voted against an appropriation except in the late seventies. Consequently foreign and defense questions remain an issue of difference between the Communists and the other parties and a major cause of popular reserve.

Weak commitment

Membership in the European Community and NATO commits Italy to a specific political, economic, and security system from which certain obligations follow. The obligations are not, however, always taken seriously, and some Italian experts have characterized the country's commitment as "passive" and "liturgical." In the case of NATO the attitude stems from a conviction that Italy faces no direct military threat from the Soviets and that its defense would in any event ultimately depend on the United States. The result – whether it springs from realism, fatalism, or irresponsibility – is deep apathy. Public opinion polls, for example, at the height of the cold war, during the period of détente, and as recently as 1979 have shown that generally no more than a third of the Italians have supported their country's continued participation in NATO. Worse still, the parties, the press, the universities, and the government itself are almost totally indifferent to strategic questions and the problems of their own armed forces. Nor has there been any effort, in either the government or universities, to develop expertise about defense matters.

Italy's security policy therefore suffers a fundamental inconsistency. For political reasons Italy is invariably loyal to NATO. It gives willing support to alliance objectives and always joins, indeed insists on joining, alliance projects such as the multilateral force, the nuclear planning group, and the Vienna negotiations on force reductions in Central Europe. Italy was one of the first to agree to the American proposal in 1979 to introduce new missiles into the European theater. And it usually meets its NATO force goals. In material terms the Italian defense effort is not negligible. The army has a strength of 254,000, the air force 70,000, and the navy 42,000, in addition to which there are 85,000 carabinieri.

But because there is little genuine conviction behind these displays of loyalty, the defense effort is essentially symbolic. The defense budget is regularly one of the lowest in the alliance, down at the bottom with Canada's and Luxembourg's, and even so was slashed in 1983. Defense spending in that year amounted to a mere 2.3 percent of GNP and 4 percent of the national budget. This downward trend was a sharp disappointment to the military forces, which were already in precarious shape, and undermined programs for modernization and improvements in quality and training.

The forces themselves are afflicted in varying degrees by inadequate manpower, training, and equipment. The most glaring deficiency is in manpower, two-thirds of which comprise ill-paid, mostly apathetic conscripts serving for one year. Much equipment is out of date, and projected purchases have had to be cut back because of high inflation and the competing demands of personnel costs. Training suffers accordingly. The armed forces also sustained a blow to their morale in the wake of the P2 scandal, which resulted in the resignation of almost 200 senior officers, including the chief of staff.

Of the three services, the navy is in the best shape, with well-trained personnel and modern ships. The air force, long weakened by its obsolete inventory, is gradually introducing new aircraft. The army is weak in almost every respect. Only 18 percent of its men are professionals and, except for the outstanding alpine and a few other units, personnel are neither well-equipped nor well-trained and are supported by war stocks and a reserve system that fall far short of adequate. In missile units, training is generally so poor that the possession of advanced weapons is almost pointless. A drastic restructuring program, which reduced conscription to twelve months and trimmed back the army from 306,000 to 251,000 men, was carried out in 1975 with the intent of reducing personnel costs so as to provide more funds for equipment. These steps were taken without the prescribed consultation with NATO and clearly derogated from Italy's defense commitments. Moreover the equipment purchases never materialized.

Behind these difficulties lie deeper problems that still further detract from the Italian defense posture. One of these is the lack of well-formulated military plans, programs, and goals. The simple reason is as, Stefano Silvestri has observed, "decision-making for Italy's military is in chaos" and as a consequence there is "a total absence of any clear or explicit planning." The defense budget is drawn up and authorized by parliament on an annual basis only. It is therefore impossible to develop long-term programs or to link missions and strategy with funds and manpower. Moreover, each service prepares its own budget and programs; these are not coordinated among the three branches, and in the end the funds are divided not according to an integrated system of priorities but simply in accordance with a long tradition decreeing that the army should receive 50 percent, the air force 30 percent, and the navy 20 percent of the defense budget. So military plans, procurement, and missions are developed on a year-by-year and service-by-service basis. Service jealousies and parochialism are problems in every country; they are more severe in Italy than in most other NATO countries because there is neither an organizational mechanism nor a psychological will to resist them. Efforts are under way to introduce long-term planning, but steps toward an integrated defense effort have yet to be taken.

An equally important set of problems arises from the fact that the Italian military has few strategic experts and does little or no strategic planning. Plans are still based on the hypothesis that the greatest threat lies in the Northeast – a land invasion by the Soviets through the Gorizia Gap. Therefore the army is considered the most important service, receives the major share of the budget, and is equipped for a land invasion. Only gradually has strategy been reassessed to take into consideration the changed political-military situation in the Mediterranean since the end of the 1960s. Italian participation in the peacekeeping forces in the Sinai in 1981 and in Lebanon between 1982 and 1984 was a striking departure from long-standing policy and indicated a recognition that Italy has a responsibility for Mediterranean security. But apart from some modernization of air defense in the South, the forces have not undergone the reshaping that is called for, in particular the establishment of a rapid-deployment force.

The problem of developing a coherent and effective security policy is further complicated by the lack of high-level policy coordination between the Defense and Foreign ministries. Matters of the greatest importance are referred to the Supreme Defense Council, which is chaired by the president and whose members include the prime minister as well as the ministers of defense, foreign affairs, interior, treasury, and the chief of the defense staff. But this body, whatever its potential, is little more than a rubber stamp for decisions already taken by individual ministries.

As a result, Italy falls back on NATO and the United States to provide a strategy, to develop plans, and to establish goals. It is for these reasons sometimes said that Italy's primary NATO contribution is one of providing bases for American forces in their NATO role on the southern flank. Certainly Italy has been among the most cooperative members of the alliance in accommodating American facilities, even when some of the installations – such as those on Sardinia and the new missiles on Sicily – are not warmly welcomed by the local populace. Although it could not agree in 1974 to the blanket transfer of NATO facilities from Greece when that country withdrew for a time from NATO military integration, the government accepted most of them. And despite a formal declaration in 1973 that American facilities could no longer be used for non-NATO missions, such as operations in the Middle East, the government acquiesced without a murmur in the American use of these bases for operations in subsequent years.

The story is much the same in the case of the European Community. Italy's role has again been exemplary in all the big institutional issues. Successive governments have been foremost champions of strengthening the Community's central authority, of enlarging the Community to include Britain and the Southern

European states, of holding direct elections to the European parliament, and of any other step leading toward greater cohesion among the partners. In 1979 Italy joined the European Monetary System even though membership seemed to some experts at the time contrary to its economic interests. Two years later it sponsored a settlement of the dispute over Britain's budgetary contribution that was disadvantageous to itself.

But in many practical areas the devotion is again passive and liturgical. Normally one of the first to follow Community initiatives and reforms, Italy is often the last to follow its decisions and regulations. Implementation of the EC regulations on a value-added tax was delayed for fully three years. Imports from Community members have been repeatedly subject to dubious or illegitimate controls. Agricultural reforms endorsed by Italian officials in Brussels are regularly ignored at home. Some of the confusion is due to government instability and inefficiency, which leaves the Italian delegation in Brussels uninstructed for long periods; some results from the difficulty of synchronizing the procedures of Italian public administration with Community regulations; but some raises suspicion of bad faith.

The European partners have also observed that Italy's devotion to the Community does not run so deep that Italians seek a career in the institution. In the Brussels bureaucracy Italians are always below their quota. Few want to serve even as commissioners. In 1970 the Italian government had great difficulty finding someone willing to take the very top position, chairman of the European Commission. Franco Maria Malfatti, then minister of post and telegraph, finally agreed but spent little time in Brussels and resigned before the end of his term to run for parliament at home.

In addition to the economic and political advantages that they confer, NATO and the European Community are Italy's principal means of having a place on the international stage and of satisfying a passion for diplomatic status. Ever since unification, and perhaps because it was achieved so late, Italy has wanted, in Altiero Spinelli's words, "to be one of the great European powers and above all to appear to be one." Appearances are indeed important. Of his official trips to Rome, Henry Kissinger wrote, again with wounding candor, ". . . Each visit left me with the feeling that its primary purpose was fulfilled by our arrival at the airport. This symbolized that the United States took Italy seriously; it produced photographic evidence that Italian leaders were being consulted." The concern with diplomatic prestige is constantly visible in Italy's insistence on being a member of every NATO group and every international organization and on participating in every international conference and forum. Conversely it is manifested in anger when excluded, as in the case of the 1979 Western summit in Guadeloupe. It can also be seen in tenacious opposition to exclusive groupings inside NATO and in nervousness toward any sort of special relationship among member states.

Italy is far from being the only country to worry about diplomatic face. Part of the problem is that it occupies an objectively ambiguous position. By certain material standards – size, population, location, and economic strength – it is roughly in the same category with France, Britain, and Germany. However, government weakness combined with a lame foreign and defense policy reduce Italy to the level of the smaller countries of Western Europe in terms of political and military weight. It therefore constantly strives to be in the former category and struggles against being relegated to the latter. In fact its "natural" position is the uncomfortable one of lying between the two.

Italian governments themselves add to the problem. By minimizing their role in international affairs, by hiding behind the EC and NATO to avoid taking independent positions, by underestimating their country's diplomatic skills, and by refusing to develop concrete positions on foreign and security issues, they diminish the rank their country could occupy. Hence the comments in international forums that Italy demands a voice but then has nothing to say. Put another way, Italy wants to enjoy the sensation of being an important power without going to the effort of being one. If Italy does not take itself seriously, others will not.

Good relations with everyone

No other large country manages better than Italy to minimize frictions and maximize smooth relations with others. Because of the lack of nationalistic sentiment, Italians may have resentments but find it difficult actually to dislike anyone. The government can therefore dispose of diplomatic problems with relative ease.

In Europe the few significant postwar bilateral disputes have been settled, and occasional lesser problems never ruffle good relations for long. The Italian government strongly supports Yugoslavia's nonaligned status and has done its best to settle bilateral issues that could strain relations between the two countries. With the Treaty of Osimo in 1975 Italy definitively renounced the territory and Italian population around Trieste, putting to rest a sensitive and protracted border dispute. In the case of Austria, the political relationship, long frayed by the South Tyrol issue, was symbolically normalized in 1973 when the Italian foreign minister visited Vienna for the first time since the war. With Switzerland the long-standing difficulties over the large Italian working community there have been settled by a series of bilateral accords. Italy has close diplomatic links with France, owing in part to a strongly francophile group in the Farnesina. Yet the deeper political relationship is weakened by what Italians regard as French disdain of Italy and France's great power posturings, which result in Italy's exclusion from inner-allied consultative groups.

Although there is no emotional warmth in the relationship, Britain and Italy have many common political and economic interests. Italy was among the most steadfast proponents of British entry into the EC, Rome seeing this both as a means of strengthening the institution and as a counterweight to France and Germany. The two countries have a keen interest in the Community's regional fund and in a reform of the common agricultural policy. In 1980 Italy sided with Britain in the bitter EC budget dispute. Relations with Greece, Spain, and Portugal receive surprisingly little attention in Rome, although Italy has supported their membership in the Common Market despite the fact that Italian agriculture stands to suffer from heightened competition.

For the Italians, the relationship with West Germany is heavily charged. On the positive side Germans enjoy a great deal of intellectual and cultural admiration. More concretely, West Germany is regarded as the model success story of European social democracy. Brandt and Schmidt have been respected by Italians of all political views and in recent years have been virtual heroes for the Italian left. For nearly 600,000 emigrant workers, the Federal Republic is home. Germany is also Italy's most important trading partner, both in terms of exports and imports. But the attraction is balanced by a countervailing and highly subjective repulsion based on pejorative stereotypes on both sides.

Although it has relatively strong commercial links to Eastern Europe and the Soviet Union, Italy has not invested any political capital there. Relations are, while uncontentious, cool and lacking in substance. Yet the irenic strain in the national character impels Italy to avoid a purely adversary East–West relationship and to encourage détente, arms control, and other means of lessening antagonism. For a long time the Soviets could leave it to the Communist party to bring their views to bear inside Italy. But even in the past decade, when this was no longer possible, Moscow has ostentatiously ignored Rome.

Outside the Atlantic community the only part of the world where Italy has any political interest is the Mediterranean and Middle East. And even this interest – stemming from Italy's historic role, geographic position, former colonial links, and feeling of being as much Mediterranean and European – is neither substantial nor constant. At times it manifests itself in a desire to be an independent influence in the area. At other times it appears as a wish to be a mediator between Europe and the Arabs. Space for an Italian role possibly existed between the mid-1950s, as British and French influence disappeared, and the late 1960s, when America became actively engaged in the Far East. For a time it looked as though Fanfani, simultaneously prime minister and foreign minister in the late fifties, intended to claim such a mission. But neither Fanfani nor Italian interest in a "Mediterranean vocation" lasted long. In the wake of the 1973 oil crisis Italian leaders lavished attention on Arab countries. But no political design has ever emerged. The Italian government has considerable expertise in the area; however, this knowledge has never been focused and brought to bear with real weight inside NATO or the European Community, where Italy's voice would merit serious attention.

None of Italy's bilateral relationships is more intense than that with the United States. However, the peculiar character of these relations is not based on the existence of any significant differences; apart from a few trade issues, relations have always been singularly free of problems and tensions. Nor does it stem from any special amicability; the American government is usually indifferent to Italy, and the Italian government feels closer to its European partners. Rather, the singular nature of the relationship is due to the depth and openness of American involvement in Italy's domestic affairs.

The critical element in American–Italian relations is the existence in Italy of a Communist party potentially strong enough to share power or lead a government. As seen in Washington, such an eventuality would create both a domestic political problem for an American president and a risk that Italy might leave NATO or reduce its alliance commitments. The overriding American aim has always been to forestall any form or degree of Communist participation in government.

So obsessive is this policy that the American government has felt free to intervene at every level of Italian domestic affairs. Much of the intervention goes on behind the scenes, is indeed covert. In the early postwar period the American government provided encouragement and funding for the establishment of a political party –

the Social Democrats – and two trade unions – the UIL and the CISL. Subsequently it has dispensed funds to a variety of individuals, groups, and parties. For instance in 1972 it provided $10 million to certain political parties to help them in the national election that year. Ambassador Graham Martin gave $800,000 to General Vito Miceli, the extreme-rightist head of Italian military intelligence, without conditions on the money's use. A 1976 report of the House of Representatives stated that the Central Intelligence Agency had passed $75 million to Italian parties and candidates during the preceding three decades. Intervention of a different sort takes the form of private consultations when American officials proffer advice on coalition formation and even on internal party matters.

Public interventions have included admonitions at election time and at other critical junctures by American government officials, including ambassadors. From the summer of 1975 to the summer of 1976, when the Communists were on the electoral offensive, President Gerald Ford, Secretary Kissinger, NATO Supreme Commander Alexander Haig, and Ambassador John Volpe engaged in an open campaign against the Communist party. In January 1978 the American government issued a formal statement, specifically directed at Italy, opposing the entry of Communists into any Western European government and calling for a reduction of their influence in any government. The immediate objective of the statement was designed to head off the formation of a Christian Democratic government with the parliamentary support of the Communists.

Italian officials and the majority of the Italian public have tolerated such interference with remarkably little resentment. The forbearance can probably be traced partly to the long experience of outside involvement in Italy's affairs. It also responds to a deep sense of vulnerability and specifically a fear that the United States might place Italy in some form of quarantine that could undermine the country's economic well-being. But Italians also put up with it because it suits their purposes. For favored parties and individuals, the American government offers an excellent source of secret funds. For the Christian Democrats the opposition to the Communists has been a convenient way of keeping the Communists out of the government while shifting the responsibility to the American government. In any case the Italians take the money and advice and do as they please. In 1978, for instance, the Christian Democrats responded with silence to the State Department's January statement; two months later they formed the government the statement was designed to forestall. All in all, therefore, official contacts between the two countries may be smooth on the surface but the basis of a solid relationship – mutual trust and respect – is lacking. Americans do not take Italy seriously, and Italians respect the United States for its power, not for any wisdom in its handling of international affairs.

14. "But it does move" – a summing up

A journey through the labyrinth of Italian politics ends as it began
– with a deep sense of the uniqueness, subtlety, tension, paradoxes,
confusion, vitality, and resilience of the Italian mode of self-government. Ultimately the question always asked is how a political
system so beset by problems has survived and whether it can go on
without a fundamental change in its institutions and style of politics. Any answer to this – perhaps unanswerable – question lies in
diagnosing the key structural problems of the system and then in
trying to discover how these defects have been counterbalanced by
the Italian genius for survival.

Government instability

The most obvious symptom of political dysfunction is the acute
instability of government. Statistics sum up the situation dramatically. Between 1945 and 1985 there were forty-five governments
and seventeen different prime ministers. Governments lasted on
an average less than ten months. Parliament itself had on four
successive occasions to be dissolved ahead of its full term because
incompatible party interests made impossible the formation of any
type of governing coalition. In the second half of the life of the
republic, twice as much time was required to form a regime as
during the first half. In arithmetic terms, Italy was without government during these four decades for periods that totaled nearly three
years. And if there are also taken into account the months of
"turnover time" – the periods spent in preparing elections, in
launching a new government, and in holding a government together after its political base had collapsed but before its formal
resignation – it is evident that the three-year figure decidedly un-
derstates the length of time the country has been without a fully
operating government.

The root cause of this situation lies in the party system, itself a
conundrum of disorders and anomalies. With parties of the left and
right excluded from government, coalition partners occupy essentially the identical middle ground and compete for essentially the
same electorate. As a result governments are fragile, their life

struggle beginning from the moment they are installed. In trying to carry out their program goals, they find that important initiatives touch vested interests, vested interests touch parties, and parties, however tiny, can bring down the government. The broader the coalition, the wider the span of interests to be protected. So proposals to deal with important – and therefore contentious – issues must be avoided or reduced to the lowest common denominator or in the end shelved. This general problem, as Samuel Beer has recalled, was the plague of the Weimar republic, where it was known as "pluralistic stagnation." A government that hoped to survive could have no policy; a government with a policy could not hope to survive.

The Italian version of this debility is more virulent still. Even when a coalition government has both a solid majority and an agreed program, none of the junior partners wants the government to succeed, since success would be turned to partisan advantage. Consequently the members of a coalition are from the start bent on reducing the government to impotence. This consideration explains why Italian governments find it extremely difficult to deal with some of the most basic issues of society – for example, why criminal and civil codes written by a Fascist government are still largely in force; why every broad economic program, from the Vanoni plan in 1955 to the Pandolfi plan over two decades later, came to nothing; why Italy was seventy years into the twentieth century before having a divorce law; why such a high proportion of the population escapes paying taxes; why it took the threat of a referendum to produce final action on an abortion law; and why a malfunctioning parliament, executive, cabinet, civil service, and judicial system are not put right.

This is the situation that as much as anything brings Italian political practices into disrepute abroad no less than at home. In the end the anguished doubts about Italy's governability concern not merely whether more durable governments can be constructed but whether they will ever be able to rule effectively once in office. It was indicative that the parliamentary commission established in 1983 to identify ways of correcting the dysfunctions of the system was charged with examining the problems from the perspective of the institutions rather than the dynamics behind them. Symptoms, therefore, were the issue rather than causes – which is ultimately the system of *partitocrazia*.

Lack of alternation

Another structural disorder is the lack of alternation of government. With the Christian Democrats permanently in, the Commu-

nists always out, and the other parties oscillating between government and opposition, there has never been a genuine change of
regime in the whole course of the republic's history. Some Italians
regard this situation as an anomaly rather than a defect. As they see
it, rotation in power is not a necessary prerequisite of democracy
and is not entirely compatible with the political character and
experience of the country. Moreover, representative democracy is
still regarded as a delicate plant whose roots should not be tam-
pered with. As evidenced in their voting behavior, for instance,
Italians are generally apprehensive of sudden and drastic change,
instinctively preferring gradual shifts to novel departures. Gentle
modulation from left to right around a center pole is reassuring to
the major vested interests. This tendency is reinforced by the country's historic contribution to political science, the art of *trasformismo,* where the clear distinction between government and
opposition – basic in most other Western democracies – is replaced by broad collaboration.

Indeed the summum bonum for Italian politicians – although
few might admit it – would be a coalition that includes all parties.
Such an arrangement would in no way diminish the savage competition for power but would greatly simplify the troublesome burden
of governing. An apt metaphor might be an orchestra. All the
components would be represented; some sections would play at
some times, others would play at other times, and on occasion all
would play together. Everyone would be on stage but few by
themselves would be essential at all times. And a sufficient number of players would always be available to perform any particular
tune.

Whatever may be said in its favor, this mode of self-government
lacks some of the most vital elements of traditional Western representative democracy. With little or no risk of being ejected from
power and relegated to the opposition, government parties have no
incentive to govern efficiently or to be responsive to popular will.
All the benefits of democratic competition are lost. Accountability
to the electorate is blunted if not completely destroyed. The voter,
normally the ultimate arbiter in liberal democracies, cannot reward
or punish the parties of government. Coalitions leave few traces of
responsibility and elections in practice turn out to be a choice
without alternatives. And so it has proved in the Italian case. The
lack of alternation left in power a long succession of governments
so absorbed in their own power struggles as to fall thoroughly out of
phase with the society they were theoretically governing. It is for
this reason that change in Italy has occurred despite rather than as a
result of the governments in power.

The art of the impossible

A further serious malfunction is the impaired relationship between the government and the governed. Although relations between the citizen and his government are everywhere imperfect, in Italy there is almost no nexus at all. In one sense Italy is the most thoroughly representative democracy in the world. With one deputy for every 80,000 electors and only 300,000 votes necessary to put a party in parliament, Italians enjoy an unrivaled representation across the political spectrum and have the opportunity of expressing a re-markably subtle political preference. In another sense, however, it is one of the least democratic. Italian voters cannot elect any of the persons who govern them – not the president of the republic, the prime minister, the president of the region or province, or the mayor of their community. They cannot determine the makeup of the coalition to be formed after or between elections or the policies it will follow since these are questions decided by party leaders following the vote. Hence the central act of democracy is devalued. The effect of voting is vitiated, and voters lose the possibility – and responsibility – of making clear-cut choices. The electorate con-sequently feels as little capable of influencing the government as of changing the weather.

Inability to change: Here is a difficulty that perhaps underlies all the structural problems. No nation is more self-critical, more aware of its faults, more alive to what needs to be done. Deficiencies and ways of correcting them are discussed endlessly in the press, at conferences, in parliament, in books, at family dinner. Studies are conducted, commissions convened, and proposals submitted. Yet in the end, resolution falters and will fails. After all the hands are wrung, interest dissipates and little action ever follows. As a psy-chological phenomenon the situation is well known: The discom-fort of the existing condition is less severe than the anticipated pain of change. Muriel Grindrod has expressed this thought in a more general way: "The Italian genius is on sure ground when working towards a practical, concrete end, whether it be building a road or making a washing-machine. It is in the more abstract spheres of government and administration that indecision creeps in."

Frustration over this sense of political impotence explains in part the outburst of social action that followed the "hot autumn," the spread of extraparliamentary activities, the rise of new-left groups, and the eruption of leftist terrorism. Forces dammed up by the immobility of the system had to find alternate outlets in other forms of political expression. More recently a rising proportion of the public has vented its frustration by the futile gesture of abstaining or casting blank ballots in national and local elections. Dissatisfaction with governing authority is a historic phenomenon in Italy; postwar leaders can be held accountable for having perpetuated it.

So for all its drama, surprises, and never-ending excitement, Italian political life is essentially an empty exercise in power brokering among the parties. Nowhere else in Europe do politics have more zest and less material purpose. Even those politicians with substantive political aims are blocked by the inertia and indifference of the government and the resistance of the parties. Italy has not lacked leaders with a vision of national purpose, but they have been few. De Gasperi was the only prime minister able to force the system to produce concrete results over any appreciable period. Since then Italy has drifted along with remarkably little central direction. The Italian political system is like an intricate machine that operates at terrific speed, throwing off a cascade of sparks but producing little more than energy for its own consumption. Asked not long before he died what his feelings were about Italy's postwar political course, Ugo La Malfa replied: "At the end a great bitterness."

"Eppur si muove"

After recanting his proposition that the earth is not stationary but rotates around the sun, Galileo is said to have murmured: *"Eppur si muove"* – "But it does move." Similarly, in the face of all the apparent evidence to the contrary, Italy does move. It in fact fascinates the world precisely because of an ability to stand at the edge of apparent political chaos and not merely to survive but prosper more markedly in some ways than its putatively better governed European partners. This paradox is one of the biggest enigmas of a country notorious for its mysteries. Why in fact does the ship, rudderless and awash, sail on instead of sinking?

The most important reason is that the substructure is solid. Despite ideological divisions, ceaseless political combat, and a vast span of political differences, there is for all practical purposes unanimous agreement on the most basic issue: the desirability of democratic self-government in a representative parliamentary system. Italians may feel a lingering sense of alienation from the state and may mistrust the institutions that govern them, but they draw a heavy line of distinction between that state and the constitutional order under which they have lived and thrived since the foundation of the republic. Perhaps nothing could prove this fact better than the way they hold on to their political system in the face of all its faults. Few European democracies have had their political institutions so severely tested – by terrorism from right and left, by political conspiracies, and by massive organized crime. Few nations have adjusted so painlessly to rapid social and psychological changes. But, at times, when the economy plunged and political uncertainty soared, Italians and non-Italians asked themselves whether the country might be going the way of the Weimar and Fourth French republics. It was exactly at such moments that the strength of the democratic system, in all its vital respects, was clear beyond question.

A particularly telling contrast to Germany in the early thirties and France in the late fifties is the fact that all sectors of society accept the established democratic system and play by the rules of the constitutional order. The role of the Communist party – given its disruptive potential – has been especially important. It had a central part in constructing the new democratic state after the fall of Fascism and, although actively opposing such government policies as the acceptance of Marshall Plan aid and adhesion to NATO, it consistently worked to bolster it. At key points, such as the "hot autumn," it acted as a moderating influence. And during the most difficult period of postwar Italy – between 1976 and 1979 – it made a vital contribution to the stability of the system. During those latter years it formed a solid front with the Christian Democrats to combat leftist terrorism. It supported the government's measures to deal with the gravest economic crisis of the republican era. It assisted in the formation of two Christian Democratic governments, which could not otherwise have existed. And it helped to bring about a number of important social reforms that the majority of Italians wanted. Had the Communists adopted an opposition stance on these issues or even merely withheld their support, the much overused and misused term "ungovernability" would have acquired all too concrete a meaning and the state of Italy in the years following would be difficult to imagine.

It was because of this near-universal acceptance of the political system that those who wanted to subvert it utterly failed. The plottings of De Lorenzo, Borghese, and Gelli – along with the squalid activities of the intelligence services and right-wing circles in the Interior Ministry – revealed an odious strain in Italian political society, but, whatever nonsense they may have fomented behind the scenes, they did not divert Italy by one millimeter from its democratic course. Similarly, the political terrorism of the seven-

ties was absorbed and finally defeated thanks ultimately to the
maturity and calm with which the Italians reacted to the havoc.

One of the most important reasons behind this loyalty is the
openness and tolerance of the system. No important group has ever
been excluded from playing some role in the country's political
and social life. Even at the height of Christian Democratic power,
there were areas outside the party's control. Private business maintained its independence. The country's intellectual and cultural
life was a monopoly of the left, a fact of great importance in a
country where artists and intellectuals hold enormous prestige.
The press, precisely because it was so politicized, conveyed a spectrum of views unexcelled anywhere else in the world. In the political area the Communists and – at some times and in some places –
the neo-Fascists played a role not only in parliament but also in
local and regional governments. In the course of the 1970s the
dispersion of power was greatly accentuated. By then the series of
referenda contributed materially to public participation in the
democratic process. The positions of president and prime minister
have several times gone to non–Christian Democrats. The lay
parties and the left occasionally joined ranks to outvote the Christian Democrats and bring about important social reforms. In such
ways power has been spread, the effects of one-party dominance
mitigated, and the blockage of the system to some extent overcome. As a result serious alienation from the constitutional order
was confined to a tiny minority of left and right extremists.

Moreover, the ship has followed a remarkably steady course. Not
only has there been no change of constitution, as in France, there
have been none of the substantial shifts of foreign and domestic
policy that have occurred from time to time in most other Western
states. Elections come and go, governments change, and crises
recur, but the direction Italy follows at home and abroad remains in
all essentials unaltered. Behind this political continuity is a
society – for all its effervescence – as stable as any in Europe. Despite the deep ideological bitterness that characterized much of the
republic's history, there has always been an underlying spirit of
peaceful coexistence, a subtle but unmistakable sense of unity.
This was the joint political legacy of De Gasperi and Togliatti.
Italy, with the largest Communist party in the West and the center
of the Catholic church, was not long ago an ideological battlefield.
In time it became a model of ideological tolerance. Today it is no
longer a matter of reconciling Antonio Gramsci and the pope, as
the antithesis was at times phrased; both have become essentially

irrelevant to politics as currently practiced. Social cohesion earned through struggle is social cohesion with real strength. Here is another support for the country's constitutional order and its underlying pluralist system.

Prosperity and peace

In short, the system is strong because it enjoys universal acceptance. A second, related, and equally important set of reasons can be traced to the very virtues of the system's defects. The long succession of Italy's postwar governments may not have accomplished much in a positive sense, but they committed few errors and by their conspicuous inaction gave free reign to the country's social forces to develop at will. The economy was the key element. Apart from its intervention in the South, no other government in postwar Europe was so singularly lacking in programs to promote economic growth, industrial modernization, or foreign trade. In part by design but in larger part by abdication, the government followed a course of laissez-faire that has probably not been seen anywhere else in the West after 1945. The "underground economy" – based on an inability or unwillingness to enforce tax regulations and other laws – is the epitome of its approach.

For a nation of such pronounced individualism, industry, and ingenuity, this unbridled freedom unleashed the native energies of the people and produced economic growth as miraculous in its way as that in Germany. Overall there has been a rise in the standard of living of all social groups, even if unequally shared, that has reinforced popular support for the constitutional order under which it occurred. The economic success is the success not of the government but of the hard work and entrepreneurial spirit of workers and managers alike. The contrasting decline of the public sector enterprises after their annexation by the Christian Democrats is clear evidence of how – and why – Italy works best when government is not involved.

Another passive success has been Italy's external policies. Through the links with the European and Atlantic worlds, Italy has not only made itself a net economic beneficiary of the European Community but has been able to transfer much of its security burden to the Atlantic Alliance and the United States. It has in effect traded its strategic geographical advantage – "the best aircraft carrier in the Mediterranean," in American naval jargon – for defense at a bargain price. This low-profile foreign and defense policy suited the postwar Italian temperament and saved Italy the stresses that have afflicted many other countries as a result of their foreign engagements.

On the upswing

For all the country's problems, the severity of Italy's difficulties has at times been exaggerated. "The political crisis which the country is going through in these months, is of the utmost gravity." This front-page comment in *La Stampa* in 1979 by the noted political writer Noberto Bobbio was the sort of message constantly being repeated by politicians, journalists, and academic observers in a crescendo throughout the seventies. The Communist party's major theme during the last half of the decade was that the country was in such dire shape it could be governed only with Communist participation in the cabinet. Hence a general impression was created that the critical moment, event, or year had arrived and that Italy was in danger of sinking into the condition of a Latin American banana republic. But Italy was never on a precipice, and the twilight-of-the-gods atmosphere of those years was vastly overdone.

In addition there are several important psychological elements that help to explain why and how the country's problems have been managed and some defects overcome. On another occasion Norberto Bobbio said that he preferred to assess political results not by the standard "things could have gone better" but by the one "things could have gone worse." This attitude lies deep in the psyche of the Italian nation. The Italian's political fatalism and mistrust of the state are a great liability but have another side: the popular capacity to absorb crises, shocks, and scandals because nothing much better is expected from the governing authority. Being skeptical, Italians have no false hopes; being on their own in an "asocial social welfare state," they know how to protect themselves by either making the system minimally effective or getting around it entirely.

There is also a more important and positive consideration. Bad as things may be, they were at any time in the past even worse. The days when Alberto Moravia's novels were banned and films questioning the established social order could not be shown, when workers could be fired because of their party or union membership, when divorce and birth control were illegal, when few houses had baths, when people in the South lacked enough to eat and had to emigrate to find work, when nightclubs could not operate in Rome because of its "holy character" – all of this well within living memory – belong to a vanished epoch. If social and political conditions are assessed as a whole, the overall trend, with few exceptions, has been in a decidedly favorable direction. There is greater social harmony, popular political involvement, and economic well-being. There is less ideological division, poverty, and illiteracy. There is no recent past to look back on with particular pride or particular shame – no lost empire, no vanished era of successful self-government, no golden age of prosperity. All in all Italy therefore suffers little or none of the sense of decline, stagnation, purposelessness, or general malaise that afflicts some other states in Western Europe.

Beneath all these various explanations of why Italy moves despite the manifold flaws of the system lies yet a deeper consideration: Italian national character. Italians have, in a word, a genius that they have learned over centuries for patience, resilience, and improvisation in the face of looming disaster. They possess a much higher tolerance for uncertainty, confusion, and complexity than any other Western people and enjoy an uncanny ability to bring at least a minimum of order out of a maximum of chaos. Although such abstract traits are easy to overlook beneath the more tangible defects and weaknesses of the political system, they ultimately provide the country with an underlying emotional strength that helps it ride out every storm.

Ultimately Italians have in their political system the sort of government that most of them want. Although they crave the security the state can offer, they are natural Jeffersonians – knowing from experience that that government governs best that governs least – and consider little and weak government safer than strong and effective government. The institutions may not work smoothly and may arouse derision, but they are the institutions Italians feel safest with.

Everything considered, Italy is one of postwar Europe's outstanding successes. Democracy is secure. The country will not go over the precipice. But whether the Italian mode of self-government will be equal to the increasingly difficult demands that confront all democracies in an era of technological complexity, economic interdependence, and worldwide insecurity is a question that worries both Italians and their friends.

Appendixes

Appendix A. Election results: Chamber of Deputies (in percentages; number of seats in parentheses)

Party[a]	1948	1953	1958	1963	1968	1972	1976	1979	1983
DC	48.5 (305)	40.1 (263)	42.4 (273)	38.3 (260)	39.1 (266)	38.8 (267)	38.7 (262)	38.3 (262)	32.9 (225)
PCI	31 (183)[b]	22.6 (143)	22.7 (140)	25.3 (166)	26.9 (177)	27.2 (179)	34.4 (228)	30.4 (201)	29.9 (198)
PSI		12.8 (75)	14.2 (84)	13.8 (87)	14.5 (91)[b]	9.6 (61)	9.6 (57)	9.8 (62)	11.4 (73)
PSDI	7.1 (33)	4.5 (19)	4.5 (22)	6.1 (33)		5.1 (29)	3.4 (15)	3.8 (20)	4.1 (23)
PRI	2.5 (9)	1.6 (5)	1.4 (6)	1.4 (6)	2 (9)	2.9 (14)	3.1 (14)	3 (16)	5.1 (29)
PLI	3.8 (19)	3 (13)	3.5 (17)	7 (39)	5.8 (31)	3.9 (21)	1.3 (5)	1.9 (9)	2.9 (16)
PR	—	—	—	—	—	—	1.1 (4)	3.5 (18)	2.2 (11)
DP	—	—	—	—	—	—	1.5 (6)	0.8 (—)	1.5 (7)
PdUP	—	—	—	—	—	—	—	1.4 (6)	—[c]
MSI	2 (6)	5.8 (29)	4.8 (24)	5.1 (27)	4.4 (24)	8.7 (56)	6.1 (35)	5.3 (30)	6.8 (42)
Monarchists	2.8 (14)	6.9 (40)	4.8 (25)	1.7 (8)	1.3 (6)	—	—	—	—
Others[d]	2.5 (5)	2.7 (3)	1.7 (5)	1.3 (4)	6.0 (26)	4.0 (4)	0.8 (4)	2.7 (6)	3.2 (6)

Source: Istituto Centrale di Statistica (ISTAT).

[a] DC (Democrazia cristiana), PCI (Partito comunista italiano), PSI (Partito socialista italiano), PSDI (Partito socialista democratico italiano), PRI (Partito repubblicano italiano), PLI (Partito liberale italiano), PR (Partito radicale), DP (Democrazia proletaria), PdUP (Partito di unità proletaria per il comunismo), MSI (Movimento sociale italiano).

[b] Parties presented joint election lists.

[c] Ran on PCI lists.

[d] Includes South Tyrol People's party (SVP), Sardinian Action party (PSA), Valdôtaine Union (UV), and Socialist Party of Proletarian Unity (PSIUP). SVP generally accounts for 3 seats; PSIUP won 23 seats in 1968.

Appendix B. *Prime ministers and their governments since the Second World War*

Prime minister	Composition of government[a]	Duration
Ferruccio Parri	anti-Fascist parties	June 1945 – Dec. 1945
Alcide De Gasperi	DC-PSI-PCI and others	Dec. 1945 – July 1946
Alcide De Gasperi	DC-PSI-PCI-PRI	July 1946 – Feb. 1947
Alcide De Gasperi	DC-PSI-PCI	Feb. 1947 – May 1947
Alcide De Gasperi	DC-PSDI-PRI-PLI	May 1947–May 1948
Alcide De Gasperi	DC-PSDI-PRI-PLI	May 1948 – Jan. 1950
Alcide De Gasperi	DC-PSDI-PRI	Jan. 1950 – July 1951
Alcide De Gasperi	DC-PRI	July 1951 – June 1953
Alcide De Gasperi	DC	July 1953
Giuseppe Pella	DC	Aug. 1953 – Jan. 1954
Amintore Fanfani	DC	Jan. 1954
Mario Scelba	DC-PSDI-PLI	Feb. 1954 – June 1955
Antonio Segni	DC-PSDI-PLI	July 1955–May 1957
Adone Zoli	DC	May 1957–June 1958
Amintore Fanfani	DC-PSDI	July 1958–Jan. 1959
Antonio Segni	DC	Feb. 1959 – Feb. 1960
Fernando Tambroni	DC	March 1960 – July 1960
Amintore Fanfani	DC	July 1960 – Feb. 1962
Amintore Fanfani	DC-PSDI-PRI	Feb. 1962 – May 1963
Giovanni Leone	DC	June 1963 – Nov. 1963
Aldo Moro	DC-PSI-PSDI-PRI	Dec. 1963 – June 1964
Aldo Moro	DC-PSI-PSDI-PRI	July 1964 – Jan. 1966
Aldo Moro	DC-PSI-PSDI-PRI	Feb. 1966 – June 1968
Giovanni Leone	DC	June 1968 – Nov. 1968
Mariano Rumor	DC-PSI-PRI	Dec. 1968 – July 1969
Mariano Rumor	DC	Aug. 1969 – Feb. 1970
Mariano Rumor	DC-PSI-PSDI-PRI	March 1970 – July 1970
Emilio Colombo	DC-PSI-PSDI-PRI	Aug. 1970–Jan. 1972
Giulio Andreotti	DC	Feb. 1972
Giulio Andreotti	DC-PSDI-PLI	June 1972 – June 1973
Mariano Rumor	DC-PSI-PSDI-PRI	July 1973 – March 1974
Mariano Rumor	DC-PSI-PSDI	March 1974 – Oct. 1974
Aldo Moro	DC-PRI	Nov. 1974 – Jan. 1976
Aldo Moro	DC	Feb. 1976 – April 1976
Giulio Andreotti	DC	July 1976 – Jan. 1978
Giulio Andreotti	DC	March 1978 – Jan. 1979
Giulio Andreotti	DC-PSDI-PRI	March 1979
Francesco Cossiga	DC-PSDI-PLI	Aug. 1979 – March 1980
Francesco Cossiga	DC-PSDI-PRI	April 1980 – Sept. 1980
Arnaldo Forlani	DC-PSI-PSDI-PRI	Oct. 1980 – May 1981
Giovanni Spadolini	DC-PSI-PSDI-PRI-PLI	June 1981 – Aug. 1982
Giovanni Spadolini	DC-PSI-PSDI-PRI-PLI	Aug. 1982 – Nov. 1982
Amintore Fanfani	DC-PSI-PSDI-PLI	Dec. 1982 – April 1983
Bettino Craxi	DC-PSI-PSDI-PRI-PLI	Aug. 1983 –

[a] For meanings of party abbreviations, see Appendix A.

Appendix C. *Presidents of the republic*

Enrico De Nicola, 1946–8
Luigi Einaudi, 1948–55
Giovanni Gronchi, 1955–62
Antonio Segni, 1962–4
Giuseppe Saragat, 1964–71
Giovanni Leone, 1971–8
Alessandro Pertini, 1978–85
Francesco Cossiga, 1985–

Appendix D. *Popes*

Pius XII (Eugenio Pacelli), 1939–58
John XXIII (Angelo Giuseppe Roncalli), 1958–63
Paul VI (Giovanni Battista Montini), 1963–78
John Paul I (Albino Luciani), 1978
John Paul II (Karol Wojtyla), 1978–

Appendix E. *Some economic indicators*

Year	GNP at constant prices (% annual variation)	Gross fixed capital formation (% annual variation)	Prices (% annual variation)	Unemployment rate (%)	Balance of payments (millions of lire)
1951					−77
1952	4.4	14.0	3.2	—	−84
1953	7.5	13.1	2.8	—	−49
1954	3.6	11.4	2.8	—	−4
1955	6.7	12.3	3.4	—	+45
1956	4.7	6.6	3.9	—	+54
1957	5.3	9.0	2.0	—	+129
1958	4.8	2.7	2.3	—	+496
1959	6.5	8.7	−0.2	7.0	+531
1960	6.3	12.3	2.0	5.6	+274
1961	8.2	11.4	3.0	5.1	+359
1962	6.2	9.5	5.8	4.5	+31
1963	5.6	8.0	8.4	3.9	−783
1964	2.6	−5.9	6.5	4.3	+483
1965	3.2	−8.4	4.3	5.4	+996
1966	5.8	4.3	2.3	5.9	+435
1967	7.0	11.7	2.9	5.4	+203
1968	6.3	10.9	1.5	5.7	+392
1969	5.7	7.4	4.2	5.7	−869
1970	5.0	2.7	6.8	5.4	+223
1971	1.6	−3.1	7.1	5.4	+489
1972	3.1	0.4	6.3	6.4	−747
1973	6.9	8.2	11.7	6.4	−208
1974	3.9	3.7	17.7	5.4	−3,588
1975	−3.5	−12.7	17.3	5.9	−1,439
1976	5.9	3.3	17.9	6.7	−1,531
1977	2.0	0.1	18.9	7.2	+1,730
1978	2.6	−0.4	12.4	7.2	+6,997
1979	4.9	5.8	15.7	7.7	+1,824
1980	3.9	9.4	21.1	7.6	−6,388
1981	0.2	0.6	18.7	8.4	+1,533
1982	−0.4	−5.2	16.3	9.1	−2,521
1983	−1.2	−5.3	15.0	9.9	+3,882

Source: ISTAT.

Appendix F. *Comparative annual average growth rates of real GNP*

	1950–60		1960–70		1971–80	
	Total	Per capita	Total	Per capita	Total	Per capita
Italy	5.5[a]	4.9[a]	5.4	4.5	4.0	3.7
France	4.4	3.5	5.7	4.6	1.2	0.7
Netherlands	4.6	3.3	5.3	4.0	0.6	−0.2
Sweden	3.6	2.9	4.3	3.5	1.8	1.6
United Kingdom	2.7	2.3	2.8	2.2	−1.4	−1.5
West Germany	7.7	6.6	4.6	3.5	1.9	1.7
Japan	8.0[b]	6.8[b]	10.9	9.7	4.4	3.5
United States	2.9	1.2	4.6	3.3	−0.3	−1.4

[a] 1951–60
[b] 1952–60

Source: United Nations, *Yearbook of National Accounts Statistics, 1969: International Tables* (New York: United Nations, 1970). U.N., *Yearbook . . . , 1971* (New York: United Nations, 1973). U.N., *Yearbook . . . , 1981* (New York: United Nations, 1983). Copyright United Nations. Reproduced by permission.

Appendix G. *Some indicators of social change*

	1951	1961	1971	1981
Population (millions)	47.5	50.6	54.1	56.6
Urbanization: % of population living in communities with				
fewer than 50,000 inhabitants	72	66.6	62.7	62.3
more than 50,000 inhabitants	28	33.4	37.3	37.7
Industrialization: labor force				
as % of total population	41.2	38.8	34.8	35.3
% in agriculture	42.2	29.1	17.2	11.2
% in industry	32.1	40.6	44.3	39.8
% in tertiary sector	25.7	30.3	38.5	49
Education				
illiterates (% of population)	12.9	8.3	5.2	3.0
semiliterates (% of population)	46.3	34.2	27.1	18.2
% of population with				
5 years of schooling	30.6	42.3	44.3	40.8
8 years of schooling	5.9	9.6	14.7	23.9
13 years of schooling	3.3	4.3	6.9	11.4
university degree	1.0	1.3	1.8	2.7
enrollment as % of appropriate group				
primary[a]	83.4	88.8	101.2	101
secondary	9.8	19.7	44.5	72
university	3.4	5	15.4	25.1
Family and related				
mean size of family	4	3.6	3.3	3
median age at death	67.4	70.3	72.5	73.9
death from infectious diseases (thousands)	61.3	25.9	15.9	6
daily caloric intake	2,235	2,679	3,197	3,330
% of homes with bathrooms	10.7	28.9	64.5	98.5
	(1953)	(1962)		
motor vehicles (% of population)	5.8	15.3	30.7	36.7
telephones (% of population)	2.9	8.1	19	36
television sets (% of population)	—	7.2	17	22

[a] Includes double enrollment (public and private schools).
Source: ISTAT (based on census figures, 1981 data provisional).

Appendix H. *Regional
variations of per capita
national income, 1979
(national average equals 100)*

Valle d'Aosta	159.9
Lombardy	132.8
Liguria	131.8
Piedmont	127.4
Emilia-Romagna	124.8
Trentino – Alto Adige	119.2
Friuli–Venezia Giulia	116.8
Tuscany	111.5
Veneto	104.2
Lazio	97.0
Marches	97.0
Umbria	94.0
Sardinia	78.0
Abruzzi	77.9
Puglia	69.8
Basilicata	69.5
Molise	68.1
Sicily	66.6
Campania	66.2
Calabria	54.4

Source: ISTAT.

Appendix I. *Religious practice and electoral preference of a sample of Catholics (in percent)*

	Religious practice	
	Attend mass regularly (25.4% of sample)	Never attend mass (35.3% of sample)
Electoral preference		
Christian Democrats	36.8	13.6
Communists	5.6	32.0
Socialists	13.9	13.3
Social Democrats	0.4	1.0
Republicans	5.0	5.1
Liberals	2.2	1.3
Neo-Fascists	1.8	3.9
Radicals	0.8	2.7
Proletarian Democrats	0.4	1.6
Do not vote	2.8	4.2
No response	30.2	21.4

Source: CeSPE Foundation, 1985.

Bibliography

Chapter 1. The political context

Background of the period

Earle, John. *Italy in the 1970s.* Newton Abbot, England: David & Charles, 1975.
Grindrod, Muriel. *Italy.* New York: Praeger, 1968.
Hughes, H. Stuart. *The United States and Italy.* 3d ed. Cambridge, Mass.:
    Harvard University Press, 1979.
Kogan, Norman. *A Political History of Italy: The Postwar Years.* New York:
    Praeger, 1983.
Mack Smith, Denis. *Italy: A Modern History.* New ed. Ann Arbor: University
    of Michigan Press, 1969.
Mammarella, Giuseppe. *Italy after Fascism: A Political History 1943-1965.*
    Notre Dame, Ind.: University of Notre Dame Press, 1966.
Nichols, Peter. *Italia, Italia.* Boston: Little, Brown, 1973.
Wiskemann, Elizabeth. *Italy since 1945.* London: Macmillan, 1971.
Woolf, S. J., ed. *The Rebirth of Italy.* London: Longmans, 1972.

Political and social analysis

Adams, John Clarke, and Paolo Barile. *The Government of Republican Italy.*
    Boston: Houghton Mifflin, 1966.
Allum, P. A. *Italy - Republic without Government?* New York: Norton, 1973.
Almond, Gabriel, and Sidney Verba. *The Civic Culture: Political Attitudes and
    Democracy in Five Nations.* Boston: Little, Brown, 1965.
Calise, Mauro, and Renato Mannheimer. *Governanti in Italia: un trentennio
    repubblicano 1946-1976.* Bologna: Il Mulino, 1982.
Cavazza, Fabio, and Stephen Graubard. *Il caso italiano.* Milan: Garzanti, 1974.
Dogan, Mattei, and Richard Rose, eds. *European Politics: A Reader.* Boston:
    Little, Brown, 1971.
Galli, Giorgio. *Il difficile governo: Un'analisi del sistema partitico italiano.*
    Bologna: Il Mulino, 1972.
I partiti politici in Italia 1861-1973. Turin: Utet, 1975.
Dal bipartismo imperfetto alla possibile alternativa. Bologna: Il Mulino, 1975.
Germino, Dante, and Stefano Passigli. *The Government and Politics of
    Contemporary Italy.* New York: Harper & Row, 1968.
Graziano, L. and S. Tarrow, eds. *La crisi italiana.* Turin: Einaudi, 1978.
Lange, Peter, and Sidney Tarrow, eds. *Italy in Transition: Conflict and
    Consensus.* London: Frank Cass, 1980.
LaPalombara, Joseph. "Italy: Fragmentation, Isolation, Alienation." In
    Political Culture and Political Development, ed. Lucien W. Pye and Sidney
    Verba. Princeton: Princeton University Press, 1965.

303

Rusconi, Gian Enrico, and Sergio Scamuzzi. *Italy Today: An Eccentric Society.* London: Sage, 1981.

Sartori, Giovanni. *Parties and Party Systems: A Framework for Analysis.* Cambridge: Cambridge University Press, 1976.

Teoria dei partiti e caso italiano. Milan: SugarCo, 1982.

Sani, Giacomo. "The Political Culture of Italy: Continuity and Change." In *The Civic Culture Revisited,* ed. Gabriel Almond and Sidney Verba. Boston: Little, Brown, 1980.

Zariski, Raphael. *The Politics of Uneven Development.* Hinsdale, Ill.: Dryden Press, 1972.

Elections

Barnes, Samuel H. *Representation in Italy: Institutionalized Tradition and Electoral Choice.* Chicago: University of Chicago Press, 1977.

Fabris, Gianpaolo. *Il comportamento politico degli italiani.* Milan: Franco Angeli, 1977.

Parisi, Arturo, and Gianfranco Pasquino, eds. *Continuità e mutamento elettorale in Italia.* Bologna: Il Mulino, 1977.

Penniman, Howard R., ed. *Italy at the Polls: The Parliamentary Elections of 1976.* Washington: American Enterprise Institute, 1977.

Italy at the Polls, 1979: A Study of the Parliamentary Elections. Washington: American Enterprise Institute, 1981.

Chapter 2. The Christian Democrats: The indispensable center?

Andreotti, Giulio. *Diari 1976 1979: Gli anni della solidarietà.* Milan: Rizzoli, 1981.

Intervista su De Gasperi. Rome: Laterza, 1977.

Baget-Bozzo, Gianni. *Il partito cristiano al potere: La DC di De Gasperi e di Dossetti 1945–1954.* Florence: Vallecchi, 1974.

Cassano, Franco. *Il teorema democristiano.* Bari: Laterza, 1979.

Cicchitto, F., G. Rocchi, B. Manghi, L. Ruggiu, and A. Cavazzani. *La DC dopo il primo ventennio.* Padua: Marsilio, 1968.

Einaudi, Mario, and François Goguel. *Christian Democracy in Italy and France.* Notre Dame, Ind.: University of Notre Dame Press, 1952.

Galli, Giorgio. *Storia della democrazia cristiana.* Bari: Laterza, 1978.

Levi, Arrigo. *La DC nell'Italia che cambia.* Bari: Laterza, 1984.

Menapace, Lidia. *La Democrazia Cristiana: Natura, struttura e organizzazione.* Milan: Mazzotta, 1975.

Orfei, Ruggero. *L'occupazione del potere.* Milan: Langenesi, 1978.

Rossi, Maurizio. "Un partito di 'anime morte'? Il tesseramento democristiano tra mito e realtà." In *Democristiani,* ed. Arturo Parisi. Bologna: Il Mulino, 1979.

Sylos Labini, Paolo. *Saggio sulle classi sociali.* Bari: Laterza, 1975.

Tamburrano, Giuseppe. *L'Iceberg democristiano.* Milan: SugarCo, 1975.

Webster, Richard. *Christian Democracy in Italy: 1860–1960.* London: Hollis & Carter, 1961.

Zuckerman, Alan S. *The Politics of Faction: Christian Democratic Rule in Italy.* New Haven: Yale University Press, 1979.

Chapter 3. The Communists' struggle for legitimacy and acceptance

Amyot, Grant. *The Communist Party: The Crisis of the Popular Front Strategy.* New York: St. Martin's Press, 1981.

Berner, Wolfgang. "The Italian Left, 1944–1978: Patterns of Cooperation, Conflict, and Compromise." In *The European Left: Italy, France and Spain,* ed. William E. Griffith. Lexington, Mass.: Heath, 1979.

Blackmer, Donald L. M. *Unity in Diversity: Italian Communism and the Communist World.* Cambridge, Mass.: M.I.T. Press, 1968.

Blackmer, Donald L. M., and Annie Kriegel. *The International Role of the Communist Parties of Italy and France.* Cambridge, Mass.: Center for International Affairs, Harvard University, 1975.

Blackmer, Donald L. M., and Sidney Tarrow, eds. *Communism in Italy and France.* Princeton: Princeton University Press, 1975.

Boggs, Carl. *The Impasse of European Communism.* Boulder, Colo.: Westview Press, 1982.

Colletti, Lucio. *Intervista politico-filosofica.* Bari: Laterza, 1975.

Galli, Giorgio. *Storia del PCI.* Milan: Bompiani, 1977.

Hobsbawm, Eric J. *The Italian Road to Socialism: An Interview by Eric Hobsbawm with Giorgio Napolitano of the Italian Communist Party.* Westport, Conn.: Lawrence Hill, 1977.

Ingrao, Pietro. *Masse e potere.* Rome: Editori Riuniti, 1977.

Kertzer, David I. *Comrades and Christians: Religion and Political Struggle in Communist Italy.* Cambridge: Cambridge University Press, 1980.

Lange, Peter, and Maurizio Vannicelli, eds. *The Communist Parties of Italy, France and Spain: Postwar Change and Continuity.* London: Allen & Unwin, 1981.

Ranney, Austin, and Giovanni Sartori, eds. *Eurocommunism: The Italian Case.* Washington: American Enterprise Institute, 1978.

Sassoon, Donald. *The Strategy of the Italian Communist Party: From the Resistance to the Historic Compromise.* New York: St. Martin's Press, 1981.

Sechi, Salvatore. *L'austero fascino del centralismo democratico.* Bologna: Il Mulino, 1978.

Serfaty, Simon, and Lawrence Gray, eds. *The Italian Communist Party: Yesterday, Today, and Tomorrow.* Westport, Conn.: Greenwood Press, 1980.

Spriano, Paolo. *Storia del partito comunista italiano.* 6 vols. Turin: Einaudi, 1967–75.

Tarrow, Sidney G. *Peasant Communism in Southern Italy.* New Haven: Yale University Press, 1967.

Urban, Joan Barth. "Moscow and the PCI in the 1970s: Kto Kovo?" *Studies in Comparative Communism,* Summer/Autumn 1980, pp. 99–167.

"Soviet Policies and Negotiating Behavior toward Nonruling Communist Parties: The Case of the Italian Communist Party." *Studies in Comparative Communism,* Autumn 1982, pp. 184–211.

Chapter 4. The ambiguous role of the Socialists

Barnes, Samuel H. *Party Democracy: Politics in an Italian Socialist Federation.* New Haven: Yale University Press, 1967.

Craxi, Bettino. *Pluralismo o Leninismo: Il dibattito ideologico nella sinistra italiana e gli interventi.* Como: SugarCo, 1978.

Galli, Giorgio. *La sinistra italiana nel dopoguerra*. Milan: Saggiatore, 1978.

Faenza, Liliano. *La crisi del socialismo in Italia (1946–1966)*. Bologna: Alfa Edizioni, 1967.

Lenin, V. I. *Sul movimento operaio italiano*. 16th ed. Rome: Editori Riuniti, 1976.

Pasquino, Gianfranco. "The Italian Socialist Party: Electoral Stagnation and Political Indispensability." In *Italy at the Polls, 1979: A Study of the Parliamentary Elections*, ed. Howard R. Penniman. Washington: American Enterprise Institute, 1981.

Pellicani, Luciano. "Il riformismo alla prova dei fatti." In *Mondoperaio*, April 1984, pp. 59–61.

Tamburrano, Giuseppe. *Storia e cronaca del centro-sinistra*, 4th ed. Milan: Feltrinelli, 1976.

Pci e Psi nel sistema democristiano. Rome: Laterza, 1978.

Chapter 5. The small parties: The lay forces and the extremes

Aghina, Guido, and Claudio Jaccarino. *Storia del Partito Radicale*. Milan: Gammalibri, 1977.

Ciani, Arnaldo. *Il partito liberale italiano da Croce a Malagodi*. Naples: Edizioni scientifiche italiane, 1968.

De Luna, Giovanni. *Storia del Partito d'Azione: La rivoluzione democratica: 1942–1947*. Milan: Feltrinelli, 1982.

Ferraresi, Franco, ed. *La destra radicale*. Milan: Feltrinelli, 1984.

La Malfa, Ugo. *L'altra Italia: Documenti su un decennio di politica italiana 1965–1975*. Milan: Mondadori, 1975.

Monicelli, Mino. *L'ultrasinistra in Italia, 1968–1978*. Bari: Laterza, 1978.

Rosenbaum, Petra. *Il nuovo fascismo: Da Salò ad Almirante: Storia del MSI*. Milan: Feltrinelli, 1974.

Spadolini, Giovanni. *L'Italia dei laici: Lotta politica e cultura dal 1925 al 1980*. Florence: Le Monnier, 1980.

Teodori, Massimo. *Storia delle nuove sinistre in Europa (1956–1976)*. Bologna: Il Mulino, 1976.

Teodori, Massimo, Piero Ignazi, and Angelo Panebianco. *I nuovi radicali*. Milan: Mondadori, 1977.

Chapter 6. Parliament, prime minister, and president

Amato, Giuliano. "Il governo." In *Attualità e attuazione della costituzione*. 2d ed. Bari: Laterza, 1982.

Cazzola, Franco. "La solidarietà nazionale dalla parte del parlamento." In *Laboratorio politico*, March–June 1982, pp. 182–210.

Governo e opposizione nel parlamento italiano. Milan: Giuffrè, 1974.

Cheli, Enzo. *Costituzione e sviluppo delle istituzioni in Italia*. Bologna: Il Mulino, 1978.

Di Palma, Giuseppe. *Political Syncretism in Italy: Historical Coalition Strategies and the Present Crisis*. Berkeley: Institute of International Studies, University of California, 1978.

Surviving without Governing: The Italian Parties in Parliament. Berkeley: University of California Press, 1977.

Martinelli, Alberto, and Gianfranco Pasquino. *La politica nell'Italia che cambia*. Milan: Feltrinelli, 1978.

Onida, Valerio. "Recenti sviluppi della forma di governo in Italia: Prime osservazioni." *Quaderni costituzionali,* April 1981, pp. 7–31.
Pasquino, Gianfranco. *Crisi dei partiti e governabilità.* Bologna: Il Mulino, 1980.
Degenerazioni dei partiti e riforme istituzionali. Bari: Laterza, 1982.
Tarrow, Sidney. "Italy since 1976: Historic Compromise or Waning of Opposition." Paper Prepared for Seminar at Washington Center of Foreign Policy Research, 1977.
"Crisis, Crises or Transition?" In Peter Lange and Sidney Tarrow, *Italy in Transition: Conflict and Consensus.* London: Frank Cass, 1980.

Chapter 7. Public administration and *sottogoverno*

Cassese, Sabino. *La formazione dello stato amministrativo.* Milan: Giuffrè, 1974.
Il sistema amministrativo italiano. Bologna: Il Mulino, 1977.
Cazzola, Franco, ed. *Anatomia del potere DC: Enti publici e "centralità democristiana."* Bari: De Donato, 1979.
Cerase, P. P., and F. Mignella Calvosa. *La burocrazia dello stato tra crisi e rinnovamento.* Venice: Marsilio, 1978.
Emiliani, Vittorio. *L'Italia mangiata.* Turin: Einaudi, 1977.
Forte, Francesco. *Industria Governo Sottogoverno.* Turin: Società Editrice Internazionale, 1976.
Giannini, Massimo Severo. *Rapporto sui principali problemi dell'amministrazione dello stato.* Rome: Istituto Poligrafico dello Stato, 1979.
Gorrieri, Ermanno. *La giungla retributiva.* 8th ed. Bologna: Il Mulino, 1975.
Graziano, Luigi. *Clientelismo e sistema politico: Il caso dell'Italia.* Milan: Franco Angeli, 1980.
Hine, David. "Italy." In *Government and Administration in Western Europe,* ed. F. F. Ridley. New York: St. Martin's Press, 1979.
Holland, Stuart, ed. *The State as Entrepreneur: New Dimensions for Public Enterprise: The IRI State Shareholding Formula.* London: Weidenfeld and Nicolson, 1972.
Posner, M. V., and S. J. Woolf. *Italian Public Enterprise.* Cambridge, Mass.: Harvard University Press, 1967.
Putnam, Robert D. *The Beliefs of Politicians: Ideology, Conflict, and Democracy in Britain and Italy.* New Haven: Yale University Press, 1973.
"The Political Attitudes of Senior Civil Servants in Britain, Germany, and Italy." In *The Mandarins of Western Europe: The Political Role of Top Civil Servants,* ed. Mattei Dogan. New York: Halsted Press, 1975.
Serrani, Donatello. *Il potere per enti: Enti pubblici e sistema politico in Italia.* Bologna: Il Mulino, 1978.
Spreafico, Alberto. *L'amministrazione e il cittadino.* Milan: Communità, 1965.

Chapter 8. The administration of justice

Barzini, Luigi. *The Italians: A Full-Length Portrait Featuring their Manners and Morals.* New York: Atheneum, 1964.
Canosa, Romano, and Pietro Federico. *La magistratura in Italia dal 1945 ad oggi.* Bologna: Il Mulino, 1974.
Cappelletti, Mauro, John Henry Merryman, and Joseph M. Perillo. *The Italian Legal System: An Introduction.* Stanford: Stanford University Press, 1967.

Freddi, Giorgio. *Tensioni e conflitti nella magistratura.* Bari: Laterza, 1978.
Galli, Giorgio. *L'Italia sotterranea: Storia, politica e scandali.* Rome: Laterza, 1983.
Mancini, Giuseppe Federico. "Politics and the Judges – The European Perspective." *The Modern Law Review,* Jan. 1980, pp. 1–17.

Chapter 9. Dangers to the state: Plots, terrorism, and the mafia

Conspiracies and terrorism

Acquaviva, Sabino. *Guerriglia e guerra rivoluzionaria.* Milan: Rizzoli, 1979.
  Il seme religioso della rivolta. Milan: Rusconi, 1979.
Barbato, Tullio. *Il terrorismo in Italia: Cronaca e documentazione.* Milan: Editrice Bibliografica, 1980.
Bocca, Giorgio. *Il terrorismo italiano 1970–1978.* Milan: Rizzoli, 1978.
Collin, Richard. *The De Lorenzo Gambit: The Italian Coup Manqué of 1964.* Beverly Hills: Sage Publications, 1976.
Galleni, Mauro, ed. *Rapporto sul terrorismo.* Milan: Rizzoli, 1981.
Minucci, Adalberto. *Terrorismo e crisi italiana.* Rome: Editori Riuniti, 1978.
Negri, Antonio. *Il dominio e il sabotaggio.* Milan: Feltrinelli, 1980.
Ronchey, Alberto. "Guns and Gray Matter: Terrorism in Italy." *Foreign Affairs,* April 1979, pp. 921–40.
  Libro bianco sull'ultima generazione. Milan: Garzanti, 1979.
Silj, Alessandro. *Never Again Without a Rifle: The Origins of Italian Terrorism.* New York: Karz, 1979.
Tessandori, Vincenzo. *Br imputazione: banda armata.* Milan: Garzanti, 1977.

The mafia

Arlacchi, Pino. "The 'Mafioso': from man of honour to entrepreneur." *New Left Review,* Nov.–Dec. 1979, pp. 53–72.
  La mafia imprendatrice: L'etica mafiosa e lo spirito del capitalismo. Bologna: Il Mulino, 1983.
Blok, Anton. *The Mafia of a Sicilian Village, 1860–1960.* New York: Harper & Row, 1975.
Hess, Henner. *Mafia.* Bari: Laterza, 1973.
Martelli, Franco. *La guerra mafiosa. Mille morti in dieci anni: La sfida della "ndrangheta" calabrese alla democrazia italiana.* Rome: Editori Riuniti, 1981.
Pantaleone, Michele. *The Mafia and Politics.* London: Chatto and Windus, 1966.

Chapter 10. Economic and social transformation

The economy

Allen, Kevin, and Andrew Stevenson. *An Introduction to the Italian Economy.* New York: Barnes & Noble, 1975.
Amato, Giuliano. *Economia, politica, istituzioni.* Bologna: Il Mulino, 1976.
Bagnasco, Arnaldo. *Tre Italie: La problematica territoriale dello sviluppo.* Bologna: Il Mulino, 1977.

Bagnasco, Arnaldo, and Marcello Messori. *Tendenze dell'economia periferica.* Turin: Valentino, 1975.
Censis Foundation. *L'occupazione occulta: Caratteristiche della partecipazione al lavoro in Italia.* Rome: Censis Foundation, 1976.
Colantoni, Marcello. *Il commercio estero dell'Italia con i paesi dell'Opec.* Milan: Giuffrè, 1979.
Graziani, Augusto. *L'economia italiana dal 1945 a oggi.* Bologna: Il Mulino, 1979.
Lutz, Vera. *Italy: A Study in Economic Development.* London: Oxford University Press, 1962.
Podbielski, Gisele. *Italy: Development and Crisis in the Post-War Economy.* Oxford: Clarendon Press, 1974.
Salvati, Michele. *Il sistema economico italiano: analisi di una crisi.* Bologna: Il Mulino, 1975.

Trade unions

Horowitz, Daniel. *The Italian Labor Movement.* Cambridge, Mass.: Harvard University Press, 1963.
Lange, Peter, George Ross, and Maurizio Vannicelli. *Unions, Change and Crisis: French and Italian Union Strategy and Political Economy, 1945– 1980.* Winchester: Allen & Unwin, 1982.
LaPalombara, Joseph. *The Italian Labor Movement: Problems and Prospects.* Ithaca: Cornell University Press, 1957.
Perna, Corrado. *Breve storia del sindacato.* Bari: De Donato, 1978.
Pizzorno, Alessandro. *I soggetti del pluralismo: Classi, partiti, sindacato.* Bologna: Il Mulino, 1980.
Pizzorno, Alessandro, and others. *Lotte operaie e sindacato: Il ciclo 1968 – 1972 in Italia.* Bologna: Il Mulino, 1978.
Turone, Sergio. *Storia del sindacato in Italia (1943 – 1969).* Bari: Laterza, 1976.

Industry

Amato, Giuliano. *Il governo dell'industria in Italia.* Bologna: Il Mulino, 1972.
Berger, Suzanne, and Michael J. Piore. *Dualism and Discontinuity in Industrial Societies.* Cambridge: Cambridge University Press, 1980.
Ferrero, Fiorenzo, and Sergio Scamuzzi, eds. *Piccola e media impresa e politica industriale.* Rome: Editori Riuniti, 1979.
Grassini, Franco, and Carlo Scognamiglio, eds. *Stato e industria in Europa: L'Italia.* Bologna: Il Mulino, 1979.
Martinelli, Alberto. "Organized Business and Italian Politics: Confindustria and the Christian Democrats in the Postwar Period." In Peter Lange and Sidney Tarrow, *Italy in Transition: Conflict and Consensus.* London: Frank Cass, 1980.
Pirzio Ammassari, Gloria. *La politica della Confindustria.* Naples: Liquori, 1976.
Votaw, Dow. *The Six-Legged Dog: Mattei and ENI – A Study in Power.* Berkeley: University of California Press, 1964.

Social developments

Acquaviva, Sabino, and Mario Santuccio. *Social Structure in Italy: Crisis of a System.* London: Robertson, 1976.

Alberoni, Francesco. *Italia in trasformazione.* Bologna: Il Mulino, 1976.
Birnbaum, Lucia Chiavola. *Liberazione della donna: A cultural history of the contemporary Italian women's movement.* Middletown: Wesleyan University Press, 1985.
Censis Foundation. *Rapporto sugli aspetti sociali ed economici della situazione universitaria italiana.* Milan: Franco Angeli, 1974.
Ergas, Yasmin. "1968–1979 – Feminism and the Italian Party System." *Comparative Politics,* April 1982, pp. 253–79.
Ferrarotti, Franco, ed. *La crisi dello stato sociale in Italia.* Bari: Edizioni Dedalo, 1983.
Ruffolo, Giorgio. *Dal '68 a oggi.* Bari: Laterza, 1979.

Chapter 11. Regional devolution and the problem of the South

Agnelli, Gianni, and others. "European Industry and Southern Italy." *Isveimer Bulletin* (27–8), June 1980.
Alcock, Anthony E. *The History of the South Tyrol Question.* London: Michael Joseph, 1970.
Allum, Percy. *Politics and Society in Post-War Naples.* Cambridge: Cambridge University Press, 1973.
Amendola, Giorgio. *Intervista sull'antifascismo.* Bari: Laterza, 1976.
Arlacchi, Pino. *Mafia, peasants, and great estates: Society in traditional Calabria.* Cambridge: Cambridge University Press, 1983.
Banfield, Edward C. *The Moral Basis of a Backward Society.* New York: Free Press, 1958.
Caciagli, Mario. *Democrazia cristiana e potere nel mezzogiorno: Il sistema democristiano a Catania.* Rimini-Florence: Guaraldi, 1977.
Cassese, Sabino, ed. *Guida per le autonomie locali '80.* Rome: Edizioni delle Autonomie, 1980.
Censis Foundation. *XIII rapporto/1979 sulla situazione sociale del paese.* Rome: Censis Foundation, 1979.
Chubb, Judith. *Patronage, power, and poverty in southern Italy: A tale of two cities.* Cambridge: Cambridge University Press, 1982.
Compagna, Francesco. *Mezzogiorno in salita.* Milan: Editoriale Nuova, 1980.
Istituto per la Scienza dell'Amministrazione Pubblica. *Le relazioni centro-periferia.* Milan: Giuffrè, 1984.
Leonardi, Robert, Rafaella Y. Nanetti, and Robert D. Putnam. "Devolution as a Political Process: The Case of Italy." *Publius: The Journal of Federalism,* Winter 1981, pp. 95–117.
Podbielski, Gisele. *Twenty-five years of Special Action for the Development of Southern Italy.* Milan: Giuffrè, 1978.
Tarrow, Sidney. *Between Center and Periphery: Grassroots Politicians in Italy and France.* New Haven: Yale University Press, 1977.

Chapter 12. The changing relations between church and state

Barnes, Samuel H. "Italy: Religion and Class in Electoral Behavior." In *Electoral Behavior: A Comparative Handbook,* ed. Richard Rose. New York: Free Press, 1974.
Biorcio, Roberto, and Renato Mannheimer. "Elettorato e fratture culturali." *Politica ed Economia,* supplement to issue of March 1985.

Bucci, P. Vincent. *Chiesa e stato: Church-State Relations in Italy within the Contemporary Constitutional Framework.* The Hague: Martinus Nijhoff, 1969.

Burgalassi, Silvano. *Il comportamento religioso degli Italiani.* Florence: Vallecchi, 1967.

Cornwell, Rupert. *God's Banker: An Account of the Life and Death of Roberto Calvi.* London: Gollancz, 1983.

Jemolo, A. C. *Church and State in Italy.* Oxford: Blackwell, 1960.

LaPalombara, Joseph. *Interest Groups in Italian Politics.* Princeton: Princeton University Press, 1964.

Longo, Raffaele Giura. *La sinistra cattolica in Italia: Dal doppoguerra al referendum.* Bari: De Donato, 1975.

Magister, Sandro. *La politica vaticana e l'Italia 1943-1978.* Rome: Editori Riuniti, 1979.

Martina, Giacomo. *La chiesa in Italia negli ultimi trent'anni.* Rome: Edizioni Studium, 1977.

Poggi, G. *Catholic Action in Italy.* Stanford: Stanford University Press, 1967.

Prandi, Alfonso. *Chiesa e politica.* Bologna: Il Mulino, 1968.

Chapter 13. Foreign and security policy

Andreotti, Giulio. *Visti da vicino.* Milan: Rizzoli, 1982.

Are, Giuseppe. *L'Italia e i mutamenti internazionali, 1971-1976.* Florence: Vallecchi, 1977.

Bonanni, Massimo, ed. *La politica estera della repubblica italiana.* Milan: Communità, 1967.

Di Nolfo, Ennio. "The Political Significance of Italian Policy." In *The Shaping of Western European Foreign Policies.* Bologna: Johns Hopkins Bologna Center, 1980.

Faenza, Roberto. *Il malaffare: Dall'America di Kennedy all'Italia, a Cuba, al Vietnam.* Milan: Mondadori, 1978.

Istituto Affari Internazionali. *L'Italia nella politica internazionale.* Milan: Communità; annual since 1972.

Kogan, Norman. *The Politics of Italian Foreign Policy.* New York: Praeger, 1963.

Quaroni, Pietro. "Chi è che fa la politica estera in Italia." In Massimo Bonanni, *op. cit.*

Ronzitti, Natalino, ed. *La politica estera italiana: Autonomia, interdipendenza, integrazione e sicurezza.* Milan: Communità, 1977.

Willis, F. Roy. *Italy Chooses Europe.* New York: Oxford University Press, 1971.

Index

abortion, 16, 36; Catholic position on, 120-1, 247, 248-9, 259-60; Christian Democrats' position on, 110, 120, 248-9; and Communist party, 58, 110; feminist position on, 121, 219; and lay parties, 89, 92, 219; legislation on, 109, 110, 114, 120, 219, 248, 284; neo-Fascists oppose, 96, 120; number of cases of, 120, 247, 248; Radicals support, 94, 121; pope campaigns against, 121, 248-9, 260; *see also* referendum: on abortion

Abruzzi, 216, 237

Acheson, Dean, 269

ACLI (Associazioni Cristiane Lavoratori Italiani), 35, 256-7

Acquaviva, Sabino, 182

Action party, 86

Adenauer, Konrad, 5, 15, 22

Administrative Reform, Ministry of, 135

Adorno, Theodor, 100

Afghanistan, 49, 50, 66, 273

Agip (Azienda Generale Italiana Petroli), 139, 148

Agnelli, Gianni, 211; and Communist party, 63-4; heads Confederation of Industry; 210; and press interests, 211; and Republicans, 88, 210; views on Southern development, 235, 236

agriculture, 279; Christian Democratic influence in, 35, 144; decline of, 194, 195, 215; in South, 232-3, 235, 238, 240; *see also* farmers

Agriculture, Ministry of, 16, 35, 214

air force, *see* armed forces

Air Ministry, 127

Alfa Romeo, 139, 179, 234, 237

Alibrandi, Antonio, 162

Alitalia, 139

Allende, Salvador, 44

Almirante, Giorgio, 98, 173

Almond, Gabriel, 3

Amalfi coast, 240

Amato, Giuliano, 78, 118

Amendola, Giorgio, 53, 59, 66, 238

American government, *see* United States

Amnesty International, 163

Andreatta, Beniamino, 253

Andreotti, Giulio, 11, 106, 112, 142, 250; on Borghese plot, 172; career in government, 15-16, 31, 35, 114; on foreign policy consensus, 273; 1976 government of, 28, 45, 114, 273; party role of, 30; quotes Togliatti, 93

"anti-system" parties, 12

anti-terrorist legislation, 164-5, 181

Aosta, 222

Arcaini, Giuseppe, 145

armed forces: condition of, 274-5; intelligence branch of, 168-9; in Lebanon, 267-8, 276; in Sinai peacekeeping force, 273, 276; size of, 129, 274; spending on, 273, 274; strategy of, 275-6

Armed Proletarian Nuclei, 181

Armed Proletarian Power, 181

Armed Revolutionary Nuclei, *see* NAR

arms sales, illegal, 156, 174, 185, 186, 187, 189, 192

army, *see* armed forces

Arnold, Matthew, 67

Assisi, 242

Atlantic Alliance, *see* North Atlantic Treaty Organization

attorney general, 151, 157, 192, 193

Austria, 278-9; and South Tyrol, 222-4

autonomous administrations, 136

"autonomous" unions, *see* trade unions

Avvenire d'Italia, 258

Baffi, Paolo, 161-2, 197, 252

Bagehot, Walter, 125

Bagnasco, Arnaldo, 217

Ballestrero, Anastasio, 254, 255, 260-1

313

316   Index

Christian Democratic party (DC) *(cont.)*
Socialists, 17, 28, 75, 76, 80, 81, 82,
147–8; and *sottogoverno,* 15, 24–5, 28,
37, 105, 141–5, 147–9; South,
dominant power in, 240; state, attitude
to, 3, 21, 104–5; subculture of, 10,
34–8, 244, 249; unions, opposes
reunification of, 205; and United States,
3, 20, 22, 28, 47, 281
Christian Workers' Associations, *see* ACLI
"Christians for Socialism," 258
Chubb, Judith, 235
church, *see* Catholic church, Italian
Churchill, Winston, 15
CIPE (Comitato Interministeriale per la
Politica Economica), 118
CISL (Confederazione Italiana Sindacati
Lavoratori), 199, 201; American
support for, 280–1; links to Christian
Democrats, 35, 199, 200, 201, 204–5;
organizes Catholic workers, 199, 256–7;
and wage indexing, 205
CISNAL (Confederazione Italiana
Sindacati Nazionali Lavoratori), 97,
179, 199
civic committees, 255, 256
civil code, 104, 156, 284
civil liberties, 89, 96, 150; abuses of,
162–3; and Constitutional Court, 152,
163; constitutional guarantees of, 103,
163; and Communist party, 58; and
ferment of sixties, 219; and Radicals, 76,
94, 163, 165; and Socialist party, 76
civil service: absenteeism in, 133; and *bus-
tarelle,* 135; conditions in, 131, 132–3;
entry into, 130; legislation for, 111;
"moonlighting" in, 133; organization
of, 128, 131; personnel, numbers of, by
category, 129–30; politicization of, 130,
131, 132; public attitude toward, 3, 132,
134, 136; and *raccomandazione,* 134–5;
reform of, 135–6; retirement in, 131;
and right to strike, 131, 157
Coco, Francesco, 180
Coldiretti, *see* Confederation of Small
Farmers
Colletti, Lucio, 54
Colombo, Emilio, 15, 30, 35, 240
Colombo, Umberto, 148–9
Cominform, 43, 269

Committee for Economic Planning, *see*
CIPE
common agriculture policy, 271, 279
Communion and Liberation, 36, 219, 257,
261
Communist party, French, 48–9
Communist party, Italian (PCI): accepts
monarchy, 43, 76; and big business,
63–4, 207, 210; and Catholic church,
64–5, 262; concordat, its support for, 43,
64, 244; constitutional order, its loyalty
to, 10, 13, 45–6, 55, 63, 66, 67, 113,
288, 289; and Chinese party, 48, 49; and
Christian Democrats, cooperation with,
11, 17–18, 27–8, 42, 44–6, 63, 107,
113–14, 257, 273, 288; and CGIL, 61,
198, 204–5, 208; and Czechoslovakia,
48, 50, 57, 66; and "democratic
centralism," 51–2, 54–5; and de-Stalinization, 43, 44; and divorce referendum,
26, 44; and *doppiezza,* 43, 47; electoral
performance of, 9, 18, 27, 45, 46, 53,
62–3; and Eurocommunism, 48–9; and
European Community, 48, 59, 67, 270,
272–3; and excommunication of its
members, 65, 244, 246, 259, 262;
expelled from government, 17, 43, 113;
factionalism repressed by, 7–8, 51–2,
55; and foreign and defense issues, 47,
92, 113, 272–3; founding of, 41–2,
66–7, 70; and "historic compromise,"
45, 46, 49, 53, 72, 147; and Hungarian
revolution, 44, 47, 60, 66, 72; its
inclusion in parliamentary resolutions,
45, 49, 273; and "Italian way to
socialism," 44, 46, 53, 56; and left
radicals, 99; and left terrorism, 63, 183,
186, 288; and Leninism, 10, 17, 27,
55–60, 66; Marshall Plan, its opposition
to, 43, 167, 288; membership in, 57,
60–1; minorities in, 51, 52, 53–4; and
NATO, 45, 48, 53, 67, 167, 269, 272–3,
288; and October Revolution, 41, 49,
50, 57, 70; and parliament, 27, 43, 45,
55, 104, 106–7, 109, 113–14; and
Poland, 50, 52, 53, 66; regional role of,
44, 62–3, 113, 225; and social and
economic issues, 43, 58–9, 63, 66, 160;
Socialists, relations with, 41, 42, 46, 62,
64, 66, 68, 70–3, 74, 79, 80, 199; and